What Readers Are Saying

Juliana, a young mother:

"This book really changed my life... I couldn't put it down, and found myself returning to its pages often to reflect and learn to deal with situations going on in my life. Jeanne clearly paints with these words from God a beautiful picture that flows from chapter to chapter, beginning to end, so that we may see the need for God in every type of grief, pain and despair that we go through..."

Corey, a new Christian:

"I've been involved with drugs/alcohol, sex, satanic heavy metal music—everything that's bad... Even though I'm only halfway through the book, I wanted to write to tell you how much the book is helping me in my new walk with the Lord."

Deborah Watson, Founder of Faithwalkers Int'l:

"Jeanne's book is so beautiful, not only because it comes straight from her heart but because it shows that even if you're serving the Lord with all your heart and soul, trials and tribulation will come. The key is what we do during those times and who we turn to. Jeanne allows us to peek into the window of her soul and see what a mighty God we serve."

M. McDonald, Pastor of Cornerstone Foursquare Church:

"I was especially encouraged by the chapter 'Strength in Crisis.' What a compelling reminder that we are to be those worshippers the Father seeks; those who truly desire to seek nothing less than to know Him and draw strength from His nearness!! Oh, may I be that worshipper!!!"

Put Down Your Anchor, Ride Out The Storm

Jeanne M. Mohr

Living Praise Publications
High Ridge, Missouri

To the Only One who can give:

"Beauty for ashes,
The oil of joy for mourning,
The garment of praise
for a spirit of heaviness;
That they may be called trees
of righteousness;
The planting of the Lord,
That He may be glorified"
(Isaiah 61:3)

ISBN 0-9660383-4-7

www.livingpraiseministries.com
e-mail: jmlivingpraise@sbcglobal.net

Original cover art by Vicki Rose.
Cover prepress by Sherry Ziegler, ZEC, Inc.

Printed in the United States of America.

Second Edition 2004
Third Printing 2006

Table of Contents

Setting Sail (Prologue)

The Anchor Holds (Epilogue)

Giving Thanks...

As I've birthed this book, special thanks and blessings: to my dear daughter-in-law Debbie Mohr for proofing the second edition; to Sally Bartnett, dear, dear friend, with me for many years in every phase and outreach of our ministry—Living Praise; to Juliana Chaney, part-time secretary—so much a part of this book, encouraging me in every step and word; to Vicki Ferguson, precious prayer partner and anointed designer of the cover; to Jon Klemmer for his inspirational editing and vision; to Penny Wattle, special treasure in preparing drafts of both editions; to Debra Peppers and all the radio staff of KJSL - AM 630 St. Louis, for the joyful Salt and Light example they continually set for me; to my sister-in-law, Helen Everett, the first one to tell me, "Jeanne, you can write!"; to Marlene Bagnull, prolific author and writer's conference founder, who first encouraged me to publish, insisting, "Jeanne, people need to read what you write."; to Living Praise Fellowship for their continual caring and support (thanks for believing in me); for friends and family everywhere who love and pray for me; and to my Lord and Savior, who's proven over and over again—He'll be my Anchor in any and every storm!

Dear Reader,

This book is **user-friendly!**

It welcomes your underlining, highlighting and comments in the margins.

No matter what you know, or don't know about God, as you read this book—He will meet you there.

The Author

Setting Sail

(Prologue)

Hopes of happiness run high in the human heart, but perhaps higher at Christmas than at any other time of the year. The resulting disappointment and discouragement when those expectations aren't realized can linger long after we've taken down our trees; long after we've packed away the wreaths and tinsel. In part, because other downers have gone before, taking their toll. We've got a whole lot of "stuff" pushed down; consisting of broken promises, shattered dreams and unfulfilled hopes. So, as Christmas approached I decided to do a series on disappointment and discouragement on my weekly radio program.

I was delighted at how much the messages helped people; and surprised as I studied to prepare for the broadcasts, that although the Bible doesn't always use the words disappointment and discouragement, it has a lot—**a lot**—to say about the situations we face that cause us sadness, loss, grief and pain.

Then I sensed the Lord telling me to expand the broadcasts into a book! I'd protested. I didn't really want to write another book. And I'd reminded Him (ever done that?) that there were already some good books on this subject. Nevertheless, He convinced me by insisting: **He had a Mission for THIS Message as well.**

So… I launched out into the deep to write and publish this book—the book you're now holding. A song I'd written years before entitled *Put Down Your Anchor, Ride Out The Storm* became this book's title and theme.

In days of old, sailors encountered storms. **All kinds of**

storms. Sometimes they occurred on regular voyages; at other times during extended ones when they ventured into uncharted waters hoping to find new treasures or undiscovered lands. I've heard that whenever they couldn't outrun a storm, they'd put down their anchor and ride it out. And in the process—become better sailors.

As Christians, while sailing in the Ship of Life following Jesus (our Treasure) and "seeking that City which is to come" (Heaven), we will encounter storms. **All kinds of storms.** Wind and raging seas of adversity, hardship, heartbreak and trial buffet our ship. I've written this book so that, like those sailors of old, we, too, can discover our Anchor, and learn how to put it down. As you read and return to each chapter, if you'll ask the Holy Spirit to minister to you just what you need, I believe you'll receive new revelation, restoration and faith—the kind that only our Lord Jesus can give in (and particularly in)—tough times.

Put Down Your Anchor

"Put down your Anchor, ride out the storm;
Jesus is with you; He'll shield you from harm;
And though waves surround you,
And no light breaks through—
You question "if He's leading,"
And you're not sure just what to do...

Put down your Anchor in the midst of your tears;
For He is the Answer to all your doubts and fears;
For He cannot fail you, when He's promised to save;
For He is the Master of the ship—and the waves!"
© *Jeanne M. Mohr, 1988*

I pray newfound hope, joy, steadfastness and freedom for you, dear reader, as together — **We...Set...Sail...**

Chapter 1

Tempest Tossed

I gripped the railing of the ship with both hands, needing every ounce of strength I could muster to keep from falling apart. In the pitch darkness, peering into the pounding sea, I willed my eyes to penetrate the crashing waves swirling below me, to find my daughter, Chris.

"Oh, Lord," I cried, my voice becoming a whisper flung back in my face by the raging storm and wind. "How can I praise You when I've lost her?" Because the question that had suddenly pierced through the storm and now hovered over my heart was, *Will you still praise Me??* The question seemed a heartless invasion, no worse—a violation. *How can You ask me that at a time like this?!*

Learning to praise the Lord in every situation and for all things had not been part of our religious background, nor of our mission school training before coming to New Guinea as medical missionaries with our eleven-year-old twin sons, Kevin and Steven, and daughters, Chris, nine, and Lori, six.

Although my husband, Bob, and I had both been raised in preachers' homes, we each had become more alive and in tune with Jesus as Lord and Savior since coming to New Guinea. I'd begun to realize that before our mission assignment, I'd worshipped God from a distance—substituting religious doctrine, dogma and formalism for a day-by-day personal relationship with the Lord.

When the stress of adjusting to missionary life in a primitive setting with people so different in culture and language laid bare my pride and self-righteousness—my arrogance and

1

"barenness"—I was devastated. I found I wasn't God's gift to them at all—I, who had the expertise and education. They were God's **Gift** to me! Simple, unlettered and unlearned people wearing Tonka leaves and living in grass huts had taught me how to trust in the Lord and His Word at all times and for all things.

Up to then I'd counted way too much on being "right" and having the "right" answers, and way too little on being led by Him. I'd depended solely on others to tell me what I should know and believe. God began weaning me away from that security blanket—one I'd clutched close to my heart throughout my whole life.

For the first time I searched the Scriptures for myself to find out what was true! In them I saw that Jesus had promised His Spirit would lead even me into all truth: *"... when He, the Spirit of Truth, has come, He will guide you into all truth"* (John 16:13).

Scripture was also clear: We needed the empowering of His Spirit to do His work. Jesus said, "... tarry in Jerusalem until you are endued with power from on high" (Luke 24:49).

"... you shall receive power when the Holy Spirit has come upon you; and you shall be witnesses to Me in Jerusalem, and in Judea and Samaria, and to the ends of the earth" (Acts 1:8).

We were to be part of the ongoing book of Acts! However, it would be *"not by [our] might and not by [our] power, but by His Spirit"* (Zech. 4:6). As enrollees in God's School of Obedience, we saw each day bring us new experiences and a heightened expectancy. What in the world would God do next!?

1 Thess. 5:18: *"In everything give thanks; for this is the will of God in Christ Jesus for you"* came alive! It sounded so

2

risky—and was! To realize that no matter what happened, God was still in control. He couldn't be caught off guard and have to scramble to make up for it. I hadn't slipped through His fingers for a moment or been left behind. Not if each hair on my head was numbered, and He knew my thoughts before I thought them (Matthew 10:30, Psalm 139). He cared; He really cared about me—everything about me, everything concerning me, and He had a plan for all of it.

It really was true that "nothing could separate me from His love" and that His perfect love could cast out all my fear of trusting and of changing. Like, praising Him at all times. A complete turnaround for me. Yet, wonderful. And so freeing!

In any school and in lessons learned, there are tests. How easy it had been to praise Him as we saw dramatic and instantaneous healings in answer to prayer. Little children with eyes fixed in death—raised up! New Guineans enslaved for generations to demonic spirit worship—SAVED—chains broken!

Revival took place in New Guineans and missionaries alike, as we, His Church, met together to testify, pray and praise the Lord! We were living the Gospel song, **Heaven Came Down and Glory Filled My Soul.**[1]

Yes, praise had been easy then. It was a little harder to praise Him when the roads washed out from mudslides and earthquakes, and we ran out of medicine and supplies; when our storage tanks for water ran dry with no rain in sight; or especially when we had to wave good-bye to our three teen-agers as they flew off to Australia for boarding school—not to be seen again for months at a time. Harder? Yes. But in each of those situations and countless others, we all saw God answer prayer; remain faithful; provide what we needed, and grow us closer to Him.

3

Harder still (for reasons I'll describe in a later chapter), after meeting with field leaders over a period of months, they decided we had to leave the mission field. Though broken-hearted over leaving the people we'd come to serve and grown to love, we discovered in the days following that as we praised the Lord while seeking His repair, incredibly He gave us **JOY** in going!

We were expectant—not defeated! All was not lost or over. For the same God who'd opened New Guinea's doors to us six-and-a-half years before was promising He'd open new ones!

"I know your works. See, I have set before you an open door, and no one can shut it; for you have a little strength, have kept My word, and have not denied My name" (Rev. 3:8).

So Bob and I had gathered our four chicks around us. Beginning our next "assignment", we had boarded the ship, Totol, the first stage in a long journey. For the twins, it would mean going back to Australia to finish their last year of high school; for Chris, now 14, and Lori, 11, it would be returning to America with us. All of us were battle-weary and in shock, and each of us had hurts we weren't even yet aware of. With adjustments of living again in America—huge ones—still before us, this south sea island boat trip sounded like just what we needed.

And on that beautiful sunny day with sea like glass it had started out that way. The kids took turns spotting dolphins at play and made friends with other travelers. However, the Totol was not a luxury boat by any stretch. In fact, at first glance it seemed barely sea worthy. As a small cargo boat, it lumbered up and down New Guinea's coast, stopping at towns and villages to take on or remove cargo.

Passage could be bought cheaply by the New Guineans or

anyone else who could stand the accommodations. The New Guineans could get the very cheapest fares by traveling in the hold of the ship, sleeping on mats or blankets they had brought, and providing their own food. What did "first class" accommodations consist of? Bunk beds nailed to the deck of the boat, close to the rail and together, providing no privacy whatsoever! (None of this had been explained when we bought tickets!)

Missionary life had trained me well. How bad can this be? I thought. It's just for a day and night. But within a few hours, the sunny skies and blue tranquil ocean changed to stormy weather and tempest-tossed seas. As the rain blew in upon the deck and into our bunks, the New Guinea crew worked rapidly to lower canvasses, tying them to the side rails to keep out the wind and rain. They didn't. Soon we were wet and cold, as night approached with no light in the darkness.

The pitching ship introduced me to seasickness. By late afternoon I'd sought my bunk, unwilling to move until we docked—or I died—whichever came first. Frequent reunions were held at the ship's railing as those the sickest staggered up to relieve themselves, then fell back into their bunks. The ship was at full capacity, every bunk taken. Everyone slept fitfully, anxious for this miserable night to end.

But the storm had increased in violence. And now I stood at the rail, facing the overwhelming certainty that Chris had been swept overboard. I felt such revulsion as the waters churned below me, yet I couldn't turn away. The unforgiving angry waves, the image of her struggling alone in them—terrified, with no one to hear, no one to rescue her—shattered my heart and threatened my sanity. Why hadn't I realized the danger? Why hadn't I gone with her when she got up? A mother was supposed to protect her child. How could I leave her in these dark waters and return to America without my precious one?

5

Earlier she'd been battling seasickness also. In the dark I'd felt her slide out of the bunk directly above me, saying she was going to the bathroom. I'd dozed off, then jerked awake, somehow sensing she hadn't returned. I'll go sit with her in the bathroom, I thought.

My first steps revealed the storm had become worse—much worse—and I had to grab the rail to keep erect. All too quickly I'd exhausted the only two places she could be—the bathroom or the tiny kitchen. Nor was she talking to the captain at the wheel, when frantically I asked if he'd seen our little girl.

Desperate now, I retraced my steps, checking our bunks again, my mind insisting, *She's back safe in her bunk now, and I've just missed her in the dark.* She wasn't! Beside myself, I grabbed two stewards, shouting above the wind, "I can't find my daughter! You've got to help me!" Looking aghast, they fanned out, searching the same places I had, bumping into me in the dark. But they didn't find our little girl!

Finally, I dragged myself from the rail, and in a zombie-like state, bent over and wakened Bob. I'd put off telling him. Not voicing my fears would keep them from being true. As I spoke, the finality of losing her swept over me like a tidal wave. My words jumped Bob to his feet. In pure panic, he ran off beginning the same search I'd made. My last hope: Her daddy would find her and bring her back to me. He didn't. He returned, anguish in his eyes, despair in his voice, announcing, "I'm going to look again."

All hope died. It was time to tell the children. We needed to face this together as a family. We'd already been through a lot. How in the world would we weather this? Yet amazingly, even in this dark hour, I realized I would somehow, some way, whisper, "Yes" to God's question, "Will you still praise Me?" For even now—even in this—He was still worthy of praise!

That had not changed.

Dreading the next moments, I touched Kevin's shoulder. "Kevin, we can't find Chris. We think she's gone overboard." Shocked awake instantly, as his eyes swept the scene his face mirrored the hopelessness I felt. There was no way anyone could survive.

As I moved to waken Steve, sleeping next to him, I heard Bob yell, "I've found her!" I turned to see him grabbing her sleeping form from one of the lower bunks at the far end of the deck. Now we really had something to praise the Lord about, as we gathered around her, grabbing her close, and all jabbering at once. And as we did, I realized that the wind had lessened and the storm had moved on...

She related that she'd sat for awhile in a lone deck chair to ease her queasy stomach. Then, becoming sleepy, she'd seen the only empty bunk, and thinking that a lower one might have less sway, crawled into it. Like Goldilocks, she'd gone fast to sleep in a strange bed, and now had no idea why she'd been jerked up and out of a sound sleep. Or what all the fuss was about!

I wasn't going to be put to the test after all, of praising the Lord in the loss of a child. Yet, I learned that whatever test God would choose to put me through in the future, He would allow nothing to come to me that He hadn't already strengthened and prepared me for.

You might say, "It's easy for her to talk about praise; she didn't really lose her child." And perhaps you have; and there's nothing more devastating than seeing our children suffer, or losing them in death. The gem I've discovered in the gold mines of God is that circumstances don't make or break God's principles. Results don't prove—or disprove— God's Word. God

Himself is His own witness; He swears by Himself. The **I AM** has spoken; there need be no other proof.

"Look to Me and be saved, all you ends of the earth! For I am God, and there is no other. I have sworn by Myself" (Isaiah 45:22,23a).

God's Word flows from God's very life—from who God is... That's why His words are not just good ideas, or "very good ideas" because God came up with them. They are never dead letters, but rather an outpouring of Himself and an impartation into us through His awesome promises.

Consequently, obeying Him becomes an opportunity, not a burden. A privilege, not a heavy yoke. Obeying Him connects us to the very God of all creation—the Alpha and Omega, the beginning and the end. Believing Him, taking Him at His Word, throwing ourselves completely upon Him allows Him to infuse and transfuse His very Self into us.

Therefore, rather than it being a hardship to trust Him (though it sometimes feels like it initially), it becomes a blessing we can't begin to fathom, measure or weigh.

Do I praise the Lord that I didn't lose Chris and have to walk that out? Oh, yes. Yet I know that if she'd died at sea, I'd have received an even greater measure of grace. Grace upon Grace.

Before boarding the Totol, I'd put down an anchor of faith in my life that said, "No matter what, I'm going to praise the Lord." **An anchor is absolutely no good unless you put it down!** For I'd settled it (I call it making transactions), that He was greater than any circumstance or tragedy, and **always** worthy of praise. No matter what happened or how it looked; no matter how I felt; and no matter if I never understood or never saw the

8

results—I would praise Him.

On the Totol, amidst the storm and darkness, the strength of that anchor was put to the test…and, praise God, proven— **MORE THAN** sufficient.

By God's grace alone, I too could say:

*"I will bless the Lord at all times; His praise shall **continually** be in my mouth. My soul shall make its boast in the Lord; the humble shall hear of it and be glad. Oh, magnify the Lord with me, And let us exalt His name together. I sought the Lord, and He heard me, and delivered me from all my fears"* (Psalm 34:1-4).

 * * * * *

Chapter 2

Strength In Crisis

The thunder of the horses' hooves increases, kicking up even more clouds of dust from the wilderness trail into the weary soldiers' eyes. The horses, without any urging from their riders, sense that they're not far away from fresh water and all the oats they can eat. Commander David ben Jesse, riding at the head of his command, straightens his tired back muscles after three days on maneuvers, knowing that just around the next curve they'll be able to see their village. He can't help but smile with satisfaction as he observes the discipline of his men riding in columns, their eyes fixed also on the road before them, knowing they are almost—home.

Home, a carved-out city between rocky prominences given to them for refuge by a neighboring king, and certainly not affording the lavish palace life David had experienced months ago when he'd had King Saul's favor. But Ziklag has provided a place where some semblance of family life could continue. Wives along with children had joined them there; and they had made, as only women can do, a place the men loved to come home to. It was amazing that from those who were "distressed, in debt, and discontented," a disciplined and loyal band was now knit with him.

They'd gathered around him when he fled for his life from King Saul's jealous rage, catching the vision and purpose: they were not to fight against the current reigning king but against Israel's enemies under David's command. David, anointed by the prophet Samuel as God's chosen king of Israel, would indeed one day ascend to the throne. But the timing for that was in Jehovah God's Hands; and could not—must not—be brought about through men's schemes or grasping hands of mortal flesh.

Now, as they round that last curve, their heartbeats quickening, expecting to see curls of smoke from cooking fires at campsites, and hear echoing out across the valley babies' cries and sounds of their children at play—they hear only silence… And see only billows of black smoke from a city burned.

The horses slow their pace, tossing their heads against the acrid smoke filling their nostrils, reined in by men who can't believe their eyes. Silently, with only the cadence of the horses' hooves marking each step, they enter what had once been their city. No loving arms are there to welcome them; no children's hands reach up to sit on daddy's horse, if but for a few minutes. Everywhere they look there's only carnage and devastation. Nothing left—nothing recognizable. And the heart-stopping realization that all wives and children have been taken captive as slaves by the wicked Amalekites. A picture their minds refuse to entertain. Then, shoving the silence aside, a wail of mourning begins; first by one, then two, then waves of moaning, weeping, screaming, crying. Fists raised to the sky, men falling on their knees groveling in the dust, their anguish in waves sweeping across the camp, and out across the valley. 'Til finally they're exhausted "with no strength to weep."

Once again there is silence. An ominous one. When we hurt, when we're in pain, we want to blame someone. Someone is responsible, someone must pay. Consequently, all eyes turn on David, though he, too, has suffered loss of loved ones. But this time the men don't want his encouragement, direction, or command. They want him dead. Their leader is responsible, and that leader must pay. David's life, his call, his anointing have caused this tragedy. And almost as one man they pick up stones to stone him. In a moment frozen in time, they've become David's judge and jury. Together they will now execute the unanimous sentence: **Death.**

What thoughts come as David faces those angry stares from

11

men who merely hours ago had gazed at him with admiration and devotion? Does he consider using his leadership skills and power of persuasion to talk them down and out of this idea? Surely if he eloquently reminds them of the prophetic words spoken over him that he will some day ascend to the throne, they will relent. Then together they can find a way to deal with this tragedy. He can remind them how far they've come, how thoroughly they've been molded into an army that's unbeatable. They've engaged in overpowering battles before, and against all odds not only have come up victorious, but stronger than ever. All he has to do now is convince them to believe in themselves, in him, and in God also, once again. He can do it; he can make it happen.

Or perhaps another voice jockeys for position. One that accuses, "You do deserve to die. You are responsible for this. If it weren't for you, they wouldn't be here, and they wouldn't have lost everything. You've made mistakes in the past. Now God is through with you, and He'll find someone else to fulfill His plan."

Then perhaps the **"Why?"** questions shove their way to the surface—tormenting, condemning. Wasn't it his decision to let the children and wives come to Ziklag? Why hadn't he realized it was too dangerous for them? What kind of a leader was he? As Commander-in chief, he was supposed to cover all the bases and think of everything. And once those taunts had marched by, leaving behind a sinking in his very soul, others now thrust the deepest wound: Why hadn't God stopped it? Why had He let this happen to innocent women and children? What kind of a God was He? David had served God and God's people, Israel, faithfully. Was this how Jehovah God rewarded those who left all to follow Him? What would people say about David, the fair-haired warrior **now**? Oh, God, **why?**

We don't know what battles he silently fought as he faced

that mob of 600 angry men. But we do know that whatever doubts or fears stormed his faith wall, whatever guilt or condemnation tormented him or caused him to trust in his own abilities—none were able to turn him away from his God. Because in the very midst of his personal agony, in that tragedy of losing everything, *"David strengthened himself in the Lord his God."*

As a young shepherd boy, David had faced the giant Goliath and, running toward him, with one stone had silenced forever his taunts and blasphemies against the Lord God of Israel. Now David, wrenching his eyes from the men's raging stares and from the stones clenched in their hands, turns away from them and runs to his God.

David pours out his heart to Him. And I don't believe he's silent (though he stands alone) in his supplications, worship and praise to The Almighty. This humble warrior is not ashamed of his total dependence on the living God. He hadn't learned to know and love the Lord in an army training camp or in King Saul's palace, but in the stillness and loneliness of shepherd fields near Bethlehem. There, on hillsides with harp in hand, he'd become God's worshipper, depending on Him alone. If they kill him now, they must do it amidst praise and heart cries to the God of his salvation ringing in the air. So that whether he "lives—or dies—he is the Lord's"!

"Whom have I in heaven but You? And there is none upon earth that I desire besides You. My flesh and my heart fail; but God is the strength of my heart and my portion forever."
"But it is good for me to draw near to God; I have put my trust in the Lord God, that I may declare all Your works" (Psalm 73:25,26,28).

At some point as he prays, as he worships, he senses God is going to give direction! So he calls for the priest, Abiathar, to come forward and bring the ephod, so that David may inquire of God. **What?** There's a priest standing there witnessing all of it? And silent? Had he, too, sided with the men? And if not picking up a stone himself, was he unopposed to them stoning David? Was he afraid—afraid they'd stone him as a witness to their deed? Or—perhaps He was allowing David to walk this out without any help from "leadership." Leadership can be wrong or they can be afraid. OR... they can rise to the occasion and step back so that we can exercise our own spiritual faith muscles. The result? We all become stronger.

David doesn't ask the priest to inquire. David asks God, "Shall I pursue this band? Shall I overtake them?" And God says to him, "Pursue, for you shall surely overtake them, and you shall surely rescue all."

After David gets his direction and promise from the Lord, I believe he may have faced yet another temptation: to turn to his men now that God has spoken and promised deliverance, and talk them into going with him. But it's not recorded that he did. Instead, I picture him just throwing back his tired shoulders, stealing his eyes toward the horizon. For the victory is already his. God, Himself, is the proof. He tightens his belt of armor and with renewed zeal steps forward to go. If necessary—by himself! For he had sought his God; he had heard; now he would obey. If others wanted to come along, fine.

And... come, they did.

How do we respond in our situations? We who are so prone to depend on everyone else, will we take that first step of faith, and if necessary, walk it alone? Our experiences, which disappoint and discourage us, God wants to use to shake and break us loose from any and all that we have depended upon. Consequently, we will be pressed to walk alone with our God. And if we will, in the process, like David we too will discover

He is more than enough!

"But what things were gain to me, these I have counted loss for Christ. But indeed I also count all things loss for the excellence of knowledge of Christ Jesus my Lord, for whom I have suffered the loss of all things, and count them as rubbish, that I may gain Christ" (Phil. 3:7,8).

Like David, amidst trial and calamity, we are bombarded with accusing thoughts and questions. Waves of discouragement break upon the shores of our lives and sweep over us, threatening to drown us in despair and defeat. What can be the most damaging of all? The feelings that God has betrayed or abandoned us (or both) though we scarcely dare think this—much less voice it, for fear we'll lose what little faith we have left.

David and his men had not led lives of ease leading up to this test. Before Ziklag, caves had been their homes, living in hiding from their pursuers, scrambling for their very lives. On King Saul's Most Wanted List. Even in Ziklag, I doubt they had three square meals and a nice soft bed at night. Life was hard. For the sake of their cause and their King, they'd given up everything. But the destruction of Ziklag, along with the tragic loss of their loved ones, was the last straw. The last in a long line of hardships. Feeling like they'd lost any semblance of control in their own lives and desperate for relief, they reached out to take matters into their own hands.

Because there is a "prince of this world" who is out for our destruction, because we live in a fallen world, because we live in a society that does not honor God and at least in some measure is under His divine judgment, because of our own human failings, weaknesses and sin, and because we are just "pilgrims passing through seeking a City which is to come"— life is hard. In our anger at the pain life brings we're determined to affix blame. We think if we can just get the "why?" question answered and turn on or away from those we find responsible, somehow life will be better. The pain less intense. Yet, none of these can heal us, nor bar the door of our lives so that hardship can never again shove its way inside.

Is there anything that will not only make our lives bearable and endurable, but miraculous and marvelous? Yes! Like David, we can turn to the Lord and strengthen ourselves in Him. And in the turning find healing and release. Sweet peace that passes all human understanding. Consequently, that situation, that hardship, which once held us captive and pressed us to the mat— no longer does!

Too often we look at the end of this story (and others like it), believing the high point is that they not only got back what was stolen—wives, children, possessions—but they got back many times over what they'd lost! (They did, you know.) Hands full of treasure; donkeys laden down. They took so much in spoils that they were able to bless the tribes of Israel with it, and rejoicing spilled all over the land because of their great deliverance. For sure a happy ending. Hallelujah! Praise the Lord!

But, as we look at our lives, we know that many times there isn't this kind of deliverance. There isn't a "happy-ever-after" ending (at least not yet). Instead, our situation worsens; the hardship grows even harder, with no end in sight, and we feel short-changed. Resentful. Especially when we look around and see that others do have their "happy-ever-after." But what if the true highpoint of the story is not in the visible tangible blessings that David and his people experienced, wonderful as they were? What if it's not in the change in circumstances, or the restoration of things? What if it's not because the ones who turned away from David once again showed him favor and followed him? What if it lies solely and only in—"David

16

strengthened himself in the Lord his God"?

Yes, he got an answer. Yes, he got specific direction. Yes, he got an outstanding victory—one that everyone took note of, both friend and foe alike! And I believe God took pleasure in blessing His people that way. But I believe He got even greater pleasure from seeing David in his deepest darkest distress run into His Everlasting Arms and find that, no matter what, all he wanted was the nearness and dearness of his God.

"But as for me, the nearness of God is my good; I have made the Lord God my refuge, that I may tell of all Thy works."
"... I am continually with Thee; Thou hast taken hold of my right hand. With Thy counsel Thou wilt guide me, and afterward receive me to glory" (Psalm 73:28,23,24 NASB).

David had stood between two enemies: the Amalekites on one side, and on the other those who had been his followers, just minutes before. Both wanted his destruction; both were being used by satan to strike him down and defeat God's plan. Though their choices took place in a wilderness dwelling place thousands of years ago amongst men with feet shod in sandals, fighting with spears and arrows, the same cosmic conflict still rages today. We, too, stand in the middle between the world and satan. And who we will turn to, and run to, determines the real victory.

If the truth be told, don't we often seek God just to get relief from the problems, a respite from the strife? But true worshippers in spirit and in truth want more than that, need more than that. They want and need the Lord. So, what does God see when he looks down on us as the storms of life bombard us? When all seems lost and nothing stands? When everything's been taken away?

17

Does God look down at me and say, "Well, she certainly wants the victory and the blessing." Or... does He look down at me and say, "She strengthens herself in Me, her God, in every situation. No matter what— I AM all she wants!"

(Story taken from 1 Samuel 30)

 * * * * *

Chapter 3

Bitter/Sweet

The aged man gazes far out across the countryside, the land more wonderful than he'd remembered. Of course it had been long ago, forty years ago, when he'd first seen this country, this land of promise; and then for such a short time.

During those years, had remembered scenes tumbled through Caleb's dreams? Dreams of lush green pastures (more than enough for his flocks and herds); sparkling streams chattering over stones; vines weighted down with gigantic grapes; and majestic mountain peaks standing as sentinels in the distance. But then would he awaken only to find that his sleeping mat lay on hard desert sand; and a goat's hair tent defined his nomadic life?

Day followed day, week followed week. Month after month, year after year, he'd traveled through the wilderness; tenting with God, and moving only when Jehovah God willed it.

No matter how much Caleb had gotten caught up in daily living, one eye had to be kept on the pillaring cloud of God's Presence hovering above the Tabernacle. For at any moment, day or night, it could lift from above the Tent of Meeting signaling to all—God was on the move. And not to follow Him meant—you were left behind! A priest would lift a silver trumpet to his lip sounding the advance, and Moses' shout would resound across Israel's campsite, echoing out across the valley 'til it was swallowed by the wilderness' vastness. *"Rise up, O Lord, let Your enemies be scattered; and let those who hate You flee before You"* (Num. 10:35).

There was absolutely no warning (no council meeting the day before, so tribal elders could decide it was time to move on). At a moment's notice (they might have been camped there weeks, months, or just settled in); yet when that call came, immediately they had to pull up tent stakes, roll together bedding, gather utensils, and grabbing kids, goats and bedroll, swing into some semblance of the order designated for their move.

Carried by the priests of the House of Aaron, the awe-inspiring Ark of the Covenant led forth. Behind it the tribe of Levi carrying the furniture, utensils and articles for tabernacle worship. Next the tribe of Judah, the tribe of praise (Caleb's tribe) going before all the other tribes, would swing into formation, its banner with a lion emblazoned on it, waving proudly in the breeze. What an amazing sight—this gigantic undertaking—as the great multitude set out, the very earth trembling under millions of sandaled feet. There would be no halting until the cloud that went before them suddenly stood still, hovering over their next encampment, signaling that God had chosen their resting place. Then Moses' voice would once again ring out: *"Return, O Lord, to the many thousands of Israel"* (Num. 10:36). For how long? Only God knew.

"Whether it was two days, a month or a year... at the command of the Lord they camped, and at the command of the Lord they set out..." (Num. 9:15-23).

Although it was wilderness living, their everyday life was sprinkled with miracles. At day's dawning, bread from heaven (called Manna) laid out on the ground for them—as much as they needed for that day. But if they gathered extra it became wormy. Except for Sabbath. For that designated day of rest, they could gather extra. Then there were the astounding provisions of water. Once, when tired and thirsty after three days journey, realizing water was up ahead they'd rushed forward only to discover when they bent down to drink—it was bitter! But their crushing disappointment along with parched tongues was short-lived; for God showed Moses a tree and told him to throw it into the water! When he did, the most amazing thing happened. The water became pure, more than quenching everyone's thirst, including Caleb's.

"So he [Moses] cried out to the Lord, and the Lord showed him a tree. When he cast it into the waters, the waters were made sweet" (Ex. 15:25).

Funny, how just placing that tree into bitter waters under God's direction could bring forth, rather than death—sweetness and life! Later again when they needed water (they were always needing water) with no spring, no well, no oasis in sight, under God's orders, with griping, complaining voices murmuring in the background, Moses had struck a rock with his rod. A rock! And amazingly, out of that flint-like stone a fountain-like stream gushed forth—enough for every man, woman and child (Ex. 17:6).

Then there was the thing with their clothing and shoes. In the hot sun and with the many miles they walked, why didn't their clothes and shoes wear out? Although life was rough and rugged, everyone seemed to thrive. There was no way to explain it other than that they were on a miraculous Journey led by a Miraculous God. Although the people continued to complain, always wanting to tuck-tail-it back to Egypt, Caleb must have sensed that God was showing them in every way (now that He had a people for Himself), that they could depend on Him and Him alone. He wanted to be close to them, and in every way possible was demonstrating that: Care, Provision, Direction, Protection. And most of all—Love!

Yes, there was a lot of life in the camp. New ones being born; flocks and herds increasing. Praise and Worship available for anyone at the Tabernacle where the Very Presence of The Living God resided. Think of it! The God of Abraham, Isaac and Jacob—right there in their midst. Close enough to touch—almost. And when He spoke, the sound of His voice like thunder, so that no one could miss His commandments or direction. No one could say they hadn't heard from God in this atmosphere.

But it was also a death camp. For God had said that, with the exception of Caleb and his friend Joshua, no one who was alive when they'd first viewed Canaan land would live to enter. *That whole spy plan,* from beginning to end, had failure written all over it. The people themselves had insisted on sending in spies ahead to see what awaited them in this proposed conquest. So, Jehovah God had designated that a leader from each tribe would go. Twelve mature men would assess the land and its people, and bring back a report. They did. And among ten of the elders it was unanimous. *"We cannot take the land; the people are giants, the cities too well fortified!!!"*

Astounded, immediately Joshua and Caleb (the other two elders) reacted. Yes, the people were giants and the land well fortified. The report was true, but not the conclusion. Joshua and Caleb pleaded with the people, "Don't believe their report!" It was "not" true, they said, that Israel could "not" prevail and take the land—for God had told them to!

"Behold, I send an Angel before you to keep you in the way and to bring you into the place which I have prepared… if you indeed obey His voice and do all that I speak, then I will be an enemy to your enemies and an adversary to your adversaries. For My Angel will go before you and bring you in…" (Ex. 23:20,22,23a).

Joshua and Caleb had seen the same giants, viewed the same defenses. As Caleb quieted the people before Moses, he implored, *"We should by all means go up and take possession*

22

of it, for we are well able to overcome it."

But the ten spies now spread these words among the people: *"We are not able to go up against the people for they are too strong for us... this is a land that devours its inhabitants... we became like grasshoppers in our own sight, and so we were in their sight."*

It would come down to a matter of faith or unbelief. *(It always does, doesn't it?)* Who would believe their eyes? Who would believe in God and His Promises? Who would obey God, no matter what? Who would turn away? Those men, respected as leaders, even though the Lord God had led them out of Egypt in the Exodus and had promised it to them, had no faith to believe that, in truth, the land was already theirs!

It wasn't as if these ten doubters had had no experiences with God. They had an intimate history with a Miracle-working God; a God who had proven Himself trustworthy in any and every circumstance they had encountered since leaving Egypt. As Egypt's slaves, they'd seen the ten awful and awesome plagues their delivering God through Moses had visited on Egypt when mighty Pharaoh refused to let God's people go. Things like frogs, and locusts and the river Nile turned to blood. Lastly, they'd trembled behind a blood-stained door hardly knowing what to think as the death angel passed over and passed by, because the Lord God had said, *"When I see the blood, I will pass over you"* (Ex. 12:13).

With the blood's protection on their lives, no Israelite's firstborn had died on that doom-filled night. But from every household that did not have the lamb's blood on their door, death took a captive. Cries of anguish and wails of grief went up all over the land as households discovered the deaths. Yet in Goshen, safe behind blood-stained doors, they'd stood huddled together with their families, their voices hushed, and eaten the unleavened bread and Passover Lamb, whose life's blood stained their doors. Then with day breaking, Moses had led them out through the blood; out through the city streets, out into the countryside, out of Egypt, out of captivity—*free at last!*

They'd seen (as Moses stretched forth his rod) God part the Red Sea right before them. Then *"the children of Israel [had] walked on dry land in the midst of the sea, and the waters were [like] a wall to them on their right hand and on their left"* (Ex. 14:29). Looking back, they'd witnessed Pharaoh's Army, with horses and chariots ready to overtake them, swallowed up as the wall of water, held back by Jehovah's Hand, crashed in upon them. As they traveled, they'd seen God defeat every tribe and nation who came out against them. Daily, these men had their stomachs filled and their bodies strengthened by God's provision. As they journeyed they'd walked under the cloud canopy that shielded them from the sun in the daytime, and gazed up at a fiery pillar glowing above them as they marched by night, lighting their way and scaring away predators (Ex. 13:21,22).

They'd felt the ground shake under their feet as the Lord God gathered the twelve tribes together at the foot of Mt. Sinai. Later, they'd watched Moses descend from that mountain, his face absolutely glowing from forty days in the presence of the Lord. Their ears had been almost deafened, their bodies had trembled when the very voice of Yahweh thundered from that mountain (Ex. 19:17-19). They'd also seen this Awesome God deal immediately and decisively with any and all who rebelled against Him (Ex. 32).

They'd experienced the joy of Tabernacle worship and praise, singing, dancing. God had created this place to meet with Him; and there they could find mercy and forgiveness whenever they carried a lamb without blemish to the priest, laid their hands upon its body as they confessed their sins, and watched while its throat was slit and its innocent life's blood drained away—for them. In the Tabernacle designed and designated by God, God Himself dwelt in their midst, desiring to be close to them, providing for them every step of the way (Ex. 33:10). Yet, in spite of all they'd seen, heard and done; in spite of the countless examples of His Mercy and Grace (along with shocking examples of what can happen if you turn away from Him), when it came time to trust God and draw from their own reservoir of faith—they came up empty—which goes to prove that signs and wonders don't necessarily build faith!

Whatever previous trust they'd had came up short in light of the seemingly gigantic task facing them. (It's always easier to talk faith than to demonstrate it, isn't it?) Quickly, their unbelief like wildfire ignited fear, spreading quickly from one to another; their words a pestilence, and soon everyone had caught the "plague!" Everyone, that is, except Caleb and Joshua. Those two stood alone as the people backed away.

A line was being drawn in the sand. Joshua and Caleb pleaded (ripping their garments in anguish, demonstrating how serious this decision was); and Joshua warned, *"If the Lord is pleased with us, then He will bring us into this land and give it to us...only do not rebel against the Lord and do not fear the people of the land for they shall be our bread. Their protection has been removed from them, and the Lord is with us; do not fear them."*

Their earnest entreaty falls on deaf ears. Minds are already made up. Hearts already hardened. Like a herd of spooked cattle, this frightened multitude wants only one thing: to turn and flee. Instead of repenting and pleading for more faith, their doubts and fears brew themselves right into rebellion (the end result of not believing God). For they, speaking with one voice, are even more determined; accusing God. *"... If only we had died in Egypt, or ... in this wilderness. Why is the Lord bringing us into this land, to fall by the sword, our wives and children becoming victims... Let us select a leader and return to Egypt."*

Driven by mob mentality, they decide to stone these faithful messengers who've opposed their turning back. That's when God steps in. His Shekinah glory descends into their midst. But not to bless (not this time). The Righteous Judge will now decide the issue and determine their fate. For forty years (a year for each day they'd been there) they would wander until a whole new generation came forth; and only that generation would inherit the land. But not until all those who'd rebelled against God were gone. Not until every man and woman over twenty died. They'd accused God of wanting them to die in the wilderness. Their prediction of death was prophetic. They would die in the wilderness. But by their own decision, through their unbelief. Only Caleb and Joshua would live to enter. They'd been faithful. They were His remnant.

Israel had repented—crying, weeping, and immediately determined they would right their wrong. They would now go up against the nation. God warned them not to go (presumption never pleases God). But go they did, resulting in massive retreat as they fled for their very lives. For the second time, Jehovah tells Moses that He will destroy these people and start over. Ten times they have turned against Him and accused Him of wanting to destroy them. Ten plagues God had used to free them from Egypt's slavery. It was as if by their willfulness they were canceling out and negating each miraculous act God had done to set them free.

As Caleb watches, Moses now pleads with God (as he has done before) not to turn His back on the people He has chosen. For the sake of His own name, to forgive and relent, God does. Mercy's plea always wins the day. Nevertheless, the people will literally have to walk out the consequences of their choice.

And so it had come to pass. Over the many years Caleb

and Joshua watched as dear friends, beloved comrades, mothers, fathers, sisters, (wives?), brothers, aunts and uncles, grandparents—men and women died. On the one hand, shouts of joy and victory in praise to their God permeated the camp. On the other hand, sadness. Rivulets of tears ran down dusty cheeks and wails of grief drifted out across the long winding caravan, as loved ones were laid to rest in the desert sand, or at an oasis; then reluctantly left behind as God's people stumbled on. *A generation on a death march.*

Over those past forty years, it would have been so easy for resentment to bore its way into Caleb's heart and like a leech fasten on his soul, sucking the very life juices out of him. After all, it wasn't Caleb's fault that God's judgment had fallen. This tragedy couldn't be laid at his door. He had believed God in the midst of his fear and had urged the people not to rebel. Along with Joshua, with all the words they could muster, with tears and pleading, they'd struggled to change minds, but to no avail. So did the questions of *"Why did he have to suffer when the fault belonged to others?"* ever enter his mind? I think it must have. Yet if it did, we find from the end of the story that in no way has this man become bitter or held onto resentment or unforgiveness. No question of *"God, this isn't fair, what did I do to deserve this?"* dominated his past forty years. No thinking now, *"God, I got robbed a generation ago, and You owe me big time."*

Incredibly (but as promised), Caleb's life has now come full circle. This is where it all began. At last it's time for Israel to take possession of the land "flowing with milk and honey" promised long ago to their Father Abraham, founder of faith, friend of God. As Caleb's eyes graze the scene laid out before him, he's hardly able to take it all in, or sort out the myriad of emotions as he remembers all that's happened, all he's seen, all he's been through. After wilderness living, the brilliant shades of greens in the meadows and hillsides and the bright array of multicolored flowers in bloom wash over him; the smell of the rich earth fills his nostrils, his whole being drinks in the overwhelming reality that finally, finally God's Chosen are home! Home, in this much longed for and promised land. And as Caleb considers who will enter, he realizes all over again that God's Word has come to pass; every one of His promises—fulfilled!

Yet for 85-year-old Caleb, surely this wilderness walker is old and tired now, weary of the walk, bent over, weak and feeble. Just glad it's finally over. At last he can take his ease. Have a real house. No… think again. This aged traveler of hundreds of moves and as many campsites comes out of that just-keep-putting-one-foot-in-front-of-another walk, not with dourness and crustiness. Nor tired and spent. He's not a wizened and embittered old man. Not at all. Not this one. For Caleb comes out of his testing with freshness and invincible strength! Though older now, much older, his passion has not lessened! And instead of the embers of his faith scattered and coals cold (or at least lukewarm), over the decades it seems a fire of faith has been building in his bones. A fire just waiting for an opportunity to flash forth into full flame. And this is that moment.

Imagine! For he declares: *"Behold, the Lord has kept me alive as He said… here I am this day eighty-five years old. As yet, **I am as strong this day as I was on that day** [that Moses sent him]… just as my strength was then, so now is my strength for war, both for going out and coming in… Give me this mountain [where the giants live in fortified cities]… and I shall drive them out as the Lord said"* (Joshua 14:10-13).

Don't you love it??? Though well advanced in years, he stands more than ready and willing to serve His God in any way needed. Still eager and still able to go the extra mile—to put his life at risk (if necessary) for the God He loves and serves!

Once again, he's center stage. And once more—he's responding magnificently! One would think that instead it was time to bring out his "due me list" relating his loyalty and faithfulness in serving the Almighty One. A list that recounts *in great detail* all he's been through; all he's endured for the sake of the Kingdom. Surely, now it's reward time—and time for him to rest. *Time for the younger ones to take over, he's done his part.* Time to kick back and coast through his remaining years.

Not Caleb. Caleb whose name means *"forcible"* doesn't add it up that way at all. Rather than seeing those forty years as wasted, or at least as just marking time ('til the Big Revival takes place—or 'til we finally get the Victory), he's counted it instead as an awesome privilege to walk with God! No matter where, no matter how! For Caleb, it's been time well spent learning God's Ways, learning God's will. Yes, he's seen the supernatural (not only seen it, but lived it), and he'll always be grateful for that. But more importantly, it seems, he's discovered something even more precious—something that has continually refreshed his soul. Like an ever-flowing fountain, it's softened the hardness of the discipline and turned the bitter into sweet. Through it all he's had the opportunity to learn God's nature, His character. *His nearness and dearness.*

That's what hardship does when embraced rightly in one's life, dear friend. God wants us to learn about His character through His power, signs and wonders, but we also learn His character through suffering and hardship. We not only **learn about** His character—we become **partakers of it** (2 Peter 1:4). Glory to God! Yet, there is more: Out of the crucible of testing, God births a testimony.

And perhaps because dear Caleb our brother in faith has not given place to resentment, even his physical body shows stamina and youth way beyond his years. Mumbling, grumbling, insisting on better, blaming God, living in doubt and unbelief, in worry and anxiety—they take a terrible toll. They infest our souls; break down our bodies, affecting and infecting anyone and everyone whose lives we touch. They bring a cloud of heaviness—a darkness—to our soul. Yet from Caleb's lips come no words like those; no complaining that he's been a *victim*. Not even a hint that God has even once treated him unfairly; or that He's ever asked too much from him.

As far as we know Caleb didn't blame leadership either. Remember, it was other leaders (mature elders from each tribe) who brought the fearful report leading to Israel's downfall and the 40-year sentence. Surely if leadership gets off track, we shouldn't be blamed for going along with them, should we? They're the ones who are supposed to hear from God and know His Word and Will! Well, perhaps Caleb realized something we've failed to grasp—that his daily walk, obedience and faithfulness to the Lord must not depend on others. ***On no one!*** Not even leaders. Not ever!

God had said about Caleb forty years earlier when he'd first seen the land that *"he had a different spirit... "* (Num. 14:24). And forty years later after all that's transpired—he still has it! Over those arduous years Caleb's spirit has not been diminished by hardships nor shrunken by circumstances. Because now from this faithful follower, this seasoned traveler, from that same spirit come words of faith and strength, "I can take that mountain; I can overcome. God has said so."

Caleb's life demonstrates that circumstances may cause us some limitations: For example, if I'm scheduled for surgery, I'm probably not planning a trip overseas. But circumstances, situations, or my past do not, and must not, define who I am. I must not let them. And they never have to define me again if I'll look out of them and beyond them to God.

It's so easy for bitterness to creep in with hardship. Has

your pain (emotional or physical), or the feelings that no one cares or understands, that you're all alone in your hardship become an excuse for bitterness? Are you plagued by thinking, *It's so unfair?* Have the waters of your life, once fresh and satisfying, become tainted by resentment?

In the natural, bitterness is difficult, perhaps impossible to dilute. You can dilute things that are too salty, or sweet, or sour by adding more liquid. But bitterness is another story. You can't cover it, or drown it. And the taste of bitterness lingers. Long after you've swallowed it, the taste remains—like a bad memory. Perhaps you've tried ways to deal with your bitterness, not knowing you can't dilute it or cover it over. Nor can you make excuses for it, or try to forget about it.

Although nothing about Caleb had been recorded for forty years, God had not lost track of Him. And dear one, He's not lost track of you. He's not forgotten you, nor has He abandoned you. Although you may have had, and still are walking through dry barren times; though others have rejected you and you've had to stand alone; though nothing has been fair about your situation, and long nights grow even longer with no end in sight—for the one who's been redeemed, *there is no excuse for bitterness.*

Though God understands, He does not excuse it. However, He will forgive it. For there is—a *Tree!* And if you'll repent of your bitterness and resentment, and let His Cross truly touch your heart and all that's happening, He will make all your bitter waters—*sweet.*

(Story taken from Numbers 13 & 14)

 * * * * *

31

Chapter 4

Calvary Covers It All

Don't you like to think that if you'd lived back then, you'd have been, if not a Joshua, *for sure* a Caleb? I know I do. I like to think that throughout those long years of testing and hardship, at times going around the same mountain again and again, I'd have come out of it like Caleb—pure and true; stronger than ever in my faith and devotion to the Lord. Not even a speck of resentment would have buried deep in my heart for what I'd had to endure, or for what I could have had, or done, during what looks like wasted years—just wandering.

Yes, I can picture on that Day of Decision, there would have been, not two, but three of us standing there believing God. Bravely joined with Joshua and Caleb and shoulder to shoulder with them facing that raging crowd, I too would have dared to stand for God. For God alone, come what may.

Or...I can go even further back than that incident. I don't think I'd have grown weary, as Abraham did waiting all those years for the child of promise, taking matters into my hands, trying to make God's promise come to pass with an Ishmael. I'd have trusted God and waited (no matter how long) for the ***true*** child of promise—Isaac (Gen. 15:6).

Or...back even further. I can imagine that I'd have heeded Noah's prophetic warning for 120 years that the earth would be destroyed by flood as he and his three sons fashioned timbers and planks together (Gen. 6). I wouldn't have decided he was crazy building that box-like thing. Although I'd never seen rain and couldn't imagine what a flood would be like, when he called out, "It's time. All aboard!" I'd have clambered up that gangplank, come on board the Ark and looked for my assigned place. (I wonder if I'm bunking with the gorillas or the giraffes.) Even if no one else joined me. Even if I had to go alone, and leave everything I knew behind me.

Or, further back in time.... I don't think I would have become so angry at my brother, Abel, jealous that his sacrifice was accepted when mine wasn't, that I would have killed him like Cain did. No, when God warned me that my heart wasn't right, along with my offering, I would have repented and sought to have my relationship with the Lord God and my brother Abel restored (Gen. 4:4-9).

Or what if I go way, way back; back to the very beginning of time itself. Back to a garden called Eden. When God said, "You may eat of every other tree in the garden, but of this one... you may not eat" I'd like to think that I'd never have eaten. I wouldn't have even gone near that tree. Not me.

Jumping ahead, fast-forwarding into Jesus' day. One of the chosen. One of those listening, following. I'd have believed Him. I wouldn't have doubted. I wouldn't have run away when He needed me, and left Him to suffer all alone. Surely I'd have done something—anything—to try to stop them from nailing Him to a Cross. I could never have been part of that...

Oh yes, I could have! And if the truth be known about my heart, I would possibly have been the first to turn and run, and done the deed quicker. Been the first to shout, "Crucify Him!" I wouldn't have necessarily been any better than any of the people I've mentioned—I could have been worse, and demonstrated even less faith than they did.

The Apostle Paul understood this when he said, "I am chief of sinners," and "in me (that is in my flesh), no good thing dwells" (1 Tim. 1:15; Rom. 7:18). Because *Pride* (thinking we're better than we are) and taking credit for what we've been given, since the beginning of time, has been the root sin.

Yes, if I'm truly honest with myself as I consider Caleb's life, I realize how easily I could have been more like the rest of Israel's multitude when they heard the ten spies' report. Quick to doubt God rather than trusting; rebelling rather than obeying. I, like they, could have been easily swayed by others whom I trusted in, rather than standing on the promises of God for myself. And have done so more than once. After all, if we've got leaders telling us we shouldn't go on, that we don't need to be foolish or take useless risks, then I better listen to them. They know more than I do. Right?

And (God forbid) I, too, could have been ready to pick up a stone. I, too, could have cast my deadly vote right along with the others against Joshua and Caleb, who were truly clinging to God's promises; who were ready, in the face of overwhelming obstacles, to obey God.

Unlike Caleb, I could have been chock full of mumblings and grumblings, as soon as things got tough and my feet hurt. My thoughts could have reeked with the regrets of *"What ifs"* and *"If onlys."* Always looking back, wishing my life had been different, morose and depressed, grieving on what it could have been like if the last forty years of my life (my best years) hadn't been spent in hardship.

Seeing those years as wasted. Seeing myself as a failure and God not faithful. Fantasizing on all I could have accomplished if my talents and "giftings" hadn't laid dormant, unused and wasted on everyday humdrum work. And…if the truth be known, harboring in my heart thoughts that I could have ordered my life better than God. (I don't know quite what that would have been, but whatever I would have come up with wouldn't have been so hard, or so unfair.) And, when I operate in the flesh—rather than in the spirit—that's exactly the way I'll be.

34

However, Caleb illustrates for us that we don't have to live in the flesh. Praise God! Are there hints in Scripture that tell us why Caleb remained faithful and true? I believe there are at least two.

1) Caleb came from the tribe of Judah (the tribe of praise). He's our example that praising God continually declares to God, man and satan that our Covenant-making and Covenant-keeping God is faithful. Sincere *praise the Lord* and *hallelujahs* proclaim that Jesus is Lord and that we are trusting and committed to Him—no matter what circumstances hand us. Never, never deciding, "You owe me, God. Satan has stolen and You must repay me a hundred fold." (We are lousy spiritual accountants.)

When we worship instead of whine, then any and every hardship will produce the sweetest of wines from the fullest of vines as they did in Caleb's life. The tribe of praise always led forth as they traveled. And whenever they went into battle, praise led forth. Praise risks. God assigned those who praised to be positioned before the army—thrust out there—completely vulnerable yet completely safe—because they were being obedient to God's Command as they followed the Ark of the Covenant (the Presence of the Lord) (2 Chron. 20:15-30).

2) The tribe of Judah was also the tribe of kings. King David came from the tribe of Judah and began a long lineage of kings. Our Jesus came from that lineage, *"and He shall reign forever and ever"* (Rev. 11:15).

Yes, kings reign. Therefore, they must not allow themselves to be swayed by majority numbers or popularity polls. Nor to be swayed by circumstances, feelings or others' opinions. They must—if they are going to be good kings and rule their people wisely and well—see the bigger picture! Kings must be willing to suffer being unpopular in order to bring about that higher, better good for their people. Caleb, with his royal bloodline, ruled over his feelings and what he saw—the fortified cities and gigantic people—when he believed God. We, too, as priests and kings can reign in every situation, for royal blood flows in our veins as well! (Rev. 1:6; 2 Peter 2:9).

However… you may think—he didn't win the victory! He had to endure forty years of tough times. So… what good does it do to trust in the Lord if your life is going to end up just as hard as others'? Is it not that Caleb acknowledged a God bigger than himself? And as he refused to let anything overrule his faith (and his God), he was lifted high above his hardship and trial, able to follow wherever God's presence led—for as long as it took!

I believe Caleb had hold of the basics. Caleb "had laid hold of the horns of the altar" and he wasn't going to let go. You see, he'd eaten daily of *heavenly bread;* he'd seen Moses, following God's command, throw a branch into bitter waters, and when that *Tree* touched the water, the bitterness—vanished! Completely. There was no waiting, no other additive, no ritual to add to that work of The *Tree*.

Yet what Caleb had seen and experienced was not enough for the others. God had so desired to have a people for Himself, a kingdom of priests with Him dwelling right in the midst of her. But as Israel came out of Egypt she was often anything but content with what God offered or provided. Her discontentment built; so that when the test came—and right in front of her was the blessing and the fulfillment of the glorious Promised Land— she couldn't see it! She couldn't recognize it because she'd grown so accustomed to doubting God.

Israel was so used to viewing Him with mistrust; so used to accusing Him of not taking care of her. As soon as anything went wrong, He was the first to be blamed—He was out for her destruction, never her good.

God so often has a different view of our circumstances than we do. He told Israel, *"You've seen what I did to the Egyptians and how I bore you on eagle's wings and brought you to Myself"* (Ex. 19:6).

Their attitude was, *Wait a minute! When did we get carried by You? We've been walking, getting tired and thirsty and it doesn't feel at all like we've been carried.*

Although some of those same thoughts may have come to Caleb (we can't keep thoughts from coming into our minds), I believe he cast them aside before they could take root. I think Caleb **made the choice** that if God said He'd carried them—He had! It might not have felt like it, it might not have looked like it. But if God said He'd carried them—He had!

With that choice to make God's view his view, Caleb's baggage of worry and concern would have dropped to the ground. And he would have walked on unencumbered—His burden lifted! He wouldn't have to figure it all out or come up with a better plan. *(Whew!)* He could now just enjoy the walk, "counting it as joy," following the One leading who had everything under control! And although the journey was arduous, Caleb could see he was part of an awesome endeavor.

That very same God, who calls us to follow Him, sees everything happening to us through the window of the Cross. There's a gospel song that says, *"Calvary covers it all."*[2]

Calvary (the Cross) and all that the Cross includes must be applied to everything: to our pride that adds up our lives and decides that God hasn't done rightly by us, just because there is hardship; to our mumblings and grumblings, our discontentment, our anger, for all of it is sin—sin that God hates (Psalm 106:24-27).

Then, if, in repentance, we'll dip all of it, along with our weariness, disappointment and discouragement into His Waters of Forgiveness, we'll discover that, yes, indeed…

Calvary does cover it all.

 * * * * *

A Personal Note from the Author

What does the phrase "Calvary covers it all" mean to you? If you're already a born-again believer who knows Jesus as Lord and Savior and are following Him—it means everything!

However, you may be reading this book and never experienced this. You may have heard about Jesus——even believed that He's the Savior of the world. However up to now, you have never bowed your head, your knee and your heart, asking Him to forgive and save——you!

Scripture says that nothing you can do, no good works can ever bridge the huge gap your sins have made between you and a Holy God. In God's Celestial Courtroom you stand guilty as charged for breaking His Laws: Like, putting others, or things, before Him; stealing (the value of the article doesn't matter); lying (there are no "white" or "little" lies. (Ex 20:1-17) And no matter how sincere you've been in what you've believed and counted on up to now——He says it's insufficient!

However, that same God loves you, and doesn't want you to be lost. That's why Jesus Christ—who had no sin—died in your place to remove all judgment against you; wash your sins away by His blood; and give you Eternal Life through His Resurrection! Jesus becomes **God's Gift of Grace to you** *through faith when you believe Him and pray to receive Him.*

Jesus said, "For out of the heart proceed evil thoughts, murders, adulteries, fornications, thefts, false witness, blasphemies. These are the things which defile a man" (Matthew 15:19,20a).

"Come now let us reason together," says the Lord, "though your sins are like scarlet they shall be as white as snow; and though they be red like crimson, they shall be as wool" (Isaiah 1:18).

"... He [Jesus] was wounded for our transgressions [the breaking of God's laws, rebellion], He was bruised for our guilt and iniquities [sins and moral violation]; the chastisement needed to obtain peace and well-being for us was upon Him, and with the stripes that wounded Him we are healed and made whole" (Isaiah 53:5, AMP).

[Jesus said] "For God so loved the world that He gave His only begotten Son, that whoever believes in (trusts, clings to, relies on) should not perish but have eternal everlasting life" (John 3:16).

"I [Jesus] am the resurrection and the life. He who believes in Me, though he may die, he shall live" (John 11:25).

Chapter 5

Why, God, Why?

The young man looks furtively around. He's put his life on the line if he's caught here. At any moment gleeful yelling soldiers could surround and take him captive. Or… slaughter him on the spot. The hated Midianites would show no mercy, retaliating with vengeance if they found him.

Whenever Israel began harvesting a crop, Midian raiders along with Amalekites would sweep down, destroying people, livestock, torching the crops and completely devastating the land. For their goal was to totally demoralize and humiliate this proud people. This siege of devastation, this degradation had dragged on, not for weeks or months, but for seven long years! Driven from their homes by the invaders, the children of Israel now scratch out a subsistence digging out dens for themselves in the mountains and caves. God's chosen ones now live no better than animals.

On this day, Gideon has snuck into a winepress, hoping to thresh out some wheat for his family. Despairing thoughts and feelings perch on his shoulder, whispering in his ear as he works frantically, ***"Where is God in all this?"***

Recently in their desperation as the *"sons of Israel cried to the Lord,"* God had sent a lone prophet traveling throughout the land crying:

"Thus says the Lord, the God of Israel, 'It was I who brought you up from Egypt, and brought you out from the house of slavery… I delivered you from the hands of all your oppressors… and gave you their land… I am the Lord your God; you shall not fear the gods of the Amorites…but you have not obeyed me'" (Judges 6:8-10 NASB)

40

Gideon didn't know if others had responded. His father hadn't. Their altar to Baal and its wooden idol to Asherah still stood. Could just getting rid of idols solve the kinds of problems they had? Perhaps he thought, *Desperate situations demanded desperate means. People needed all the help they could get; what could it hurt to call on some other gods, especially if Jehovah God wasn't listening anymore?*

Gideon slashes at the grain, feeling helpless, hopeless and trapped. Stories of how God had worked wondrous deliverances for Israel in years past seemed like old men's tales. A man couldn't exist on stories; nor feed a family on memories. If only Jehovah would once again take up their cause…

Suddenly Gideon is no longer alone… His hand on the threshing fork freezes. A voice like none he's ever heard before speaks, *"The Lord is with you, O valiant warrior." Whoever this person is, he certainly doesn't know whom he's talking to,* Gideon thinks. *My name may mean "warrior/destroyer", but hiding in this winepress is proof that I'm more wimp than warrior (although it had taken some courage to do even that).*

All his pent-up doubts, fears, even accusations long caged in Gideon's mind, now break forth, one tumbling after the other, *"Oh my Lord, **if the Lord is with us, why then** has all this happened to us? And **where are all His miracles,** which our fathers told us about…. But now **the Lord has abandoned us** and given us into the hand of the Midianites"* (Judges 6:13).

Don't we often have the same questions Gideon had? Like **WHY???** (which God never seems to answer). Yet, we know from the text that God had told them what was wrong: They were worshipping false gods, and were no longer listening to or following Him. And He'd offered them the remedy, "Repent and turn back to Me"—which they'd ignored.

Like Gideon, we also fault God for not working miracles, signs and wonders that we can see, hear, touch and feel to lift our burdens. If God will only manifest His Power, then we'll believe He truly cares, and that we're special. Gideon looks at the circumstances and (like us) adds up the score.

His conclusion? God has abandoned them. He's given them into the hand of the enemy. God has let them down. *It's God's fault.* God's the villain. Once we begin to question—invariably we decide God could have done a better job of taking care of us!

Gideon was about to get—NOT answers, but an assignment! Not comfort, but a Call. Not a way out, but a way through. Then the Lord looked at him and said, *"Go in this your strength, and deliver Israel from the hand of Midian. Have I not sent you?"* (Judges 6:14 NASB).

In Gideon's blindness, in his blame-shifting, even amidst his sins of doubt, anger and idolatry—the Lord came looking for him. Those wondrous eyes saw the future and the man in that future. The **I AM's** vision was not limited to that moment in time; nor was He swayed or influenced by the circumstances. Conditions and situations, tragedies and trials never cause Him to change His character! Nor His ultimate plan.

The Shepherd of Israel has stepped on to the scene. Those Shepherd eyes are searching, searching for a heart that will listen, turn and obey. This "angel of the Lord" (a visitation from the pre-incarnate Christ) doesn't answer any of Gideon's questions. Nor does He defend Himself against any of Gideon's accusations. Not one word of theological discussion or explanation is given. For God is not accountable to us. Only we—to Him.

God's answer is in His look. In turning to Gideon, He, the Creator of the Universe, has taken note of him. And… looked at him. *"For the eyes of the Lord move to and fro throughout the earth, that He may strongly support those whose heart is completely His"* (2 Chron. 16:9 NASB).

Don't you wonder what was in that look? Was it a look that said, *"With men this is impossible, but with God all things are possible"* (Matthew 19:23)? Was it the same kind of look that gazed down from Calvary and said, *"Father, forgive them, for they do not know not what they do"* (Luke 23:34)? Conviction cradled in Compassion. A look that held Love's Future and Love's Plan; and at least a glimpse of Eternity's Fullness...

Whatever it was, whatever it held, that gaze silenced Gideon's questions. Stilled his anxious heart. Stirred new hope, and kindled a spark of faith. Suddenly, his bone-weariness and hunger-panged stomach are forgotten; the heart-wrenching feelings of abandonment and years of discouragement fade off the screen of his life. His eyes and thoughts that up to then were fixed solely on hating his enemy (and being angry at God) begin finding their peace and sweet release in The One who is looking at him. Whose attention he has: The-Lord-Shalom: God of Peace.

Those eyes and that voice say to him, ***"Go!"*** Do you mean to tell me that just looking at Jesus—"looking full into His wonderful face"—will give me all the strength and resources I need to change me, overcome my enemy, my situation, and become a mighty instrument for Almighty God? Well, it did for Gideon.

" My eyes are ever toward the Lord, for He shall pluck my feet out of the net" (Psalm 25:15).

"My heart said to You, 'Your face, Lord, I will seek...'" (Psalm 27:8).

Gideon's eyes turn from his hardship. Yet, Gideon has more, much more, to learn from this Heaven-sent Mentor. For when Gideon is faced with a way out and that he's to be part of that way out, his accusations change to protest and excuses. You can't mean me! *"Oh my Lord, how shall I deliver Israel? Behold, my family is the least in Manasseh, and I am the youngest in my father's house."* Don't ask me to be part of the solution. I'm not even a two-bit player in this production. Don't look to me to take center stage and make a difference—an Eternal one!

As if He had not heard Gideon, *"...the Lord said to him, 'Surely I will be with you, and you shall defeat the Midianites as **one man**."* Like the "Why?" questions, God didn't buy Gideon's excuses. And guess what? He won't buy yours and mine, either. Because... we're not the issue—God is. He didn't try to build up Gideon's poor self-esteem. "Come on Gideon, you can do it." He didn't tell him to dream his own dream; or have him listen to motivational tapes day and night. The issue was what God had decided to do and whom He'd decided to use. He delights in using the unqualified and un-proficient—the weak and wobbly! *"...that the surpassing greatness of the power may be of God and not from ourselves"* (2 Cor. 4:7 NASB).

We know from the rest of the story that the Lord was oh, so patient with Gideon and his lack of faith. After starting out with 3,000 men, God narrowed the number to 300! Those *few* became Gideon's mighty band. Under The Commander-in-Chief's direction, with trumpet and torch in hand, they did indeed rout the enemy and win the victory. However...throughout the story, Gideon remained weak and faltering, constantly needing proof that he was truly hearing from God. Therefore, the lessons from Gideon's life are not so much how to prevail with God and overcome the enemy, but rather how little faith it takes for God to still show Himself strong on our behalf! *"If God is for us, who is against us?"* (Rom. 8:31 NASB).

You see, He delights in leaning down to where we are, lifting us up and out of our self-pity, dusting off our excuses, and washing our eyes with His vision so that we might finally truly SEE—HIM!

Will we put down the *Anchor of Faith* that says, "I may not understand why this situation has happened to me, but this one thing I know: *God is not my enemy!* And maybe, just maybe, there are some things in my life that the Lord wants me to examine: How long has it been since I have (or have I ever) taken inventory asking Him to show me anything and everything in my life that has edged Him aside? What has crept in and stolen time and attention from what is eternally important?

He also wants me to quit making excuses for not being in the *Fight for Faith.* For always looking around and counting on someone else to fight the battle and lead the way. For saying, "I'm not talented enough; or smart enough. I haven't been a Christian long enough. Therefore, God wouldn't want to use me...."

Throughout Scripture and Church history (and in my own life), I see that my lack will not deter God from His Plan. But my fear-filled excuses and blame-shifting will most certainly limit the blessing of my getting to be a part of it.

In Gideon's case, the root problem was not that the Midianites were oppressing and persecuting Israel. The issue was not other people. (It seldom is.) The issue was not the world, nor its beliefs and actions. The problem was that God's people had turned from Him to worship other gods. Part of Gideon's wearing down and depression was not because of what the enemy was doing; nor was it because of what had been stolen from Gideon. It was because he had idols in his own heart and life.

Like Gideon, when we're feeling oppressed and

discouraged, we often overlook sin. Especially, the sin of idolatry. Like Israel, idolatry will allow our enemy to ransack our lands: pillaging, plundering, stealing our fruit and grain, putting us in a virtual den of our own making. We know we don't bow down before golden calves or burn offerings of bullocks on altars of stone today, so the idea that we might have idols we shrug off. God's commandment *"Thou shalt have no other gods before Me"* rarely do we investigate. Rarely do we ask, "Lord, what are the idols in my life? What do I spend way too much time on? Who or what engulfs my thought life and takes my full attention? Is Jesus Lord of how I spend my money and the plans I make? And what priorities of mine crowd out time and attention with the Lord and kingdom endeavors?"

When we go through hardship and long hours of trial—weeks—months—stretching into years, our faith may weaken, seeming almost non-existent. However, at that same kind of low in Gideon's life, God brought him back to square one, commanding that he must destroy the altar of Baal and its idol. In their place he was to erect a new altar to the Living God and offer sacrifices to Him. Gideon agreed—but with some friends did it hidden by the curtain of night. It was a serious breach of patriarchal order for him to tear down his father's shrine and destroy the idols at his front door.

Yet, despite his not-so-brave act of obedience to the God of Abraham, Isaac and Jacob, his own father, Joash, gained newfound faith and courage. Rather than turn his son over to be killed for his blasphemous deed, Joash turned, faced the vengeful mob, and announced, *"If Baal is a god, let him contend for himself!!!"* (NASB). We, too, will find that when we obey and destroy any and all idols in our lives, we'll reap the awesome result that others too will follow suit. Joash's name means **Jehovah-fired**. Gideon's act of obedience rekindled Joash's faith, setting new fire to it. **Christian Courage is Contagious—it's Catching—praise God!**

You see, unless we remove and destroy our own personal idols—anything that we're looking to or relying upon—we'll not be able to look fully into our Lord and Master's face. We'll be double-minded and two-faced, looking at everything and everyone else for help, solutions and satisfaction. In every situation against the enemy that Israel faced before and after Gideon (and there were many), the final outcome *always* depended solely on one thing: Would she throw off idol worship and follow only the Lord?

And for me, for you, in our lives, in our hardships, in our pain, in that thing that presses us down and presses in upon us, only one thing counts both now and forever: ***Who will we live for??***

(Story taken from Judges Chapters 6 & 7)

 * * * * *

Chapter 6

Correcting Our Course

The long wide driveway at our daughter Chris's home seemed perfect for our five-year-old grandson, Jared, to practice riding his cousin's bike for the first time without training wheels. With only a smidgen of fear and a big bunch of confidence, Jared climbed aboard, lined up his bike perfectly for a straight shot and with his grandpa steadying him took off. Yet before we knew it, he lay in a tumble and tangle of bike and legs in the grass. Only a few feet after starting he'd run off the driveway and into an oak tree growing right at the driveway's edge. Not to be denied, with five-year-old determination, Jared had quickly picked himself up, pushed his bike back to the starting line, and begun his ride again, only to crash moments later into that same tree.

Watching from the sidelines, I walked over to the dejected teary-eyed boy and gave him a hug while checking for injuries. As I looked into his face there was a look in his eyes that said, *Maybe I can't do this after all.*

"Jared, honey, where do you want to go?" I asked. "I want to go down the driveway," he answered, blinking back tears. "OK," I replied, "now I want you to look at the end of the driveway—don't take your eyes off it, don't look at the tree. Don't look at anything else, and GO!" Off he went; this time, no detour. No crash. From the far end of the driveway, waving and hollering, he yelled, "Grandma, I did it. I rode the bike!"

I've discovered when it comes to matters of faith in the matters of life—focus is everything. In the counseling I do at Open Door Counseling Centre, I often use Jared's bike ride as an illustration that, whatever we focus on—we'll go toward.

And when that something is off of God's path, it's an obstacle to faith. A crash is inevitable. And unless and until we get an entirely new focus and point ourselves in that direction—refusing to even look at the obstacle—we'll keep on gravitating toward it and getting knocked down. Finally, weary of crashing, we may give up and give in, saying, "I don't think I can change. It hurts too much. I doubt I can run the race and finish the course. It's too hard."

Although thoughts can rush through our minds at racecar-like speed, one right on top of another, it remains true—we cannot think of two things at the same time. (Try it, if you doubt me.) If the predominance of my thoughts is on my bad situation, then that's my focus and that's where I'll stay unless and until I get a new one. By an act of my will, I have to choose to focus on what God has said and what He's like.

Walking in the Spirit is realizing—and then doing something about—what rules and reigns in my thought life. (I didn't used to know this!) Scripture describes it as *"casting down arguments and every high thing that exalts itself against the knowledge of God, bringing every thought into captivity to the obedience of Christ..."* (2 Cor. 10:5).

I can't keep wrong thoughts from coming, but when they do, I can replace them, thereby resisting that which is opposed to God. Martin Luther once said something like, "You can't keep birds from flying into the branches of a tree, but you can keep them from building a nest." Faith is all about getting God's viewpoint and "riding" towards it for all we're worth.

However it's not a mental trick we learn so we feel better and our behavior changes. And it isn't mind over matter or positive thinking, either. If it has to do with faith (and it does) it's **always** about a relationship. As we choose God's viewpoint, we're yielding to Him. We're stepping **into** Him. And as soon as we do this, His Grace and Power pick us up and He carries us. In an instant we're on the ride of a lifetime; with no wrecks, no crashes, no battering—not even bruised knees!

"The eternal God is your refuge, and underneath are the everlasting arms..." (Deut. 33:27).

*"Listen to me, O house of Jacob, and all the remnant of the house of Israel, who have been upheld from birth, who have been carried from the womb: Even to your old age, I am He, and even to gray hairs, **I will carry you!** I have made you, and **I will bear you:** even I will carry, and will deliver you"* (Isaiah 46:3,4).

We so often think the problem is *out there*; and if we could just get rid of *it*, we'd be fine. Yet in Jared's case, the problem wasn't *"the tree!!"* For him to ride his bike successfully, we didn't have to call Acme Tree Service to come and cut down the tree. The problem was Jared's focus. Once he ran into the tree the first time, then a second, it was pretty hard for him to see anything else. Or to believe that a life of tree crashing wasn't his future. Rather than having the fun of riding a bike, his painful experience almost caused him to believe that bike riding wasn't for him.

Many of us spend our lives waiting for Acme Tree Service (God) to come and cut down our trees. We invest a lot of time and money in the world's answers of how to divest our lives of trees. In the meantime we've fallen off to the side of life, nursing our bruises and crying because no one has come and removed our problem.

Whenever we operate in our own strength and ideas, we'll find ourselves striving and consequently worn out and disillusioned. *I'm really trying, but this isn't working!* Such thinking can never bring us the fullness of life available in Christ

Jesus; and that's why we're often disappointed, discouraged, disillusioned and resentful. Rather than having the abundant life Jesus promises in John 10:10, we feel like continual losers in this game called "life."

Beloved, there are always going to be "trees" along our driveways *(you can count on it)*. Their wide branches beckon us toward them. Trees are great, but they're not for running into. And we don't have to. Too often we're waiting for feelings to change, or leave, before we make a new response.

A lie that I listened to and believed at an early age was that I shouldn't read my Bible or pray if I didn't feel like it. *Why?* Because God hated hypocrites. So I would wait for the right mood, or the right feeling. I thought my feelings were the real me, and that they were the barometer of how I should respond. As you can imagine, my devotional life was pretty weak and "iffy"—the enemy saw to that.

Living in my **"feelings"** was a "tree" along the highway of my life that continually beckoned me towards it. This "tree" hindered me from the close relationship God wanted to have with me. No wonder I was lukewarm and bruised, off to the side of life, believing that being a Christian didn't really change your life that much. And that it was very hard. It was no wonder, also, that satan was able to get me to believe other deceptions about myself, about him, and about God. I was focused on me—not Him!

We can test our focus by looking at our conversation. For example if I say, "I know God answers prayer, **but** He doesn't seem to be answering mine," my emphasis is on the words that came after the "but". I may truly believe God answers prayer, yet I'm emphasizing—He isn't answering mine. See what happens when I turn the sentence around. "God doesn't seem to be answering my prayers, **BUT** I know God answers prayer!"

Then, faith lingers; faith remains.

I may not have yet experienced a breakthrough, but I'm still trusting and believing Him. And this makes all the difference in the world if we're feeling down, disappointed, weary in the walk, fatigued in the fight. It makes all the difference in the world, whether I'm declaring God is trustworthy, or thinking that He doesn't care; or that my situation is too hard for Him to do anything about.

When I'm focused on, *this isn't fair; I didn't do anything to deserve this,* the enemy has big ears and is always listening. Therefore, with a **decision** to think this way *(yes, it's a choice),* your adversary rushes to give you feelings to match your unbelief, making you all the more certain that God has let you down. You're helpless. A victim. Things just happen.

However... if you say, **"But God..."** My dear friend and helper of many years in the ministry, Sally Bartnett, calls this the *"But God" principle.* And we find it over and over in scriptures. The book of Proverbs is plumb full of examples! (Sometimes Scripture uses the word *nevertheless,* which is even more descriptive.)

The Prophet Habakkuk had plunged into overwhelming despair as he looked at Israel's situation and realized that invasion by a cruel nation was imminent. *Yet* in the very midst of that terrible future, a soaring declaration of faith rose up and out of his very being. He used the worst case scenario to describe his choice to trust God no matter what.

*"Though the fig tree should not blossom, and there be no fruit on the vines, though the yield of the olive should fail, and the fields produce no food, though the flocks should be cut off from the fold, and there be no cattle in the stall, **yet will I exult in the Lord.** I will rejoice in the God of my salvation. The Lord*

God is my strength, and He has made my feet like hinds' feet, and makes me walk on my high places" (Hab. 3:17-19 NASB).

What changed? Not his situation. His focus changed, and thereby his faith.

The Master of the "But God" principle was Jesus. Time and time again He would tell them what others said, then say, *"But I say to you...."*

*"You have heard it was said, 'An eye for an eye and a tooth for a tooth,' **but I say to you,** love your enemies and pray for those who persecute you..."* (Matthew 5:43,44).

Jesus wasn't ignoring what others said or thought, but rather bringing their words into the light of examination so that the disciples' choices were clear: Believe what others said, or believe Him! Believe what they'd always believed, or believe Him—the One who claimed to *be "the Way and the Truth and the Life"* (John 14: 6).

In effect wasn't He saying, "Don't steer toward the 'trees' of what others believe; don't get caught in the 'branches' of their ideas; don't crash into the 'trunks' of others' opinions? Look at me. Steer your course only toward Me! **Follow Me!"**

Just as sailors of old used the North Star to hold their course, and to correct their course, we too have a star to keep us on course: Our **Bright and Morning Star**—Jesus!

Words like these from Him check us and correct us—(or should): *"No one, having put his hand to the plow, and looking back is fit for the kingdom of God,"* (Luke 9:62), and *"He who is not with me is against Me, and he who does not gather with Me scatters abroad"* (Matthew 12:30).

While writing this book, I got a letter from Marian Mephan, a woman I met in 1990 when I joined with a ministry engaged in smuggling Bibles into Communist China. It was a two-week stint. And those two weeks turned out to be even harder than I'd imagined: the excessive humidity and heat; the language barrier; the humongous crowds; the stress of feeling like I wasn't prepared to cross the borders alone carrying contraband Bibles; and finally getting separated from my team behind the Bamboo Curtain; and thinking for several hours that I'd be arrested as a CIA spy and vanish forever!

Marian was a team leader, and upon meeting her I was immediately drawn to her. Her commitment to her Lord and the maturity and stability that she offered the group impressed me. She was never flashy, yet there was a *boldness*, a holy fire, constant and burning in her gentle and humble life. At a moment's notice—off she'd go—to witness, hand out tracts and minister.

One evening Marian said, "Come on, Jeanne, go with us." So with a few others, we began winding our way through narrow crooked streets that seemed to lead nowhere. I felt hopelessly lost within a few minutes, as we plunged into the dense darkness and sinister depths of Hong Kong—with sights, sounds, and smells I would never have imagined. I found out that, of all things, a large Buddhist Temple was our destination! And there, right there on its steps, we set up microphones, sang songs, witnessed and handed out tracts. With Marian orchestrating the whole thing.

And always there was prayer. Earnest intercession was Marian's watchword at all times and for all things. It was so evident that she had laid her life down for the sake of Christ— come what may. In the past few years she's taken another difficult assignment to teach English at a university deep in China. It's the only way a Christian witness can be present. We've continued to keep in touch by mail. Her letter, while I wrote this chapter, told of a fire in her apartment destroying nearly everything she had—in a place where it's very difficult to replace anything. She shared what she'd lost, and tears filled my eyes. She's given up so much to serve Jesus. I could tell that it wasn't only things— clothes, computer, personal items—but also, that her very faith had been put to a test once again. (We're all tempted to say, *"Why me, Lord? Have I missed Your leading? Have I displeased You in some way? **Are you angry with me**??")*

Yet, after she outlined the loss and that she had no idea how she was going to be able to replace things that she needed to live there, there came a "But God". Knowing Marian, I knew there would be. For she closed by quoting that much-used but never-gets-old text, Romans 8:28: ***"But"*** she declared, *"all things work together for good to those who love God...."* Then she added, "The enemy wants to get me down and possibly out, but one thing I know—God is faithful!"

Making the exchange of "But God" has become Marian's way of life. Is it yours? It will make such a difference. Focus *is* everything. Either it will be on what I've lost, what I don't have, what's happened to me, etc. Or, on the goodness and faithfulness of God. That He's not, and never will be, against me as long as I follow Him. And if I'll just correct my course toward Him, my way will be made plain and straight.

My choice of how I describe my situation will either add to my bondage or liberate me in the very midst of it. The *right choice* liberated three young Israelite men who were captives in Babylon. King Nebuchadnezzar demanded that they bow down and worship a golden image, or be thrown into a fiery furnace. Contemptuously, the King asked, "What god is there who can deliver you out of my hands?" Facing the absolute monarch, the searing flames and an immanent agonizing death, they still declared, *"If it be so, our God whom we serve is able to deliver us from the furnace of blazing fire; and He will deliver us out of your hand, O King.* **But even if He does not,** *let it be known to you, O king, that we are not going to serve your gods or worship the golden image that you have set up"* (Daniel 3:17-18).

Whether He delivered—or didn't; whether they lived—or died; they would worship none other! Amazingly, the King and all who watched saw that the fire (which had already destroyed those who merely came close to it), didn't incinerate them! Bound, when thrown into the furnace, these three lads now walked unfettered and free in the flames. And a fourth walked with them. Called out of the furnace by the King, there wasn't even a stench of smoke and fire on them, nor were their garments, those used to bind them—singed!

That fourth man (our Jesus) met them in that fire and walked with them in the flames. And, dear one, although you cannot see Him, He's walking with you in yours. For this same one says: *"...Do not fear, for I have redeemed you; I have called you by name; you are Mine! When you pass through the waters, I will be with you; and through the rivers, they will not overflow you. When you walk through the fire, you will not be scorched, nor will the flame burn you, for I am the Lord your God..."* (Isaiah 43: 1-3a).

No matter what we go through, God will be with us, and that whatever happens, it need not defeat us. Is this an empty promise? The Apostle Paul didn't think so! And he'd walked through more than we probably ever will. Because he had the right relationship, he had the right focus when he testified: *"We are afflicted in every way,* **but not crushed;** *perplexed,* **but not despairing;** *persecuted,* **but not forsaken;** *struck down,* **but not destroyed"** (2 Cor. 4:7,8).

As you look at your life in the light of this chapter you

may agree: Yes, I have spent my life crashing into "trees" instead of driving down the driveway. Nonetheless, just changing my focus along with my conversation is such a small thing; it can't help. It's too simple. My problem is huge, and it's been going on for years. I need God to do something BIG in my life to free me. I need a POWERFUL remedy.

Well, it only took *one small stone* in the hands of David, a simple shepherd boy, to defeat a giant, didn't it? Little is more than enough; it's having something left over. Remember the loaves and fishes, when placed in the Hands of Jesus? It didn't seem like a big thing for Jared to look down the driveway instead of at the tree. It didn't seem like a big thing to make a slight course correction.

Yet, didn't it make all the difference in the world whether he crashed or rode his bike?

 * * * * *

Chapter 7

You Better Believe It!

Throwing his Bible to the floor, our pastor announced: "We're not going to worship this book anymore! We're just going to worship Jesus. Recent post-grad studies at the seminary have shown me new ways of looking at Christianity!"

I sat in stunned silence with others in our Bible study, shocked at his action; feeling betrayed by a man of God we'd trusted to hold to the Word. I didn't know quite why, but somehow this was wrong, terribly wrong—this separating Jesus from the Scriptures. That moment with the Bible lying on the floor was a defining moment that would forever change me.

As a child I'd come to Jesus as my Savior, and believed that the Bible was true and without error. However… I'd also believed that God was distant and remote! After setting everything in motion, He was far away in Heaven waiting for me. Meanwhile, I had to get through life the best way I could. So, although I knew and loved all the Bible stories, and "religiously" read my Bible every day, I saw almost no connection with it and my moment-by-moment life. Its words were *a mental reminder* of God—not a touch point. The Book I defended had not (as yet)—captured me!

Though he staunchly preached explicitly from God's Word each Sunday, my pastor dad never referred to Scripture as our answer and hope throughout the week. My school friends also attended churches; yet we never talked about God as we shared our roller coaster ups and downs, hopes and dreams. God was not relevant.

As I moved into adulthood, got married and had children,

I trusted in my church to point me in the right direction and keep me on course. Mentally I agreed (and faithfully argued in defense of Christianity), not knowing that my heart wasn't fully engaged.

However, I'd come to feel somewhat apologetic about believing the Bible as altogether true. Some Biblical scholars in their critique of the Bible doubted certain passages and texts—not atheists trying to prove there was no God, but professors in seminaries.

Now, our pastor urged me to read their books. "Don't you want a more mature and intelligent faith?" he asked me. Flattered that he thought I could understand—and not wanting to be dumb or foolish—I tried to read them! But I couldn't. They made me feel angry and sick inside.

Yet I had no defense. Who was I to disagree? Nevertheless, something within me did—intensely! *For if they were right, if some portions of the Bible were not true, how could I be sure about the portions having to do with Jesus and my salvation?*

And so my frail little craft entered unknown waters. Instead of assuming answers, instead of mimicking words I'd been taught and had memorized, instead of trusting in others' faith— I examined my own. To my surprise, I realized I loved having "right" answers, but didn't want to struggle to find Truth. I wanted answers handed to me (as they had been by my church and pastors) so I could just go on with my life; have all the necessary bases covered; with no worries about getting into error. Now, I felt all confused and overwhelmed as new questions bombarded me. Where could I go for my answers, and who could I trust?

Amidst this confusion, one clear question stood out above the others: *if* God had created us in His image; *if* He loves us; *if*

He has a plan and destiny for each one of us (as the Bible says), would He set us loose on the ocean of life without maps, compass and provisions? Would He push us far out into treacherous currents to drift and flounder on the storm-tossed open sea, leaving it up to us to get safely through life? Or... through His Word and by His Spirit would He not—with Map and Compass—establish us upon the high seas, so that we ride them out and ride them safely Home?

As if this upheaval weren't enough at that time, our family was also getting ready to go overseas as missionaries! Two books I came across told of those who trusted fully in God's Word and Spirit to lead them. The way they believed—and lived—it was amazing—but so scary. I determined to go overseas and leave this whole struggle behind me. I didn't go far enough. Because, overseas I came face to face with New Guineans, who took the Bible *literally!* They believed everything it said and acted upon it. For them, faith was about life—real life!

Finally at the end of myself, hesitantly, fearfully, I asked God's Spirit of Truth to lead me and be my Teacher—no matter what the cost. As I did, I came to see that the two—Jesus (the Word who became flesh) and the Bible—were intricately and inseparably interwoven and intertwined. They could never be separated. How could I fully trust one without fully trusting the other? I couldn't. As I committed to one, I committed to both. And my long-held mental agreement with the Bible turned into grab-hold, heart-felt faith!

Once I chose to believe God and take Him fully at His word, *faith brought sight* (not the other way around). And power! Believing meant—seeing!

"... *faith comes by hearing, and hearing by the word of God*" (Rom. 10:17).

Believing meant: ***trusting in, relying upon and clinging to.*** Although I would never understand or comprehend all that was in the Bible—I would ***believe*** it ***all!*** In doing so I found a Ship that would sail—gloriously. Absolutely! This Ship alone could take me safely through high tides, blustering winds, overwhelming waves, and unknown waters. Yes!

Doesn't it all come down to faith? We can spend our faith on believing in ourselves, with no map or compass—go it alone—and perish. Or… we can invest our faith in totally believing that, yes, God's Word is true—for me! And like the compass, knowing that just a few degrees off will soon lead me far off course, I need to clutch it close and hold it near and dear.

However, we don't like hearing "God's way—or no way!" We want ***The Way*** to be broader, less narrow and restrictive than the one the Bible describes. That's why television talk shows easily convince us we're *spiritual* people, without need of church or fellowship! After all, we pray for "higher power" help. We may even read the Bible occasionally. We're quick to admit, "Sure, we've made some mistakes [God calls them sins], but mistakes are only a negative if you don't learn from them. There's nothing wrong with adding Jesus to whatever belief system we already hold."

Nonetheless, God views such beliefs, compromise and mixture as downright dangerous.

Jesus said, *"Enter by the narrow gate; **for wide is the gate and broad** is **the way that leads to destruction**, and there are many who go in by it.… Not everyone who says to Me, 'Lord, Lord,' shall enter the kingdom of heaven, but he who does the will of My Father in heaven"* (Matthew 7:13,17).

*"I am **the way**, the truth, and the life. No man comes to the Father but by Me"* (John 14:6).

61

*"See to it that no one takes you captive through philosophy and empty deception, according to the tradition of men, according to the elementary principles of the world, rather than **according to Christ**"* (Col. 2:8 NASB).

Isn't it interesting that we have no problem believing in and yielding to God's absolute natural laws? Like the Law *(His Law)* of Gravity—you know, the one that keeps us from banging our heads on the ceiling when we get up in the morning? We know such laws are good for us; they keep us safe. However, when it comes to *spiritual one-ways*—we rebel!

Haven't we heard for years that science disproves the Bible, and that evolution disproves Creation? Yet evolution remains, and always will remain, a theory requiring faith—*yes, faith*—because no one can prove it! No one was there!

We're not told that scientists as they now examine what they once thought to be the *simple* human cell, have discovered that in that *single* cell is crammed enough information to make a rich library of 4,000 books! There are at least thirty trillion cells in the body (you can do the math). When God said "we are fearfully and wonderfully made" did He know what He was saying, or what?[3]

Nor are we told that as scientists have attempted to simulate evolution on the computer, they've reached the conclusion: Creation *couldn't* have evolved! It required Intelligent Design and Control.[4]

In other words, **true science** says, "Behind it all—*because creation is so awesome*—there's a Creator—a Creator whose Word reveals He is absolutely God, and His Word is wholly and absolutely true."

I'm no longer ashamed or apologetic about believing that

the Bible is altogether factual, accurate and without error. For it is there that I see that God never second-guesses Himself; never issues disclaimers; and He doesn't publish updated versions to correct mistakes He's made. [He doesn't make any.] Nor does The All-knowing One publish new discoveries, as scientists must do. He's committed Himself to one book—*this one Book*—to speak life into our very being. To offer us everything we need for this life; and ready us for the next!

The good, the bad, and the ugly march across its pages. Nothing is sugar-coated. Since God is Truth—He tells it like it is.

"God is not a man that he should lie; nor a son of man that He should repent; has He said, and will He not do it? Or has He spoken, and will He not make it good?" (Num. 23:19).

Devious, even devilish intentions of the human heart are disclosed as God focuses His searchlight of Truth. In this most *sacred book*, sublime faith and undying devotion as well as character flaws and deep deeds of darkness are exposed. Meanwhile, His wondrous wisdom and relentless love pursue us page after page.

History is predominantly—His-story! The enfolding of His plan and destiny for mankind as told in the Scriptures. From Genesis 1 right on through the book of Revelation, the Bible tells what it took—and all it took—to redeem man from his rebellion against his Maker and give him eternal life. Sixty-six books, written over a period of 1,500 years by a variety of writers—shepherds, prophets, kings and fishermen—most with little education and no knowledge of, or contact with, one another.[5]

If God inspired everyday people to write the Scriptures, won't He inspire everyday people to understand them? Even critics and unbelievers agree it has one Author![4] As someone once said, "It's the oldest book in the library whose author is still living." An Author who never insists that His Word is totally true in its entirety. He just declares, "Thus says the Lord."

"The entirety of Your word is truth, and every one of Your righteous judgments endures forever" (Psalm 119:160).

Like an immoveable rock on the ocean's shoreline that year after year resists the pounding surf of each wave and the pull of the tides—the Bible has stood the test of time. It has withstood every challenge; and remains the "#1" bookseller year after year. Confirmed skeptics seeking to disprove it have, instead, fallen on their knees crying out, "This is truly God's Word, and Jesus Christ is Savior and Lord."

Every attempt over the centuries to destroy and eradicate the Bible has failed, because the Bible is God's Divine Document. Kill the messenger? They may. Kill the Message? Never! For no might of mere mortal man will ever erase that Message—or diminish its power. And anyone who dissects and tears at the Scriptures and in doing so shipwrecks others' faith is left with ***"life-less" faith.***

" '...Be astonished O heavens, at this, and be horribly afraid; be very desolate,' says the Lord. 'For My people have committed two evils: They have forsaken Me, the fountain of living waters, and hewned themselves cisterns—broken cisterns that can hold no water'" (Jer. 2:12-13).

In days gone by, pirates lurking on the high seas attacked and plundered ships for their valuable cargo: gold, silver, jewels, precious spices. How wonderful to discover we have even greater riches always available in the treasure chest of God's Word.

"The law of the Lord is perfect, converting the soul; the

64

testimony of the Lord is sure, making wise the simple... More to be desired are they than gold, yea, than much fine gold; sweeter also than honey and the honey comb" (Psalm 19:7,10,11).

Satan plots to rob us of our **gold and honey** by casting doubt about the Bible. He trembles that we might truly believe Jesus' words, *"Heaven and earth will pass away, but My words will by no means pass away"* (Matthew 24:35).

So... battling desperately to steal (or at least dilute) our faith, satan seeks to pirate away our priceless and vast treasure by *whispering,* "Has God said?" and "Are you sure?" Any of us can be deceived—*even* church leaders and pastors like the one who threw his Bible on the floor.

Those wicked pirates of old often raised a friendly flag in order to draw near an unsuspecting ship without being recognized. Not until they were upon their prey would they lower the counterfeit flag and raise their own, revealing their true identity and evil purpose. With the pirate ship suddenly upon them, it was too late to fire the big cannons. And so the pirates would swarm aboard, and midst flashing swords and fiendish screams, they'd capture the ship, the crew and its treasure with little opposition. Recognition and resistance had come too late. *"The thief had stolen, killed and destroyed..."* For satan works to either keep the Bible from us (as in lands where it's a crime to have a Bible), or he'll keep us from the Bible through unbelief and ignorance. Or...through deception.

Like the pirates, "Captain Hook" draws near disguised as our friend and ally. He, too, flies the false flag of current opinions and philosophies while appealing to our pride. "Don't be limited by one book; it's too narrow in its views!"

Beware! Satan's true colors and flag remain the same as the pirates': Skull and crossbones. Death and Deception.

However, when we're far out on the turbulent sea of life with its conflicts and trials; when waves of life's pain and hardship crash up against us threatening to plunge us under; when we see no visible landmarks (we've never faced this situation before); in the mist and the fog with no stars and no light, we feel confused and overwhelmed. When we're surrounded by those who don't believe, it's easy to become shaky, and doubt our Compass, isn't it? How can we be sure—in the complexity and stress of hi-tech life—that the Bible really is our answer?

Because God says so! The Word of God is divinely inspired by the One who says, *"It is written!"* The turbulent waves of our troubles don't shake Him. Nor is He ever intimidated, or even influenced, by the gusting winds of what others think.

*"The grass withers and the flower fades, but **the Word of our God endures forever"** (Isaiah 40:8).

His enduring Word produces enduring faith. Such Faith finally overrode my reservations, objections, apologies, exceptions, and excuses. When we finally surrender to the Lover of our souls—praise God—we board the right ship! And our Heavenly Father puts the Compass of His Word into our hands to hold tightly, check often, love dearly, and trust fully. It alone has the power to guide, keep us on course, and correct our course when we begin to drift. It's divinely set to keep us close to Him and safe with Him every moment of every hour. It holds full provisions—*the promises of God*—no matter how long the voyage takes!

Our Compass points to *only one way* to be saved. *Only One* loved us enough to send His Son to die for us; and *only Jesus* could suffer on the Cross and accomplish our Salvation. Does all that sound extremely narrow and uncompromising? *Absolutely.*

That's because on any ship the Captain is the law—the sole person in authority! He alone makes the rules. Yet in that position, He assumes full responsibility for the ship, its passengers, its provisions; and to sail the ship safely to its destination. That's because he alone knows the vessel, the waters and the way! The Captain of our *Faith Ship*—who owns the ship, mans the wheel, and keeps the watch—is the Lord Jesus. And under His command, He's absolutely committed to us. What's more, He extends faith to believe—*the Bible!*

 * * * * *

Chapter 8

Driven ...

"...that we should no longer be children, tossed to and fro **and carried about with every wind of doctrine,** *by the trickery of men, in the cunning of craftiness by which they lie in wait to deceive, but, speaking the truth in love, may grow up in all things into Him who is the head—Christ...."* (Eph. 4:14).

Wrong beliefs bring us false expectations. They, in turn, lead to heaviness, even hardness of heart. As in the case when a young woman seated before me in my counseling office, looking like a poster model for distress, wearily told of daily pain due to chronic illness and separation from a husband. He'd gambled all their money away and left her responsible for large gambling debts through maxed-out credit cards. She and her three young children had returned to her parents and were living in their basement.

Staci (not her real name) had come to Christ several years before. What was bothering her most? She was failing God! "I can't bring Him glory," she explained, "because I'm still sick (she'd not yet received her healing) and poor. How can anyone under the "curse" of poverty bring Him praise?"

She reached for a tissue as tears welled up in her eyes. "I'm bringing shame to His name. Yet," she insisted, "I'm doing all I know to do. I'm in church for all the services. And I have a list of scriptures about healing and wealth I confess each morning, night and sometimes throughout the day, because I carry them with me."

I asked, "Aren't you tired?"

"Oh, yes," she admitted. Her wan smile said she was glad I understood. "But I don't know what I'm doing wrong. Why I haven't gotten the victory. Maybe God's angry with me—but if He is I don't know why." Then she hesitantly confessed, "Sometimes I'm just too tired or sick to do all the verses. Do you think that's what's keeping me from the blessing?" Now her voice held a hint of anger. "God's asking more from me than I can do." With that she slumped further into her chair.

Unfortunately, I'd heard such stories before. I said to her, "Jesus said in Mathew 11:28-30 *'Come to Me all who are weary and heavy laden and I will give you rest. Take My yoke upon you and learn of Me, for I am meek and lowly of heart and you shall find rest for your souls.'* Do you have that rest?"

"No," she admitted, "just the opposite." I opened my Bible to Paul's warning in Galatians 3:3, *"Are you so foolish? Having begun by the Spirit, are you now being perfected by the flesh?"*

I asked her, "What works did you have to do to get saved?" "None," she responded, her eyes widening. I continued, "Scripture says, *'Our sufficiency is from God, who also made us sufficient as ministers of the new covenant, not of the letter but of the Spirit; for the letter [the law] kills, but the Spirit gives life'"* (2 Cor. 3:5b,6).

"Tell me, what would you think of someone who demanded you run a marathon race with a broken leg? Can you picture Jesus doing that?" "Oh no!" She answered quickly. "Why, then," I asked, "do you think God is requiring so much from you?" Staci was silent.

"And, where does it say that God hates the poor? God says in His Word that it would be the poor who would receive Him and His Kingdom—and they did. And it's still true today. Scripture says He defends them: *'For He shall stand at the right* hand of the poor, to save him from those who **condemn him'** (Psalm 109:31). Or where does it say that He's ashamed of the poor? *'He who oppresses the poor reproaches his Maker, but he who is gracious to the needy honors Him'* (Prov. 14:31). In fact, because riches are such a snare to us, Jesus warned, *'...how hard it is for those who have riches to enter the kingdom of God!'"* (Mark 10:23).

"Well," she retorted, "God wants us to have the blessings of Abraham. If we don't, we're not walking in what He wants for us."

"Let's read about it," I responded. As she read, I showed her it said *"blessing"*, not blessings. Galatians 3:6,13,14: *"Even so, Abraham believed God, and it was reckoned to him as righteousness... Christ redeemed us from the curse of the Law... in order that in Christ Jesus the **blessing** of Abraham might come to the Gentiles, so that we might **receive the promise of the Spirit through faith!"**

"It's the Messiah—JESUS! That's our inheritance, Staci. Our covenant relationship through faith makes us sons of Abraham; we get to come by faith to Jesus and be made righteous!!!" I continued. "If I'm not satisfied with this, if my devotion to Jesus hinges on what He'll do or give me in the future, then *I won't be content now."*

"Scripture says, *'But godliness actually is a means of great gain, when accompanied by contentment... and if we have food and covering, with these we shall be content. **But those who want to get rich fall into temptation** and a snare and many foolish and harmful desires, which plunge men into ruin and destruction...."'* (1 Tim. 6:6-10).

"Paul's declaration, *'I can do all things through Christ who strengthens me'* (Phil. 4:12,13) followed his confession that he'd learned to be content in whatever circumstance he found himself. Wrenching verses out of context causes us to come up with wrong beliefs and false expectations. And that's when we get into works. We're trying—really hard—but it's not working. That's why we become disappointed, weary, and often angry at God. However, God can't be talked into (or worked into) being someone He's not. When we try to do that, instead of pleasing Him, we grieve Him and quench His Spirit. And we're well on our way to getting a counterfeit Jesus and a false faith. Paul warned in 2 Corinthians 11:3,4: '...*I fear, lest somehow, as the serpent deceived Eve by his craftiness, so your minds may be corrupted from **the simplicity** that is in Christ.*' "

As I talked and shared the scriptures, I could see the burden of *"working the word so that it worked for her"* lifting. Somewhat. Because her look also said, *This is too easy. It's got to be harder than this.* The yoke of religious works, of having to perform in order to move God's Hand on her behalf, was hard to let go of. Material "blessings" were due her. What if she let go of the *"way to get blessed"* when her *"breakthrough"* was right at the door? (The enemy will dangle that fat carrot before us as long as we'll run after it.)

Many, like Staci, are literally worn out from chasing after blessings and doing an ongoing inventory to see if they're measuring up to others. They must watch every word they utter to insure their confession is right. Whenever we strive to win God's approval and get His blessings, we become driven! Driven to perform! Driven to excel! Driven to compete! Driven to receive!

When I asked another person in a discipling session if she wanted God's will in her life, she replied indignantly, "Of course I do. I don't want to miss the blessings!" After only a little time, praise the Lord, she saw her need to repent of self-centeredness and began to glory only in the Cross and in her Savior.

There's a "God just wants to bless me and I just need to figure out how to get that to happen" **mindset** running rampant. Couldn't that be one of the reasons why some churches grow so quickly? They're teaching what we want to hear. Couldn't that be why some books are an overnight success? In them, authors state that they can teach us how to pray daring prayers that God *always answers.* Included in such books are always testimonies by those who have prayed such prayers (often daily for years) and had their lives and ministries revolutionized. Yet even if many testify that this works, didn't Jesus warn us about vain repetitions when we prayed?

Often books like these bring fear because we're told: "If you don't follow the method we are prescribing, you'll not only lose the blessings, but you'll not be a part of God's mighty move for these end times."

Some of these books become not only best sellers on the Christian Bookseller lists but on secular ones as well. Shouldn't that raise a question of why the unsaved are buying them? Isn't there **only one prayer** that the unsaved can pray that *God always* answers—the prayer of a sinner asking the Savior to save him?

God promises blessings when we give, but some churches today overemphasize material blessings. Members are encouraged (sometimes coerced) into "sowing their seed", and God must return to them many times over. They use Luke 6:38 as proof text.[5]

So—it's give to get!!

Doesn't that sound more like investing than giving? If I invest in a company, I expect to make a profit. When I don't—I feel cheated. It's true, we can't out-give God, and He does promise *"to provide seed for the sower"* (2 Cor. 9:10-12).

Yet... any truth over-emphasized and maximized becomes error.

What if God's looking down and saying, "Where are the people who just want to give because they love Me—with no strings attached?" Isn't God searching for people who are seeking the Giver rather than the gifts? The "Blesser" rather than the blessing? His worshippers in spirit and in truth?

There's also a running after miracles and experiences—ones that can be seen, felt, touched and heard. We're told that the signs of the end times are such manifestations, that they will increase to the point of becoming almost commonplace. They should be happening now. And if they aren't, something's wrong—with us! Scripture does predict signs and wonders toward the end. However, aren't we also warned that there will be "lying signs and wonders" from a false source leading many astray?! (2 Thess. 2:9)

I treasure the experiences I've had and the miracles I've seen. Yet, wonderful as they are, I mustn't make doctrine of them. Nor insist God do more. If I do, my heart will become parched; true faith will lessen; I'll get leanness of soul: and I'll be wooed away from the Anchor of Christianity: Jesus Christ and Him crucified.

When Jesus sent out the seventy to preach and heal, and they returned overjoyed that even the demons were subject to them, Jesus rejoiced with them. "Nevertheless," He reminded them *"... do not rejoice in this, that the spirits are subject to you, **but rather rejoice because your names are recorded in heaven"** (Luke 10:20).

People coming to Jesus for other than their need for salvation (fleeing from the wrath to come, Matthew 3:7*) will at some time be disappointed. They came to Him wanting a better life; He hasn't delivered! Many today don't know that Christianity isn't about us—it's about Jesus!!! Too often our focus (see previous chapter) is on ourselves, and what God will do for us, rather than on what we can do for Him. If it's on Him blessing us instead of His Lordship over us, we're going to reap fruit—bitter fruit that will set our spiritual teeth on edge.

What is my focus? That the Lord has come into my life to help and bless me? Or, that I've stepped into His life to be conformed to His image and to serve Him with all my heart. There's a big difference. (Please read Luke 17:5-10, to find Jesus' answer to how to have more faith.).

The **demanding** and **powerful** undertow of our own "self-centered" wants will fashion a god into what we want him to be, pulling us away from *"so great a salvation"* (Heb. 2:1-3). As a result we'll be driven to find something different, better, bigger—MORE! For flesh is never satisfied. Without the Anchor of "true-saved-and-kept-by-grace" Faith, which fastens us securely to ꂆhe Rock, our selfish expectations will drag us farther and farther out to sea. The winds of false doctrine, which always fan the fire of our own selfish passions, will drive our Salvation Ship off course. If you and I as sailors decide to ignore the compass readings, if we don't make the necessary corrections by really finding out what Scripture says, our ships will veer off course—no matter how sincere we are.

Too often today, the salvation preached and offered is one without the Law to bring us as sinners under conviction about the real reason for Christ's coming. Scripture says, *"I would not have come to know sin except through the Law"* (Rom. 7:8). Breaking God's Law (the Ten Commandments) carries eternal punishment of death and hell. You and I stand guilty of breaking that Law. But if we never hear and never believe we've earned death and hell through our law breaking, we won't become truly convicted of our need for a Savior.

74

Evangelist and author, Ray Comfort, in his book, ***Revival's Golden Key[6]***, gives statistics gathered from crusade follow-ups here and abroad. They reveal a shocking story. Some ***87-95% fall away*** in a very short time after going forward and making a decision for Christ!!! He states, "These statistics are not confined to crusades, but are general throughout local church evangelism." He contrasts this with years ago, when over ***95% stayed*** and remained committed and sold out to Jesus. "What was the difference," he asks? *Preachers and evangelists preached the Law to show sinners their need for a Savior.*

The message that "God loves us and has a wonderful plan for our lives" (though He does) brings no one under conviction. Nor does it lead to true repentance. It draws seekers of, "God, make my life better," not "God, if you don't save me—I perish!" ***It draws seekers of happiness—not holiness. Seekers of comfort and ease—not commitment and sacrifice.*** Such seekers will soon be disappointed, dissatisfied, discouraged. And they'll walk away seeking something—or someone else. Jesus described them in the parable of the Sower and the Seed (Luke 8:5-15). They tried Christianity and it "didn't work for them." They came to Christ for life enhancement and embellishment—not crucifixion. They go to the Scriptures for comfort—not correction, for blessing—not breaking. Then when life doesn't turn out as they expected, they feel foolish for trusting God—set up, then let down by Him.

Many stay in churches, yet they're never truly committed to loving and serving Jesus no matter what, because their hearts aren't ***engaged.*** They may never have been truly converted. Jesus said, *"Truly, I say to you, unless you are converted and become like children, you shall not enter the kingdom of heaven"* (Matthew 18:3). *"Repent therefore and be converted, that your sins may be blotted out, so that times of refreshing may come from the presence of the Lord..."* (Acts 3:9).

Christ's assignment was to do a finished and complete work at the Cross. He did. Adding anything, **anything at all** to that distances and cuts us off from the Blood of the Lamb. When we go to a doctor with symptoms of weariness, no energy, and blood tests that show a low blood count—we're often anemic. We don't have enough red blood cells, and the blood gives life. True also in the spiritual, for scripture declares: The *"life is in the blood"* (Lev. 17:11, Heb. 9:22).

Without knowing it, have you cut yourself off from the blood of the Lamb by substituting your works for His? Such a yoke of works is a heavy one, indeed; and we take it on so easily. All too soon it presses us down, wears us out, and stifles the very breath of God in us. Just the opposite of *"...where the spirit of the Lord is, there is liberty..."* (2 Cor. 3:17).

When our hearts are heavy and weary from trying to be a *"good"* Christian, when life seems to take more from us than it gives, don't we yearn for Strength and Joy? Since Scripture says, "the joy of the Lord is our strength," let's find out what gives the Lord joy. What gives Him pleasure? Isn't it when He sees us loving what He loves and hating what He hates?!

What gave Jesus joy??? *"For the **joy set before Him** Jesus endured the Cross, despising the shame"* (Heb. 12:2). What did the Apostle Paul glory in? *"But may it never be that I should boast (glory), except in the cross of our Lord Jesus Christ"* (Gal. 6:14).

When all our expectations are in the true Christ Jesus, Crucified Savior and Risen Lord (not a false one), we'll have satisfaction, completion and *"JOY unspeakable and full of glory."* That joy springs from the Well of Salvation that was opened for us at the Cross. There we're to drink often and freely. In Jesus' ***finished work*** we enter into our *Sabbath* rest (Heb.4:3). There we cease from striving to get God to bless us.

No longer driven, **but led** by our Good Shepherd, fed and resting in His place of Grace. Hidden in Him and established in His Work, we won't be blown off course by the winds of false doctrines. Or, find our faith shipwrecked on the shoals of false expectations. No longer will we be under **the curse** that Scripture says comes from trusting in ourselves and in our own strivings! (Jer. 17:5).

It's *Jesus alone* who reaches out to give us Blessed Life—reviving life, full and free—found only in His restoring stream that continually flows from Him to you and me. God promises to bless us when we trust in the Lord rather than in our own flesh; that we'll be like a tree having roots that spread out by the river; and we'll not fear when heat comes; nor be anxious in the year of drought. Nor will we ever ever cease from yielding fruit—glory to God! (Jer. 17:7,8).

*"Therefore you will joyously draw water from the **springs of salvation,** and in that day you will say, 'Give thanks to the Lord, call on His name... '"* (Isaiah 12:3,4).

Come. Repent. Cease from your strivings. Drink deeply. And... *Rest.*

 * * * * *

Chapter 9

Broken – Yet Whole

As she slowly straightens up and squints at the strange looking man suddenly standing before her, the little emaciated woman could have had a hard time believing her eyes. Perhaps so many days with little food and rationed water are causing her to hallucinate. Where on earth has he come from? This man, whose skin is burnt and wizened by the relentless sun; his beard and hair long and scraggly; his robe dirty and tattered; his eyes searching.

Yet his words are even more surprising: *"Please, bring me a little drink of water,"* and to her amazement she finds herself turning to obey him! Then he adds, almost as an afterthought, *"and with it a piece of bread from your hand."* If this day weren't so pregnant with gloom she'd have laughed out loud at his ridiculous words. But laughing takes energy. Energy for that kind of luxury is only a memory. Still, she finds herself explaining softly (speaking takes energy too) why she's out here. Why she's picking up sticks. Why she can't bring him a piece of bread. For as soon as she finds enough sticks to build a fire she'll take the very last measure of flour and oil, bake a little cake for her son and herself, and together—they'll eat their last meal.

No sooner has she spoken than the stranger's voice changes from supplication, *"Do not fear... make me a cake first ..."* to one of authority. *"For thus says the Lord God of Israel: 'The bin of flour shall not be used up, nor shall the jar of oil run dry, until the day the Lord sends rain on the earth.'"*

This woman, though surprised by these events, isn't the only one. Elijah, too, is amazed. A man of the house of Israel doesn't talk to a woman alone—much less ask for food from a woman's hand—and most certainly not from a heathen woman. In any case, widows were to be given to, not taken from. Jehovah God was very clear in His Law about this! But when God had said to Elijah, *"Go!"*—he'd gone. The command had been followed by a promise: A widow will feed you. Evidently, this was that woman!

The prophet had seen God fulfill His Word before. In obedience to God's command, Elijah had stood before King Ahab and denounced him for polluting the land through the shedding of innocent blood in offering human sacrifices to false gods. Boldly he'd announced: *"As the Lord God of Israel lives, before whom I stand, there shall not be dew nor rain these years, except at my word."* From that moment on, not one drop of rain had fallen; nor had dew kissed the earth. Days of drought had marched into weeks, then months, and the cloudless sky above them still held no hint of rain.

Immediately after confronting Ahab and pronouncing God's judgment, Yahweh had led and hid Elijah in the wilderness. There, the creek Cherith had sustained him with water, and ravens had brought him *"bread and meat."* That, too, had been a test of Elijah's faith: To eat whatever ravens brought, unclean birds—yet he'd done so. Once the creek dried up, new orders had come. In obedience to them, he'd trudged across many miles of mountain and desert terrain until he found himself foot weary, hungry and thirsty now standing before this withered woman. She seems like such an unlikely candidate to be used for a miracle. But then again, a perfect one... Miraculous moments come at just such times, with just such unlikely people.

In this country of Sidon where Baal is worshipped, the reputation of the God of Israel, Elijah's God, has preceded him, drifting over the hundreds of miles crossing into her country's borders, finding its way to her village of Zarephath (a place of refining) and into her simple dwelling. And now, though close to death as she speaks, she gives that God reverence: *"As the Lord, your God lives...."*

For her it's the last minute of the midnight hour with no reprieve in sight. It's as bad as it gets, and she's as low as she can go. She's in lonely desperate straights with death imminent, for both her and her only child. For all too soon she'll have to watch that son die from starvation.

As I look at this story I'm amazed at this woman. She's probably never thought, not even in her wildest dreams, that any god would take note of her. And her circumstances certainly confirmed that no one, and certainly not any god—cared. Yet, when God's Word is spoken to her by this unkempt and unsettling messenger—she believes! And immediately obeys. First, to get him precious water; then to serve him and give him all she has! She's not an Israelite—(God's chosen), yet now, with only a few words from God to act on—she acts! And in the process begins to spend, and thereby risk, all she has. She has so little— just a bit of oil and a small measure of flour for herself and her son. Yet she gives it.

Instead of believing, instead of obeying, she could have angrily accused him. After all, what has she got to lose? She's already a dead woman walking. Life is hard. She's all alone. No one cares. She's sole support for her child. Death's specter has completely drained her of any hope. And despair's heavy blanket hugs her so tightly she can scarcely breathe. So why not with her last spending of emotion pour out all her pent-up frustration, anger, resentment and despair on him—the one who'd caused the drought in the first place?

She doesn't.

The prophet's words to her are few: It's not as if he preached a sermon to convince her. Nor did he try to scare her with

80

warnings; or try to intimidate her because of his call as God's chosen prophet—the one who'd confronted the King and lived to tell it! These two people, opposites in so many ways, thrown— no, brought together—find themselves in extreme situations and unsettling circumstances. Neither one has walked this way before. Nevertheless, one of them knows and serves the living God.

And this **knowing** burns in Elijah's bones hotter than the noonday sun, fills his mouth with God's Word, anoints his parched voice and shines out of his piercing eyes rimmed with fine lines from sun's rays. That kind of faith is *contagious*; his confidence is *catching*. So that although his God-breathed words are few, some measure of faith inches its way into her heart; some measure of hope zings into her being. Only a few words convince her.

Yet when God's Words are mixed with faith—look out! Miracles are on the way... (Heb. 4:2).

And so begins a union between Jehovah God, His Prophet, a poor widow woman, and her son. As Elijah takes up residence with these two, the oil and flour never run out! Each and every day—they have just enough. They don't have anything extra— they have just enough. What they have isn't king's fair, but each day they have a meal from The King's Hand! And each day they have—a MIRACLE!

True faith means risking. It means acting on whatever measure of faith we have. This woman hadn't heard much and knew little. As opposed to those of us who've heard a lot of sermons and still know little. Nevertheless, she stepped *out* on what she had, and consequently *into* what God had planned. And, at a time when she probably didn't feel like it. Nor did she engage in a debate on the benefits of worshipping Baal as opposed to worshipping Israel's God. For it wasn't debate time.

It wasn't even talk time. It was "trust" time. Because… there wasn't much time.

I love this story because that little destitute woman is such a challenge to my own life. To my own faith. Some years ago I asked the Lord if there was a story from Scripture that was similar to my ministry? He led me to this one because we minister to the poor and needy; and often we face a dried-up creek, an empty cupboard—with no rain in sight!

Yet as I pondered this story, I realized that *my* responsibility was to be obedient to whatever God said, be His words many or few. And *His* responsibility was to take care of us. And I saw in looking back over the years, that although most of the time we didn't have extra, we didn't have lavish—we always had enough. And the fact that we'd been able to continue each day was—for me— a miracle! That widow lady held nothing back—she gave what she had. Consequently, Jehovah-Jireh became her Savior (saving her out of a bad situation), and her Provider. She gave not only *what* she could give, she gave *all* she could give. In desperate straights rather than clutching—she gave. "Lord, I pray, help me to be like her."

Someone once said, "It's not how much you give to the Lord that counts—it's how much you retain." *Ouch!* I wonder how well we Christians in this nation will do as the financial belt around America's waistline continues to tighten notch after notch? As God's judgments cause our rain of blessings to cease, as our streams of plenty go dry, as the burning sun of God's displeasure glares on us and there are few places to take shelter— what will we do? (Isa. 26:20; Jer. 10:10; Rom. 1; 2 Peter 2:4-9)

As our circumstances worsen, when we find that what we thought were necessities are, in truth, luxuries; as drought and famine invade our homes; as pestilence (diseases), terrorism, and financial meltdown are not just items on the evening news, and as persecution comes—will we still trust? Will we still give? Will we still obey? Will we still risk? Will we still witness that God is good? Will we recognize that whatever we have and all that we have is sufficient, because it's what God has ordered and what He's supplied?

Don't we all need to choose not to look at what we have in the natural, but whom we know who is Supernatural? All Powerful. Our Jehovah-Jireh. Savior. In the story we never learn the woman's or the son's name. (Names of people or ministries aren't nearly as important as their faith and obedience.) So... I can put my name in that story and ask God to work what happened to them into my heart. (And you can, too.)

You may think few know your name, or that you don't count for much. Have sadness and loss, drought and despair drained your life, also? Well, there is a God Who reaches out to that destitute one in the far country with little or no social standing. The least of the least. And that's the one—the very one—He'll speak to, impart faith to, feed and dwell with. Praise Him!

As in the past, I've asked God to keep me and all I do at the place of Zarephath, the place of refining. For that's where God's people, whether they've got much faith or little, whether they're prophet, widow woman, or child, will be fed on Heavenly Bread. If we'll be content in that place of refining, that place of pruning—no matter how far down we get, no matter how disastrous the circumstances (few of us will ever face what that woman faced)—won't God be faithful to speak His **REVIVING** Word to us? And, won't He also be faithful as our Provider to sustain and increase our faith—the very same One who multiplied a little oil and flour and made it miracle food?

Like that widow, when we suffer hardship, when we feel drained of every drop of emotion except depression, it's easy to think, *I have nothing to give—to anyone. I just need to wait 'til I feel better and more spiritual.* Or... *God doesn't care about me like He cares for others. It's hopeless—I'm hopeless.*

Until we feel fuller; until we've eaten well; until God's rain has finally come, broken the drought and overflowed our barrels; until the feelings of depression at least lift a little—not until then will we reach out. Then we'll step forth for God. But God is trying to teach us that we receive in giving. That's what the widow learned. The same situation that threatened to *break* her *made* her a woman of faith! Right at the time when we don't feel we can, it's impossible—that's the very time that God wants us to stretch, to reach out, to spend ourselves for Him—on Him. And that's faith.

Years ago if you needed water you had to go outdoors to the pump. If it hadn't been used for a while, no matter how long you pumped and how much you perspired, the only way to get water was to take some and pour it into the pump. (It's called priming.) Much of it splashed on the ground. Yet the little bit that got into the pump caused the seal to hold, and suddenly as you pumped—there was water. Lots of water! You couldn't catch it fast enough, and you know what? You always got back more than you'd lost—even though it looked like you'd wasted it. To get water you had to spend water.

I wonder how often we're dry and barren, unfulfilled and barely dragging along simply because we're waiting for our circumstances to change and our feelings to improve... We have thoughts like: *You're weary, worn out, you're empty. You don't have anything to give. Maybe later...After all, no one cares. You're not worth much, anyhow; and no one really needs you.* Such thoughts can keep each of us from following hard after God. And they bring fear of what could happen if we really did.

Ah, but if we, just like "Widow No Name" will believe Him in spite of our thoughts, fears of what ifs, feelings and circumstances, and then *offer* what we have to God, we'll be absolutely astounded at what can happen. That's because God's not just into addition, He's into miraculous multiplication *through... **brokenness!***

Isn't He the One who broke a few loaves of bread and fed a multitude? Twice. The same One who commended a woman for breaking an alabaster box and anointing Him with its precious perfume, then rebuked the one who called it "a waste"? As our Vinedresser, He knows that unless vines are pruned (drastically, down to the nubbins), there can be no fruit; and unless grapes are crushed, there'll be no wine. No new and fresh wine. For He has said: ***"To this one will I look.*** *To him who is humble and of a contrite (broken) spirit and who trembles at My Word"* (Isaiah 66:2).

Isn't this our answer? Isn't this our consolation and hope—that *"the righteous cry out, and the Lord hears, and delivers them out of all their troubles. The Lord is near to those who have a broken heart, and saves such as have a contrite [crushed] spirit"* (Psalm 34:17,18)?

Broken—yet WHOLE!

(Story taken from 1 Kings 16:29-34, 17:1-16)

 * * * * *

85

Chapter 10

Be Prepared!

Out in the Atlantic a hurricane is brewing and heading for the mainland. A big one. Hurricane warning flags fly furiously. On-shore residents, watching, alerted by the radio or short-wave reports begin preparing for the onslaught. Hurriedly they check cupboards for food supplies, candles and lantern oil. If supplies are low, they rush to stores to stock up. Discerningly, they examine their homes, boarding up windows and nailing down anything and everything that's loose and could blow away. They store food and water and test for auxiliary power. They also warn neighbors and help them prepare.

The prudent, listening carefully and often to weather reports, prepare to leave immediately if told to by authority. Only the foolish ones decide to remain, no matter what, and despite the warnings—"party" through it.

Although God wants us prepared ahead of time for adversity, all too often we haven't stored up what we need to ride out any storm. We think we're exempt; it'll pass us by. When it doesn't, we're caught off guard. Unprepared. We haven't bothered to turn on our "radios" or heed The Voice of Warning. We've tried maintaining our spiritual life on yesterday's manna, just getting by on Sunday-to-Sunday sermons. Then "Hurricane Hannah" hits full force, and we find that our supply of both food and water is dreadfully short. We've got no back-up power, or enough fuel to carry us out of the danger. We've taken no time to fasten down anything with Truth. We've never seriously thought that we needed to board up the doors and windows of our lives against anything! And our homes, which should have been built on rock—we discover are built on shifting sand.

"'Now everyone who hears these sayings of Mine and does not do them,' Jesus said, 'will be like a foolish man who built his house on the sand; and the rain descended, the floods came, and the winds blew and beat on that house; and it fell; and great was its fall'" (Matthew 7:26,27).

In contrast, a storm may reveal that we have stored up what we needed to not only survive—but thrive! As we've followed the Lord, He has put a reserve of faith within us that we never knew we had until the tempest hit! The trial, the test, revealed God's best in us and for us! He'd already prepared us. For the storm only revealed the strength of the Rope —Faith, and the Anchor—Jesus.

"I would hasten to my place of refuge from the stormy wind and tempest" (Psalm 55:8).

"For You have been a shelter for me, and a strong tower from the enemy... I will trust in the shelter of Your wings" (Psalm 61:3,4).

However, when we find ourselves unprepared for life's storms, it isn't always the result of carelessness or lack of commitment. Sometimes, it's because we think we don't measure up. Secretly, we don't believe we're "smart enough" to be a "good" Christian. The Bible is a *"how to"* book—and we were never good in school. We sat in a circle in the poor readers group. Oh, they didn't give us that name, but we—and all the other kids—knew we were the poor readers. Tests scared us to death; even though we knew the answers going into them, we could count on it that somehow our knowledge would scurry away at the door and we'd flunk the test. For various reasons we quit school early, and feeling that we're dumb *is* the skeleton in our closet.

Everyone who truly becomes a Christian yearns to learn

87

more about God. However, to do so, we have to come face to face with—a book. *The Book!* Old memories of fears, failure and shame scramble to the surface. Walls of wishing we were different and barriers of hurtful memories rise to limit our faith and push God away.

Although we've been Christian for some time, God's Word still remains out of reach—too high above us, we think. Consequently, we depend on others, and get much of our faith secondhand. However, that just makes us feel like we're on the outside looking in. We don't quite fit. We hesitate to volunteer anything having to do with faith—for what can we know? Sometimes those in authority reinforce the idea that Christianity is based on a smart mind and education; that only those who know the Greek and Hebrew, only those who are seminary trained can truly understand the Bible and get the "correct" meaning from it. (I used to believe that one.)

Consequently, we carry a hidden burden of shame and little expectation that we can ever truly know and follow the Lord the way others do. We're destined to follow from a distance, never a part of the *"inner circle."* Christianity is presented as a pass/fail issue—and all too often—we're failing. Yet... would the God who wants to be so intimate with us set such a standard? If we all stand equal at The Cross—and we do—and each person needs salvation as badly as the other—and we do—would God make it a requirement to follow Him based on our mental accomplishments? OR, that we're able to read well?

Didn't He tell Israel:

"For this commandment which I command you today, it is not too mysterious for you, nor is it far off. It is not in heaven, that you should say, 'Who will ascend into heaven for us and bring it to us, that we may hear and do it?' Nor is it beyond the sea, that you should say, 'Who will go over the sea for us and bring it to us, that we may hear and do it?' **But the word is very near you,** *in your*

mouth and in your heart, that you may do it" (Deut. 30:11-14).

And didn't Jesus say that we needed to be converted and become like **little children?** (Matthew 18:3).

Doesn't Scripture also say: *"Knowledge puffs up, but love builds up"* (1 Cor. 8:1). *"For consider your calling, brethren, that there were **not many wise according to the flesh**, not many mighty, not many noble, but God has chosen the foolish things to shame the wise, and God has chosen the weak things... to put to shame the things that are mighty... that no flesh should glory in His presence"* (1 Cor. 1:26,27,29).

You may not have the problem I've described. Yet, many do—and it's hidden. As you minister to such people who are discouraged and downcast, your well-meant advice—"You just need to get into the Word more"—rather than helping, will only add to their burden and frustration.

What if God has made a way for us to learn—all of us— no matter what our mental capacity? A way that will strengthen and prepare each of us for whatever lies ahead; a way that draws us closer to God, not one that shuts us out. What if Christianity is not like classrooms with pass or fail grades as our western culture often makes it? What if it's more about the heart than the head? What if it's not so much about teacher and student as it is about mentoring?

What if it's more like when a young man apprentices himself to a carpenter? Once accepted into the apprenticeship, the young man (we'll call him Jason) learns the trade mostly by following the older man around (we'll call him Joshua) as he watches and listens to him. It's a lot like Jesus probably did in Nazareth with His father, Joseph. Beginning with very simple tasks like sweeping up shavings, and separating and sorting nails. As Jason is faithful in the smaller jobs, he soon advances to others like carving the wood and crafting the cupboard. He travels to the lumberyard with Joshua to choose wood, and watches how he greets and serves customers in the shop.

Day after day and through the months that follow, Joshua shares what he knows with the eager young man. Without even realizing it, Jason is learning and absorbing what he needs to know and do, naturally, without being forced. And throughout the days a relationship forms—one of respect, friendship and trust. Over shared lunches, they discuss, along with upcoming projects, what's going on in their lives.

In this apprenticeship (another word for discipleship), facts are not the issue (although there are facts). Rather, it's a way of life shared and experienced by both the older and the younger. Joshua gives Jason no written tests. There's no chance of flunking out—only the choice of walking away from the relationship. The "learning" takes place simply because the master carpenter is demonstrating what he knows and imparting who he is to Jason. And Jason wants that. Before you know it, Jason has become a true carpenter in every sense of the word. For it's been worked into his will and into his heart.

Carpentry, along with friendship, has become a way of life for him—never to be held lightly, nor taken from him easily (as opposed to learning material for a test, then forgetting it as soon as one passes the course). Jason's training, experience, and the trust he now feels will stand him well, no matter what reverses or what challenges life brings. Because absolutely nothing can take away from Jason what he knows, or who he is! He's a carpenter. And he knows and loves the Master Carpenter.

Discovering that God wanted to apprentice me to Himself changed my life! It took my focus off my being His student and He the Teacher to one of friendship and trust. The Bible is the

Carpenter's Shop. He invites all of us to join Him there. **All of us!**

In order to become like Him, all we have to do is watch Him and follow Him around in His shop—The Bible. There we see what He's like and how He deals with situations and people. There we hear His voice, ponder His goodness, and wonder at His power. There we search out and discover—He has the very answers we need! There we can heed His warnings and make new choices. There we can hear the promises He makes *to us* then watch Him come through on every one of them.

You know what? I think we've made knowing our God far too hard. Apprenticeship doesn't require a great mind, or the ability to read well and comprehend a lot of material. *If so, many need not apply.* It only requires a **willing and surrendered heart**—and can't we all have that? It doesn't require pride in learning, but humility in receiving. God's so good. He saw our need, and made it possible for each one of us to come and be fed.

"He would have fed them also with the finest of wheat; and with honey from the rock, I [the Lord] would have satisfied you" (Psalm 81:16).

Along with apprenticeship, there is yet another way to view God's Word that prepares and strengthens us, that energizes and deepens our love for Him. So that having "done all, we can stand." We know that on the night on which He was betrayed, Jesus girded Himself with a towel and began washing His disciples' feet, demonstrating servanthood and humility.

Perhaps there's an added meaning in His action? What if He were also showing them that the Word is very accessible? Close enough to touch—and be touched. Because *It* (He—The Word) was kneeling right before them. Pride and

91

misunderstanding— "Never shall You wash my feet"—stood in their way. Jesus would later tell them, *"You're already clean because of the word which I've spoken to you."* But now He insists, *"If I do not wash you, you have no part with Me"* (John 15:3; 13:8).

We know that the Word shows us our sin and keeps us from sin. But have we known that it also cleanses us from the daily grime—the kind of stuff that sticks to us just because we're walking in a human body in a fallen world?

On that last night of all nights, as far as we know, Jesus gave no grades, no evaluation to decide who could move up higher in ministry and closer to Him. In fact, He rebuked those who were thinking along those lines. In those final moments before the disciples' darkest hour, He didn't give them a final exam. Instead, He ministered to each one's weariness. The weariness and grime that just comes from everyday living. They had tired and dirty feet. He knew they needed refreshing. So, although His greatest challenge and final battle lay before Him, He saw it as crucial that He take time to bend low before them and love on them with the water. And through this simple act He was preparing them for the agony about to break upon them.

How awesome God is to make provision for any and everything that comes our way. We can be prepared—no matter what. Despite any lack in training and talents, we can have sufficient oil, food, fuel and water. Even though the "radio" reports are ominous, and the storm flags fly furiously. What a relief to find it's all in His Word, yet so easily obtained. A Word, not just for learning, but His Word to minister to us whenever we present our weariness to Him and let Him wash us.

No more pretending that we're keeping up in the "contest" of "Who knows the most?" The Good News—there's no contest! Rather, there's a love relationship. Glory to God! In my concordance the word "study" occurs a few times; the word "meditate"—many times! Scripture does talk a lot about learning, but it's in the context of watching, listening, following, doing…

Once I felt the Lord impressed upon me that my capacity to learn wasn't nearly as great as I thought. I needed to be content with small portions from His banqueting table so that they could take root in my heart, fasten on my soul and become my strong anchor—part and fiber of who I am. I've been thankful ever since, for it caused me to cease from striving and from taking any pride in what I've learned. I realized it isn't God who's mandated that we read the Bible through in a year, or read at least a chapter a day. Consequently, the "religious" yoke of **having to read** large portions lifted.

The power of His Word is so great that it doesn't take a lot. So… I can sit at His feet (even if it's just for a few moments); and whatever He decides I need from Him will be just fine. I've found also, that when I let Him wash me in His Word, as I'm revived by it I often go on to more study —sometimes for hours…

As you meditate on just a small portion (perhaps just a phrase), He'll draw near to revive and restore you. And who doesn't need that? Who doesn't get weary? Who doesn't have weary dusty feet from walking life's daily paths? No wonder God tells us over and over in Scripture to meditate on His Word. He knows what we need most: To mull it over, chew on it like a satisfying cud; hold it close, speak it, pray it, memorize it, sing it, share it—love it! Oh, yes.

"Your words were found, and I ate them, and Your word was to me the joy and rejoicing of my heart; for I am called by Your name, O Lord God of hosts" (Jer. 15:16).

Suppose I've walked a long way on a hot day and come upon a small lake and sit down beside it. Entranced by its beauty, the breeze fanning my cheeks, and slipping off my sandals I dangle my feet in the cool water. Information about the lake is not a priority. I don't care how it got there, how deep it is, or if it has fish (unless I'm an avid fisherman!). I'm just thankful it's there. It's ministering to me in its simplicity just like the Psalmist David described, *"He leads me beside the still waters. He restores my soul"* (Psalm 23:2b,3a).

Over and over again God makes water synonymous with His Word: to drink, to wash in and be revived by. *"My soul cleaves to the dust; revive me according to Your word"* (Psalm 119:25).

Dear one, we need to get better acquainted with The Foot-washer; the One who has given us His Word, like the lake, like a fountain to refresh and revive us. For when He ministers to us through His Word, we're revived, we're prepared—for anything! When we go through hardships and trials, pain and long sleepless nights, crushing situations with no relief in sight—we know we need equipping. Yet we're drained; we're too weary for serious study. Just to pick up our Bibles seems like too much. We can't keep coherent thoughts together—let alone **learn anything.**

It's at just those times, right when we need Him the most that we often push God away thinking, *He's asking too much.* We feel guilty and feel we've failed Him when we think, *Lord, I can't learn anything now.* Believing that serious Bible study is the only thing that connects us to God, we sigh. *It's too much and too hard. I'll read later.*

Consequently, as we turn away from the Word, we turn away from the very One who will equip us for every fight and hold us strong and true no matter what we have to go through.

94

Ah… but when we realize we have a Savior like no other, One who wants to apprentice us to Himself, who understands what it's like to walk in human flesh, who has experienced weakness and weariness. One who stands waiting to bend before us so that He can—and wants to—wash and refresh us with the Living Water of His Word—well, then, there's hope. There's relief. There's reviving. And so much more…

Foot-washing, anyone?

 * * * * *

Reflections:

Have you ever apprenticed yourself to the Lord? Can you see how thinking of learning from Him in this way lifts a yoke of works and performance? Remember… shepherds in Israel lead their sheep—they don't drive them. "My sheep hear My voice…, and they follow Me" (John 10:27).

*I write Scriptures on 3x5 cards (words that have especially spoken to me) so I have them available anytime, anywhere, to refresh and revive me. Our handwriting is unique; it's our very own. So when we write the Word we're putting our hand and our heart to it. As we meditate, as we memorize, as we store it in our hearts, the results are **awesome**—results that will make you even more aware of how very powerful God's Word is.*

Chapter 11

No Pain – No Gain

When we're sick, quite often a doctor must hurt us in order to heal us. For very often what he prescribes to heal—hurts! (Or, at least tastes bad.) However, he's not supposed to harm us. Hurt is acceptable (and there may be a lot of it—painful injections, drastic rehabilitation), but harm and damage—no. And so it is with our Heavenly Father. He may use pain in our treatment and for our recovery—yet He will never harm us. It's just that His assessment of what constitutes the difference between hurt and harm—often differs from ours!

Now it's 3 a.m. and ideas for this chapter have wakened me from a sound sleep. I've tried to push them out of my mind, burrowing deep down under the covers, because I don't want to lose sleep. Yet, here I am. For as I struggle out of bed and stagger to the computer, I realize the Lord loves me too much to let me get away with disobedience. For when I disobey, for my own good, shouldn't I want His corrective Hand to stop me?

He loves all of us too much to let us keep on doing what will draw us away. Unfortunately, all too often the only way He can draw us back to Him (or closer) is by allowing the onslaught to hit—and hit hard.

Didn't Jesus ask, *"Why do you call Me, 'Lord, Lord, and do not do the things which I say'"* (Luke 6:46)? Don't I want these words to be as true of me as they were for David? *"Sacrifice and offering You did not desire; my ears You have opened... Then I said, 'Behold, I come; in the scroll of the Book it is written of me.* ***I delight to do Your will, O my God...'"*** (Psalm 40:6-8).

Yet I'm still resisting, for just the thought of the discipline of the Lord, and chastening through hardship makes me want to take off running, hoping they won't catch up with me. They make me cringe and look for a place to hide. I don't even want to write about God's discipline; it's like if I do I might be hanging a *"Come on in"* sign on my door. And... because others have gone through much more testing and trial than I, I question even writing about it. However, my writer friend, JoAnn Conboy, insisted, "Yes, you can! What you're writing about is generic. One size fits all; what you've learned will apply to others."

I struggle with discipline, correction and His loving me in the same breath. Because, I'd like Him (the One I call Father) to spoil and indulge me; give to me; bless me. And spankings not to be an option. I don't want to have to overcome—or struggle. It certainly has become that way in America. We want life easy for us and for our children. We want our kids to like us; we want to be their friend, and not bring them any displeasure.

Although the Scriptures are to discipline and train us (2 Tim. 3:15,16)—all too often we look for "bless me" verses, and jump right over the "correct me, change me, rearrange me" verses. We've got those *"bless me's"* highlighted in our Bibles and know just where to find them. So... when we avoid His first line of correction, He has to move Phase 2 into operation.

I like to use the Sheep and Shepherd analogy in counseling situations. Along with pictures, I have a statue my friend Kathy Thornburgh gave me of Jesus holding a lamb tenderly close to His heart. An older sheep leans against Him, looking up at Him in full trust. It's beautiful; yet as tender as that looks, behind it there's a story of tough love.

I've read that shepherds had a drastic measure whenever a lamb continued to stray and lead others in its straying and dangerous pursuits. The shepherd would break one of its legs.

After mending it, he would carry the lamb close to his heart. While its leg healed, the shepherd would hand feed it, taking care of all its needs, talking to it, stroking it, loving it. By the time the lamb's leg was fully healed, it wouldn't ever want to stray. This former rebel, this one who had roving eyes and straying feet, would now cling to its master, never wanting to leave his side.

Yes, the shepherd had hurt the lamb; but only to keep it from the harm and danger of straying. He'd bring it close to his side to demonstrate his faithfulness, love and care for it. That lamb would now be an example to the others of what it means to closely follow the shepherd—any time, anywhere!

[Our Lord] *"... will feed His flock like a shepherd; He will gather the lambs with His arm, and carry them in His bosom, and gently lead those who are with young..." "My sheep hear My voice, and I know them, and **they follow Me....**"* (Isaiah 40:11, John 10:27).

What if at times our wayward ways give The Shepherd cause to regretfully "break our legs"? Many of us came to the Lord at just those times. Our rebellion, our disregard for His call, our wanting our own way, set in motion what at first seemed harsh and too hard. For God's chastening Hand grabbed hold of the scruff of our necks, and with some shaking He stopped us cold in our tracks.

It's choice time: To believe He knows best, that He wants to forgive us, then carry us close to His heart while we heal; or to think He doesn't love us because the leg He's broken hurts— a lot. If the latter is our choice, we'll push Him aside, angry at his treatment of us. We'll hobble off dragging a broken limb with a resentful heart. And carrying a burden of even more guilt.

"The rebellious dwell in a dry [parched] land..." (Psalm 68:6b).

Through *Open Door Counseling Centre* come people who are products of more than a generation who've lived without the reality of God's laws in their lives, or in the culture around them. Consequently, they bear the chains of sin forged through self-centeredness, abuse, addictions, indulgence of children, law breaking, immorality and divorce. They've set standards for themselves based on psychology and what seems right at the time. And they get their answers for life from the liberal/secular media, humanistic education and "TV talk shows." Although they may come to Christ (praise the Lord), and immediate and awesome change takes place, oftentimes they still have the attitude, *I'm gonna do it my way,* which God must deal with.

Through a songwriter's group I organized years ago, I met Jesse Williams, a guitarist who writes soul-searching songs. Though raised in a Christian home, as a teenager he strayed from faith and became heavily involved in drug use and in dealing drugs. Eventually he served time in prison, and saw his marriage break up. This prodigal, while in prison returned to the Lord—full force. His loving, humble and inspiring testimony in word and song has touched many lives.

As a single parent raising a son by himself, his one desire has been to use his music in ministry for the Lord—and for a while that was happening. Because he used contaminated needles, Hepatitis C will be his companion for the rest of his life, unless the Lord heals him.

However, not every hardship that comes our way is the result of rebellion or disobedience. In the past few years, added health problems—several knee surgeries, back surgery and neurological problems—have completely shut down his musical outreach.

99

I called him while writing this chapter to see if he could minister at our fellowship. I ended up not asking him as I could hear the weakness, weariness and pain in his voice. Yet, I sensed no anger, no distancing from God. I was sure of it when after I told him I was working on this book he asked, "Are you going to talk about *the gift of pain*?" When I asked what he meant, he replied, "Pain is the only tool sharp enough to cut away the fatness of our own wayward will." As soon as he spoke those words, he exclaimed, "Wow! I never said anything like that before—it just came out of my mouth. But it's true."

Yet, Jesse doesn't seem to have a wayward will. He doesn't appear to be a "strayer"—not at all. Is it that Jesse sees through his suffering, God working a deeper, necessary and greater work in him—even though others can't see it's needed? Something, some quality, some perception, some depth, some purification, some new level of trust or surrender seemingly doesn't take place through any other means than suffering. Jesse continually professes, "God does all things well; God will perfect the thing which concerns me; and His grace is sufficient."

Today, Jesse's life revolves around long trips to the doctors, much time spent in waiting rooms, stressful therapy, and pain— lots of pain. And, most of all, that Jesus is Lord—Lord of all!

"It is good for me that I have been afflicted, that I might learn Your statutes" (Psalm 119:71).

I believe that when God disciplines us He will show us if it's because of wrongdoing. For He wants us to know our sin so that we can repent and receive the cleansing that comes from repentance (1 John 1:7-9). His deepest desire is that we know Him and His ways. So He isn't unclear or vague; He won't leave us stumbling around in the darkness, unsure of what we've done, or how to deal with it. A good father wouldn't tell his child, "You've done something very wrong and this is your

100

punishment for it. But I'm not going to tell you what you've done."

The Holy Spirit's work is to speak clearly to us about our sin, and point us to the loving Savior, who so desires to forgive and restore us. Part of the heaviness of our hardship and its resulting depression is that we haven't sought God about it. So... we wrongly assume He's punishing us. Like Job's friends, we think, *God's angry with us.*

Instead of it being punishment, God uses the everyday setbacks and failures that we experience, the heartaches and heartbreaks—the things that come to us just because we live in a fallen world, in fallen bodies, in the midst of fallen people— to train us!

When a horse trainer first puts the bit in a young colt's mouth, attaches it to a bridle, and tries to lead him around in the paddock, he rears and bucks. The bit hurts. The young stallion, Starburst, wants no part of it, and sees no good in it. Left to himself, he would never put that bit in his mouth and be led around. And for sure he would never, never allow anyone to climb on his back and decide where he should go!

Once trained, however, it's another story. Starburst loves being ridden, and loves the one who's trained him. He now throws up his head, tosses his mane in anticipation, and greets his trainer with a glad whinny, as he gallops to meet him—ready and willing to carry him—anywhere! And Starburst knows (because of the excellent training he's had) he can enter a race and finish a winner! Kentucky Derby—here I come!

"Do you not know that those who run in a race all run, but one receives the prize. Run in such a way that you may obtain it" (2 Cor. 9:24).

101

Years ago as a student nurse, we all dreaded being assigned to the Coronary Care Floor because the work was so physically draining. There were no ICU's, and desperately ill patients were ours to care for. Back then (way back then), the treatment for heart attacks was bed rest. Complete bed rest—meaning that the patient wasn't allowed to do anything—not even hand himself a glass of water. The medical opinion then was that the heart needed absolute rest to recover and to prevent further attacks or damage.

How different treatment is today. Today it's, "Don't rest the heart—it's a muscle. Exercise it back to health." Muscles not used will weaken and wither. To get stronger, muscles must be stretched, pressed, and used. Any athlete knows this.

As runners in the Christian race of life though, don't we often resist the stretching and pressing that people and situations bring us? Yet, what if they're just the very things that will hammer our hearts into holiness, the very things that will form us into His Frame so we can run the race of faith and finish victoriously?!

*"...let us **lay aside every weight**, and the sin which so easily ensnares us, and let us **run with endurance** the race that is set before us, **looking unto Jesus**, the author and finisher of our faith, who for the joy that was set before Him **endured** the cross..."* (Heb. 12:1,2).

Together reaching! Stretching!
Pressing onward!

 * * * * *

Chapter 12

Faith Under Fire

During our years in New Guinea from 1967-1973, we saw God move in ways then new to us.

By becoming more surrendered to Jesus as Lord, empowered and led by His Word and Spirit, we saw things like this: Eight year old Trevor (name changed), an Australian government worker's son, had been caught in an out-of-control-grass fire. The third degree burns on his legs had failed to heal rightly, leaving contractures so that he couldn't walk upright. He was scheduled on a Monday to fly to Australia for surgery. The Friday before, his mother had seen Bob at the hospital. Having heard that we believed in the power of God for today, brushing away tears she'd pleaded, "Will you and Jeanne come and pray for Trevor?" Saturday morning we went, talked to Trevor about Jesus as his Savior, laid hands on his legs as we prayed a simple prayer for his healing, and left.

Monday morning when the doctor unwrapped his bandages to re-dress his burns for the flight, they saw no grafts were needed. His legs were completely healed with new skin! He returned to school telling his classmates, "I've been healed!"

Then there was Jim (name changed). Within a very short time this vibrant teenage top-of-his-class New Guinean student had become so incapacitated that he'd been finally and reluctantly released from the hospital to die. As his culture demanded, he was sent home to die on his own land—but only after the staff had exhausted all attempts to diagnose and treat him. That same Friday evening, Jim, unable to eat, speak or hear, was carried into our home. Missionaries and New Guineans met together knowing only God could set him free. And He did!

Monday morning Jim was back in his school, totally restored, declaring, "Medicine is good; hospitals are good. But they didn't help me. The hospital sent me home to die; but Jesus, and His name alone, healed and set me free!"

However, such happenings made waves within our mission family. Our experiences—like those described in the Bible—while building faith and unity in some, disturbed others. Those with concerns went to mission leadership insisting there must be a committee formed to meet with those of us who believed in God's promised supernatural power for today.

Church leaders assured us, "Such meetings will clear up misunderstandings." Although some pastors told us they had grave misgivings, I thought it was a great opportunity! I'd have a chance to share some of the wonderful things Jesus had taught me since making Him my Lord and Teacher. And I could glean from these learned men, their faith, their wisdom. *What an opportunity*, I thought, *to share and grow together!*

To my dismay, at our first meeting it became immediately and abundantly clear that the committee's goal was not to find common faith ground, as I had naively assumed. They called our beliefs too simplistic, and that we took Scriptures too literally when we shared promises from God's Word about being led by Him.

Yet hadn't Jesus said, *"My sheep hear My voice, and I know them, and they follow Me"* (John 10:27)? And wasn't that because, *"Jesus Christ is the same yesterday, today and forever"* (Heb. 13:8)?

At the close of the second session, we were told that rather than using the Bible as we had been doing, future meetings would rest solely on the church's beliefs defined in its doctrine. Documents of creeds and confessions—written earlier by church

104

leaders—would be the only standard allowed thereafter—and our judge! Yet, hadn't Jesus Himself warned about this very thing?

"...you have made the commandment of God of no effect by your tradition." "...In vain they worship Me, teaching as doctrines the commandments of men" (Matt. 15:6,9*)*.

As a young person, I'd felt such safety, such confidence, in knowing my church's foundational stand was **Scripture alone, faith alone.** Now I felt betrayed, because it seemed that those in leadership were willing to set this aside in order to find *their* safety in doctrine and dogma alone. And insisting I do the same.

Returning home, my hurt and even the anger I felt at the way that meeting had gone spilled over. "Lord, this isn't fair. We're just trying to be obedient and walk in the Spirit. This is too hard," and I felt altogether justified until these words invaded my mind stopping me cold: *You have not yet resisted to the point of shedding blood, have you?* It was so real that I instantly looked down at my hands and feet to see if there was blood. There wasn't.

I quickly went to the Scripture where I knew this verse was found and read:

*"For **consider Him** who endured such hostility from sinners against Himself, **lest you become weary and discouraged in your souls.** You have not yet resisted to bloodshed, striving against sin. And you have forgotten the exhortation, which speaks to you as to sons: 'My son, do not despise the chastening of the Lord, nor be discouraged when you are rebuked by Him; **for whom the Lord loves He chastens and scourges every son whom He receives'"* (Heb. 12:3-6).

He chastens us for our profit *that we may be partakers of His holiness*! *"Now no chastening seems to be joyful for the present, but grievous; nevertheless, afterward it yields the peaceable fruit of righteousness* **to those who have been trained by it"** (Heb. 12:10,11).

When God reached down and corrected me with His question, then humbled me with those verses, the extreme heaviness I'd felt since the meetings began suddenly lifted completely. I hadn't been *considering Jesus*—only my own discomfort! From that day on (after repenting for my **sin of complaining**), I was able to go back into other meetings with a new attitude, even one of peace and joy! And I clung to the verses, verses the Lord had put on my heart right before our first meeting:

"Beloved, do not think it strange concerning the fiery trial which is to try you, as though some strange thing happened to you; but rejoice to the extent that you partake of Christ's sufferings, that when his glory is revealed, you may also be glad with exceeding joy. If you are reproached for the name of Christ, blessed are you, for the Spirit of glory and of God rests upon you" (1 Peter 4:12-14).

Verses that hadn't seemed to fit back then, did now; comforted me now; and strengthened me for what lay ahead.

Because nothing we said—no Bible passages (and there were many), the evidence of changed and transformed lives (and there were many), the testimonies by others of healings, miracles, deliverances like Jim's—surely at least some of these were evidence that the living Lord through His Spirit was in our midst and bringing revival! We stood at a crossroad: We could move together by faith—or "not." Leadership decided "not."

For Bob and I, it came down to this: God's Word had come alive to us in a new and promised way; we *couldn't* go back to what we'd known before. And those in charge *wouldn't* go forward. We had once held the form of religion but denied the power. Now we could no longer do so! (2 Tim. 3:5).

Sadly, we couldn't find enough common ground and had to leave the mission field. It wasn't that the leaders making the decision didn't love us. It wasn't even that they didn't believe what they'd seen, or what they'd heard about. It was more like when Jesus had healed the man with the withered hand in the Synagogue. For the leaders back then, the issue was not the healing. The healed one stood before them. In fact, they'd wanted Jesus to heal the man, so that they could accuse Him of breaking the Sabbath!!! (Mark 3:1-6).What Jesus was teaching and doing—everything about Him—threatened the religious structure of that day with its prescribed and controlled boundaries.

In our case, mission leaders decided that even if what we believed was Scriptural, even if there were God-glorifying results, if it didn't fit within their written doctrine, it couldn't be included within their church structure. It wasn't worth the cost, or, the risk—the risk of stepping through and out of old boundaries into new waters of trust—ones that hadn't been tested by them, or approved by those higher than they. They weighed on one hand the unknown, the untried; and on the other what they'd always had. And they decided in a stroke of time that what they knew and believed to be tried and true would prevail! While we disagreed with their reasoning and were grieved by their choices, Bob and I respected their right and authority to make their decisions.

I understood their struggle, for it had been mine. No one knows better than I what a scary thing it is to throw off what we've loved and believed in for years—and launch out into the deep. Our craft looks so frail, and the ocean so immense. How will we ever survive if there's a storm? And, we know there'll be one.

Yet faith, true faith in the Lord Jesus Christ, and ***His ability to lead and keep His Church***—and our need to let Him, or it's not true faith—is almost never about safety. Or, comfort. And almost always about risking. Despite our fears! If that weren't so, what would there have been to write about in the Book of Acts? Wasn't that book about new believers launching out into unknown waters led by God's Spirit? They, too, had a lot to lose—more than we do today—but look at what they gained! And aren't we Christians today because of it?

Faith, ***true faith***—not merely agreement—is about a Christian embarking on the sea of life in what looks like a flimsy craft indeed; one that's counting on the wind in its sails to carry it to its destination. Jesus likened the Holy Spirit to the wind that's unpredictable—blowing wherever it wills. (John 3:5-8).

Such wind—***His Wind***—can be relied upon to carry us. But it cannot be contained by man. For, "...*the Word of God is not chained*" (2 Tim. 2:9b). "...*and where the Spirit of the Lord is, there is liberty*" (2 Cor. 3:17).

At those meetings in New Guinea; as we talked with pastors, teachers, and others who were also being questioned; as we sat across the table from those who disagreed, I saw that all of us were involved in more than an ideological struggle. Although our conflict seemed to be about doctrine and dogma, creeds and beliefs, varying expressions of faith and interpretations of Scripture—it wasn't!

Against our little craft called ***Faith,*** the true battle was being waged by satan's forces! They were the ones totally opposed to our living solely and wholly for Jesus, empowered by His Holy Spirit. They were the ones hurling fiery rounds of intimidation and doubt across our bow, hoping we'd surrender our ship, deciding the war wasn't worth it. The fires of revival—*the fires of passion for Jesus*—will always draw the enemy's fire in return.

Of course, satan didn't want us to believe all of God's Word! Or in obedience to that Word, stretch forth our hands in Jesus' name to heal and set free.

"And these signs will follow those who believe: In My name they will cast out demons; ...they will lay hands on the sick and they will recover" (Mark 16:17,18).

"Behold, I [Jesus] give you [believers] authority to trample on serpents and scorpions, and over all the power of the enemy, and nothing shall by any means hurt you" (Luke 10:19).

Ultimately, it was satan who didn't want the power of God's Spirit flowing in, through, and out of us in revival, so that souls were saved, and the name of Jesus was exalted and glorified!

We were part of a Cosmic Conflict. And, Glory to God, our eyes were being opened to see that for us who'd set sail in Jesus—there would be times of war!

 * * * * *

Reflections

Can you see that surrendering to Jesus Christ as Lord of your life means risking rejection and paying whatever is the cost to follow him?

Up to now, have you believed that Christianity was about God doing things for you, and blessing you, rather than you serving and blessing Him?

Have you ever asked Jesus to fill and empower you with His Spirit of Holiness as promised? (John 7:37-39; Luke 24:49; Acts 1:8; Acts 2:1-21; Acts 8:14-17; Acts 10:38; Acts 19:1-6; Eph. 5:18-20; 2 Cor. 12:1-12)

Have you, or those you love, been hurt or let down by the church, perhaps at a time when you were just beginning your search for, or walk with, God? When you badly needed someone to encourage you, but you were condemned, did that cause you to say: "I'll still keep my faith, but I don't want church?" Can you see from this chapter that satan was behind it all, hoping you'd do just that?

If we turn away from Christ's Body, doesn't that mean we're turning away from the One who's the Head of His Body?

If you're in church leadership in some capacity, how has this chapter spoken to you?

God's shepherds need to protect His flock from error. However, in what ways can tradition and what's familiar become a hindrance for you in following the Chief Shepherd into paths not yet traveled or known by you?

Prayer: Talk to the Lord about whatever has spoken to your heart. Ask Him to show you where you need forgiveness; and where you need new discernment about the enemy. As your choice, step

110

*through your fears and ask Him to give you **fresh faith** to follow*
Jesus Christ, the Lord, no matter where, no matter what the cost.

Chapter 13

Battle Weary, or Battle Ready?

In the past chapter, we came to realize we were in the middle of spiritual warfare—but we were raw recruits! We'd found ourselves in combat without preparation.

In our armed forces, new recruits upon induction are introduced and initiated into the wonderful experience of military life through boot camp! It's called, "Basic Training"—innocent words for "agonizingly difficult!" And it doesn't take long before each inductee realizes that his or her flesh doesn't like any of it.

My flesh as well wants to avoid the warfare training I so badly need. But if I really want to be a faithful follower of Christ, right in the very midst of my problems and trials, right in the midst of satan's attacks I need to spiritually throw off my covers (it's no time to sleep!)—jump out of bed; stand to attention; keep my eyes fixed straight ahead; listen only to my Commander's voice; and instantly obey! Despite my feelings. Even though I'd like to pull the covers up around my ears, snooze right on through the bugle call, ignoring roll call in God's Army. *(Yet, what if I'm "sleeping" when the Final trumpet sounds.)*

When young people enter military service, they often set their sights on a special service assignment. (It's why they enlisted.) However, before that can ever happen, boot camp and basic training are a must. *No one* gets a special assignment without first being **trained in the trenches**.

I think there are some of us in the Body of Christ wanting special assignments—**minus boot camp!** In basic training each recruit is fine tuned, taught to listen and obey and work together as a single unit. 24/7. And although the regimen is rigorous and downright painful at times, because of it each one becomes a well-disciplined and loyal soldier. One who is able to fight faithfully and well.

Most soldiers hate basic training. They even have dreams of getting even with their drill sergeant—the one who adds dozens of push-ups for the slightest infraction, and screams in their ears while they grunt and strain. Yet when they finally pass basic, those same soldiers are thankful, even grateful, that mean old Sarge was as hard on them as he was. For now they see the benefits. The discipline, the hardship—yes, even the seeming unfairness of it—held a high purpose. In the long run, the difficult training worked for their good and for the good of the whole army. Although trained as a unit, each one now has a new identity and strength of character they never had before. Isn't that because **they're trained** to serve something other and higher than themselves?

"You therefore must endure hardship as a good soldier of Jesus Christ. No one engaged in warfare entangles himself with the affairs of this life, that he may please him who enlisted him as a soldier" (2 Tim. 2:3,4).

Any well-trained soldier studies his enemy—his armor and ammunition, his tactics and position—very much aware that the one out to destroy him will use every advantage he can. The soldier knows his adversary has painstakingly gathered intelligence; and if he can discover weakness he'll attack with vengeance at that very place. In contrast, when satan and his cohorts fight us, too often we don't suspect anything. We forget—or never really believed—that satan uses **everything and anything** to cause us to doubt God, be ineffective and stray. That includes illness, accidents, misunderstandings, and any and all problems. (When we read that Jesus *rebuked* sicknesses and storms, doesn't that mean that at those times **He knew** the devil was behind them?)

113

If we want to be truly trained in spiritual warfare and protected from *"all the fiery darts of the evil one"* so that we don't retreat *"when the enemy comes in like a flood,"* then we must first realize that our enemy will use anything and everything to steal our peace—anything to distance us from God; anything to strike us down, and keep us down; anything to make us doubt or fear.

*"Put on the whole armor of God, that you may be able to stand against the **whiles** of the devil"* (Eph. 6:11).

At a recent retreat, my dear friend from New Guinea, Elise Arndt, described what we should be doing. "We need to quit telling God how big our storm is and start telling the storm how big our God is!!!"

When we came to Christ, we were inducted into the Army of God —whether we realized it or not! And our Commander-in-Chief is going to do whatever it takes, and use whatever it takes to get us in shape and **teach us warfare.** He'll use it all: every hard situation, every difficult person who treats us badly—yes, even that one who judges us unfairly, continually criticizes us, or calls us before them for questioning; anything and anyone who tries to limit our walk and silence our witness.

For He has a Plan and a Goal: to make us loyal and faithful soldiers, ready at a moment's notice to *"fight the good fight of faith."* As the Captain of our Salvation, and as the Lord of Hosts [armies], He has the right —every right— to do with us as He wills. ***"Yes, Sir!"***

Job understood this when he acknowledged in his misery, *"Though He slay me, yet will I trust Him…"* (Job 13:15).

On September 11th, 2001, life not only changed drastically for America, but for the whole world as well. When the Twin

Towers of the World Trade Center crumbled and fell; when passenger planes became devastating missiles; when terrorists invaded our soil and sought to intimidate, paralyze and take us captive through fear of what they might do next—a new battle line was drawn in the sand. A new war was declared in the heavenlies. That's why we see *"men's hearts failing them for fear, and the expectation of what is coming on the earth..."* (Luke 21:26).

This new war we find ourselves in parallels closely to the spiritual warfare that continually wages against us—to steal our peace and sabotage our faith. Demonic spirits in this war will work tirelessly to reinforce our weariness. They'll hang their hats on our hardship and coax us in times of illness or loss to give up and give in. Often satan has either orchestrated the circumstance, or rides in on the waves of it. Yet, way too often, we don't discern we're under attack, or know what to do if we do realize it.

"For we do not wrestle against flesh and blood, but against principalities, against powers, against the rulers of the darkness of this age, against spiritual hosts of wickedness in the heavenly places" (Eph 6:12).

The terrorist today often goes undetected because he lives in the same apartment house as we do, shops at the same supermarket, and looks and acts much like anyone else. In the same manner, the enemy of our souls has observed us for years and doesn't seem different or dangerous. And the words he whispers in our "ears" don't set off any alarm bells, either.

We are ***both blind and deaf*** soldiers without Our God's Word and Presence! God alone sees the scope of the battle. He wants us strengthened by the fight—not weakened. He doesn't want us struck down any longer by the enemy's accusations and actions, or by our life's experiences. It grieves Him to see us lying weak and wounded on life's battlefield when He's given us everything we need to overcome: His Word. His Spirit. His name. His armor!

"For though we walk in the flesh, we do not war according to the flesh. For the weapons of our warfare are not carnal but mighty in God for pulling down strongholds" (2 Cor. 10:3-4).

"And they overcame him [satan] by the blood of the Lamb and by the word of their testimony, and they did not love their lives to death" (Rev. 12:11).

So... overcoming means ***remaining faithful***—to the very end. Overcoming is recognizing the enemy's works and ways wherever that might be: home and family; job; school; relationships; and yes, even inside the church. It means resisting him firm in the faith!

"Therefore submit to God. Resist the devil and he will flee from you" (James 4:7). Hallelujah!

It means clinging more tightly than ever to Jesus, because He's made us **full partakers** of His Holiness, and **beloved heirs** of His Righteousness, praise God! Overcoming means continually living as if *"For to me, to live is Christ, and to die is gain"* (Phil. 1:21).

And when we **"Fight"** this way—**His Way**—we'll be no longer struck down, but standing—**in Him!** No longer ***battle weary, but*** **revived** (even in the fight), and ***battle ready!*** Able to say words like: *"I have fought the good fight, I have finished the race, I have kept the faith..."* (2 Tim. 4:7).

 * * * * *

Chapter 14

When One Suffers...

Suffering is universal—with no one exempt. Suffering is promised to Christians. Is it a promise we'd rather not claim?

"... all who desire to live a godly life in Christ Jesus will suffer persecution." "For to you it has been granted on behalf of Christ [is God saying it's a privilege?], not only to believe in Him, but also to suffer for His sake" (2 Tim. 3:12, Phil. 1:29).

Each month *"The Voice of the Martyrs"* magazine[8] relates gut-wrenching stories with pictures of the lives and testimonies across the globe of those suffering for the sake of Christ—our brothers and sisters. These stories open our eyes to this stark reality: It isn't just Christians who died for their faith centuries ago, but it's men, women and, yes, children persecuted for the sake of the Gospel—today! In sixty countries (some we can easily name, others we can't pronounce or find on the map), **200 million Christians** are denied basic fundamental rights *solely* because of their faith. And an estimated **164,000 Christians** are martyred every year for their faith![9] Yet amazingly, in such countries where the Church suffers, and even has to go underground—it flourishes! In contrast, where Christianity is tolerated—faith flounders. Polycarp said centuries ago, "The blood of the martyrs is the seed of the church." Proof, is it not, that suffering for the Lord doesn't weaken the Church, it only strengthens?

As I write, in northern Nigeria they're worshipping in burned-out churches with death threats upon their heads if they gather. And I can't help but wonder—would I do the same? If there were risk to my life and limb would I take that risk and pay the cost? I want to believe I would; yet I'm so aware that only by His Grace and Power could I.

"The Spirit Himself bears witness with our spirit that we are children of God and joint heirs with Christ, if indeed we suffer with Him that we may also be glorified together. For I consider that the sufferings of this present time are not worthy to be compared with the glory that shall be revealed in us" (Rom. 8:16-18).

Throughout this book, I've used examples from people's lives that have encouraged, humbled, corrected, taught, strengthened and changed me. That's what's supposed to happen in the Body of Christ. And suffering—whether it's for the sake of Christ, or from life's hardships—has its own gifts and lessons to impart. As always, our Jesus has gone before us. *"... although he was a Son, he learned obedience from the things which He suffered..." "For it was fitting for Him...in bringing many sons to glory to make the Author of their Salvation **perfect through sufferings**"* (Heb. 5:9, 2:10).

Though *Suffering 101* may be a class we'd like to skip in God's School of Obedience, we mustn't. It's a course requirement. If we don't accept the cup of suffering (though it may be through clenched lips), we'll be the loser. We're members of His body. Hurt that happens to one happens to all. And our All-powerful, All-knowing, Ever-present God is able to impart a measure of the blessing to us that comes from the suffering of others—even when we haven't undergone the same thing. Isn't that incredible?

We don't suffer alone. Yet it surely feels like we're alone and isolated in the furnace of our affliction, doesn't it? St. Paul urged the early church to remember those in bonds as if they were also in bonds; for spiritually, they were. He wrote, *"If we are afflicted, it is for your comfort and salvation"* (2 Cor. 1:6). In the same way our human body is knit together with a single beating heart and blood flow, the Body of Christ transcends color, language and culture across the miles and across the ages. Intrinsically joined. One Body (1 Cor. 12:12,26,27).

Yet, there is even more that suffering provides. Through exposure to one another's afflictions and infirmities, we're humbled. (And tell me we don't need that!) Spontaneously, gifts of compassion, mercy and service rise up in us to meet such need. Compassion for the hurting and suffering moved our Jesus into the midst of the crowd, so He could touch the untouchable, heal and deliver. *"And when Jesus went out He saw a great multitude; and He was moved with compassion for them, and healed their sick"* (Matthew 14:14). That same Spirit of compassion *yearns to reach out and touch* those who are hurting and suffering—through us!

I saw this body ministry of compassion and helps exemplified in a fellowship Bob and I joined in 1980. I first saw Rosa (not her real name) during an evening service in a tent at our summer Bible Camp. During praise and worship she remained seated in her wheelchair. It was obvious she was only able to whisper the words of praise and exultation that the rest of us were shouting so exuberantly. As I watched Rosa, her face glowing, though marked by disease, what was my first conviction? That I'd taken for granted the ability to stand, raise my hands and shout to the Lord. On the spot, I prayed that by the grace of God I never would again. Nor did I want to ever play it safe or slack off when it was taking every ounce of strength she could muster just to whisper in song, "I love you, Lord, and I lift my voice…"

The disease of Multiple Sclerosis had ravaged her; her weight—she barely weighed anything; her strength—her inability to move anything except her head. Because her respiratory muscles were also damaged, every sentence uttered—she gasped. She could do absolutely nothing for herself. MS had stolen everything, everything from her—except her spirit! Always, always there was

119

a smile on her face and love blazing out of her eyes. I never heard a complaint, only words of praise and trust in her Jesus. (And occasionally a little joke to make those of us around her feel more at ease.)

She required 24-hour care. Her husband, Ben (name changed) and their five children, as they cared for her, were amazing to watch. Her condition and their shared faith had worked such mercy, tenderness and steadfastness in each one that it brought awe to my heart and tears to my eyes. (And still does as I write this, remembering...) No one seemed to see caring for her as a duty or burden, but rather as an opportunity and a privilege. Their home held no heaviness—*joy* greeted you at the door and tagged you home. And despite her great limitations, her family included her in every decision, every operation of the household. It was obvious—she was the hub on which the rest of the wheel turned.

When Ben was at work and the children at school, members of our congregation took turns staying with her. That's when I got to know how real, how concrete Rosa's faith was. (It's behind closed doors that the real "us" stands up.) Thinking I'd go to help and cheer her, I always left with far more faith and encouragement than I'd come with. Each time I left, I left shaking my head because I'd been the one ministered to.

Everyone involved believed in healing; and we'd seen miracles take place. She was constantly lifted up for such healing and deliverance. There was much fasting, yet the MS remained. Do we know why? No. Has the Lord been able to use her illness to the glory of God? Oh, Yes! And shame on those today who add to the burden of those suffering by saying, "God can't be glorified in this."

Paul wrote: *"Therefore we do not lose heart. Even though our outward man is perishing, yet the inward man is*

120

being renewed day by day. For our light affliction which is but for a moment, is working for us a far more exceeding and eternal weight of glory..." (2 Cor. 4:16,17).

Pat Riley, one of my closest friends of many years, became a diabetic as a young mother of two at the age of twenty-five. From the very beginning, her disease was difficult to regulate and control; and she could quickly swing from insulin coma to insulin shock. Over the years there were complications from the disease. At one time she was studying Braille because her doctor said she was going blind. BUT she didn't. Because there would be healings—over and over again healings—but never from the Diabetes itself.

One day she described a vision to me she received when she questioned, "God, why haven't I been healed of the Diabetes, when I've been healed of other things?" In the vision as she walked down a narrow path, a bush with huge thorns suddenly appeared across the path blocking her way. She asked, "Lord, what should I do?" "Tell it to leave in the name of Jesus," was the reply; and as she did so, the bush disappeared. She walked farther, and again the bush dropped into her path. "What shall I do, Lord?" she questioned. "While it is here, I shall use it for a season to teach you." Then, a path was shown to her around the bush, so she skirted it and walked on.

A third time the bush appeared, blocking her way and once again she asked, "Lord, what should I do?" This time the Lord said, "Pick it up." "But Lord," she protested, "the thorns will hurt me." "Pick it up," came the command once more. And as she did, bringing those brambles close to her heart, beautiful fragrant red roses burst into bloom. Then she walked on carrying armloads of sweet smelling blossoms, enveloped by their fragrance.

I've related her vision over the years as I've taught and

ministered; and I never tell it without choking back tears, for I know Pat's life of trust. And, I know the God who gave her that vision. Those who don't understand this dimension of *"faith,"* those who insist God isn't like that and would never do that, often reject her. She still believes ardently in healing (while walking in the "word" she believes God has given her). And… she walks in peace. Pat believes that one of the reasons the Diabetes has remained is so that she can give encouragement—instead of rejection, to those who are not (yet?) healed. *Suffering used—not wasted!*

As in Pat's vision, for us also there are times when hardships, when obstacles and hindrances, and yes, sicknesses and disease, are removed and lifted by words we speak—words of power and authority given to us to use by Jesus Himself: *"In My name …they will lay hands on the sick and they will recover." "Behold, I give you authority to trample on serpents and scorpions, and over all the power of the enemy, and nothing shall by any means hurt you"* (Mark 16:17,18, Luke 10:19). And it's glorious to experience this.[10]

Then at other times God shows us a way around the prickly situation, the thorny problem (*or person?*), the snare or trap the enemy has laid for us. Once we've learned the lesson and God has used it to change us (and others), He shows us a way around it and we walk on unhindered and unhampered.

Still… there are those times—those crushing ongoing situations when the "obstacle," the lingering ongoing problem that seems to have no answer or solution (like Pat's Diabetes) are not taken away. Neither does God make a way around it, or through it. What if the Lord then says to us, "Pick it up? Embrace it. Don't avoid it, for it's come by My permission and by My nail-pierced Hand"?

"… that I may know Him and the power of His resurrection,

and the fellowship of His sufferings, being conformed to His death"
(Phil. 3:10).

When we obey, not understanding or comprehending—like Pat—instead of more thorns, instead of more hurt and heaviness of heart, won't we also experience wondrous blossoms of His nearness and faithfulness? As we walk on and *walk through,* carrying what we've been told to embrace (no matter what others may think or say, no matter if we never fully understand this side of Glory), won't we be walking—*in Him*? And doesn't Scripture guarantee when we do that, we're the fragrance of Christ? An aroma from life—to LIFE?

*"Now thanks be to God who always leads us **in triumph in Christ,** and through us diffuses the fragrance of His knowledge in every place. For **we are** to God **the fragrance of Christ** among those who are being saved and among those who are perishing..."*
(2 Cor. 2:14,15).

There's no doubt, suffering molds and changes us. Another dear friend taught me about being molded and changed, and she did it through classes she'd taken in pottery. I learned—potters love clay! They actually like putting their hands on the clay, working it, kneading it, molding and shaping it! Now, I don't like to get my hands dirty, and I wear gloves if I do any gardening. But not potters. They like the feel of the clay in their hands. As I learned this, I got a new understanding of why God calls Himself—The Potter. *"O house of Israel, can I not do with you as this potter?"* says the Lord. *"Look, as the clay is in the potter's hand, so are you in My hand, O house of Israel!"* (Jer. 18:6).

My view used to be (before I really knew about potters) that God could hardly wait to get the vessel (*me*) finished. He just kind of put up with the process (*all that kneading and molding stuff*) in order to get the end result: *a beautiful finished vessel.* So… whatever situation I was going through, I just wanted it over—Quickly! My eyes were on the finished product; and I was ashamed of the impurities in me that kept rising to the surface as He worked the clay.

I see it differently now. I see Him differently now. And I see me differently. Now my eyes are on 𝔖he 𝔓otter—not the vessel. Being a true Potter, He likes—no loves—the clay!!! He enjoys putting His hands on us; molding, forming us, working the impurities out of us (the things we make excuses for, that He wants to remove); adding just the right amount of water (the Word) to keep us supple and pliable. (Clay does dry out quickly, you know.) Throwing us back on the wheel (*ouch, Lord*), adding more clay to stretch us, enlarging the pot's capacity (*oh, no*), patiently firing the kiln to just the right temperature and placing us in it (*double ouch, Lord*), then removing the pot just in time— He LOVES IT ALL. Since learning this, I don't so easily shun His Hand that holds sharp tools. And I'm not looking around for a way to jump off the wheel, as he works this lumpy clump of clay. Nor am I quite so quick to want and sometimes insist, "Lord, I've been in the furnace long enough. Haven't you made a mistake and turned the temperature up too high? It's *too hot* in here!"

Although I can't explain it, and I can't begin to fully understand it, He's enjoying the hands-on work it's taking to conform me to His Son. And He's promised to perfect and complete what He's begun.

"Being confident of this very thing, that He who has begun a good work in you will complete it until the day of Jesus Christ" (Phil. 1:6).

"…may the God of all grace who called us to His eternal glory by Christ Jesus, after you have suffered a while, perfect, establish, strengthen and settle you" (1 Peter 5:10).

This God of ours isn't far off—He's near! Near enough to put His very own hands upon us as He molds and fashions us. *"But now, O Lord, You are our Father; we are the clay, and You* ***our Potter****; and all we are the work of Your Hand"* (Isaiah 64:8).

And yes, suffering and surrender are tools The Potter uses. Suffering makes us vulnerable; the masks go off. There are no walls of pretense to hide behind, for suffering is the common denominator of human life. (I learned this early on in nurses' training, for everyone looks amazingly alike in a hospital gown lying in a hospital bed.) Although we'd much rather lead and prefer to give help rather than take it, suffering requires we surrender our pride and put on humility as we whisper, "Please, I need help."

Suffering remains for me (as for others) a mystery, with the full answer not to be revealed until THE DAY when all is revealed. What we can see and know here and now is that suffering is to be seen and received as a ***"gift"*** to us—and to others. It's necessary and needed, essential and crucial, in order for the Body of Christ to fully be His Body. As Paul explained:

*"I now **rejoice in my sufferings for you**, and fill up in my flesh what is lacking in the afflictions of Christ, for the sake of His Body, which is the Church"* (Col. 1:24).

I don't know where I'd be today if I hadn't received all that I have from those in the Body of Christ. And as I remember what I've personally gone through, there's no pain with my memories—just the beauty of how God used them, as only He can, to make "something beautiful out of my life." It's as the great French painter, Renoir, once said, "The ***pain passes,*** but the ***beauty remains.***"

And we become, glory to God "...*a vessel of honor [of gold and silver], sanctified and useful for the Master, prepared for every good work*" (2 Tim. 2:21).

 * * * * *

Chapter 15

In The Fullness of Time

We're a country, a culture, a people, individuals—who hate to wait. And American technology makes it possible that we seldom have to wait—for anything! Express Lanes. Fast Foods. Meals-In-A-Minute. Quick-Change oil change. Fast forward VCR's. Instant Replay. Quick! Fast! Instant! Such advertising words get our attention.

Busy signals, red lights, long lines of traffic upset us, causing road rage in some. I confess that people who are late for appointments are one of my pet peeves, because I don't like wasting my time waiting for them. If I'm not careful, I'll put my relationship with the Lord on the clock as well. Then when I spend some time in Bible study and devotions, expecting God to show me something and it doesn't happen, I can feel disappointed and think He's let me down. When tangible prayer answers are delayed, I may be tempted to think, *He isn't going to answer. He doesn't care.*

We see people looking for fast *express lanes* in some of our churches, as well. If the service goes over the allotted or expected time, they start shuffling feet and checking their watches. The designated time for God has gone into overtime. And unlike an exciting tied-score basketball game where the next few minutes decide the championship, our God-time is over. Let's move on to something else.

Likewise, this *express* mentality can affect how much time we invest in presenting the gospel. In the last few remaining minutes of the service, the question is asked, "Is there anyone here who would like to get saved? Is there anyone here who would like to have Jesus in their hearts?" Those who raise their hands are invited to the front and led in a "sinner's prayer"—then—told they're saved. And it's all happened in less than ten minutes!

The result? The most important decision of their lives about the most important Person for their lives has been given less time and attention than it takes most of us to pick out a new pair of shoes.

However, when we examine Bible history we find God has a different view of time. He's never in a hurry; and He often makes those He loves—wait. Some examples: Abraham and Sarah's long wait for the child of promise, causing them both to try to hurry things along, resulting in an Ishmael. Joseph's years of imprisonment for a crime he didn't commit, before being raised up to be ruler in Egypt next to Pharaoh. King Saul's disobedience when told to wait for Samuel, God's prophet and priest, who would come and offer the sacrifice before Israel's battle began. Israel's long, long wait for her Messiah. Our over-two-thousand-years' wait to welcome back the King of Kings and Lord of Lords. And the Bride of Christ still waiting for her Bridegroom to come like a thief in the night and spirit her away.

God knows we don't like to wait and that our flesh wants instant gratification. Nevertheless... we need to wait. Scripture says, *"The testing of your faith produces patience. But let patience have its perfect work, that you may be perfect and complete, lacking nothing"* (James 1:2,3).

Perfect work takes time. Whether we're talking about answers to prayer, a release from our situations, or relief from pain, Scripture says, *"Let us not grow weary while doing good, for in due season we shall reap if we do not lose heart"* (Gal. 6:9).

Mary and Martha of Bethany, anxiously watching their much loved brother Lazarus become more and more ill, waited and worried, "Why doesn't Jesus get here? He knows Lazarus is sick, and He loves him so. We've seen Him heal great crowds of people. He can heal our brother—if He'll only come in time." He didn't. He came too late. Lazarus died.

However, it turns out (as it always does) they'd not waited in vain. For when Jesus finally did arrive, it wasn't to heal Lazarus—it was to raise him from the dead! And bring forth a powerful testimony that Jesus was the Resurrection and the Life... He who believed on Him would live even if he died (John 11: 25). Jesus wasn't late after all; turns out, He was right on time. Jesus' delay and Mary and Martha's wait resulted in a greater miracle and stronger faith.

Too often, while hoping and praying for our circumstances to change, Jesus seems to be asleep in our boat. Once, on the Sea of Galilee, after battling the wind and waves 'til they were exhausted, as they watched their boat fill with water, His disciples (those once full-time fishermen, now full-time fishers of men) thought as fear overtook them, *How can He be sleeping when we're sinking? Doesn't He care that we're all going to perish?* When awakened from sound sleep, did Jesus apologize for not taking care of them? For neglecting them in their need? Or, for sleeping? Not on your life. Rather, He rebuked them for being timid and having no faith (Mark 4: 35-41).

Throughout Jesus' life and ministry, others often pressed Him to respond differently and more quickly. When, after seeing the miracles that He performed, the crowds tried to take Him by force to be their King, He slipped through their grasp. It wasn't time (John 6:15).

On that first Palm Sunday, as Jesus rides into Jerusalem sitting on a donkey (fulfilling Old Testament prophecies), joy-filled throngs shout praises and lay down palm branches and their garments in his path. Finally their long awaited Messiah, their King, has come. Their shouts of *"Hosanna!"* (save now) ring out across the streets until the whole city is energized (Matthew 21:9).

The people shouting exuberant *"Hosannahs!"* want deliverance from tyranny. They want a king who will throw off Rome's yoke and set them free from Roman oppression. They want Release and Relief—now! They're tired of waiting, weary of enduring. Their immediate need is all they see or care about. *(Sounds a lot like us, doesn't it?)*

What are Jesus' thoughts and emotions as this triumphant procession in His honor winds its way through the narrow streets of the Holy City? Gladness, no doubt, as He sees and hears their rejoicing, and knows this is ordained. Yet, was there sadness also, for the people still didn't understand His mission? Nor their true need. His cousin, John the Baptist, had understood. Three years earlier, he'd announced prophetically as Jesus approached him at the river Jordan, *"Behold the Lamb of God who takes away the sins of the world"* (John 1:29).

From the beginning of His ministry, Jesus had pointed to His sacrificial death as His reason for coming. If Jesus had answered the need they now clamored for, if He'd answered their prayer then and there, if He'd climbed off the donkey announcing, "You're right. I am the Messiah—I am the King of Kings" and taken Israel's throne in the way they were demanding, there would never have been: *a Cross, a Sacrifice for Sin, Salvation, Redemption, Eternal Life. The Plan of Salvation* would have been thwarted and aborted. Death without life. And never able to give Life— to us!

As the crowds shouted and rejoiced on that "10ᵗʰ Day of Nisan", they thought it was time for their King to come. Past time. God knew better. (*Doesn't He always?*) On this particular day, it wasn't the hour for Him to rule and reign in Jerusalem, or the time for Him to be King. Not yet. We talk about God's Will, and sometimes God's Way, but God's timing is an integral part of that. On that special day, it was ***time for the Lamb***.

Jesus, as The Lamb commissioned to take away the sin of the world, rode into *David's City* on the very day that all over Jerusalem, lambs for Passover were being selected. Ones without spot or blemish, pure and undefiled, chosen to be the Passover lamb for each household. This special lamb would first be examined to be absolutely sure it was perfect. Then kept and watched closely to be sure it remained pure and undefiled (Ex. 12:5,6).

Our Jesus had lived His life openly before the people. Pure and spotless—He qualified. So, on this day of days it wasn't King-crowning time; it was Lamb-choosing time. They wanted a Ruler: They needed a Redeemer—One Who would redeem their debt of sin. They wanted a King: They needed a Lamb! And unknowingly, they'd chosen One. Jesus would provide more—much more—for them than deliverance from Rome. He would provide deliverance from Sin, Death, and Hell through His Crucifixion, Resurrection and Ascension to the Father. Eternal Life to anyone who in faith would come to Him (John 10:27,28).

God's Will in God's perfect timing would provide a way— ***The Way***—for them (and for millions who came after them) to have true liberty. To live free—no matter what the situation or circumstance! For Jesus had promised, *"... if the Son makes you free, you shall be free indeed"* (John 8:36).

Because Christ completed his assignment, and through the atonement brings us into full fellowship with God, nothing can separate us *ever* from His love.

*"For I am persuaded that neither death nor life, nor angels nor principalities, nor powers, nor things present nor things to come, nor height nor depth, **nor any other created thing,** shall be able to separate us from the love of God which is in Christ Jesus our Lord"* (Rom. 8:38,39).

Time is one of those "created things". But in the midst and muddle of difficulties sometimes it's hard to believe that I can't be separated from God's love. It can *feel like* I've been abandoned and forgotten, and that He doesn't care about what I'm going through. *If He cares, why doesn't He stop it?*

Wouldn't you think the Apostle Paul would have felt the same way? In a dark dank prison cell, chained to guards, with a death sentence hanging over his head—how was he able to write such a joy-filled *"Rejoice in the Lord always. Again I will say, rejoice!"* letter to the saints (Phil. 4:4)? How could he be joyful when his résumé described him as: Repeat offender with numerous incarcerations. Beaten many times with rod and whip. Once stoned. Three times shipwrecked. A day and a night in the sea. In perils from robbers, countrymen and false brethren. In hunger, cold and nakedness, without home and family… (2 Cor. 11:23-28).

How could he be *joy-filled* when his miracle-working revivals had been cut short? Why wasn't he in perpetual pity and despair, asking, "Why, God, why?" If anyone had reasons to, Paul did. Because, to all intents and purposes, the enemy had succeeded in shutting him down and out for some time. He was no longer able to preach the Gospel and establish new churches as he'd done before being imprisoned. This great evangelist was now under lock and key, his life almost over.

How could this be God's will when the early church still needed him? Hadn't Jesus Himself appeared to Paul in a vision and told him he was set apart for the Gentiles? (Acts 22:21).

132

How could he fulfill his call and ministry in prison? All he could do was *just write letters* of encouragement, training and correction to those He loved in the Lord and to the young churches (while having to remind friends on the outside to bring him writing supplies). How could this be part of "The Plan?"

Well, Paul's passionate epistles—with prison as the return address—now constitute two-thirds of the New Testament! The very situation that looked like death to all he was called to do reached more people (and continues to) than all his missionary trips put together! Yet, did he, when he dipped pen into ink, know how much those letters would be used? I doubt it. I don't think he saw the magnitude and scope of what he wrote. Yet without knowing, no tears of self-pity and regret craft his sentences or anoint the pages. Rather, it's joy, contentment, zeal and Holy Ghost power that empower each one.

"... holding fast the word of life, so that in the day of Christ I may have cause to glory because I did not run in vain nor toil in vain. But even if I am poured out as a drink offering upon the **sacrifice and service of your faith, I rejoice and share my joy with you all.** *And you too, I urge you,* **rejoice in the same way and share your joy with me"** (Phil. 2:16-18, NASB).

Is your excuse, "I'm not Paul—I don't have that kind of faith"? Well... do you want that kind of faith? Are you seeking more? Perhaps you have more faith than you think. One way God builds faith is to test it. Do you think Abraham was ever the same after offering up his son Isaac to God? He already had a lot of faith when, in obedience to God's command he slowly climbed Mount Moriah, built an altar, then tied his son to it, preparing to slay him. For Scripture says he believed God would raise his son from the dead! (Heb. 11:19)

Along with Isaac (remember Isaac had yielded to being the sacrifice), can't you almost see Abraham floating down that mountain, his feet barely touching the ground, so elated that instead of his son, Isaac, *Jehovah-Jireh* (their Provider) had provided a ram in the thicket for the sacrifice? (Gen. 23:13) In this way, Abraham, the aged patriarch, and Isaac, the young man, had the privilege of being the foreshadowing of the wondrous event when God, our Father, would offer up His only begotten Son as a sacrifice for our sins (John 3:16, Isaiah 53:10).

God will allow difficult situations to strengthen and increase your faith through testing. He wants you to know that He has placed far more faith in your heart than you've known was there. Waiting never weakens God's plan nor limits it. Instead it allows it to become better, much better; richer, fuller than if we'd never had to wait. When we realize this, waiting will be easier. For while we wait, He's working faithfulness in us, which He's looking forward to rewarding when we see Him face to face!

"Be faithful until death, and I will give you the crown of life" (Rev. 2:10b).

In gardening, when we see plants burst into bloom, it all seems so spontaneous and effortless. Yet, their blooming is really a result of all that's been accomplished during the long winter months when they were hidden away in the dark recesses of the soil. Waiting turned out to be incubation time for new life and growth. Needed time.

God won't be rushed—ever. It's still ***"in the fullness of time"*** that He acts on our behalf. He wouldn't be rushed on that first Palm Sunday (*thank God*), and He won't be rushed in your situation. He cares too much for you, and has too much invested.

He won't remove what you're going through 'til He's wrung ***the very last drop*** of His Grace and Power from it. And not until He's used it in as many lives as possible. No trial that He allows need crush you or break you, but He does want you stretched. Stretched so far that your arms reach out wider than ever to embrace Jesus and draw Him close, closer than ever to your heart.

Once in talking to a pastor friend, Bob Lehman, about a family situation that had brought our family sadness and loss, he told me, "Just remember, the last line of that story isn't written yet. God's building a testimony." That's come back to me on so many occasions when I've been tempted to doubt that a person or situation could change.

Beloved, can you look at your life as a book still being written, with surprises yet in store? Books take time to write—especially good ones! And as someone said, "God's delays are not necessarily God's denial." God is ever-writing on the tablets of hearts. He's always at work in the hidden places, unobserved and unseen by our eyes. And our adversities have His fingerprints, handwriting and DNA all over them.

"You are our epistle [letter] written in our hearts, known and read by all men" "... written not with ink but by the Spirit of the living God..." (2 Cor. 3:2,3).

When I once looked up the word "wait" in my Strong's Concordance, I was surprised to find that it can mean being woven together like a three strand cord. What if that means: As I wait on the Lord He's knitting me together with Him in His plans and purposes so that it's hard to tell where one leaves off and another begins? Could it mean that He and I are united in something that is amazingly strong, wonderful and Eternal? His Plans and Purposes—mine; and my plans and purposes—His? Wow!

"O Lord, we have waited for You; the desire of our soul is for your name and for the remembrance of you. With my soul I have desired you. Yes, by my spirit within me I will seek you early" (Isaiah 26:8-9a).

However, the kind of waiting He requires is ***never passive.*** It's never "fold your arms, sit back and give up time." And there's nothing wrong in praying as the Psalmist did, *"...I am poor and needy; make haste to me, O God! You are my help and my deliverer; O Lord, do not delay"* (Psalm 70:5). In other words, *answer quickly*, as long as we've surrendered the What, Where, How and When—to Him!

The Psalmist wrote, *"My times are in Your hands."* So, will you place yourself, along with what you're going through, completely into His Hands—*for as long as it takes?* Will you choose to rest—instead of fret? Will you lay down instant results—for Eternal Ones? Will you?

"Wait on the Lord; be of good courage and He shall strengthen your heart; wait, I say, on the Lord" (Psalm 27:14).

"...those who wait on the Lord shall renew their strength; they shall mount up with wings as eagles. They shall run and not be weary, they shall walk and not faint" (Isaiah 40:31).

 * * * * *

Chapter 16

I Thought I Could Trust You

"Even my own familiar friend in whom I trusted, who ate my bread, has lifted up his heel against me" (Psalm 40:9).

I couldn't believe my ears. A woman who'd been one of my dearest friends for the past two years had just told me she could no longer be my friend. "Jeanne, there's something terribly wrong with you," she informed me. "But," she added quickly, "I can't tell you what it is because I know you won't deal with it."

In shock I pleaded, "Jan (name changed), please tell me what I've done; whatever it is—I'll repent of it." Although her voice and face showed no emotion, no caring, she did offer one hint of hope: "If I ever see that you'll deal with it, I'll let you know." With that she closed her front door, leaving me standing outside. In a daze I made my way home thinking, *This has to be a mistake—some horrible joke gone amuck. She'll rethink this; tell me what she sees, or what's wrong; I'll repent or change, and we'll go on as before—dear friends in ministry together.*

She didn't. She refused every phone call, every attempt to talk again. Thus began one of the hardest tests and trials of my life, lasting over two years. Yet, as is always the case—the one I learned the most from and grew the most in.

As we voyage through life, devastating loss and heartbreak are often caused by those we've loved and trusted. Those who should support and encourage us are all too often the very ones who turn against us, neglect, abandon, betray, and even abuse us. Those we've loved can become—in a moment of time—our worst enemy! They hurt us, sometimes in ignorance, but often on purpose, for reasons we can't figure out or understand, no matter how hard we try. They falsely accuse us, slashing and shredding our reputations. The resulting shame, confusion, anger and fear of trusting or loving, affect our other relationships—including our one with the Lord.

Jesus told us we couldn't serve two masters. Those who've damaged or dominated us can still loom larger than life, overshadowing and overpowering our thoughts, memories, and imaginations—even though we may be miles apart and seldom if ever see them. When that happens (until we get free) we can never be fully yoked with Him, because we're still bound to those who've hurt or harmed us.

Crisis situations, hardships, tragedies shake us, threaten us, throw us into panic, and zap our energy. The kinds of situations we've talked about earlier in the book steal our time, emotions, strength, and finances. But when those we care about hurt or harm us or those we love with cutting words and unspeakable actions, they exact a much higher toll.

"For it is not an enemy who approaches me; then I could bear it. Nor is it one who hates me... then I could hide from him. But it was you, a man my equal, my companion and my acquaintance. We took sweet counsel together and walked to the house of God in the throng" (Psalm 55:12-14).

"Flesh and blood" inflict deep and lasting wounds. If left untended or ignored, such wounds become a seedbed of infection for all kinds of ugly, ungodly attitudes and actions. They erupt out of us suddenly, violently. Appalled we think, *Where did that come from? Why did I react that way? I'm a Christian. Why am I still like this? I don't want to be.*

Since time began, we see people inflicting damage and destruction on those who loved and trusted them. From Abel's pleasing sacrifice that triggered his brother's jealousy and resulted in Cain murdering him, to Joseph's betrayal and abandonment by brothers, landing him as a slave in Egypt. From King Saul who lovingly had called David "my son" then persistently sought to kill him, to the prophet Jeremiah—imprisoned—in stocks and thrown into a pit of mud up to his waist by those he'd wept over. Betrayal, shattered trust and broken hearts.

We know for sure Jesus wasn't exempt. It had been prophesied that He'd be *"despised and rejected by men, a man of sorrows and acquainted with grief."* He first suffered rejection when *"He came to His own, and His own received Him not"* (Isaiah 53:3; John 1:11).

We know that later, avid followers turn and want nothing more to do with Him. Why? Because the Messiah's face is "set like flint for Jerusalem" and His words about a Cross have struck *choice* into their hearts. Finally… in those last crucial hours, from those who are His nearest and dearest, He suffers betrayal and abandonment.

Yes, rejection, betrayal, and broken trust are common to each generation. They began in The Garden with Adam and Eve. Yet, they don't get my full attention until they happen *to me*! Haven't we thought at times we'd go crazy, as painful encounters and conversations replay on our mental screens, echoing again and again in our ears throughout the long nights? Memories taunt and torment us as unwanted and uninvited guests in the "wide-awakeness" of sleepless nights: *What went wrong??? How could he or she have done this to me?* John Donne once wrote, "No man is an island entire of itself." However, at such times, don't we wish we were?

Yet, islands are lonely. The breakup of my friendship with Jan isolated me from others, wrapping me in a cocoon where

I felt muffled and all alone. And I withdrew myself because I felt I didn't deserve to be around others until I found out what Jan meant. I fasted, prayed, wept tears saying, "Oh God, please show me what this can be." I found nothing. Depression deepened. My husband and children insisted they didn't know what she meant. Our nineteen-year-old daughter Chris said, "Mom, there's nothing wrong with you—it's her—not you," but I shrugged off her words. I trusted Jan's discernment in the Lord, and felt Chris loved me too much to be objective.

I went to a close friend who knew both Jan and me. Neither she nor her husband had a clue what Jan meant. If I'd listened to and believed others who knew me well back then, I'd have saved myself a lot of heartache. I'm not proud that the situation with Jan held me down and back for so long. Yet, the Lord redeemed my not listening then by showing me so much as I trudged my way through. (Later there would be release and redemption; and spiritual keys that would unlock every door that was closing around me.)

I knew I had to forgive Jan and try my best not to inflict the same loss she was causing me. For very soon Jan went to mutual friends, friends I'd introduced her to, and told them she'd had to break off our friendship. By saying she couldn't say why, through her sighs and innuendos suspicion spread: *What could be so bad that she couldn't explain it?* (I wondered the same thing.) Yet, it wasn't long before her hints became outright warnings. "I was dangerous to be around." Friends (including the ones I'd gone to), and some I'd brought to the Lord, became distant—a wary look in their eyes whenever we met. I was experiencing in some measure what King David had meant when he wrote in Psalm 55:20b,21: *"He has broken his covenant. The words of his mouth were smoother than butter, but war was in his heart; his words were softer than oil, yet they were drawn swords."*

Unknowingly, we were all caught in a web of deceit, with satan spinning the web ever larger.

From the very beginning and throughout the long ordeal, the Holy Spirit impressed upon me that I mustn't defend or explain myself in any way. Nor was I to say anything against Jan. I believed she had valid reasons for breaking off the friendship, and I didn't want to hinder what I thought God still needed to show me. I needed to discover what was wrong— with me! True, she wasn't walking it rightly, but I needed to find my own guilt. (And true guilt was there; it just wasn't for what I thought.)

No matter what's been done to us, we must want to see and acknowledge our part (no matter how small) instead of seeking vindication. And never retaliate. No one, absolutely no one, sees any situation without some bias, some blind spots. We think we alone see the issue perfectly; we remember exactly what happened and what was said. We don't. Focusing on what's been done to us keeps us from owning and fully repenting of our part. (I'll tell you what I needed to repent of later.)

Seeking answers, praying in desperation, I clung to the Lord in a way I never had before. *"Be merciful to me, O God, for my soul trusts in You; and in the shadow of Your wings I will make my refuge until these calamities have passed by"* (Psalm 57:1). The same hymn that had strengthened me in New Guinea played over and over in my mind: *"My Hope Is Built"*[11] with this recurrent theme: *"On Christ the solid rock I stand, all other ground is sinking sand."* And especially this verse: *"When darkness veils His lovely face, I rest on His unchanging grace; in every high and stormy gale, **my anchor holds within the veil.**"*

When I found scriptures like these, I'd grab them like a life preserver: *"You shall hide them in the secret place of Your presence from the plots of man; You shall keep them secretly in a shelter from the strife of tongues"* (Psalm 31:20). Yet, a part of me doubted these promises could really be for me when there was something so wrong.

At my lowest point, when I had no song—God gave me a song. The words taken from Isaiah 43 showed me His view of me: streams of water in a dry land, waters in the wilderness, rivers in the desert, drink to His chosen people!

In an incredible way, when I chose to believe what He said rather than what I had been thinking and feeling, He lifted me up and out of the pit of introspection, self-examination, doubt and despair. And I saw that no matter what others thought about me or were saying, my ministry was first and foremost unto the Lord.

Jan's and my life were still intertwined. We traveled in the same circles, and were often thrown together. With her husband and mine, we'd helped start a Christian school. Her husband, Don (name changed) and I served together on the school board. However, my most difficult time was when I led worship and praise at our weekly Prayer and Praise meeting that they both attended. Still, it was there that I learned the blessings of pressing into praise even though I felt shame and struggled to hold back tears.

".... I am poor and sorrowful; let Your salvation, O God set me up on high. I will praise the name of God with a song, and will magnify Him with thanksgiving" (Psalm 69:29,30). For directly across from me as I played my instrument, sang and encouraged others to praise sat Jan—staring.

Many of you know that when you go through tough times, you're attacked on more than one front. I had to have surgery for Cervical Cancer. But—praise God—I "knew" before going in, that I'd been healed! And, sure enough, they found nothing. Our family was still learning how to relate to one another after separations in the mission field. Kevin and Steve, our twin sons who were attending college, were trying to make the transition from Australian schools and culture to America's. Lori, now a teenager in high school, faced issues new to her. And, we grieved with our daughter Chris and her husband Steve at the loss of several babies through miscarriage.

We went through some of the same trials in our local church (the one my dad had pastored) that we'd undergone in the mission field due to what we'd believed the Scriptures said concerning the power and work of the Holy Spirit. When we felt led by the Holy Spirit to go another church, criticism flourished: "How could she leave her father's church?"

Also, my mother began having problems of senility which required more of my attention. Crisis became commonplace.

In the midst of all this, God was bringing people to me for counseling and help with some of the most serious problems I'd ever encountered. Yet through the Scriptures and by His Spirit, they were being restored and made whole from things like mental illness, addiction and abuse. How could that be happening if what Jan had said about me were true? I swung back and forth from confidence in the Lord to questioning—so many questions.

At the end of two years, I traveled to visit my dear friend, Pat Riley. We shared ministry gifts, and our husbands were also close. As I related the ongoing saga of Jan—I still didn't know what was wrong with me—she stopped me. "Jeanne," she said, "Use your counseling gifts. Your respect and caring for her is keeping you from seeing what's really happening." In that moment God sent forth His light and His truth, and they began to lead me and bring me to His Holy Hill (Psalm 43:3). For as

I slowly retold the story and began sorting it out on the basis of what was truth and what was sin, I could see for the first time what had really taken place.

"The secret [intimacy, or counsel] of the Lord is with those who fear Him; He will show them His covenant. My eyes are ever toward the Lord, for He will pluck my feet out of the net" (Psalm 25:14,15).

Praise the Lord—it was feet plucking time! God was untangling the net of deception and suspicion from my feet, and removing the blinders from my eyes.

I realized that an incident occurring before the break-up was pivotal. Late one night, Jan had called me sobbing, then came to my home, and with more tears had confessed a serious besetting sin, one that involved others. She wanted me to hear her confession and pray for her, which I did. And, I realized something else was relevant. Several times before the break-up, for want of a better description, I'd seen Jan turn for a few minutes into a totally different person! One that almost frightened me. At the time, I'd excused those glimpses—she was a fairly new Christian; what I'd seen was so completely out of character I'd probably imagined it... Now I saw that in order to protect herself and her sin, she had projected her problem—to me! To do this, it was imperative she remove me from her life. In doing so, whatever evil thing I'd seen only glimpses of before had risen up in her, and was out to destroy me! I discerned my true enemy.

"For we do not wrestle against flesh and blood, but against principalities, against powers, against rulers of the darkness of this age, against spiritual hosts of wickedness in the heavenly places" (Eph. 6:12).

However in the days following, God showed me my part.

144

I'd trusted her way too much, and God not enough. I'd been more willing to blame myself (though I knew not why) than to look with discerning eyes at Jan and the situation. Her seemingly deep spirituality had overly impressed me. I'd been flattered when she praised me as I mentored and taught. And when she'd tried to isolate me from others, I'd excused, rather than confronted it. Worst of all, and these are the most important lessons:

1) I'd let her vague accusation be truth for me. Never, never by God's Grace would I allow that to happen again. The Holy Spirit, who is in the world to "convict of sin, righteousness and judgment" is specific. Never, never vague. He either convicts of sin, or is silent until another time. If there'd been anything in my life like Jan had hinted at, God Himself would have shown me as I sought Him. He's greater than our flesh; greater than any deception; and perfectly capable of showing us our sin and His redemption. Because I'd yielded the Holy Spirit's work to Jan, the enemy had ground to torment me with false guilt and condemnation. (And he's good at that!)

2) Because I'd seen Jan get so much from God's Word, heard her pray sincerely and minister effectively, I'd accepted her judgment of me. When I did this I let her and her opinion of me take up residence in the Holy of Holies of my life—*the place where only the Holy Spirit is to live and reign.* When we do this, when we let anyone be that important to us—for any reason—it's ***idolatry!*** Only what God says and His opinion counts. Only His Truth, His Way counts. Anything else is deception and idolatry. For God says that we must have no other gods—no one else or thing—before Him!

I had much to repent of and be cleansed from. I also needed to ask God to forgive me for not handling the situation Scripturally. I'd been ignorant and deceived; yet that was no excuse. Because I was afraid and ashamed that there was something seriously wrong with me, I'd kept the whole thing hidden. Just what satan wanted. Now, cleansed and free, I could pray that God vindicate me, for He promises to uphold the righteous. (I couldn't pray that before when I thought I had hidden sin.) *"Cast your burden on the Lord, and He shall sustain you; He shall never permit the righteous to be moved"* (Psalm 55:22).

And I also began praying that whatever was hidden in the darkness in this situation would now be exposed and brought into the light. (A prayer that I've seen God answer over and over since then!)

Operating now under a Banner of Truth with newfound courage, according to Matthew 18:15-17, I went to Jan asking for reconciliation, hoping she'd repent. She refused to even listen. I then went to the two head elders of the prayer group and told them what I'd been facing for two years. They knew some of it, but were appalled at the rest. Within a few days they went to her home. When they faced Jan and Don with her accusations and slander of me, she admitted no fault. Instead, she insisted that her discernment was right. And she warned them further about me. This time it didn't work.

"O God the Lord, the strength of my salvation, You have covered my head in the day of battle...." *"By this I know that You are well pleased with me, because my enemy does not triumph over me. As for me, You uphold me in my integrity, and set me before your face forever"* (Psalm 140:7;41:11,12).

God says He will pursue the wicked and drive them out before Him (Psalm 18:37-39). Within the month, Don resigned from the school board; they removed their daughter from the Christian school; Don quit his job, took a job out of state and they were gone! Gone.

" ...the Lord is with me as a mighty awesome one. Therefore my persecutors will stumble, and will not prevail. They will be greatly ashamed for they will not prosper... " (Jer. 20:11).

The ordeal was over; the storm moved on. *"He calms the storm so that its waves are still"* (Psalm 107:29). What the enemy had meant for evil, God would now use for good. Through what I'd learned about His ability to keep me, hold me close, and teach me—even in the midst of continual waves of suspicion, slander and deception—He'd sunk His anchor of hope deeper than ever into the cleft of my soul. All praise to my glorious Redeemer. *"And now my head shall be lifted up above my enemies all around me; therefore I will offer sacrifices of joy in His tabernacle... "* (Psalm 27:6).

In the wake of any terrible storm or flood, we sadly view loss and damage. Our possessions have been ripped apart by strong winds and ruined by high, turbulent waters—some of which can never be repaired or restored. When we're rejected, abandoned or abused; when we experience broken relationships, we need to know that there is a way to live with that loss. Although I can't explain it (it's one of those God-things), no matter what—we ourselves can't lose—*in* Christ! Because *"... in all these things we are more than conquerors through Him who loved us"* (Rom. 8:37).

In the tempests that batter and try to shatter our lives, slashing at our sails and sometimes stripping us, ripping away from us those we hold dear, we can't deny we get wounded. And, yes, we bear scars, deep scars from those wounds. However, beloved... scars are not just proof of wounds. ***They're proof of healing!***

What do we experience after a tempestuous tempest? Freshness and newness! Everything's sparkling and washed clean as we look out at the bright sun, brilliant blue sky and tranquil seas. A time to begin again with more than we had within ourselves when the tempest first struck. We weathered it.

The same is true of spiritual storms. For there is a peace following the onslaught. And an assurance, a confidence, even a fresh expectancy as we lift our eyes to the horizon that we're stepping—though hesitantly, slowly perhaps—into something fresh and brand new!

And we will never, NEVER, **NEVER** be the same!

 * * * * *

Reflections:

One of the reasons this was hard to sort out was that everyone involved was Christian. Satan wants us to turn away from church and Christian relationships because of a wounded and disappointed heart. Don't!

1) Forgiving seems at first to be one of the hardest things to do because everything rises up in us to say, "They don't deserve my forgiveness." But forgiveness is about mercy—and no one deserves that. Forgiving isn't saying that no wrong was done. It's praying words like these: "Lord, You forgave me of all my sins and I certainly didn't deserve it. I forgive_____, and I ask You for mercy for _____ and all those concerned. Do with _____ as you will; I turn them over to You. I bless them in Your name, Lord Jesus, for

Your Word says to bless those who curse us, and pray for those who despitefully use us..." (Matt. 5:43-45). Continue to pray as the Spirit leads you, then thank and praise Him for healing you and setting you free.

Forgiveness is a choice, an act of our will, of volition, apart from our feelings.

2) Whom have you looked to for your identity? Any time we look to another to complete us, to tell us who we are to be, whenever we allow others to dominate and control us, we give them access and power in our lives that is to belong to God alone. To be free, we have to repent of giving the person that position in our life; by calling it idolatry; and in the name of Jesus, separate ourselves from that kind of soulish tie and domination.

Chapter 17

Life-Line

A serious and solemn occasion involves two Israelites. They stand facing one another with weapons drawn. But Nahum and Josiah have not come to fight; they've come to "cut a covenant." Let us watch.

As Nahum speaks words of loyalty and protection, he places his favorite weapon into Josiah's hand. All enemies of either man had better beware! For as they exchange weapons, each one if need be will fight to the death defending the other.

Josiah removes one of his own garments and places it carefully over Nahum's shoulders, pledging, "I give myself to you. My possessions, talents, liabilities—all that I have is at your disposal." Nahum responds in the same manner, adding, "Receive my strength," as he hands his belt to Josiah.

Both men then turn to the animals they have brought to the covenant. The slain carcasses are cut down the middle and separated. Nahum and Josiah then walk between them, winding through them in a figure eight, and return to the middle to meet face to face. With words and actions, each vows, "I give up all rights to myself. As I stand in this blood, my old life is dead and I take up my new life with you. Should I break this covenant, I deserve to be cut asunder."

The ceremony now becomes even more intense. A cut is made in each man's right wrist. And as the blood pulses forth, they raise their hands, pressing the wounds together. In this covenant clasp, their blood becomes one. As blood brothers, Nahum accepts Josiah's name to be linked forever with his. Both take the other's name, adding it to their own.

Clay or roots are now pressed into the painful wounds so that the scars will heal stained—a visible and undeniable *seal* and evidence of this ceremony. There is no secrecy, nor shame in this blood bonding. They've not entered into it lightly; they've counted the cost and are proud to be in covenant with one another. Witnesses are listening to their promises and gravely watching each step of the ceremony.

They sit down and begin feeding one another bread and wine which has been brought for this special meal. Each affirms as he eats and drinks, "Through this bread and wine I come into you; I now am part of you, just as you are part of me." Salt (an eastern preservative) may be touched to their tongues, signifying that their covenant will be preserved forever.

Next, they take some of the blood from the slain animals and sprinkle it upon a young tree. Together they plant it, demonstrating that their relationship is a living one. Should it not be possible to plant a tree, they would instead gather large stones, placing one upon another to make a permanent landmark and testimony to their new and binding union—a union which includes their wives and any children now living or who will be born afterward. These are already included in this covenant— heirs to all that has been promised and given.

Not only have these two men become covenant brothers, but their families are now covenant families.

Before this day there may have been grave disagreements, even enmity between the two. But covenant brings close together those who have been far off. Those who once were sworn enemies become closer than kin. In and through covenant, their hearts are now forever knit together, going past friendship and loyalty, extending beyond death, farther than the grave. A cut-blood covenant has been made.

151

What a fascinating ceremony! But what does it mean to us in this sophisticated twenty-first century? Let's find out.

Whenever we look at ourselves, we have to acknowledge that many times although we have good intentions, don't we sometimes fail to keep our promises? Hasn't it ever happened that sometimes through no fault of your own you were unable to fulfill a commitment? Haven't you ever secretly questioned, "Is God really able to keep His promises to me? Is He able to fulfill all of His commitments to me in a fallen world?"

In turn, have you earnestly wished you could believe more? Or perhaps you've become tired of trying to figure out the life of faith. Are you worn out trying to have more faith? Are you doing a lot of spiritual pretending, going through the motions, saying the right words, but feeling dead inside?

Beloved, God understands how difficult it is for you and me to believe Him. He knows better than we do that our nature has a tendency to doubt. He knows we tend to view the promises in His Word as lovely and inspiring, nice to think about but easy to forget in the stress of daily life.

He knows that His promises slip so easily out of our remembrance. Or that we move to an extreme, constantly confessing certain promises, words and phrases as if saying them often enough will somehow set in motion a reluctant God who will finally do our bidding. Where does Truth lie?

Well, Abram (before his name was changed to Abraham) who is called the **Father of Faith** was having trouble believing God's promises to him also. In Genesis 15, we read that God was promising him more descendants than he could count, and a land to possess which was already inhabited!

But Abram was by this time in his nineties, and there was

still no child of promise. To capture and hold a land required descendants. Many decendants. And so Abram, friend of God, dared to ask his God, "How may I know?"

To answer Abram's question, God comes down to earth and visibly demonstrates to His friend—His faithfulness!

He begins by instructing Abram to gather some animals together, split them apart, and separate them. Abram knows what that means. A covenant is going to be cut and he is no stranger to covenants. It's a familiar, life-changing ceremony in his culture. What kinds of questions must have whirled through his mind as he prepared the animals?

What can I give Jehovah God to show my loyalty?
What vows shall I make to Him?
What will be required of me?

Throughout the day, in the midst of such speculation, he's kept busy driving away birds of prey which swoop down, threatening to attack and steal the covenant sacrifice. Abram becomes weary. Finally, the day is over. The sun sets. It becomes very dark. It is time for God to act.

Drawing near, God causes deep sleep to come over His beloved friend. Abram is set aside and then can only watch as God Himself in the form of a smoking oven and flaming torch, passes between the dead carcasses and through the blood.

Abram is terrified by the awesome scene—yet strangely comforted and strengthened as He hears God's further words of promises, foretelling events to come—all because God loves him and has chosen him!

Jehovah God, his *"shield and exceeding great reward"*

(Gen 15:1) has cut a blood covenant with him. But it is not the kind of covenant Abram is accustomed to. In this one God has provided all and done all! What has God required from him? *Only* that Abram **believe** what he sees and hears taking place.

Centuries later Jesus would say to the Jews, *"Your father Abraham rejoiced to see My day and He saw it and was glad"* (John 8:56).

Covenant. Cut-blood Covenant. Stronger than a contract, more binding than a promise. These are terms and ceremony very dear to the heart of God. Why? Because they so ably typify and express the union which He wants to establish with us—through faith.

Our God and Savior, Christ Jesus has been willing to come down to earth and prove not only His great love for us, but also His reliability and credibility through Covenant. **He can, and will, keep His promises?**

From God's point of view—the only one that counts—the concept of Covenant with man is so important that He has established His entire Plan of Redemption upon the grounds of one. Awesome! Yet sadly, we've not even known that our Old and New Testaments should more accurately be called Old and New Cut-blood Covenants. What a loss.

Did you know that God has placed such a high value on Covenant that the idea and practice of it are found worldwide in the hearts of tribes and tongues who have yet to learn of Him?

So... whether you visit an Indian tribe in the southwest, travel into deep jungles of South America, watch a tribal dance in dark Africa, huddle around a fire with the Highland people of New Guinea or roam with the nomadic Aborigines in the outback in Australia—there is covenant.

Although it is distorted and for the purpose of worshipping other gods, covenant remains a perfect vehicle for missionaries to witness about the Good News of the Gospel.

Many Christians do not witness to a Covenant-making and Covenant keeping God. Why? We in our western culture have not known its importance because we're a culture of the mind. And this idea of Covenant has remained vague, foreign and a mystery to us. Is it because it is too personal? (It is, you know.) Is it because Covenant requires (and makes a way) for us to come very close to Him—and remain so. Forever bound to Him with cords of Covenant Love.

God is not talking about mere contracts; these can be broken or written with loopholes. He is talking about, and demonstrating through Himself, something which is more than a legal agreement. Covenant is a permanent relationship incorporating all of life; more than a thought or concept—it's **a way of life.**

What has happened to allow us to be so ignorant about that which God esteems so highly? You guessed it. The enemy has swooped down and stolen from us the concept and therefore the experience of Covenant. Just as surely as the birds of prey swooped down and sought to rob Abram of his. (The devil's plot and ways have not changed over the years. He is a dirty bird.)

But by God's Grace, we are able to drive him off and lay hold of our Covenant experience. Glory! Let's do it. And so, with God's eyes and His viewpoint, attend with me one more Covenant and watch with new vision as it is cut—for you!

Come with me to Calvary. Approach (as if you've never been there before) that place of destruction and death where God is doing more than erasing, eliminating and crossing out your sin. He is cutting a new Cut-Blood Covenant for you. But

155

as He does, you, like Abram, are set aside and can only watch from a distance as Jesus, Son of Man, enters in your place into this Everlasting and Eternal Covenant with the Holy Father.

Like Abram, you have nothing to bring, nothing to offer. Only Jesus, your Kinsman Redeemer and your Representative, can cut this Covenant for you. Only He has been able to live the perfect life, eat the Covenant meal and drink the Covenant cup—the Last Supper. Therefore, only He can pledge and demonstrate complete faithfulness and loyalty.

As His life blood is sprinkled on the Tree planted at Calvary, *that Tree* becomes a testimony forever—to friend and foe alike—that you are in Covenant with God Himself!!!

He is not ashamed to call you "brother." And as His hands willingly receive the Covenant cut, as His blood becomes yours by faith, you and He become Covenant-kin. Blood brothers. One with Him and the Father. He has carved you on the palms of His hands and holds you there in a Covenant clasp.

"See, I have inscribed you on the palms of my hands..." (Isaiah 49:16). You are now forever His, bone of His bone, flesh of His flesh (Eph. 5:30 KJV).

Just as Josiah and Nahum's Covenant was sealed with a blood-stained scar, the *seal* upon your life that this has taken place is the Holy Spirit. And also, as there were witnesses to their Covenant, all of Heaven has stood in witness to ours. Because of this Covenant, you who were once far off, even at enmity with Him, have become one with Him, and the dividing wall between Jew and Gentile is broken down (Eph. 2:12-15). GLORY!

Through this New Covenant *"...you are all sons of God through faith in Christ Jesus. For all of you who are baptized* *into Christ **have clothed yourselves** with Christ. There is neither Jew nor Greek, there is neither slave nor free man, there is neither male nor female; for you are all one in Christ Jesus. And if you belong to Christ, you are Abraham's offspring, heirs according to promise"* (Gal. 3:25-29).

Because of Covenant you have the Lord of Hosts (Armies) to defend you now. What can any enemy do to you? In that moment of Covenant-making, His treasures and all the glories of Heaven become yours as your inheritance. His nature is now yours as He comes to live His life through you. He gives you His name to wear, the name Christian—anointed one. His name to use with authority.

"In The Name of Jesus Christ, I ..."

Scripture terms suddenly come alive, with both Old and New Testament verses now taking on new and deeper meaning: "Put on Christ" "Put off the old man" "You in Me and I in you" "garments of Salvation and robes of Righteousness." Yes!

Father God's stamp of approval upon this Covenant is witnessed by an empty tomb, a resurrected glorified Christ, an overcoming and ascended Lord, an indwelling Holy Spirit, a Great High Priest seated in the heavenlies, ever living to make intercession for you. And... a soon-coming King, with whom you'll reign forever and ever. Praise You, Precious Lord.

And so, son or daughter of Abraham, whenever you doubt; whenever you fear; whenever you think the enemy looms too large; whenever you question "How may I really know God's Word is true and God Himself is faithful?"—look through the eyes of faith to Calvary. There, God has stretched a ***life-line*** from here to Eternity—from God's heart to yours! One that no one can sever and no one can steal.

"Dear one, look and see what He has done. Look and live!"

 * * * * *

Chapter 18

Missing Pieces

Excitement, like bees around honey, buzzed around my twin sister and I as the center of attention in Grandmother's living room on that warm summer day. But everything had been exciting for Joanne and me since the moment we'd heard the train conductor cry "All aboard" and with Mother and Daddy we'd come all the way from Ohio to Detroit, Michigan. In a few weeks our first day of school would start. Yes, life was exciting all right.

For some of the relatives gathered that day, this was the first time they'd seen "the twins." With dark eyes dancing and brightly colored hair ribbons bobbing, matching exactly our look-alike dresses Mother had made, we were used to drawing attention. And by the age of six, both Joanne and I were already adept at answering the kind of questions twins get asked no matter where they go: Which of you is the oldest? By how much? How do your parents tell you apart?

Suddenly there was a flurry in the doorway, and another great aunt burst into the room. Flustered because she'd arrived late, moving quickly toward us with arms outstretched to gather us into her ample bosom, she exclaimed, "Oh, here are the little adopted darlings!"

Instantly, time was suspended. Then Mother's voice broke through. "They don't know they're adopted; they haven't been told yet," she exclaimed angrily. Daddy's words filled with disgust echoed hers, while the aunt who'd been rushing towards us to wrap us in a huge hug now collapsed in a chair sobbing, "I'm so sorry; I wouldn't have said anything if I'd known they hadn't been told."

I saw and heard what was happening as if separate scenes were circling around me in slow motion. For I'd stumbled upon and was still stuck on that new and strange word "adoption." What on earth did it mean? And why had it made Mother and Daddy so upset and angry. I felt ashamed because it must have something to do with Joanne and me—but what? What had we done now that was so bad?

At some point minutes later Mother and Daddy took us into the adjoining dining room. There, they hurriedly told us that we'd first been born to another mother, a mother who'd given us away. Mother and Daddy hadn't been able to have children of their own, and wanting children, they'd taken us. It was called adoption. "We'd planned to tell you right before school began," they explained, "because we didn't want you to learn of it from other kids." (So…that meant that others knew about this? Other kids knew?)

My parents very well may have tried to assure us at that time of their love for us, that we were special and chosen. I have no memory of it. What I did have was the realization in my little-girl heart that finally I had the answer to questions that had always been with me but had never had permission to surface. Like, why didn't I feel loved and accepted? Why did I feel like I didn't really belong? And, what was wrong?

Now I knew. Now I had my answer. And although confused and distressed because I didn't know what it all meant, somehow I felt—relieved! What hadn't made sense before did now. And, I would return home with a gut feeling of being different, separate, with something missing.

Joanne took the news of our adoption in stride. I was angry. Back at home, it wasn't long before I began sassing my parents, telling them I didn't have to listen to them because I wasn't really theirs, and they weren't really my parents. I'm sure I hurt them; they saw me as ungrateful. I longed for proof that I was loved and belonged. They informed me they'd done us a favor because they'd rescued us. "If we hadn't taken you," they scolded, "you could have ended up in an orphanage. Times were hard at the end of the depression years when you were born," they continued. "People didn't have money to adopt one baby, much less two baby girls two weeks old. Well, we adopted you and had to give up a lot to do it. We had to cash in some insurance policies just to buy baby furniture. And now you aren't even grateful!"

Their accusations shut me down and shamed me. I was immediately awash with guilt. Of course they didn't love me; I'd never done what I needed to do to make them love me. I owed them everything. How could I ever make all that up to them? I knew what I would do. I would prove to them that their sacrifice hadn't been in vain. And from that day on I would spend the following years of my life trying to do just that.

But unknowingly I had set for myself an impossible mission—a mountain far too steep and slippery to climb. Because both Mother and Daddy were perfectionists, they expected perfection from themselves, from others; and they were often critical. To my eyes they performed perfectly in everything they said and did. In contrast, continually and consistently both Joanne and I failed miserably. We were always falling short of their expectations. I was sloppy, careless; thoughtless at times. Although I got fairly good grades without much effort, I could count on having a check mark in the column of my report card, "Capable of doing much better." Even though I'd done well, even though I'd improved, that was the column I'd hear about.

At a very early age, Joanne and I began singing together at church and community functions, songs Mother taught us. Later we learned to harmonize. And people praised us. But what about the two I yearned to please? They never volunteered comments.

161

So when I'd hesitantly ask, "How'd we do?" and they'd say, "it was nice," or "you did OK," I'd know it hadn't been good enough. (In retrospect, I think they may have believed praise could spoil us or that we wouldn't keep trying.)

Growing up, Daddy was also my pastor; and Mother carried the responsibility of being his right hand for a large congregation. They worked flawlessly together. I loved church from the very beginning, and I believed it was there that God would draw near and come closer.

Because I hadn't experienced anything personal being shared or spoken in my home about what God would do, I deduced that God was too distant and holy to be at our house. Church was that *holy place* where we could meet with Him. He'd come there.

My father preached inspiring sermons of Jesus and the Cross with eloquent simplicity that warmed my heart. Each Sunday I could hardly wait until he stepped into the pulpit. I hung onto his every word (no one had to keep me quiet with coloring books and crayons). I'd sit spellbound, scarcely breathing, as through his words I was transported into the very scenes of the Bible. Oh, how I'd wish I could have walked with Jesus and known Him then.

Although I felt my greatest peace at church, I also felt the most confused there. We always sat in the second row on the left with Mother in the middle. Throughout the service she'd lovingly touch us, stroke our hair, or cuddle us close. However, quite often she'd been very angry with us before we'd come, punishing us with, "If you don't know what you've done, I'm not going to tell you." Even worse—long periods of silence would follow her harsh words.

But now her tenderness must mean we were forgiven, I'd

think, basking in the attention. Now everything would be all right. But no. Once back home, as soon as the door closed behind us—as if there'd been no pause—her anger returned full force.

Whenever others came to the house, or whenever we left home with her, she was friendly, smiling, gracious, admired and loved by all; and always loving to us. But immediately after others left, or we returned home, all too often we faced another person. And we faced her all alone. Surely Joanne and I were the cause, because around others, Mother could be wonderful. Since being alone with us brought out the worst in her—it must be our fault. One more thing I felt guilty about and didn't know how to fix. I assumed again that it had to do with our being adopted, rather than realizing, as I do now, that she had serious emotional problems.

As Joanne's twin, I also felt responsible for her actions. I saw us as one; if she messed up, in a way, I had as well. When she did poorly, I took it personally; it reflected on me. She, in turn, was faced with constant comparisons to me. At school (we were always in the same class) and at home, she was told repeatedly, "You need to get better grades like Jeanne." There were times when she and I had scratching, kicking, down-on-the-floor fights. (How much, I wonder, now, did that have to do with turning the anger and pent-up frustrations we felt against Mother on one another?)

When I learned that God, the Father, had adopted us as His children, instead of being excited my heart sank. This was not good news to me. God was holy and perfect. How much more then would He expect from me than my parents? And how much more would I fail in living up to His expectations? Surely I would disappoint Him over and over again as well. Yet I must try. As with my parents, I must somehow prove to Him by being good that His investment had not been wasted, for He had gone to such great lengths to save me.

163

When as a young child I saw a movie of the crucifixion, I understood—it was my sin He'd gone to a cross for, my sins had nailed Him there! (In my household there was no problem with realizing you were a sinner.) I knew without a shadow of a doubt I needed forgiveness. And I knew in that moment of believing that Jesus was my Savior, that I was forgiven and saved from Hell. However, the debt I thought I owed to those I loved—first to my parents and now to God—was mounting. And the burden of my efforts to prove to all of them that their sacrifices hadn't been in vain was becoming increasingly heavy indeed.

In our teen years both Joanne and I dared to ask our parents for more details about our birth parents. There really was little known, and our asking upset them. It showed we didn't really appreciate them or see them as the only parents we loved or needed. And they warned us, "If you ever try to locate or contact your birth parents, it will hurt us so much we doubt we'll ever want to have anything to do with you again."

Yet, that threat didn't keep Joanne from secretly daydreaming of finding our birth mother. Lying on our beds, scanning movie magazines with full color photos of beautiful starlets, she'd fantasize that our mother would turn out to be someone at least rich, and perhaps famous! Someone with connections to the music world. Once we'd find her we'd learn she'd been yearning to find us, and searching, also. She'd immediately swing wide the doors for us to be discovered, and we'd be on our way to stardom.

I had no such fantasies; no daydreams. Oh, I wanted to be the discovered singer, all right. But I wanted absolutely nothing to do with finding another person who I assumed might not want me either; or one I could never fully please or satisfy. And in my teen years I began hardening my heart and rebelling. My efforts weren't making a difference and I was angry and tired. So very tired.

164

I chose nursing over music as a profession because I knew I'd fall short in music; and nursing education was much cheaper then than college. High on my list was to cost my parents as little as possible for my education. However, nursing also demanded not only near perfection, but constant performance! Throughout the three years of training, supervisors watched and checked our procedures. And I had a constant fear of making a serious error. Nevertheless, I loved nursing because I loved helping people. It was so refreshing to be thanked instead of criticized. And for the first time in my life, my parents took pride in what I'd accomplished.

Thankfully, when I met, then later married my husband, Bob, he held me to no standards. He thought I was wonderful! Surely, love was blind. His family welcomed me in just as I was. In fact, they all thought I was wonderful which seemed way too good to be true. Nevertheless, with the birth of twin boys, and then two little girls, I still felt the need to perform. In my eyes I was continually missing the mark as a person, a wife, a mother, a Christian. (Like an unseen shadow, I could almost see Mother's image standing just behind me, constantly watching me disapprovingly.) However, my Jericho wall of striving and perfection was about to come down. Utterly!

While overseas as a medical missionary (one more situation where I was pressed to perform) I read Catherine Marshall's book, *"Beyond Our Selves."*[12] In it she told of finally surrendering to Jesus as Lord of her life. She said that He would take full control and full responsibility for our lives if we'd yield them to Him. I'd never heard of such a thing. But when I finally made that surrender, giving Him all—my past, present, future— I felt a tremendous weight leave me. What a relief.

How many sermons had I heard on Grace, yet not 'til then had I ever known how to live by it! Jesus' yoke was easy and His burden light because it was His yoke—not mine! Up 'til then I'd only experienced the kind of frustrations Paul describes in Romans 7:19: *"...the good that I will to do, I do not; and the evil I will not to do, I practice."* Now, for the first time in my life I stepped into, *"But thanks be to God, who gives the victory through our Lord Jesus Christ"* (1 Cor. 15:57).

One day this verse leapt off the page: *"When your mother and father forsake you, the Lord will take you up"* (Psalm 27:10*)*. Suddenly, I realized that the One I owed my life to, the One I owed my adoption to—was the Lord! He'd been the one in charge all along. My birth had not been an accident; certainly not a mistake.

"You made all the delicate, inner parts of my body, and knit them together in my mother's womb" "... you saw me before I was born and scheduled each day of my life before I began to breathe" (Psalm 139:13,16 TLB).

It was God who'd placed me with my parents; I had been His gift to them— whether they ever realized it or not. *"By You I have been upheld [sustained] from my birth; You are He who took me out of my mother's womb. My praise shall be continually of you"* (Psalm 71:6).

For the first time in my life, shame was exchanged for belonging. "Not knowing who I was" for "NOW I know! And I am known!" I not only had a present, my past and future as well were already laid out for me—in the Bible!

Though others had not wanted me for whatever reasons, Father God had always wanted me. And He didn't see me as a liability. I could do absolutely nothing to earn His love (it wasn't for sale); and I wasn't supposed to try. Later I would learn I couldn't do anything to get God to love me more. His love was absolute and couldn't be added to. I was commanded to cease from my own efforts and enter His rest—resting and trusting *in His finished work.*

"There remains therefore a rest for the people of God. For he who has entered His rest has himself also ceased from his works as God did from His. Let us therefore be diligent to enter that rest..." (Heb. 4:9,10,11a).

Life with Him wasn't about pass/fail; it was about love and obedience. It wasn't about trying then being angry because it wasn't working. It wasn't supposed to work. Life with Him was about dying (dying to self and other's expectations of me) and becoming alive—*in Him!*

"For in Him we live and move and have our being" (Acts 17:28).

Yet there was even more. Not only did I have a new Father—I had a family tree! I too had a genealogy. I could now trace my heritage much farther back than the Mayflower! And there were no missing links as so often happens when people try to trace their roots. My genealogy went as far back as you could go! Back to Adam and Eve, living in a Garden called Eden, fellowshipping with God.

The God of Abraham, Isaac and Jacob—the God of Israel was my God as well; and all the stories of the Old Testament were stories of *my* ancestors. Spiritually, as I was *"in Him"* I was *in them.* Grafted in! (Rom. 11:17-24)

My genealogy even revealed a royal bloodline! *"...you are a chosen generation, a royal priesthood, a holy nation, His own special people, that you may proclaim the praises of Him who called you out of darkness into His marvelous light; who once were not a people but are now the people of God, who had not obtained mercy but now have obtained mercy"* (1 Peter 2:9-10).

The Old Testament wasn't just a historical book with some good object lessons. It was God's Covenant record—God's Covenant Book—to introduce me to my very own Covenant kin.

As I read, I found God imparting even transfusing what I needed for my life today from their lives of yesteryears. Since my Family of Faith had its roots when God made Covenant with Abraham—the Father of Faith, He tells me to *"look to the Rock from which you were hewn... look to Abraham your father"* (Isaiah 51:1-2), the father of us all (Rom. 4:16-18).

At Calvary, when God cut the New Covenant in Christ Jesus, God forever bound Himself in an eternal relationship to those who would believe on Him and follow Him. A Covenant based solely on His love and His provision as He provided (and became) the Sacrificial Lamb. Therefore, our search for our identity ends there. For there He has inscribed us on the palms of His Hands to proclaim to Heaven and Earth alike (and to all the dominions of darkness)—we are His! (Isaiah 49:16)

There's a story in the Bible that describes my search. King David is remembering the covenant He'd made years before with his dearest friend, King Saul's son, Jonathan. Jonathan is dead. Nevertheless David, the covenant-maker, remembering his deep love for Jonathan, yearns to fulfill the promises he'd made to him in their covenant. And so he searches earnestly to find a relative. Meanwhile out in Lodebar—the "far country"— there's a son of Jonathan who doesn't know about the covenant. In fact, Mephibosheth is in hiding, thinking that if David ever found him, he'd destroy him because he's the natural heir to the throne.

Mephibosheth's name means "destroyer of shame." He must have felt he'd been misnamed, for his whole life has been one of shame. Even his legs are crippled because His nurse had dropped him when she rescued him from possible death as they fled the palace.

However, David's servant finds Jonathan's son, with orders to bring him to the palace. What anger and resentment against David had festered in Mephibosheth's heart over the long wearying years? And now what fears ride with him as he journeys? Naturally, he expects to die. Instead, as he stands before the King—a new life is granted! He's welcomed as royalty. David announces to all that every promise made to Jonathan will be fulfilled to Mephibosheth, along with his family. Lands and possessions. And for Mephibosheth—a favored seat at the King's table will be forever his assignment. **And all because of covenant** (2 Sam. 9).

I lived a long time not knowing that The King had made a Covenant through the One He loved so much that included me. When His "Word" came that He was searching for me, and I presented myself before Him I found that truly my shame had been exterminated. It didn't even matter if life had crippled me. A new inheritance was mine. I had a place at the King's table—forever. **And all because of Calvary's Covenant.**

Another finishing piece of the puzzle of my life was added when I fulfilled a long-held dream and visited Israel. Even before our plane landed I had the distinct and overwhelming impression that The Father was welcoming me Home!

At the beautiful Sea of Galilee and in the surrounding villages where Jesus spent so much time ministering and being refreshed, my heart nestled in and found rest. There was an incredible sensing that not only had I come Home, I didn't ever want to leave. And if I did leave, I'd want to come back as soon as possible! (Others sensed the same thing.)

When I walked up to Jerusalem (as pilgrims had done for

thousands of years) and looked out over that eternal city, I wept tears of intercession. Throughout the tour, on every highway and at every bend in the road, I continued to sense that the Spirit of the Lord was knitting me with His Covenant Land and His Covenant people—my people. Somehow, my life had come full circle.

With pieces missing, like a reed shaken in the wind, with no identity of my own, this lost one was finally found, thanks to Jesus. Not only was I found, but firmly anchored in place. Cemented there *by the blood of the Lamb.* Consequently, I am "through faith" forever connected to the Father and to the Family of God. Forever accepted. Forever anchored. Forever whole! Forever free!

 * * * * *

Reflections:

I now know that adopting a child can be awesome for both parents and children alike. I have two precious adopted grandchildren who are very loved and accepted, and demonstrate daily how wonderful adoption can be. Sadly in my case, the enemy was able to distort that Word and the wonder of it, and we all suffered loss.

Like Mephibosheth, so many live without knowing their true identity or position. If you've been neglected, rejected, abandoned, battered or abused by parents, or those you loved—no one else can make it up to you, dear one. No matter what's happened to you or been done to you, only the Lord Jesus can gather the missing pieces and restore you, through Covenant.

Will you let Him?

Chapter 19

Good Grief

The phone's shrill ring at 3 a.m. startles you out of sound sleep. Fumbling, almost dropping the receiver, you hear, "This is Sergeant Miller of the Police Department—there's been a serious accident—you need to come right away!" In that instant you're more awake than you've ever been. And your life is forever changed.

****

You dash into your doctor's office to pick up your daughter's OK to play soccer on your way to her game. She's such a great player—good enough to earn a college scholarship this fall. Then she'll be on her way to fulfilling her dream to be a medical missionary. However, a very sober doctor ushers you into his office; the tests show there'll be no college in the fall. Or... fulfilled dream.

****

As you relax on the patio, the afternoon sun casts filtered light on the yard and garden you and your husband have made the envy of the neighborhood. Just a few more months remain before his early retirement; then there will be more time for the two of you for gardens, hobbies and vacations. The doorbell interrupts your reverie. A messenger has papers you must sign: Divorce papers. And now there will be no more gardens, hobbies, vacations or time together. He will do that with another.

****

Words can't adequately describe what situations like these do to us. Death of hopes, dreams and life itself; indescribable and devastating loss. Charlie Brown, the cartoon character in the Peanuts series is fond of saying in response to situations, "Good grief!" It's a catchy phrase—'til grief happens. When Grief shoves its way into our lives uninvited, unplanned and unwelcome, bringing along its comrades—pain, shock and sorrow—there's no way (at least at first) that we can see anything "good" at all about grief.

When Bob, my husband of forty-four years, became ill, then very ill, then terminally ill, in coma, then dead and buried in less than four weeks, *Grief* faced me front and center. How would I deal with Bob's death and my loss? What would grief be like for me? I determined God would be my answer.

Psalm 46:1 had been the sure anchor that had held me fast throughout those turbulent weeks: *"God is our refuge and strength, a very present help in times of trouble."* (*"Abundantly available for help in tight places."*)

He had ways to heal me, and provide for me in every way. His Word said so. In Isaiah 54:4,5, He promised to be Israel's Husband; He would be mine, as well.

There are so many variables when we consider grief and mourning, because we're all so different in our emotional make-up and personality. One size does not fit all. Nor are there pat answers, or quick fixes. For some, their feelings splash out on everyone—literally. They feel emotions quickly, deeply—and show them. Others are more reserved. Some have been taught not to exhibit feelings, so difficulties seem to slide off them more quickly and easily. They're the cool ones. The ones with strong shoulders we can cry on.

The depth and degree of our grief also depend on how close we were to the ones we've lost. Were we intimate and dependent—have we lost not only our lover, but also our "best

173

friend"? Or were we distant and estranged? Are we grieving the death of a marriage through divorce or desertion—something we never imagined would ever happen to us? Is it a child we mourn, leaving a huge hole in our heart and home? Has the one who's left us been our caregiver, or we his? With this death did our financial picture change drastically—for the worse? Do we have to "sell the farm" and face the added loss of being uprooted and living somewhere else, or with others?

Yet, no matter what constitutes the many differences in our make-up, or in our situation, for a Christian, *one principle* must stand heads higher above all others: *What has God said about grief and mourning?* And, what is He saying to us now about our own personal loss? How does He want us to view it and walk it?

The Bible tells us in Ecclesiastes 3:4 that there are times to mourn and times to weep. In Romans 12:15, to comfort one another we're enjoined to weep with those who weep. The Bible mentions times of mourning set aside so that all of Israel could mourn a leader's passing. Yet on a few occasions God told people *not* to mourn—at all!

Before Bob's death, I'd already done some personal study on grief because of the counseling/discipling I do. Now as I began my own walk through widowhood, I sensed I needed to learn more; and what I'd taught others would now be tested. I was certain God did not want me shipwrecked and abandoned on grief's beach!

I sensed that He'd laid buoys through these troubled waters that would keep me safe in the channel of His will. Although these waters looked dark and uncharted, I could set my compass for the *North Star,* trusting I'd have safe passage.

Psychology had already stepped up to the plate and

defined stages of grief and how to respond to such loss. Its views were heralded and embraced. In our society where psychology (in my view) has become our national religion, many churches, unfortunately, embraced its ideas, also. We're often ignorant of how much we allow the world to conform us to its image, its views and its ways.

Oswald Chambers once said that Christianity is as much about *"unlearning"* as it is about learning. If that were true in his day (and I believe it was), how much more is it true in our age, which is dominated by this philosophy: There are no absolutes of truth; and whatever works for you is valid?

Rather than letting our minds be transformed by the Word of God (as promised) and having the mind of Christ (as promised), many Christians today make their choices and behave based on their feelings, opinions of "experts," and psychological evaluations. When that happens, they don't question (or realize) that Scripture says something entirely different. They don't realize that it's **unlearning** time—time to throw off what everyone else is saying, and cling and cleave to the full counsel of God!

I'm not denying there are stages of grief. Like unbelief and denial as one thinks, *I can't believe this is happening to me. It feels like I've suddenly appeared on a stage and been handed a part in a play. I'm reading the lines, but I've never rehearsed them. It's all make-believe, and none of it is real.*

Psychological "experts" focus on **us** as the center of the universe—our hurt, our pain, our victimization. Many are involved in psychic phenomena. Some even receive their philosophy and ideas by communicating with "spirits" and are not ashamed to say so. When they insist: "It's okay to be angry at God for taking your loved one. You need to stay in that mode just as long as you feel like it. There's nothing wrong with it..."

What is their source? Is this something God has declared? Or... something whispered from *"the Pit"*?

Satan often wraps a little truth around a whole bunch of lies hoping we'll take the bait and swallow the whole hook. *The **truth** in this case?* Yes, God understands your grief and pain. *The **lie**?* It's OK to be angry at God and stay angry for as long as you feel like it.

I believe doing this will only prolong our sadness; deepen our sense of loss and depression; and spiral us down into more self-absorption. Perfect ground that gives the enemy permission and power to press us down and out.

My Bible says I can fault God for nothing. *"The Lord is righteous **in all His ways,** and kind in all His deeds"* (Psalm 145:17).

Although I may not understand why things have happened—I am commanded to trust Him with all my heart and not lean on my own understanding. I'm to acknowledge Him in all my ways, and He will direct my paths (Prov. 3:5,6). Scripture says, *"Whatever is not from faith—is sin"* (Rom. 14:23).

Our sin of unbelief and mistrust, rather than easing our burden of grief, adds to it. For now we carry guilt—the guilt of turning away from our *Loving Father*, rather than running to Him!

That's why we see grief and depression lasting for years, even for Christians. Grieving as they, the "experts," have instructed them to do to "plunge the depth of their pain," they become mired in its murky mire. Stuck in their grief like quicksand, it clings to them, sucking at every footstep. Not knowing any better, they think this is the way it's supposed to be.

Will this heavy cloud of mourning never lift?

Support groups flourish because we think only those who've gone through the same thing can help us. We're told that only they are able to understand and help us to heal. I say instead, "We need more trust in and obedience to our Shepherd!" For He is the **only One** who knows how to *"lead us through the valley of the shadow of death."*

When I'm sick and go to a doctor, I don't require that he's had the same disease and therefore understands what I'm going through (although that would be interesting). I just want him to be able to *diagnose me properly* and *have a remedy*—a remedy I must take and use in order to recover!

In contrast, we're instructed, right at the time we need the Lord more than ever: "Be angry at Him! It's OK. He can take it. He already knows how you feel, so just scream and yell at Him."

Once, I heard a "Christian therapist" on the radio give an example of good therapy. She took her counselee out into some woods at the back of her house, handed her a box of old dishes she'd bought at a thrift shop, and told her to throw and smash them at trees while screaming her pain and anger at God until she felt better. Such "experts" tell us we must vent our anger rather than control it (as Scripture tells us to do); that if we don't express it, it will eat away at us, causing us all kinds of illness.

You know what? I've never seen anger draw people together. Anger always pushes away. Separates. Divides. Wounds. When was the last time you were drawn to someone angry? Don't you want to just get up and run? Anger destroys relationships—love draws and heals. We get angry at those who: 1) harm us; 2) treat us unfairly; 3) expect too much from us; and 4) try to dominate us.

Although we may decide that God fits into at least one of those categories—He doesn't! He may allow hurt to come to us, but never harm. On God's Eternal Scale—He's treating us with perfect righteousness.

He never expects too much from us, for He promises to give us all we need for every situation. Although He leads us, and insists we follow, we get to make the choice to do so. *Never does He chain us to Himself* with fetters of manipulation and domination. No, rather He draws us to Himself with *"cords of lovingkindness"* and tender mercies.

A little more than 72 hours following Bob's death, at his memorial service, though tearfully leading worship and praise, I found myself testifying before those gathered to honor him and comfort me, "Don't expect me to mourn as others, for Jesus has given me this example: One man, when Jesus called him to follow him, answered that he would as soon as he buried his father. Jesus didn't reply 'Oh, I understand perfectly; take all the time you need.' *No!* Instead, He said, *'Let the dead bury their own dead, but you go and preach the kingdom of God'"* (Luke 9:57-62).

Through that Scripture, I made my choice. I'd already begun my voyage through grief. I'd put the Lord at the helm of my ship. In and through Him I'd find my way through. His Word was my Compass—His Spirit my Counselor. No matter what others might think.

When we name the name of Jesus, when we testify He is Lord, isn't the most important issue Christ and the furtherance of His kingdom? Should we allow grief to derail or delay that? Where does it say in Scripture that grief should hold us back, or shut us down? Shouldn't we even in our grief glorify the One who holds the keys to death and hell? (Rev. 1:18)

178

Who says there should be extended time off? Who would tell us we should lay aside the standard of Righteousness; drop the banner of Truth; or leave the wall of Salvation half-finished?

We must never be ashamed of grieving, of sadness and many tears—of missing someone terribly. But neither must we let grief rule and reign over us. For when we do, grief will move us away from God's will, purpose and plans. Every time.

The thief who comes to steal, kill and destroy loves to take advantage of us at our most vulnerable times. And grief is one of those times. It's difficult for us to truly come to grips with satan's nature of evil, for we've never known anyone totally evil. For instance, if we think of someone like Adolph Hitler—he loved dogs and treated his mistress well.

However, satan has no such "redeeming" qualities. He's incapable of showing mercy. That's why our grief doesn't cause him to back off until we've had a chance to regroup and heal. He pounces—before the death certificate is signed, or the divorce decree granted. Then he works tirelessly to intensify and prolong feelings of sadness, despair, loneliness, hopelessness and abandonment.

Satan is hoping he can get us to feel overwhelmed by our new and harsh circumstances, unable to focus, and discouraged: *I'll never be able to do this now that I'm alone; I'll never get over this.* His all-consuming plan is to get us to doubt God and His goodness.

Consequently, in the days and weeks following, he can give us weakness and extreme weariness to the point of utter exhaustion. New symptoms of physical illness, traveling pains, headaches, nausea, insomnia, loss of appetite, dizziness, shortness of breath, lapses of memory—all of which we excuse and allow because of what we're going through. Sudden anxiousness, feelings of

179

oppression, of being weighed down by an unbearable weight, or of groping our way through a dense fog are not uncommon.

We may "see" the deceased, or "hear" voices...There can be a great longing for the way things once were; a dread of the future and what it may hold; and a death wish entertained along with thoughts of suicide. That's why people say, "I thought it would get easier; isn't time supposed to heal all wounds? I'm not getting over this; it hurts more than when it first happened."

Grief experts will say this is "normal"—while prescribing prescription drugs to alleviate the symptoms. Yet, what if it's not "normal"? What if a sneak thief is robbing us? When we state, "I'll never get over this," we give the enemy permission and power to hold us in grief's clutches.

When we let this kind of grieving continue undetected and un-resisted, the life in Christ which *"always causes us to triumph in Christ Jesus"* will seem unavailable, unattainable and very far away. That's because we lose whenever—*whenever*—we focus on ourselves instead of the Lord and His Way. Although the experts insist we focus only on ourselves—and it seems right—*it's wrong and reaps ruin!*

The *"God of all comfort"* comes. Always, He's available. But does He come saying, "There, there, Honey, someday this will pass?" Or does He not say, *"Rejoice! I will turn your mourning into dancing [if you'll let Me]; I'll put off your sackcloth [if you'll let Me]; I'll clothe you with gladness [if you'll let me], that your glory may sing praise to Me and not be silent..." "for I heal the brokenhearted..., I give beauty for ashes, the oil of joy for mourning and the garment of praise for the spirit of heaviness..."* (Psalm 30:11,12; Isaiah 61:1-3).

Shortly after Bob's death amidst tears and heartache, still I was walking in the light and power of those verses, holding tightly to my Shepherd's Hand.

Then the enemy of my soul tried another tactic. I had lunch with an author at a Christian conference and she urged me to get her book on grief. (I'm sure she was troubled by my peace and joy and thought I was in denial.) Sure enough, when I read her book it insisted we must not miss any of the stages of grief, and that some of the stages could last for years! For if we skipped stages, she warned, we were burying our feelings and in denial. At some point in time, those feelings, hurts and anger would surface bringing serious emotional and/or physical problems. She sounded very credible, citing numerous case histories and statistics to prove her theory.

With that book, fear entered my heart. She was the "expert"—I wasn't. She had the credentials—I didn't. What if I were in denial? What if I weren't in touch with my true feelings, but had stuffed them so that I could be this wonderful Christian example? What if at some unforeseen time, suddenly all my repressed anger and feelings would surface and I would be overwhelmed, sick in mind and body? It would be my own fault because I hadn't grieved rightly.

And… worst of all, what if my lack of deep and lingering grief meant I hadn't really cared for my husband as I should have? Through this parade of "what ifs" I spiraled into introspection and you guessed it—depression!

But praise God, not for long! For in the midst of this pit, His voice sounded, **"Warning! Warning!"** He reminded me of the Scripture He'd spoken to my heart before the Memorial Service: "Didn't I tell you that you were to let the dead bury the dead and that you were to go and preach the kingdom?"

Immediately, through His Word and by His Spirit, the

heaviness, oppression, the uncertainty and (false) guilt began lifting as I marched through my house proclaiming—**"Yes, Lord!"** With renewed intensity I purposed once again to listen to my Shepherd's voice—and no other's. I rebuked a spirit of heaviness and mourning, and sensed it departing, scurrying away as I praised the One who has made me *"more than a conqueror"* in Christ Jesus.

You see, the devil and his demons will try to make us feel guilty for not grieving enough! He whispers that we're being disloyal—that we didn't truly care. At that time, many people enshrine the person and memories about their loved ones to push away such false guilt. And prove they still care. One more trap; one more cage. For others, the attention they get as they mourn is hard to let go. They're the center of attention; and their loss is an excuse for not coping or assuming responsibility.

Bob's death seemed to be bad timing. It was right before we broke ground for our new ministry building. A real step of faith—together. Now it became an even bigger step—alone: *I must go ahead and build without him.* Thoughts and feelings of being overwhelmed and abandoned attacked me, as I faced this huge undertaking alone.

Roadblock after roadblock opposed me. The County didn't want me to live in the building, although we passed all codes. My builder, one I had trusted and become close to, had to be discharged, costing me more time and money. Consequently, I had to subcontract the whole project and be in charge of it all. One day, facing multiple decisions and feeling helpless, I cried, "Lord, I can't do this; it's too much!" Immediately came His whisper, "Can you do **this** hour?"

I considered this and whispered back, "Yes, Lord, I can do **this** hour." He answered, "That's all you have to do—just one hour, one day at a time. Don't look at what lies ahead. Look at

Me and just **this** hour." And so I did, refusing the concerns that tempted me to look ahead: *How would I manage? What would I do?*

Did the work, the decisions, the obstacles get easier? No, in fact, harder ones were yet to come. But, today we have the ministry building—I live in it. And the lesson I learned—*to live in this moment and for this moment*—is one I go back to again and again.

Grief and tragedy will rob us—the enemy will see to that. Unless we do it—life—one step at a time, one hour at a time— clinging closely to Jesus, counting on Him, praising Him. If in the big or (small) situations, if in every one with no exceptions, I turn them to worship rather than regret, the enemy is defeated and Jesus is glorified.

None of us needs to be captured, chained and caged by Grief. And it doesn't take a "super" saint either to be free. Just an informed and obedient one.

The choice is ours: to be struck down and out, benched by our loss—or… to resist the devil, and say, "O Lord, this is too hard for me, but it's not too hard for You! It's going to be really neat to see how You work even this situation for my good and Your Glory. Let's **GO!**"

And that's when even grief becomes—Good!

 * * * * *

Chapter 20

I Finally Looked Up

I like to walk; and one late afternoon while walking my dog Missy I realized just how much my eyes had been glued to the path and the sides of the road. For when I finally looked up, I was astounded at the beauty above me. My Creator had outdone Himself. He had painted the sky a brilliant azure blue, scattering across it puffy white cottonball clouds—all shapes, all sizes—some silver lined, others edged in glistening gold. He'd brushed broad strokes of pink and purple (my favorite colors) as far as my eyes could see. Then, in the midst of it all, shafts of golden radiance streamed down as if Heaven itself were beckoning me to rise and come away.

It was so glorious that I almost expected to see Jacob's ladder appear with angels ascending and descending! And I found myself eagerly scanning the sky. Could this be the moment of Jesus' appearing?

"Oh, Lord," I breathed, "I can't believe I've been focusing on gray dirty sidewalks and dying grass when right above me was all this splendor. What a waste of time. *Why did it take me so long to look up?*"

Then I sobered as I sensed Him saying that it takes a lot to get us to finally look up to Him. We plod along, our heads down, our eyes fixed on our immediate surroundings and circumstances. Or, on what lies just ahead. All the while, The Answer, The Glory, Heaven reaching down to us is found at A Cross and in a Savior! The next day I wrote this song:

I Finally Looked Up

I finally looked up and saw the One who died for me;
Saw the nails in His hands, His wounded side
Where His blood flowed free;
Though blinded by my doubt and sin,
His Love reached down and He drew me in;
I finally looked up and saw the Lord.
     Jesus said, "If I be lifted up
     I will draw all men to Myself;"
     So if we'll just look up—
     Look up, and believe—
     Our blind eyes shall be open—
     We shall see!
I finally looked up and saw the One who died for me;
Saw the nails in His Hands, His wounded side
Where His blood flowed free;
Though blinded by my doubt and sin,
His Love reached out—and He took me in;
I finally looked up and saw the Lord.

©Jeanne M. Mohr

In the days following, I saw even more clearly that, although I'm saved and committed to Jesus as Lord, at times I still let myself get overly absorbed in the immediate. So many things in my life jostle and compete for my time and attention. Yet on Eternity's Scale, how important are they? How do they measure up? Even my ministry endeavors can be done too much *for Him*, rather than *with Him!* (I'm still pondering this one.)

Whenever we neglect to look up, when we put off spending time with Him, when we keep putting Him off to the side rather than center stage, when we decide to lead instead of follow—we'll find ourselves driven! Driven to be the best, have the most, keep the busiest, maxing out each hour, each day, toppling into bed exhausted, wondering as sleep overtakes us: *Where did my day go? What did I accomplish? And why am I feeling so dry, discouraged, and defeated?*

It seems that Mary and Martha had differing viewpoints and mindsets as they prepared to serve Jesus and His disciples in their home. Martha, the consummate hostess, wanted to do her best and demonstrate her best to Jesus. Mary wasn't co-operating. She seemed to think *"simple"* was best if it allowed them to spend more time with Jesus. Martha saw it as unfair— she was doing all the work! She appealed to the Master, for surely He would see the injustice and tell Mary to help her. By this time Mary had positioned herself at Jesus' feet to look up— listen—and live! She was going to give her time to her King and His Kingdom. Jesus commended her choice; then told Martha she was too bothered and worried. Mary had chosen the good part. And that part wouldn't be taken away (Luke 10:38-42).

We so badly need to take the same position Mary took (at Jesus' feet), and look up and out of ourselves. To wrench our focus out of our introspection and self-pity, out of our hurt feelings, exaggerated slights and perceived rejections. Up and out of insisting we be indulged and entertained during all our waking moments. Up and out of thoughts like: *No one appreciates me.* Up and out—to God!

Without a Kingdom vision ever before us, we'll continue trudging along in the grayness and dullness of dirty sidewalks and dying grass. And never even think to ask, *If it doesn't hold Kingdom benefits or consequences, then how important is it, and how important should it be?* (Mark 8:36)

When we lived in New Guinea as medical missionaries, we raised chickens. I noticed that they hardly ever looked up. From dawn to dusk, they only looked at the ground right in front of them, pecking and picking at it. Even when a chicken hawk circled above, they didn't look up 'til its shadow loomed on the ground before them, ominously shutting out the sun. By then it was often too late. Chickens are so unlike the rafter birds we see soaring high, looking up and away, riding the winds of currents and effortlessly gliding across the sky. I think God wants me to be a rafter—I think being "born again" turns me into a rafter!!! However, if left to myself I'll still peck and pick away at life, more like a chicken. Seldom looking up.

God's Plan is always bigger, fuller, deeper, stronger, wider, higher than our eyes can see. I'm myopic (nearsighted), so I only see well up close. (Maybe chickens are nearsighted, too!) I need lenses carefully crafted to allow me to see at a distance. However, if we hold anything too closely to our eyes, everything blurs. (Try it.) I say we're *"myopic"* about God and how our situations fit into God's timing and plan. We hold what's happening to us way too close, making everything blurry. When we do this, life is confusing and wearying; we want to turn away and not even deal with it. That's when we turn to drink or drugs, keep too busy, or try to entertain ourselves out of thinking about what's truly important.

I was in the fifth grade when I got my first pair of glasses. In some ways I hated them, because I was the only girl in my class who had them. I thought they made me look ugly. And why wouldn't I? On that first day when I hesitantly wore them to class, some kids called me "four eyes" and sang the ditty, "Boys never make passes at girls that wear glasses."

Yet I remember the first time I put those glasses on and looked out through those lenses. It was like I'd been asleep all my life and just awakened. Much like Dorothy in the Wizard of Oz, I'd lived in black and white and woke up to vivid Technicolor! I couldn't believe how beautiful the trees and flowers were. And the world was so big!!! My nearsightedness had locked me in and kept me focused on only my immediate surroundings.

With my new glasses I looked up and out. I'd been

imprisoned and never known it. Everything up to then had been blurred—limited—distorted. My poor vision had held me back in so many ways. No wonder I had always struck out in baseball games—I couldn't see the ball! Learning wouldn't be such an effort, now that I could see the blackboard. I wouldn't have to pretend I could see—when I really couldn't. It was wonderful.

I have to admit however that as wonderful as it was to be able to see with my glasses, my vanity and pride often caused me to take them off, hide them in my purse and pretend I didn't need them. I was ashamed. It was more important to me to look good than to see well.

God has special, carefully crafted lenses to correct all that's wrong with our vision. However, PRIDE says, "I don't need them; I can see just fine without them!" Immediately, our world shrinks; and we only see what's up close and affecting us. Consequently, we're self-centered and self-seeking individuals incapable of seeing the bigger picture. We're imprisoned, and like the chicken, only what's right before us consumes us as we peck and pick at it.

Just as poor eyesight runs in families, we inherited our spiritual myopia from our parents, Adam and Eve. When they disobeyed God *"their eyes were opened;"* their once clear vision had changed—of themselves, their world, and God. With their choice to disobey—in one moment of time they were changed from God-centered to self-centered. Their eyes also became light sensitive; i.e., they would now tend to turn away from the Light of Truth. Blind to their own sin, they would think they had 20/20 vision when it came to seeing what was wrong with others! In this inherited fallen state we suffer from "night blindness," as Jesus described in John 3:19: *"Men love darkness rather than light, because their deeds are evil."* In addition, our "astigmatism" causes us to see people and situations with distortions, bias and prejudice—all the while thinking we're the only ones seeing clearly and rightly!

Such self-centered sight is hazardous. It's like trying to make our way through a fog, drifting off the trail and falling into a deep pit. Sight is limited in the pit, for there's little light. As we grope and feel our way along the slippery sides, there's no way out! We're stuck there unless someone hears our cry, calls out that he's come to save us, and we look up and reach out for the one who's reaching down to us.

"I waited patiently for the Lord; and He inclined to me, and heard my cry. He also brought me up out of a horrible pit, out of the miry clay, and set my feet upon a Rock, and established my steps" (Psalm 40:1,2).

These verses are a tremendous account of what happens when we get saved. Glory to God! Our blessed Redeemer has come into the midst of our "mess" and shown us His Salvation. Yet I believe those verses also describe our lives in the pit of situations like abandonment and abuse; of wearying relationships and on-going hardships; of burdens and pain; of what looks like failures.

Rummaging around within ourselves for the answers, ruminating on regret—*why did this have to happen to me?*—does nothing to get us out of the pit. Nor does taking medications that cause us to not care if we're in a pit. *(And there are plenty of those available today.)* We won't find heart answers or real release until and unless we look up, reach out and grab hold of the Mighty Right Hand of the Lord.

"Fear not, for I am with you; be not dismayed for I am your God. I will strengthen you, yes, I will help you, I will uphold you with **My righteous Right Hand**" (Isaiah 41:10).

However, most people don't think they're self-absorbed

with tunnel vision. I was one of them. Then I read an article which opened my eyes. It said that if you don't think you're self-centered, prove it by answering just one question. I thought, *Whatever the question is, I'll pass it! I've lived way too much of my life serving others, and in giving up and giving in to others to be self-centered.* The question was: If there's a group picture taken with you in the group and you're handed the picture, who do you look for first? I failed the test—miserably. (*How about you?*)

Since then God has been teaching me in oh so many ways that self-centeredness is the taproot of our lives. It's BIG, strong and goes down deep, deeper than we can ever imagine. We're born with it; and the only instrument strong enough and sharp enough to cut us loose from it is the work of the Cross and the Sword of the Spirit (Heb. 4:12).

Can you see that if I don't recognize such egoism and count it dead, it will always be easy to think that I'm living for others, when in reality my focus is still on *me*.

"Likewise you also, reckon [consider] yourselves to be dead indeed to sin, but alive to God in Christ Jesus our Lord" (Rom. 6:11).

Such deception will always distort my view of the Lord and lessen the degree of my surrender. I may talk surrender, sing songs of surrender, give testimony about surrender (even write about it like I'm doing now). Nevertheless, if I haven't dealt with my "selfness" through the Cross, my degree of yielding will be limited. I may be using spiritual talk, yet I'm still focused on *I, me, my and mine.* And songs that say "*I Did It My Way*" will apply to me, even though I bear the name "Christian".

What's the eye "prescription" I must have to clearly see my situation, my God and myself? This special prescription asks such questions as, *"What does God have to say about this? What has He promised? What is His full counsel (not just one verse picked out of context)? What's the Bigger Picture?"* The Lens of Truth which asks, ***"What is God's Truth?"*** in any and every situation and circumstance will clear my vision and enable me to see life as God sees it. With Truth, my view expands up and out of myself.

Along with my New Lenses, my Heavenly Eye Doctor has a precious and costly eye ointment. Purchased at Calvary, it's called **Eternity.** And as He touches the eyes of my heart with it, Eternity is stamped upon them. And, oh my, once Eternity's applied—suddenly I can see forever!

"...Eye has not seen, nor ear heard, nor have entered into the heart of man the things which God has prepared for those who love Him" (1 Cor. 2:9).

With Eternity stamped on my eyes, I begin to see that what I suffer or endure ***here*** is preparing me—*for* ***There!*** I'm being trained for glory—to rule and reign with Him some day! (Rev. 1:5,6; 20:6).

"This is a faithful saying: For if we died with Him, we shall also live with Him: if we endure, we shall also reign with Him" (2 Tim. 2:11,12).

What He works in me through faith HERE will shine for all eternity—THERE! Because, what He's been able to work in me by faith, He can't work in me by sight. Here, He's working in each of us qualities of character.

"We also glory in tribulations, knowing that tribulation produces perseverance; and perseverance, character; and character, hope..." (Rom. 5:5).

This side of glory we can't begin to comprehend or understand (we can't see) how all we've gone through (or are going through) will be used in our next life. Nor what a Treasure they will be in the trophy room of God's Son. Precious to Him, for they've been forged on the anvil of Faith and purified in the fire.

For, beloved, we have *"an **inheritance, incorruptible** and **undefiled**...that **does not fade away, reserved in heaven** for those who are kept by faith...In this you greatly rejoice, though for a little while, if need be, you have been grieved by various trials, that the genuineness of your faith being much **more precious than gold** that perishes, though it is **tested by fire** may be found to praise, honor and glory at the revelation of Jesus Christ..."* (1 Peter 1:3-5). Awesome!

That's when we'll know that it was truly worth it all to serve and love Jesus. Our wonderful Bridegroom has said to His Bride, *"I go to prepare a place for you... and I will come again and receive you to Myself, that where I am you may be also"* (John 14:3). Until then, He's sent His Spirit, the Spirit of Hope and Strength, **to prepare us for that place.**

I believe that EVERYTHING that touches our lives—everything we go through—is part of that preparation, equipping each of us for the life to come and for our assignments there. Because absolutely nothing is ever wasted by our Savior. You can't receive my equipping, and I can't receive yours. So, instead of resisting it—why not embrace it? Some day we'll see Him as He is and be changed to be like Him—praise God. *"When Christ who is our life appears, then you also will appear with Him in glory"* (Col. 3:4).

*"Beloved, now we are children of God; and it has **not yet** been revealed what we shall be, but we know that when He is*

revealed, we shall be like Him, for we shall see Him as He is" (1 John 3:2).

Scripture calls looking, longing and loving His appearing the "Blessed Hope"—"the hope that purifies" (Titus 2:13; 1 John 3:3). And no wonder, for it can make every shell of hardship produce a ***precious pearl of Hope.***

We count on our own hopes and dreams; yet when those hopes become dashed and those dreams become smashed, we're devastated—or at least depressed. But when we truly put our hope in the Lord, the Hope He ***is*** and the Hope He *gives* does not—cannot—disappoint (Rom.5:5).

For God cannot lie. Therefore we have strong consolation, we *"who have fled for refuge to **lay hold of the hope** set before us. This hope we have as an **Anchor of the Soul**, both **sure and steadfast** and which enters the Presence behind the veil..."* (Heb. 6:18b,19). Such Hope ***always*** looks up. And keeps on looking up!

"If then you were raised with Christ, seek those things which are above, where Christ is, sitting at the right hand of God. Set your mind on things above, not on things on the earth. For you died, and your life is hidden with Christ in God. When Christ who is our life appears, then you also will appear with Him in glory" (Col. 3:1-4).

For Splendor and Glory await us. Just like those golden beams that shone down on me that day I walked. Even now in the midst of your life as you purpose to look up, He'll shine glimpses of splendor and glory into your most desperate, devastating and destructive storm. In a life that can't even remember anything but ongoing sadness and gloom (perhaps like yours right now), you'll find yourself looking up exclaiming, "I once was blind, but now I see!"

Because He's the *Eternal One*, preparing an Eternity *with us*, our gaze doesn't need to be fastened on dirty gray sidewalks and dead grass anymore. Hallelujah! We don't need to behave like chickens—we're rafters! Praise the Lord! We can get *"Cross-correction" lenses* for our self-centered vision. Thank You, Jesus! And… no more pit stops. Glory! For Heaven's Hand beckons, the Trumpet will sound and we—you and I—shall be raised incorruptible!

"Behold, I tell you a mystery: We shall not all sleep, but we shall all be changed—in a moment, in the twinkling of an eye, at the last trumpet. For the trumpet will sound, and the dead will be raised incorruptible, and we shall be changed" (1 Cor. 15:51,52).

So, beloved, together, through every storm that satan and this old life can throw at us—in putting down That Awesome Anchor, we lift up our heads. And we **keep looking up!** For our **R**edemption, and our **R**edeemer, draweth nigh.

*"For the Lord Himself will descend from heaven with a shout, with the voice of an archangel, with the trumpet of God. And the dead in Christ will rise first. Then we who are alive and remain shall be caught up together with them in the clouds to meet the Lord in the air. And **thus we shall always be with the Lord"*** (1 Thes. 4:16,17).

*"**Therefore comfort one another with these words"*** (vs. 18).

 * * * * *

The Anchor Holds

(Epilogue)

Praise God, we can draw strength and direction from those who've sailed before us! A shared faith binds us together across the ages with those who've weathered the onslaught and come through life's trials stronger than ever. One of my favorite hymns is *"It Is Well With My Soul"*[13] by Horatio Spafford.

He suffered the loss of his four little daughters at sea in 1873, when the supposedly unsinkable *Villa due Havre* was rammed and in fifteen minutes sank. Anna, his wife, was saved miraculously out of the waters—but not before her infant daughter was wrenched from her arms by the relentless sea. Anna sent him this cable: **"Saved alone."**

While traveling to reunite with his grieving wife, the captain of the ship pointed to the ocean below them, saying, "This is where they were lost." Seeing their watery grave, in the midst of darkness of soul, of loss and grief, Spafford penned these God-glorifying words ministering comfort, strength and peace to millions over the years.

"When peace like a river attendeth my soul;
When sorrows like sea billows roar.
Whatever my task, Thou hast taught me to know,
It is well, it is well with my soul."

Oh, friend, is it not part of the *Good News* that there is no sin so sinful, no tragedy so great, no hardship so heavy, no grief so grievous that God is not *Greater*?

Throughout this book, you've learned to put down your anchor of trust in the Lord and ride out every storm. *No matter*

195

what. You'll be quicker now to reach for your Anchor because you'll sense the storm's approach even before it begins raging against your ship.

Is it not part of God's Powerful Provision that there is no storm of life that can swamp our ship, sink or capsize it?

Ships of old carried special anchors called "storm anchors." They were much heavier than the ones used in harbor or in calm seas. Realizing that a horrendous storm was fast approaching, the captain would order that the ship be turned into the storm and the storm anchors lowered. Those anchors—as the storm was faced—were fashioned and weighted to hold! Even in the worst of storms.

I told you earlier, I'd questioned whether I should write this book. And on the day that I took some time to fast, pray, and get sure direction, I opened a new CD by Ray Boltz.[14] As he began singing the first song—one I'd never heard before—I knew I had my answer and my confirmation.

As he sang *"The Anchor Holds"* and his song filled the room, I was awed. The theme of this book had been completely captured in the compelling words and music I was hearing. For it is in the storms of life that we truly experience God's love and faithfulness. After each verse, this powerful chorus rings out:

> *"The anchor holds though the ship is battered;*
> *The anchor holds though the sails are torn.*
> *I have fallen on my knees as I've faced the raging seas,*
> *But the anchor holds in spite of the storm."*

Praise God, we can put down our Anchor and know beyond any shadow of any doubt — The ANCHOR holds. The Captain of our Salvation holds. *Jesus holds*.

With our lives hidden securely and completely in Him, in the midst of every storm—in spite of every storm and for as long as the storm lasts—the One who alone is 𝔉aithful and 𝔗rue—holds!

 * * * * *

References and Acknowledgements

Chapter 1

[1]*Heaven Came Down and Glory Filled My Soul*, words & music by John W. Peterson ©1961.

Chapter 4

[2]Hymn: *Calvary Covers It All*, words and music Mrs. Walter G. Taylor, © 1934, renewal 1962, The Rodeheaver Co. Sacred Music Publishers, Winona Lake, IN 46590.

Chapter 7

[3]*Science, Creation, and the Bible*, VHS by Walter T. Brown, Jr., produced by American Portrait Films, P.O. Box 19266, Cleveland, Ohio, 44119

[4]*Creation or Evolution? Part II-The Historical Record,* by Winkie Pratney, published by Pretty Good Printing, ©1980, 1983, 1984 Last Days Ministries

[5]*The Holy Bible-Wholly True,* by Winkie Pratney, published by Pretty Good Printing, ©1979, 1985 Last Days Ministries

Chapter 8

[6]Luke 6:38. If you will look up this verse in its context, you'll find that Jesus has been talking before and after about mercy and forgiveness—not finances.

[7]*Revival's Golden Key*, by Ray Comfort....pg. 67-71, Bridge-Logos Publishers, P.O Box 141630, Gainesville, Fl. 32614

Chapter 14

[8]*The Voice of the Martyrs* Magazine, P.O. Box 443, Bartlesville, OK 74005. Tel.#(918) 337-8015. Order this important ministry magazine today. No cost.

[9]*Global Mission* Inter-bulletin on Mission Research. David B. Barrett. Tel.#(203) 624-6672.

[10]Read Luke 13:11-17 to see how Jesus dealt with *a spirit of infirmity*. Too often we don't recognize the spiritual warfare we're in, nor do we discern our need for personal deliverance. God's made provision—still we remain bound.

Chapter 16

[11]*My Hope Is Built,* by Edward Mote and William B. Bradbury. Church Service Hymns, ©1948 The Rodeheaver Co., Winona Lake, IN 46590

Chapter 17

Chapter taken from author's book: *Battle Plan*

Chapter 18

[12]*Beyond Our Selves*, Catherine Marshall, McGraw-Hill Book Company, 1221 Avenue of the Americas. New York, NY 10020

Epilogue

[13]*It Is Well With My Soul,* Horatio Spafford, P.P. Bliss, Church Service Hymns, The Rodeheaver Co., Winona Lake, IN 46590

[14]*The Anchor Holds,* words by Lawrence Chewning and Ray Boltz, ©1994 Shepherd Boy Music and Word Music. Used by permission.

God's Word To You In Time Of Need

Anger   Eph. 4:26,31,32; James 1:19,20;
                      Rom. 12:19-21; Col. 3:8,12,13

Burdened   Matt. 11:28-30; Psalm 55:22; 1 Peter 5:7;
                      Rom. 8:28

Christ's Return   1 Thess. 4:13-18; 1 Cor. 15:50-58;
                      John 14:1-3; Col. 3:4

Comfort/Counsel   2 Cor. 1:3,4; Psalm 119:97-99;
                      Psalm 1:1-3; Heb. 10:24

Commandments   Ex. 20:1-17; John 14:21,24;
                      Matt. 22:36-40; Matt. 7:22-28

Deliverance   Psalm 60:11,12; Psalm 37:39,40;
                      Micah 7:7,8; 2 Cor. 2:14

Faith   Heb. 11:6; Heb. 12:1,2; Eph. 2:8;
                      Rom. 10:8-13; Prov. 3:3-8

Fear   Isaiah 41:10; Heb. 13:6; Psalm 31:14,15;
                      2 Tim. 1:7

Following Jesus   John 10:27-29; Luke 9:23-26;
                      Matt. 12:30; Phil. 3:3,8-10

God's Word To You In Time Of Need

Forgiveness   Matt. 6:14; Eph. 1:17; Col. 2:13,14;
Luke 15:10

Freedom/Victory   John 8:31,32,36; Gal. 6:1; Rom. 8:1,2;
Rom. 6:1-11

God's Word   Psalm 119:105,160; Heb. 4:12;
2 Tim. 3:15,16; John 1:14

Gospel Salvation   John 3:36, Acts 4:12; Rom. 10:9-13;
Eph. 2:1-9; John 3:3,5,8

Healing   Psalm 103:3; Jer. 17:14; Matt. 8:16,17;
James 5:13-16

Heaven   John 14:1-3; Rev. 21:22; 2 Cor. 5:1-8;
John 5:28,29

Hell   Luke 16:19-31; Mark 9:43; Psalm 9:17;
Matt. 13:49,50

Hope   1 Peter 1:3, Jer. 17:7,8; Titus 2:13;
Col. 1:27

Love & Mercy   Psalm 103:9-14; Micah 7:18-20;
Rom. 8:38,39; Eph. 3:14-21

God's Word To You In Time Of Need

Mind Renewal   Rom. 12:1,2; Phil. 2:1-6; 1 Cor. 2:16;
Rom. 8:5-6

Peace   Isaiah 26:3; John 14:27; Col. 3:15-17;
Isaiah 54:10

Praise & Worship   John 14:23,24; Psalm 103:1-5; Psalm 34;
Col. 3:15-17

Promises of God   2 Cor. 1:18-22; 2 Peter 1:3-4;
Heb. 10:23; Psalm 119:89-90

Purity (sexual)   2 Tim. 2:22; Col. 3:18,19;
1 Cor. 6:15-20; Eph. 5:25-31

Protection   Psalm 9:9-10; Psalm 32:7; Psalm 18:1-3;
John 16:13-15

Repentance   Acts 3:19; Psalm 51; Matt. 9:13;
2 Peter 3:9

Spiritual Dryness   Psalm 63:1-8; Psalm 42:1-8; Psalm 23;
Psalm 73:25-28

Spiritual Warfare   Eph. 6:10-18; 1 John 2:15-17;
James 4:7,8; 1 Peter 5:8-9

God's Word To You In Time Of Need

Strength   Isaiah 40:28-31; Psalm 46:1-5;
                                Psalm 61:1-4; Psalm 37:39-40

Trials   James 1:2-4; 2 Tim. 3:12; Matt. 5:10-12;
                                John 15:18,21

Temptations   1 Cor. 10:12-14; Psalm 119:9-11;
                                2 Peter 2:9; Heb. 4:15,16

Worry/Anxiety   Matt. 6:25-34; Phil. 4:6,7,19;
                                Luke 11:9,10; Psalm 91:1,2,14-16

* * * * *

Personal Notes

Personal Notes

Personal Notes

Books by the Author

BATTLEPLAN – A counseling, discipling manual, which exposes the enemy's work in our lives and how to walk free! This book ministers even as it teaches and equips us to know our God, understand ourselves, and discern the enemy.

ALL THAT GLITTERS - The author believes that something like 'gold fever' is running rampant in the church today. Writing from her own experiences, she traces Christianity's movement away from the foundations that keep it safe and close to God's Word. In ALL THAT GLITTERS, learn how to discern the "Pure Gold of God's Kingdom and Power" from 'fools gold'.

AND THE BEAT GOES ON... The culture, the media and our flesh draw and drive us with their beat. For sound communicates its own message. Yet isn't it God's heartbeat and His Song that we need to hear and follow? Isn't becoming His worshippers our highest calling?

These books and other materials, as well as information on seminars and retreats, can be obtained by contacting the ministry.

Living Praise Ministries
P.O. Box 1431
High Ridge, MO 63049
(636) 376-4009
e-mail: jmlivingpraise@sbcglobal.net

ALL ABOARD . . .
For Anchor Share Groups!

Dear Reader,

I invite you to join together with friends and acquaintances to share what God has done in your hearts and lives through this book.

It's easy to do. Simply agree to meet three times for sharing. Start each session with this one question, "What did you read that helped you in some way?"

Then watch the Holy Spirit take over.

If you decide to keep your group small (5 or less), the gathering can be held almost anywhere, any time! Go for a coffee break at your favorite place; have breakfast at the local diner; discuss the book during lunch hour at work; meet before or after baseball or soccer practice; or use the book as a family devotion or as inspiration for your prayer group.

Will you invest just an hour a week for three weeks? If so, I think you'll agree, it's always more fun to share experiences when you set sail with others.

Jeanne Mohr

See what can happen if you give a copy of this book to someone facing a struggle . . .

Cynthia W. writes:

Is God blessing others with your latest book? You bet He is. Here's just one example.

I was just about to head out the front door on my way to have two new tires mounted on my car, when the small still voice of the Lord instructed, "Take a book with you...I will show you who has need of it." I reached for one of my extra copies of "Put Down Your Anchor, Ride Out the Storm."

Over the years, I have learned (the hard way) not to question that Voice, and became excited at the thought of how the Lord was going to touch someone in need.

As I sat in the small waiting room at the car garage, a tall, distinguished gray-haired man walked through the door, smiled, and nodded "hello". Once again, the Voice of the Holy Spirit spoke: "This is the one, give him the book!"

He was friendly and very easy to speak with, and it didn't take long to know why he was in need of this book. He was in the middle of a horrific storm.

"My wife and I recently lost our only granddaughter in a terrible car accident. She just turned sixteen years old. We are Christians, but to tell you the truth, we're having a terrible time trying to deal with this grief."

His personal loss deeply saddened me. "Would you please take this book and read it?" I asked, placing it gently on his lap. He looked at the book cover and smiled. "Yes, yes, and...thank you. We'll read every page of it!"

A loud voice bellowed over the intercom, "Number seventeen, your car's ready to go!" I said, "Well, my number's been called—I'd better go." The elderly man didn't even hear me say goodbye; he was already emerged in **"Setting Sail"**!

Meet The Author

While serving as a medical missionary with her husband and children in the Highlands of New Guinea, Jeanne's life turned "down-side up" when she reached out to Jesus in His fullness, His Lordship, His promises—His all!

Since returning from the mission field, she's traveled extensively in the states and abroad as teacher and exhorter in the Body of Christ.

"Living Praise Bible Institute and Seminary" was founded as a result of her ministry trip to Benin City, Nigeria, and is still training pastors and evangelists today.

Jeanne directs **Living Praise Ministries,** which includes Living Praise Publications and Open Door Counseling Centre, where Biblical counseling is offered free to the public.

She ministers in worship and praise through the songs God inspires, and holds retreats and seminars, including a one-day writer's workshop—"Let's Write For Jesus".

Jeanne's desire: To make ready a people prepared for the Lord!

Living to the praise of His glory
as we make ready a people prepared for the Lord.

Living Praise Ministries
P.O. Box 1431
High Ridge, MO 63049
e-mail: jmlivingpraise@sbcglobal.net

210

THE GREENBOOK® GUIDE TO
DEPARTMENT 56
VILLAGES

SIXTH EDITION
1996/1997

Including

THE ORIGINAL SNOW VILLAGE®
THE ORIGINAL SNOW VILLAGE® ACCESSORIES

THE HERITAGE VILLAGE COLLECTION®
Dickens' Village
New England Village
Alpine Village
Christmas In The City
Little Town Of Bethlehem
North Pole
Disney Parks Village
THE HERITAGE VILLAGE ACCESSORIES

ADDITIONAL VILLAGE ACCESSORIES

CHRISTMAS
IN THE CITY

GREENBOOK®

**The Most Respected Guides To Popular Collectibles
& Their After Market Values**
Old Coach at Main, Box 515
East Setauket, NY   11733
516.689.8466
FAX 516.689.8177

Printed in the United States, on recyclable paper.

ISBN 0-923628-37-1

GREENBOOK TRUMARKET™ PRICES are compiled from trades and information provided by retailers, dealers and collectors. Manufacturers verify factual information only and are not consulted or involved in any way in determining our TRUMARKET™ Secondary Market Prices.

The GREENBOOK would like to thank –

Department 56–with special thanks to **Judith Price**, **Glen Sorenson** and **Bill Kirchner**.

Mitch Warde, Photographer.

The Terrific Crew at Genna's Gift Gallery on Main Street in Rochester, Michigan:

Mary Jacowiak - Manager

Chris Nobels - Display Artist who un-displayed Retired items so we could photograph them.

Mary & Chris who are walking encyclopedias of Department 56 Villages. They know the line intimately and were a tremendous help, organizing and directing the other helpers.

Elaine Pierce, **Jessica Coughlin**, **Jane Sturgell** and **Cathy Kobus** were wonderful and **Betty Pannozzo** pitched in when called upon.

And, finally, **John and Cathy Genna** for the generous use of the store as our photo studio, and stock as photo subjects.

Peter George, **Jeff McDermott**, **Patsy Fryberger**, **Log Gift Shoppe** of Johnston, RI and **G & L Christmas Barn** of Windham, CT.

The **collectors**, **retailers**, **secondary market dealers** and **newsletter publishers** across the country who take their valuable time to supply us with information including secondary market status and price.

Acknowledgments

As my eight year-old would say, **"YES!"**

We hope your reaction is the same to our completely redesigned Villages Guide.

Is wasn't exactly a year like any other—

- Limited Editions are back; the hyphens are gone,

- Sets are sold by the individual piece,

- Retirement Day moved,

- The entire Disney Parks Village is retired, and,

- GREENBOOK is in FULL-COLOR

—not necessarily in that order.

If you'd like an Update Bookmark around the first of the year to keep your book current until midyear and the 7th Edition, please send a SASE with "D56 Update" written in the lower left corner.

Additionally, many of you have asked for reproductions of our exclusive cover art as lithographs. We would like you to know we are pursuing it. If you'd like to know the outcome of our efforts, please send a SASE with "D56 Cover Lithos" written in the lower left corner.

And, if you're not already busy enough, while you have your paper and pen out, we'd love to hear your comments on our new format.

Till then, as always, thanks for buying the Guide.

Louise Patterson Langenfeld
Editor & Publisher

Note From The Publisher

GREENBOOK
WHAT WE DO & HOW WE DO IT

ARTCHARTS & LISTINGS

The GREENBOOK ARTCHARTS developed for the Department 56 Villages feature color photographs, factual information and TRUMARKET PRICES for each piece.

Factual information consists of:

> Year Of Introduction
> Name
> Item Number
> Material
> Description
> Size
> Variations
> Item Particulars
> Status

GREENBOOK TRUMARKET PRICE Listings include:

> Original Suggested Retail Price
> GREENBOOK TRUMARKET Secondary Market Price
> Percentage up or down as compared to Last Year
> (NC = No Change.)

GREENBOOK TRUMARKET PRICES

Secondary Market Prices are reported to us by retailers and collectors. The data is compiled, checked for accuracy, and a price established as a benchmark as a result of this research. There are many factors which determine the price a collector will pay for a piece; most acquisitions are a matter of personal judgement. The price will fluctuate with the time of year, section of the country and type of sale; i.e. prices may be more competitive at a well-attended Swap & Sell than in a Want–Ad. GREENBOOK takes all of these factors into consideration when determining TRUMARKET Prices, and so **GREENBOOK TRUMARKET Prices are never an absolute number**. Use them as a basis for comparison, as a point of information when considering an acquisition, and as a guide when insuring for replacement value.

The GREENBOOK does not trade on the Secondary Market. The GREENBOOK monitors and reports prices, in the same way as the Wall Street Journal reports trades on the stock markets in the United States and abroad.

HOW TO USE THIS GUIDE

This Guide is divided into three main sections: The Original Snow Village, The Heritage Village and Village Accessories. Within The Snow Village and Heritage Village sections, GREENBOOK Listings are in chronological date of introduction order. It's important to remember "the year of introduction indicates the year in which the piece was designed, sculpted and copyrighted" and the piece is generally available to collectors the following calendar year.

Within each year, the Listings are in Department 56 Item Number order.

The Village Accessories Section is divided into categories such as Trees, Electrical, Fences etc. Within each of these sections, current items appear in Department 56 Item Number order. Discontinued accessories are referenced separately.

What We Do

Q&Ask The Historian

Hello! It's been a very exciting year since I wrote the Historian section for the previous edition of GREENBOOK. Think about everything that has taken place since then—especially the unexpected things. Most notable is the introduction of a numbered limited edition piece. Many collectors doubted they would ever see another. I think it is great for the collectible and the collectors. What is truly spectacular is that the Ramsford Palace, the first limited edition for Dickens' Village in eight years, is a marvelous building and is part of a set of seventeen—the largest set ever sold by Department 56.

Could you believe Department 56 had a midyear retirement? I was somewhat surprised that they retired the entire Disney Parks Village. But I was shocked when it was done in May—seven months before their contract with Disney was to expire. You never know what Department 56 is going to do or when they'll do it. Now they'll keep us guessing if there will ever be another midyear retirement or not. But that's part of the fun, isn't it?

What would a year be without a new twist? I know there are collectors who have added the mechanics necessary to make smoke rise from the chimneys on their buildings, but who expected Department 56 to introduce buildings with the required equipment already in place? Once again they showed us that they have ideas that will keep them as the number one manufacturer of lit buildings in their industry and in our hearts. I can't wait to see what they will introduce next year.

These events and others have have given us a lot to write about in my magazine, *the Village Chronicle*. As publisher of the magazine, I speak at gatherings, open houses, club meetings, and other special events around the country. This offers me the opportunity to enjoy the best thing about collecting...the collectors. As I travel, I reunite with old friends and meet new ones, too. It's truly a pleasure to be able meet so many people who have a similar interest. When we're at an event together, be sure to stop by and say hello!

Aside from publishing the magazine and traveling, Jeanne and I continue to add to our collection. It includes pieces from every village—the emphasis is on Dickens' Village, Christmas in the City, and North Pole—as well as many other Department 56 products. Our favorite aspect about the buildings is taking a piece out of a box after it has been in storage for a while and "seeing it again for the first time." It seems we always see something that we missed before.

I'm sure you will enjoy the new format of GREENBOOK. When we get together, let me know what you think! Until then...

May your home be merry and your houses be many!

Peter George

From Our Historian

I would like to share something that, to my surprise, I have been asked to speak about quite often lately. I spoke about it once at a small event, and it has become quite popular. I'm not saying collectors run home and do this, but they certainly enjoy hearing about the way I "re-configure" pieces. I've always said that these buildings are manufactured for us to enjoy, and they certainly are enjoyable as they are intended to be displayed. But, what if you don't always agree with how the Department 56 artist thought the item should appear? Why not change things a little bit? There's nothing wrong with re-configuring a piece to make it fit *your* ideas. Here's some thoughts. How about a sewer worker for Christmas in the City? It's easy to have him coming out of the sewer. First, you'll need a black container from 35mm film. Make a hole in your display so you can push the container down into the street until the top is flush with the road—that's your sewer. Now for the worker. The best character I've found yet is the Chimney Sweep from Dickens' Village; he even comes with his own brush and ladder. The only problem is that he doesn't fit into the container. Here's where the "re-configuring" comes in. You have to break off his left arm and the bottom of his legs. There...now he fits perfectly.

Don't throw away the cap to the film container. Use it as a manhole cover.

Want someone to drive your Village Express Van? First you'll have to remove the seat assembly from the bottom of the van. Simply use a screwdriver to pry the assembly out. Now place the van over the little boy from Playing in the Snow—the one holding the scarf at arms' length. Because he has his arms out, it appears that he's holding onto a steering wheel. Vroom!

Use the same little boy in a lake scene where he has fallen through the ice and is being rescued. First, cut him in half at the waist. Next, remove the scarf from his hands by pulling down at each side where it's glued. Then place him wherever you'd like on the frozen pond. His outstretched hands will be reaching for the ladder that the CIC Fire Brigade will be sending out to rescue him.

One day I was including a few new pieces in my Christmas in the City display and accidentally knocked over a fire hydrant. Instantly I thought a stream of water should be gushing skyward. And that's just what's happening now. All you have to do is use hot glue to make a vertical stream. It takes a while because you have to put down a drop and let it cool, then put a drop on top of the previous one—repeating this until the stream is about four inches high. Then work your way outward in all directions to create the crest. Place it next to the now-horizontal hydrant and you're all set.

From Our Historian

I decided that Fagin's Hide-Away needed a 55-gallon drum outside so people in the area could warm their hands during the cold nights. It was much easier to do than I anticipated. Take a 35mm film container and sand the surface so that it will accept a rust color paint. Cut a hole in the bottom, and slide a flickering bulb through the bottom into the "barrel." This is the fire. Put some glue on the rim of the barrel and apply a bit of cotton. This is the rising smoke. The only thing I needed was a person warming his hands. After looking around, I saw him…the Old Puppeteer—his hands are outstretched in order to manipulate the puppets. I snapped him off his perch and placed him in a snowbank next to the barrel. Now his hands are nice and warm. I did this for a retailer's display, too. The only problem? You guessed it! It was one of his most requested accessories.

My favorite "re-configuration" was created to fit a specific part of A Christmas Carol. I wanted Scrooge to be pleading with the Ghost of Christmas Yet to Come. But Department 56 has him pleading to the Ghost of Christmas Past. I "removed" that spirit and replaced him with the black-cloaked one. Now I have Scrooge and the spirit next to an open grave in a church's graveyard…just like in the story.

I realize that most collectors would never entertain the idea of such acts, and I can understand that. But, I am receiving more and more mail with photos enclosed that show how collectors have re-configured their own pieces. I want to stress that any time you alter a piece in any way, you void its value entirely…its monetary value, that is. If you have increased its intrinsic value to you, however, it's worth it.

Here's an actual example. While at a dealer's event, a woman told me that she loved the Dickens' Village King's Road Post Office, except for the fact that it had silver downspouts. She disliked the downspouts so much, she would not buy the building. I suggested to her that she should buy it and paint the downspouts brown. You can imagine the look on her face. She replied that painting a piece was unthinkable—it would nullify any value the piece might have in the future. I then asked her how valuable the piece would be if she didn't own it. She thought for a moment and then informed the salesperson that she would like to purchase the Post Office.

I always finish my seminars about "re-configuring" by reiterating this advice. It is your imagination, they are your pieces, and they were manufactured for your enjoyment. So do just that….Enjoy!

From Our Historian

Often Asked Questions

(Look for more questions and answers throughout the book.)

Q. I've noticed that the secondary prices on many older pieces have decreased. Why is this happening?

A. This is not unique to Department 56. Many other collectibles, especially those that are very popular and have been established for a number of years, experience the same thing. It is the result of a number of factors. One of these is the fact that newer collectors are not as sentimental about older pieces as now-experienced collectors were a few years back. This is greatly influenced by the number of current pieces, and the quality of those pieces.

Think about it. Consider collectors who were new to the hobby five or six years ago. When they started collecting there were fewer pieces available both on the secondary market and at retail. They could buy the then-current pieces they liked and, with the desire for even more pieces, look to the secondary market as another option. With relatively few retired pieces, it was feasible to purchase some of them.

New collectors, however, see an ocean of retired pieces. With pieces retiring every year, it will continue to grow. Certainly, there are some retired pieces a collector may want, but it's still not like it was in the past. Furthermore, collectors in general are looking at the quality of the pieces. New collectors often prefer the designs of the newer pieces to the styles of the older ones. For instance a new collector might think, "Should I buy this new mill for $50, or should I buy that older one for almost $5000? The new one is more colorful, and I really like the design. If I buy it as opposed to the other one, I can use the money I save to buy all the pieces for my village for the next five or six years." This may be a slight exaggeration, but you get the idea!

Q. Why have so many prices remained stagnant over the past year or two? Has the collector's enthusiasm decreased?

A. No, I don't believe it has. In fact, I think the level of enthusiasm is at an all-time high. There are more collectors than ever before. There are more collectors clubs, and more are forming all the time. There are more Department 56-related events than there has ever been.

These factors, those that indicate enthusiasm is on an increase, are to a large degree responsible for the stagnant secondary market values. These values are determined by supply and demand. Because values

Q&Ask The Historian

have not risen, however, does not necessarily mean that demand has decreased. It can also mean that supply has increased at an even greater rate than demand. This is what I believe to be the case.

Five, six, or seven years ago, there were many fewer resources from which to purchase retired pieces. Few outlets create less supply. Now, however, there are many more places where collectors may make a purchase. They may buy a piece at an event. They may ask collectors at their club if they have any pieces for sale. They may contact numerous secondary market dealers. With so many avenues available, collectors can be very particular where they make their purchases. This causes values to remain even, increase more slowly, or even decrease in some instances.

Q. *How should I go about insuring my collection?*

A. Talk to your insurance agent. Notify him that you want to insure a collectible—one that often increases in value. Describe the characteristics of the collectible in detail including the retirement process and what happens to the value of a piece after that point. Be certain to tell him that you want to insure each piece for its replacement value. Explain that, once retired, pieces are purchased through the secondary market. You may want to bring a piece or two with you when you meet. Take your GREENBOOK along as well. Show the original suggested retail prices and the current secondary market values of the pieces you own. Don't forget to mention that boxes and sleeves make up a portion of the overall value. Ask about all possible loss possibilities including fire, theft, accidental breakage, and floods, tornados, hurricanes, or earthquakes, if they are prone to your area.

Your agent will most likely suggest a rider where you will "schedule" each piece for its replacement value. This is an added cost to your home owner's or renter's policy, but it's not very expensive.

Keep as much information as possible for each piece. It will be required, or at least helpful, in case you need to file a claim. This information should include receipts indicating the prices you paid or, if the case of gifts, notes stating when you received them and their values at that time. If a piece is a limited edition, include its number. Take photographs of each piece. If you have a camcorder, use it instead. You can take advantage of its audio capabilities and describe what you are video taping. Make a copy of the tape and/or photographs and keep one copy with your collection and one copy off the premises, possibly in a safe deposit box.

Q&Ask The Historian

It will be your responsibility to notify your agent when the secondary market values change. You should do this at least once a year or when the value of a piece has increased drastically.

Q. *Why are the variations of some buildings acknowledged, while those of other buildings are disregarded?*

A. I'm not certain there is an answer for this. It's the collectors who decide which variations they're going to recognize. Many variations have gone unnoticed or totally disregarded. There are buildings with mold changes, color variations, different sleeves, and a variety of other differences, but no one seems to care. For instance, many of the early Christmas In The City pieces have both dark and light variations. Those pieces are bought and sold on the secondary market as if there were no variations at all. Collectors simply call and ask for the piece. Seldom do they request the darker one or lighter one—either is fine. But, for some reason, collectors have decided as a group to pay more for one particular variation of a piece than for another. When these pieces are purchased on the secondary market, collectors are certain to request the first issue or the second, this mold or that one. I think this process is part of what makes variations so much fun.

Q. *I collect all the villages, but can't keep up with the pace in which they are introduced. Any suggestions?*

A. I can understand your predicament. Collecting that many villages requires a large investment in both money and space. The first answer that comes to mind is to collect fewer villages—maybe the one or two you like most. But there are more creative possibilities as well. Why let yourself be confined to the parameters set by Department 56 or their villages. You can set your own.

First set up a budget—the number of buildings, accessories, and peripheral items you can both afford and house. Now, within that budget, select the pieces you want to purchase. You may work within the parameters that consist of one village perhaps. Or, it may include only those pieces you really like regardless of the village for which they were intended. Churches may be another possibility. Many collectors focus solely on the vast number of churches that Department 56 has to offer. You might consider just urban buildings. Buildings from both Snow Village and Christmas in the City would fit nicely in this scenario. Conversely, you might decide on only rural scenes. Many of the villages offer pieces that work well in this type of collection.

Q&Ask The Historian

The possibilities are endless. If you can't think of parameters for your collection, look at those that already exist. These are mini collections within collections. Snow Village has the American Architecture Series. New England Village has numerous buildings and accessories that are designed to be on or near a waterfront. Give some thought to the buildings and accessories in Dickens' Village that pertain to the Christmas Carol collections. If that is too small a collection, you might include the pieces that are associated with Charles Dickens' works. The possibilities are as vast as your imagination.

If space is a major problem—sooner or later it is for everyone—you may consider selling some of the pieces that, let's say, aren't your favorites. This might be difficult to deal with at first, but give it some thought. Why have pieces you don't really like taking up space that could be allotted for new pieces you do like? There is a bonus to this idea, too. The pieces you bought in the past have escalated in value from their original suggested retail price. Not only will you have additional room, you'll have more money to spend on new pieces.

Q. *Why does Department 56 continue to introduce so many pieces each year?*

A. There are a number of reasons. But before we get into them, do you realize that in each village (except, of course, North Pole and Disney Parks) they introduce approximately the same number of buildings, if not less, than they did nine or ten years ago? It's true! Thumb through the pages of GREEN-BOOK and count the number of introductions. You'll be surprised.

To answer your question: You have to keep in mind that Department 56 is a company and must remain profitable. This is not to say that they couldn't introduce one or two fewer buildings a year per village and not remain profitable. But they have other concerns as well. They must address the fact that collectors are in various stages of their collections. Some collectors have been collecting for many years. Others have been enjoying the hobby for just a few years, and others are new collectors. Because of this, they cannot market their product as they did five or six years ago when the majority of the collector base was fairly new.

Imagine if Department 56 drastically reduced the number of yearly introductions. Many collectors would be very disgruntled to learn that their new collections had only two new pieces introduced in December and none at the midyear introductions next May. What about that school or bank you've been wanting to be introduced? With only two or three introductions a year, it may take six or seven years before they get here. With seven or ten introductions per village, collectors have an assortment from which to choose.

Q&Ask The Historian

Q. How can I learn even more about Department 56 and the villages?

A. Subscribe to *the Village Chronicle* magazine. It is a bimonthly magazine that I publish for the enjoyment of Department 56 collectors. Each issue entertains and informs you with page after page of:
- accurate, timely information
- articles written by nationally recognized Department 56 authorities
- display advice & tips
- product highlights
- the "New Stand" for new collectors
- secondary market updates
- a calendar of Department 56 events
- classified ads so you can buy, sell, and trade
- and always much more

Learn things that you never knew about these wonderful little houses…refresh those that you did. Stay current with the latest trends and market values. Enjoy your collection like you never have before. Discover why so many collectors consider *the Village Chronicle* magazine to be the premier source of information about Department 56.

Don't miss another issue. Subscribe today!

$24 for one year   (Canadian res: $29 US funds)
$44 for two years (Canadian res: $49 US funds)
R.I. residents add 7% sales tax.

Visa, MasterCard, Discover, American Express, Checks accepted

Subscribe by phone, fax, mail, internet, or visit our web site.

Phone: 401-467-9343
Fax: 401-467-9359
Internet: d56er@aol.com
Web Site: http://www.villagechronicle.com
mail: the Village Chronicle
           757 Park Ave.
           Cranston, RI 02910

Q&Ask The Historian

THE VILLAGES

Snow Village

Dickens' Village

NEW ENGLAND VILLAGE

ALPINE VILLAGE

CHRISTMAS IN THE CITY

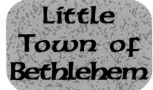

Little Town of Bethlehem

North Pole

Disney Parks Village

THE ACCESSORIES

Snow Village Accessories

Heritage Village Accessories

Add'l Village Accessories

☐ **NAME:** Mountain Lodge   1976
     ITEM #: 5001-3
     STATUS: Retired 1979

MATERIAL: Ceramic
DESCRIPTION: Bright colored skis lean against two-story lodge, upper windows painted to appear as lead panes, sunburst painted above door, snow laden tree at side.
PARTICULARS: Lighted.

OSRP: $20.00
GBTru: $325.00   ↓13%

Gabled Cottage

☐ **NAME:** Gabled Cottage   1976
     ITEM #: 5002-1
     STATUS: Retired 1979

MATERIAL: Ceramic
DESCRIPTION: Four-peaked roof with two chimneys, curtained windows, welcome mat. Ivy climbs walls to roof and door, several windows have wreath design. Attached snow laden tree with bluebird.
PARTICULARS: Lighted.

OSRP: $20.00
GBTru: $350.00   NC

The Inn

☐ **NAME:** The Inn   1976
     ITEM #: 5003-9
     STATUS: Retired 1979

MATERIAL: Ceramic
DESCRIPTION: Two large brick chimneys, full length covered porch, welcome mat at timbered front doors, attached snow laden tree on side, bright yellow door on opposite side.
PARTICULARS: Lighted.

OSRP: $20.00
GBTru: $365.00   ↓19%

Country Church

☐ **NAME:** Country Church   1976
     ITEM #: 5004-7
     STATUS: Retired 1979

MATERIAL: Ceramic
DESCRIPTION: Vines and painted welcome on walls, short-spired, door ajar, circular upper window, painted side windows, snow laden tree shades one wall.
PARTICULARS: Lighted. Also known as "Wayside Chapel".

OSRP: $18.00
GBTru: $345.00   ↓10%

☐ **NAME:** Steepled Church 1976
ITEM #: 5005-4
STATUS: Retired 1979

MATERIAL: Ceramic
DESCRIPTION: One spire, large circular window over double wood front doors flanked by leaded lattice design windows, side Chapel, snow covered tree, bluebird on steeple.
PARTICULARS: Lighted.

OSRP: $25.00
GBTru: $515.00 ↓18%

Small Chalet

☐ **NAME:** Small Chalet 1976
ITEM #: 5006-2
STATUS: Retired 1979

MATERIAL: Ceramic
DESCRIPTION: Two-story small gingerbread look home, flower box with snow covered plants set off large windows on upper story. Bluebirds decorate corners of flower box. Attached tree.
PARTICULARS: Lighted. Also known as "Gingerbread Chalet".
VARIATIONS: In number of flowers in box and color–tan to dark brown.

OSRP: $15.00
GBTru: $375.00 ↓6%

Victorian House

☐ **NAME:** Victorian House 1977
ITEM #: 5007-0
STATUS: Retired 1979

MATERIAL: Ceramic
DESCRIPTION: Textured to portray shingles and clapboard. Steps lead up to front door. Stained glass inserts above windows. Attached snow laden evergreen tree.
PARTICULARS: Lighted.
VARIATIONS: In color, with and without three birds on roof, and with and without attached tree.

OSRP: $30.00
GBTru: $395.00 ↓13%

Mansion

☐ **NAME:** Mansion 1977
ITEM #: 5008-8
STATUS: Retired 1979

MATERIAL: Ceramic
DESCRIPTION: White brick with porch supported by pillars, windows are shuttered, two chimneys plus cupola on roof. Attached snow laden evergreen tree.
PARTICULARS: Lighted.
VARIATIONS: In roof color.

OSRP: $30.00
GBTru: $495.00 NC

The Original Snow Village

❒ **NAME:** Stone Church   1977
    ITEM #: 5009-6
    STATUS: Retired 1979

MATERIAL: Ceramic
DESCRIPTION: Norman style stone building, steeple with ceramic bell. Double doors with circular window above, snow laden evergreen tree.
PARTICULARS: Lighted. This is the original Stone Church. Ceramic bell is separate, attached by wire. See 1979, #5059-1 and 1982, #5083-0.

OSRP: $35.00
GBTru: $555.00 ↓11%

Homestead

❒ **NAME:** Homestead   1978
    ITEM #: 5011-2
    STATUS: Retired 1984

MATERIAL: Ceramic
DESCRIPTION: Old fashioned farmhouse, front porch full length of house. Second floor bay windows. Triple window in front gable. Attached tree.
PARTICULARS: Lighted.

OSRP: $30.00
GBTru: $195.00 ↓22%

General Store

❒ **NAME:** General Store   1978
    ITEM #: 5012-0
    STATUS: Retired 1980

MATERIAL: Ceramic
DESCRIPTION: Full length porch supported by pillars. Sign above porch. Christmas tree on porch roof. Store supplied food, postal service and gas.
PARTICULARS: Lighted.
VARIATIONS: Variations in color–White, Tan and Gold–and in **sign lettering:** "Y & L" and "S & L Brothers." Variations affect GREENBOOK Trumarket Price. White–$435.00 (↓3%), Tan–$535.00 (↓8%) and Gold–$545.00 (↓1%).

OSRP: $25.00
GBTru: See Variations

Cape Cod

❒ **NAME:** Cape Cod   1978
    ITEM #: 5013-8
    STATUS: Retired 1980

MATERIAL: Ceramic
DESCRIPTION: Steep gabled roof with chimney, small dormer and painted landscaping. Attached snow laden tree.
PARTICULARS: Lighted.

OSRP: $20.00
GBTru: $385.00 ↑3%

❐ **NAME:** Nantucket   1978
   ITEM #: 5014-6
   STATUS: Retired 1986

MATERIAL: Ceramic
DESCRIPTION: Yellow cottage with green roof. Small front porch, attached greenhouse.
PARTICULARS: Lighted. See *Nantucket Renovation*, 1993, #5441-0.

OSRP: $25.00
GBTru: $235.00 ↓15%

Skating Rink/Duck Pond Set

❐ **NAME:** Skating Rink/Duck Pond Set   1978
   ITEM #: 5015-3
   STATUS: Retired 1979

MATERIAL: Ceramic
DESCRIPTION: One large snow laden tree with snowman and log pile. Other large snow laden tree with park bench and birds.
PARTICULARS: Set of 2. Lighted. One of the first non-house accessory pieces. (Skating Rink is the piece with the snowman.) Trees were attached directly to pond bases–their size and weight caused frequent breakage, therefore retired in 1979. Revised Skating Pond in 1982, #5017-2, with trees molded separately.

OSRP: $16.00
GBTru: $970.00 ↓3%

Small Double Trees

❐ **NAME:** Small Double Trees   1978
   ITEM #: 5016-1
   STATUS: Retired 1989

MATERIAL: Ceramic
DESCRIPTION: Small lighted snow laden trees with birds.
PARTICULARS: Lighted. One of the first non-house accessory pieces. Approximately 8 to 8 ½" tall.
VARIATIONS: Variations affect GREENBOOK Trumarket Price. First, with blue birds–$175.00 (NC), then red birds–$40.00 (↓20%). Mold changes and variations in amount of snow over the years as well.

OSRP: $13.50
GBTru: See Variations

Victorian

❐ **NAME:** Victorian   1979
   ITEM #: 5054-2
   STATUS: Retired 1982

MATERIAL: Ceramic
DESCRIPTION: Steps lead to covered porch entry, three story turret, small balcony on third floor front room.
PARTICULARS: Lighted.
VARIATIONS: In color and exterior finish. They are–in order of desirability–Peach, Gold and Gold Clapboard.

OSRP: $30.00
GBTru: $315.00 ↓10%

Knob Hill

☐ **NAME:** Knob Hill   1979
ITEM #: 5055-9
STATUS: Retired 1981

MATERIAL: Ceramic
DESCRIPTION: Three story San Francisco-style Victorian row house, steep steps to entry level.
PARTICULARS: Lighted.
VARIATIONS: Two color variations–gray or yellow. Variations affect GREENBOOK Trumarket Price. Gray–$265.00 (↓10%), yellow–$345.00 (↓8%).

OSRP: $30.00
GBTru: See Variations

Brownstone

☐ **NAME:** Brownstone   1979
ITEM #: 5056-7
STATUS: Retired 1981

MATERIAL: Ceramic
DESCRIPTION: Three stories with wreath trimmed bay windows on all floors, overall flat roof.
PARTICULARS: Lighted.
VARIATIONS: In roof color–gray and red. Red most desired.

OSRP: $36.00
GBTru: $545.00 ↓5%

Log Cabin

☐ **NAME:** Log Cabin   1979
ITEM #: 5057-5
STATUS: Retired 1981

MATERIAL: Ceramic
DESCRIPTION: Rustic log house with stone chimney, roof extends to cover porch, log pile at side, skis by door.
PARTICULARS: Lighted.

OSRP: $22.00
GBTru: $400.00 ↓16%

Countryside Church

☐ **NAME:** Countryside Church   1979
ITEM #: 5058-3
STATUS: Retired 1984

MATERIAL: Ceramic
DESCRIPTION: White clapboard church with central bell steeple, attached tree has all lower branches pruned.
PARTICULARS: Lighted. For no snow version, see MEADOWLAND 1979, *Countryside Church*, #5051-8.

OSRP: $27.50
GBTru: $260.00 ↓12%

Stone Church

☐ **NAME:** Stone Church   1979
ITEM #: 5059-1
STATUS: Retired 1980

MATERIAL: Ceramic
DESCRIPTION: Steeple attached to one side has separate entry. Circular window above front doors.
PARTICULARS: Lighted. Height is 8 ½". Ceramic bell is separate, attaches with wire. See 1977, #5009-6 and 1982, #5083-0.

OSRP: $32.00
GBTru: $915.00 ↓8%

School House

☐ **NAME:** School House   1979
ITEM #: 5060-9
STATUS: Retired 1982

MATERIAL: Ceramic–removable Metal flag
DESCRIPTION: American flag flies from roof peak above red brick one-room school.
PARTICULARS: Lighted. First design to feature the American flag.

OSRP: $30.00
GBTru: $365.00 ↑6%

Tudor House

☐ **NAME:** Tudor House   1979
ITEM #: 5061-7
STATUS: Retired 1981

MATERIAL: Ceramic
DESCRIPTION: Brick chimney and fireplace on simple L-shaped timber trimmed home, split-shingle roof.
PARTICULARS: Lighted.

OSRP: $25.00
GBTru: $285.00 ↓12%

Mission Church

☐ **NAME:** Mission Church   1979
ITEM #: 5062-5
STATUS: Retired 1980

MATERIAL: Ceramic
DESCRIPTION: Sun dried clay with structural timbers visible at roof line. Small arched bell tower above entry.
PARTICULARS: Lighted. Ceramic bell is attached by wire.

OSRP: $30.00
GBTru: $1100.00 ↓12%

The Original Snow Village

NAME: Mobile Home   1979
ITEM #: 5063-3
STATUS: Retired 1980

MATERIAL: Ceramic
DESCRIPTION: Similar to aluminum skinned Airstream mobile home. To be towed by car or truck for travel.
PARTICULARS: Lighted.

OSRP: $18.00
GBTru: $1865.00   ↑7%

❏ **NAME:** Giant Trees   1979
ITEM #: 5065-8
STATUS: Retired 1982

MATERIAL: Ceramic
DESCRIPTION: Snow covered large evergreen trees. Birds perch on branches.
PARTICULARS: Lighted. Approximately 11" tall.

OSRP: $20.00
GBTru: $335.00   ↓7%

❏ **NAME:** Adobe House   1979
ITEM #: 5066-6
STATUS: Retired 1980

MATERIAL: Ceramic
DESCRIPTION: Small sun dried clay home. Outside oven on side, chili peppers hang from roof beams.
PARTICULARS: Lighted.

OSRP: $18.00
GBTru: $2150.00   ↓14%

❏ **NAME:** Cathedral Church   1980
ITEM #: 5067-4
STATUS: Retired 1981

MATERIAL: Ceramic–stained glass windows are Acrylic
DESCRIPTION: Central dome with two shorter bell towers.
PARTICULARS: Lighted. Production problems (fragile domes) forced retirement after one year. Inspired by St. Paul's Cathedral in St. Paul, MN.

OSRP: $36.00
GBTru: $2100.00   ↑5%

Stone Mill House

❒ **NAME:** Stone Mill House   1980
ITEM #: 5068-2
STATUS: Retired 1982

MATERIAL: Ceramic
DESCRIPTION: Water wheel on dark weathered stone block mill, bag of grain hangs from block and tackle, another bag propped by door.
PARTICULARS: Lighted. Separate bag of oats hung with wire. *GREENBOOK Trumarket Price for pieces without the bag of oats is $350.00.

OSRP: $30.00
GBTru: $425.00*↓14%

Colonial Farm House

❒ **NAME:** Colonial Farm House   1980
ITEM #: 5070-9
STATUS: Retired 1982

MATERIAL: Ceramic
DESCRIPTION: Wide front porch, two front dormers in attic, symmetrical layout of windows.
PARTICULARS: Lighted. Same Item # was used for the 1986 *All Saints Church.*

OSRP: $30.00
GBTru: $315.00 ↓16%

Town Church

❒ **NAME:** Town Church   1980
ITEM #: 5071-7
STATUS: Retired 1982

MATERIAL: Ceramic
DESCRIPTION: Short bell tower rises from central nave area, attached tree tucks in close to side chapel.
PARTICULARS: Lighted. Same Item # was used for the 1986 *Carriage House.*

OSRP: $33.00
GBTru: $355.00 ↓5%

Train Station With 3 Train Cars

❒ **NAME:** Train Station With 3 Train Cars   1980
ITEM #: 5085-6
STATUS: Retired 1985

MATERIAL: Ceramic
DESCRIPTION: Station clock over entry door, 2 small wings on either side of main room, brick and timbered design. Train-engine, passenger car, baggage/mail caboose. "G&N RR" on all cars.
PARTICULARS: Set of 4. Lighted. First Original Snow Village train and station design. All 4 pieces are lit. (Train not pictured.)
VARIATIONS: Original Station–smaller in size, 6 window panes, round window in door, brick on front only. GBTru: $425 (↑8%).
Revised Station–8 window panes, 2 square windows in door, brick on front and sides. GBTru: $330 (↑2%).

OSRP: $100.00
GBTru: See Variations

NAME: Wooden Clapboard 1981
ITEM #: 5072-5
STATUS: Retired 1984

MATERIAL: Ceramic
DESCRIPTION: White house with green roof and trim and wrap-around porch. Red brick chimney.
PARTICULARS: Lighted.

OSRP: $32.00
GBTru: $210.00 ↓19%

English Cottage

NAME: English Cottage 1981
ITEM #: 5073-3
STATUS: Retired 1982

MATERIAL: Ceramic
DESCRIPTION: Thatched roof and timbered frame, two chimneys. 1 ½ stories. Roof comes down to meet top of first story.
PARTICULARS: Lighted.
VARIATIONS: In color of thatched roof.

OSRP: $25.00
GBTru: $275.00 ↓7%

Barn

NAME: Barn 1981
ITEM #: 5074-1
STATUS: Retired 1984

MATERIAL: Ceramic
DESCRIPTION: Red barn and silo. Gray roof, two vents on roof ridge, root cellar on side, hay loft over animals and equipment.
PARTICULARS: Lighted. Aka "Original Barn".

OSRP: $32.00
GBTru: $410.00 ↓11%

Corner Store

NAME: Corner Store 1981
ITEM #: 5076-8
STATUS: Retired 1983

MATERIAL: Ceramic
DESCRIPTION: Red brick with one large display window, entry door on corner, bay window in family living area, shutters on windows, shingled roof.
PARTICULARS: Lighted. Same Item # was used for the 1986 *Apothecary*.

OSRP: $30.00
GBTru: $205.00 ↓16%

☐ **NAME:** Bakery   1981
ITEM #: 5077-6
STATUS: Retired 1983

MATERIAL: Ceramic
DESCRIPTION: Bakery store beneath family living area, half-turret form gives unique angle to front and second story bay window.
PARTICULARS: Lighted. This is the original *Bakery*. Same Item # was used for the 1986 *Bakery*–a new and different design. Designed after The Scofield Building in Northfield, MN.

OSRP: $30.00
GBTru: $255.00 ↑2%

English Church

☐ **NAME:** English Church   1981
ITEM #: 5078-4
STATUS: Retired 1982

MATERIAL: Ceramic
DESCRIPTION: Steep pitched roof, side chapel, steeple topped by gold cross, arched windows, triangular window in gable above entry double doors.
PARTICULARS: Lighted. The Cross is separate and inserts into the steeple. Same Item # was used for the 1986 *Diner*.

OSRP: $30.00
GBTru: $365.00 ↓8%

Large Single Tree

☐ **NAME:** Large Single Tree   1981
ITEM #: 5080-6
STATUS: Retired 1989

MATERIAL: Ceramic
DESCRIPTION: One snow covered evergreen tree. Birds perch on branches.
PARTICULARS: Lighted. Approximately 9" tall.
VARIATIONS: Mold changes and variations in amount of snow over the years.

OSRP: $17.00
GBTru: $35.00 ↓22%

Skating Pond

☐ **NAME:** Skating Pond   1982
ITEM #: 5017-2
STATUS: Retired 1984

MATERIAL: Ceramic
DESCRIPTION: Snowman on edge of small snow covered skating pond. Tree trunks piled together provide seating. Two evergreen trees complete the set.
PARTICULARS: Set of 2. Lighted. Replaces the *Skating Rink/ Duck Pond Set*, 1978. #5015-3. Has two trees. Trees are separate from the pond.

OSRP: $25.00
GBTru: $360.00 ↓5%

Street Car

❐ **NAME:** Street Car
ITEM #: 5019-9
STATUS: Retired 1984

1982

MATERIAL: Ceramic
DESCRIPTION: Bright yellow with green "Main Street" sign on side. #2 car, hook-up on top for pole to connect to electric power.
PARTICULARS: Lighted.

OSRP: $16.00
GBTru: $325.00 ↓18%

Centennial House

❐ **NAME:** Centennial House
ITEM #: 5020-2
STATUS: Retired 1984

1982

MATERIAL: Ceramic
DESCRIPTION: Two story clapboard, square tower, carved and curved window frames, "wooden" balcony and porch.
PARTICULARS: Lighted.

OSRP: $32.00
GBTru: $305.00 ↓13%

Carriage House

❐ **NAME:** Carriage House
ITEM #: 5021-0
STATUS: Retired 1984

1982

MATERIAL: Ceramic
DESCRIPTION: Bright lamps flank entry to storage area for carriages. Driver has small apartment above.
PARTICULARS: Lighted.

OSRP: $28.00
GBTru: $290.00 ↓11%

Pioneer Church

❐ **NAME:** Pioneer Church
ITEM #: 5022-9
STATUS: Retired 1984

1982

MATERIAL: Ceramic
DESCRIPTION: Simple design appears to be of wood construction, front notice board sends joy to all who pass, short steeple on front of roof ridge.
PARTICULARS: Lighted.

OSRP: $30.00
GBTru: $310.00 ↑3%

☐ **NAME:** Swiss Chalet   1982
     ITEM #: 5023-7
     STATUS: Retired 1984

MATERIAL: Ceramic
DESCRIPTION: Stone base walls support timber upper stories.
Upper floor has front balcony with railing and is enclosed by
roof overhang. Unusual roof.
PARTICULARS: Lighted.

OSRP: $28.00
GBTru: $410.00   ↓9%

☐ **NAME:** Bank   1982
     ITEM #: 5024-5
     STATUS: Retired 1983

MATERIAL: Ceramic
DESCRIPTION: Corner building with entry by revolving door.
Outside covered stairway leads to second story. Sign becomes
part of corner design.
PARTICULARS: Lighted. Same Item # was used for the 1987
Cumberland House.

OSRP: $32.00
GBTru: $585.00   ↓2%

☐ **NAME:** Gabled House   1982
     ITEM #: 5081-4
     STATUS: Retired 1983

MATERIAL: Ceramic
DESCRIPTION: Shingled house with four-gabled roof, two
small covered porches, one lower and one upper window
to each side.
PARTICULARS: Lighted. Same Item # was used for the 1987
Red Barn. Early release to Gift Creations Concepts (GCC).

OSRP: $30.00
GBTru: $320.00 ↓18%

☐ **NAME:** Flower Shop   1982
     ITEM #: 5082-2
     STATUS: Retired 1983

MATERIAL: Ceramic
DESCRIPTION: Flower boxes rest outside by large display
window. Rolled up awnings above front windows.
PARTICULARS: Lighted. Same Item # was used for the 1987
Jefferson School.
VARIATIONS: In color.

OSRP: $25.00
GBTru: $450.00   NC

	NAME:	New Stone Church	1982
	ITEM #:	5083-0	
	STATUS:	Retired 1984	

MATERIAL: Ceramic
DESCRIPTION: Long nave with side chapel, stone block construction, steeple rises on side opposite chapel. Front has arched windows and two lamps.
PARTICULARS: Lighted. Early release to Gift Creations Concepts (GCC).

OSRP: $32.00
GBTru: $330.00 ↓16%

Town Hall

	NAME:	Town Hall	1983
	ITEM #:	5000-8	
	STATUS:	Retired 1984	

MATERIAL: Ceramic–stamped Metal weather vane is separate
DESCRIPTION: Brick and stone, two corner covered side entries, symmetrical design (window over window), steeple above front main wall.
PARTICULARS: Lighted. Ceramic bell in tower.

OSRP: $32.00
GBTru: $315.00 ↓9%

Grocery

	NAME:	Grocery	1983
	ITEM #:	5001-6	
	STATUS:	Retired 1985	

MATERIAL: Ceramic
DESCRIPTION: Red brick, full painted display windows, decorative cornice trim above/below front windows. Outside staircase leads to family quarters.
PARTICULARS: Lighted.

OSRP: $35.00
GBTru: $325.00 NC

Victorian Cottage

	NAME:	Victorian Cottage	1983
	ITEM #:	5002-4	
	STATUS:	Retired 1984	

MATERIAL: Ceramic
DESCRIPTION: Ornate carved woodwork on house front, ornamental arched entry design. First floor French windows separated by pillars.
PARTICULARS: Lighted.

OSRP: $35.00
GBTru: $305.00 ↓16%

Governor's Mansion

☐ **NAME:** Governor's Mansion 1983
ITEM #: 5003-2
STATUS: Retired 1985

MATERIAL: Ceramic–Metal trim on front tower
DESCRIPTION: Brick, metal ironwork featured on roof cupola, wide entry steps, repetitive design above door, second story, and central attic windows.
PARTICULARS: Lighted.

OSRP: $32.00
GBTru: $280.00 ↑2%

Turn Of The Century

☐ **NAME:** Turn Of The Century 1983
ITEM #: 5004-0
STATUS: Retired 1986

MATERIAL: Ceramic
DESCRIPTION: Steps lead to covered entry, front triangular ornate design crowns front gable, squared turret rises from left front corner and ends in highest roof peak.
PARTICULARS: Lighted.

OSRP: $36.00
GBTru: $245.00 ↓4%

Village Church

☐ **NAME:** Village Church 1983
ITEM #: 5026-1
STATUS: Retired 1984

MATERIAL: Ceramic
DESCRIPTION: Stone steps lead to double carved doors, design repeats on roof trim. Steeple has long narrow openings. Pointed arch windows are featured.
PARTICULARS: Lighted. Early release to Gift Creations Concepts (GCC).

OSRP: $30.00
GBTru: $385.00 ↑3%

Gothic Church

☐ **NAME:** Gothic Church 1983
ITEM #: 5028-8
STATUS: Retired 1986

MATERIAL: Ceramic
DESCRIPTION: Stone block, steeple rises straight from large double doors ending in a cross. Bell chamber has ornate grillwork. Smaller entry doors flank central area repeating design.
PARTICULARS: Lighted.

OSRP: $36.00
GBTru: $235.00 ↓15%

Parsonage

☐ **NAME:** Parsonage   1983
ITEM #: 5029-6
STATUS: Retired 1985

MATERIAL: Ceramic
DESCRIPTION: Tower rises above entry. Ornate coping on front gable topped by Cross. Coping details repeated around windows, doors and small balcony. Community rooms on first floor, family lives upstairs.
PARTICULARS: Lighted.

OSRP: $35.00
GBTru: $300.00 ↓14%

Wooden Church

☐ **NAME:** Wooden Church   1983
ITEM #: 5031-8
STATUS: Retired 1985

MATERIAL: Ceramic
DESCRIPTION: White clapboard, crossed timber design repeats over door, roof peak, and steeple. Side chapel has separate entry door.
PARTICULARS: Lighted.

OSRP: $30.00
GBTru: $285.00 ↓19%

Fire Station

☐ **NAME:** Fire Station   1983
ITEM #: 5032-6
STATUS: Retired 1984

MATERIAL: Ceramic
DESCRIPTION: Central door opens to reveal red fire truck. Brick columns from base to roof add to sturdy look. Dalmatian sits by entry, ready when necessary.
PARTICULARS: Lighted.
VARIATIONS: Without dog.

OSRP: $32.00
GBTru: $550.00 ↓12%

English Tudor

☐ **NAME:** English Tudor   1983
ITEM #: 5033-4
STATUS: Retired 1985

MATERIAL: Ceramic
DESCRIPTION: Stucco finish. Brick chimneys. Three front roof peaks create front gable design.
PARTICULARS: Lighted.

OSRP: $30.00
GBTru: $225.00 ↓24%

❏ **NAME:** Chateau   1983
    ITEM #: 5084-9
    STATUS: Retired 1984

MATERIAL: Ceramic
DESCRIPTION: First story large windows which include front and side bow windows are a feature. Diamond design on roof shingles, stone for walls, cylindrical chimney with domed flue cap. Front dormers and side peaks exhibit ornate carved design.
PARTICULARS: Lighted. Early release to Gift Creations Concepts (GCC).

OSRP: $35.00
GBTru: $445.00 ↓6%

❏ **NAME:** Main Street House   1984
    ITEM #: 5005-9
    STATUS: Retired 1986

MATERIAL: Ceramic
DESCRIPTION: White and green 1-1/2 story house. Clapboard lower story with timbered upper story, two lamps outside front door.
PARTICULARS: Lighted. Early release to Gift Creations Concepts (GCC).

OSRP: $27.00
GBTru: $225.00 ↓18%

❏ **NAME:** Stratford House   1984
    ITEM #: 5007-5
    STATUS: Retired 1986

MATERIAL: Ceramic
DESCRIPTION: Vertical ornamental timbers featured, gables all rise to same height.
PARTICULARS: Lighted.

OSRP: $28.00
GBTru: $165.00 ↓15%

❏ **NAME:** Haversham House   1984
    ITEM #: 5008-3
    STATUS: Retired 1987

MATERIAL: Ceramic
DESCRIPTION: All gables, balconies, porch, decorated with ornately carved woodwork.
PARTICULARS: Lighted. Early release to Gift Creations Concepts (GCC).
VARIATIONS: Size: Early release pieces are larger than subsequent ones.

OSRP: $37.00
GBTru: $240.00 ↓20%

❏ **NAME:** Galena House   1984
ITEM #: 5009-1
STATUS: Retired 1985

MATERIAL: Ceramic
DESCRIPTION: Steps lead to double entry doors of brick home. Bay window fills one side. Second floor incorporated into roof construction.
PARTICULARS: Lighted.

OSRP: $32.00
GBTru: $285.00 ↓17%

River Road House

❏ **NAME:** River Road House   1984
ITEM #: 5010-5
STATUS: Retired 1987

MATERIAL: Ceramic
DESCRIPTION: White house, large and grand with many windows, first floor front windows are highlighted with half circle paned glass above them, side bay windows project out from house wall.
PARTICULARS: Lighted. Early release to Gift Creations Concepts (GCC).
VARIATIONS: In window cuts.

OSRP: $36.00
GBTru: $185.00 ↓14%

Delta House

❏ **NAME:** Delta House   1984
ITEM #: 5012-1
STATUS: Retired 1986

MATERIAL: Ceramic–"Iron works" atop tower
DESCRIPTION: Brick house with balcony above wrap-around porch which is separate from entry. Porch design is repeated where roof and brick meet and on turret.
PARTICULARS: Lighted.

OSRP: $32.00
GBTru: $260.00 ↓16%

Bayport

❏ **NAME:** Bayport   1984
ITEM #: 5015-6
STATUS: Retired 1986

MATERIAL: Ceramic
DESCRIPTION: Corner entry with a turret addition positioned between the two main wings of two story house.
PARTICULARS: Lighted.

OSRP: $30.00
GBTru: $210.00 ↓11%

Congregational Church

❏ **NAME:** Congregational Church   1984
     ITEM #: 5034-2
     STATUS: Retired 1985

MATERIAL: Ceramic
DESCRIPTION: Brick with fieldstone front. Stone repeated on steeple. Louver vents on belfry.
PARTICULARS: Lighted.

OSRP: $28.00
GBTru: $615.00   ⬆3%

Trinity Church

❏ **NAME:** Trinity Church   1984
     ITEM #: 5035-0
     STATUS: Retired 1986

MATERIAL: Ceramic
DESCRIPTION: Steeples of different heights, clerestory windows to bring additional light to nave, two large wreaths by front doors.
PARTICULARS: Lighted.

OSRP: $32.00
GBTru: $245.00   ⬇20%

Summit House

❏ **NAME:** Summit House   1984
     ITEM #: 5036-9
     STATUS: Retired 1985

MATERIAL: Ceramic
DESCRIPTION: Corner house features rounded turret, large entry door with side lights, cornices appear to support roof edge. Each second story window capped by a molded projection.
PARTICULARS: Lighted.

OSRP: $28.00
GBTru: $310.00   ⬇19%

New School House

❏ **NAME:** New School House   1984
     ITEM #: 5037-7
     STATUS: Retired 1986

MATERIAL: Ceramic–separate Paper flag has a Wooden pole
DESCRIPTION: Two story schoolhouse with bell tower and clock.
PARTICULARS: Lighted.

OSRP: $35.00
GBTru: $215.00   ⬇22%

☐ **NAME:** Parish Church   1984
ITEM #: 5039-3
STATUS: Retired 1986

MATERIAL: Ceramic
DESCRIPTION: White country church with unique three-level steeple. Arched windows, red door, circular window over entry.
PARTICULARS: Lighted.

OSRP: $32.00
GBTru: $285.00 ↓23%

☐ **NAME:** Stucco Bungalow   1985
ITEM #: 5045-8
STATUS: Retired 1986

MATERIAL: Ceramic
DESCRIPTION: Two story small house with one roof dormer as mini tower, second dormer features timbered design. Entry door built into archway under a low roof peak. Wreath and garland decorate door.
PARTICULARS: Lighted.

OSRP: $30.00
GBTru: $340.00 ↓14%

☐ **NAME:** Williamsburg House   1985
ITEM #: 5046-6
STATUS: Retired 1988

MATERIAL: Ceramic
DESCRIPTION: Traditional two story colonial, all windows shuttered, three dormers, two chimneys, covered entry topped by second floor balcony.
PARTICULARS: Lighted.

OSRP: $37.00
GBTru: $165.00 ↑22%

☐ **NAME:** Plantation House   1985
ITEM #: 5047-4
STATUS: Retired 1987

MATERIAL: Ceramic
DESCRIPTION: Entry features two story wood columns, three dormers, two chimneys, four first floor front windows have canopies.
PARTICULARS: Lighted.

OSRP: $37.00
GBTru: $120.00 ↑4%

Church Of The Open Door

☐ **NAME:** Church Of The Open Door   1985
    ITEM #: 5048-2
    STATUS: Retired 1988

MATERIAL: Ceramic
DESCRIPTION: Steeple is on side chapel. Design over front entry above circular window has small repeated motif on eaves.
PARTICULARS: Lighted.

OSRP: $34.00
GBTru: $130.00   ↑4%

Spruce Place

☐ **NAME:** Spruce Place   1985
    ITEM #: 5049-0
    STATUS: Retired 1987

MATERIAL: Ceramic
DESCRIPTION: Victorian with windowed turret rising above covered porch. Decorative molding above porch, windows, dormer. Circular window over porch decorated with wreath.
PARTICULARS: Lighted.

OSRP: $33.00
GBTru: $255.00   ↓7%

Duplex

☐ **NAME:** Duplex   1985
    ITEM #: 5050-4
    STATUS: Retired 1987

MATERIAL: Ceramic
DESCRIPTION: A two-family house with shared entry. Each family had up/down rooms and a bay window. Design has small second story balcony and roof dormers.
PARTICULARS: Lighted.

OSRP: $35.00
GBTru: $155.00   ↓6%

Depot And Train With 2 Train Cars

☐ **NAME:** Depot And Train With 2 Train Cars   1985
    ITEM #: 5051-2
    STATUS: Retired 1988

MATERIAL: Ceramic–Coal Car has Plastic bag of coal
DESCRIPTION: Two wings connected by a central area, each wing has its own chimney, corners of building fortified with stone blocks.
PARTICULARS: Set of 4. Lighted. Train is non-lighting. Second Original Snow Village train and station design.

OSRP: $65.00
GBTru: $150.00   ↑3%

The Original Snow Village   35

Ridgewood

❐ **NAME:** Ridgewood   1985
    ITEM #: 5052-0
    STATUS: Retired 1987

MATERIAL: Ceramic
DESCRIPTION: Porches run length of both first and second story. First floor front windows are arched and design is repeated over front door and on attic windows.
PARTICULARS: Lighted.

OSRP: $35.00
GBTru: $180.00   ↑6%

Waverly Place

❐ **NAME:** Waverly Place   1986
    ITEM #: 5041-5
    STATUS: Retired 1986

MATERIAL: Ceramic
DESCRIPTION: Ornate Victorian home has two different turret-like window designs. Second story features half moon window highlights and carved moldings.
PARTICULARS: Lighted. Early release to Gift Creations Concepts (GCC), Fall 1985. Designed after the Gingerbread Mansion in Ferndale, CA.

OSRP: $35.00
GBTru: $290.00   ↓11%

Twin Peaks

❐ **NAME:** Twin Peaks   1986
    ITEM #: 5042-3
    STATUS: Retired 1986

MATERIAL: Ceramic
DESCRIPTION: Two matching three story stone turrets, a multitude of windows on each story soften fortress look. Red entry doors reached by wide steps.
PARTICULARS: Lighted. Early release to Gift Creations Concepts (GCC), Fall 1985.

OSRP: $32.00
GBTru: $445.00   ↓15%

2101 Maple

❐ **NAME:** 2101 Maple   1986
    ITEM #: 5043-1
    STATUS: Retired 1986

MATERIAL: Ceramic
DESCRIPTION: Brick two story home. Side of front porch built out from stone turret. Second story windows capped by half circle window.
PARTICULARS: Lighted. Early release to Gift Creations Concepts (GCC), Fall 1985.

OSRP: $32.00
GBTru: $325.00   ↓13%

incoln Park Duplex

☐ **NAME:** Lincoln Park Duplex   1986
    ITEM #: 5060-1
    STATUS: Retired 1988

MATERIAL: Ceramic
DESCRIPTION: Two-family attached home. Each has two story bay windows and share a front door. Floor plan's unique feature is placement of chimneys–as if floor plans reversed, one is at front, other is at rear.
PARTICULARS: Lighted.

OSRP: $33.00
GBTru: $135.00 ↑8%

onoma House

☐ **NAME:** Sonoma House   1986
    ITEM #: 5062-8
    STATUS: Retired 1988

MATERIAL: Ceramic
DESCRIPTION: Flavor of Southwest. Stucco walls, red roof. Decorative curved front rises 2 $\frac{1}{2}$ stories. Square turret adjacent to front door capped by same design which repeats on chimney.
PARTICULARS: Lighted. Early release to Gift Creations Concepts (GCC), Fall 1986.

OSRP: $33.00
GBTru: $140.00 ↑17%

Highland Park House

☐ **NAME:** Highland Park House   1986
    ITEM #: 5063-6
    STATUS: Retired 1988

MATERIAL: Ceramic
DESCRIPTION: Brick, timbered, and gabled house brings English Tudor design to cozy home. Rounded arch front door repeats theme in two windows in mid-roof gable. Brick chimney on side.
PARTICULARS: Lighted. Early release to Gift Creations Concepts (GCC), Fall 1986.

OSRP: $35.00
GBTru: $160.00   ↑7%

Beacon Hill House

☐ **NAME:** Beacon Hill House   1986
    ITEM #: 5065-2
    STATUS: Retired 1988

MATERIAL: Ceramic
DESCRIPTION: A row house, typical of urban Boston, MA neighborhoods. Has a solid compact look. Features bay windows on first and second story highlighted by paneled framing.
PARTICULARS: Lighted.

OSRP: $31.00
GBTru: $165.00 ↑10%

☐ **NAME:** Pacific Heights House   1986
ITEM #: 5066-0
STATUS: Retired 1988

MATERIAL: Ceramic
DESCRIPTION: A West Coast row house that appears tall and narrow based on repeated vertical theme of front porch/balcony support columns.
PARTICULARS: Lighted.

OSRP: $33.00
GBTru: $105.00 ↑5%

☐ **NAME:** Ramsey Hill House   1986
ITEM #: 5067-9
STATUS: Retired 1989

MATERIAL: Ceramic
DESCRIPTION: Victorian with double chimneys. Steps to front door, porch is adjacent to entry. Side door also features small porch. Low balustrade fronts second story windows. Hand painting adds detailing to design.
PARTICULARS: Lighted. Early release to Gift Creations Concepts (GCC), Fall 1986.

OSRP: $36.00
GBTru: $95.00 NC

☐ **NAME:** Saint James Church   1986
ITEM #: 5068-7
STATUS: Retired 1988

MATERIAL: Ceramic
DESCRIPTION: Long central nave flanked by lower roofed side sections fronted by two towers. Gold main cross reinforced by smaller crosses on each section of tower roof. Smaller round windows repeat central window shape.
PARTICULARS: Lighted.

OSRP: $37.00
GBTru: $155.00 ↓11%

☐ **NAME:** All Saints Church   1986
ITEM #: 5070-9
STATUS: Current

MATERIAL: Ceramic
DESCRIPTION: Smaller country church, simple design of long nave with entry door in base of bell tower.
PARTICULARS: Lighted. Same Item # was used for the 1980 *Colonial Farm House.*

OSRP: $38.00
GBTru: $45.00 NC

Carriage House

☐ **NAME:** Carriage House   1986
    ITEM #: 5071-7
    STATUS: Retired 1988

MATERIAL: Ceramic
DESCRIPTION: Small home from building used originally for carriages. A second story is achieved with many dormer windows. Fieldstone makes up the foundation allowing great weight during original function.
PARTICULARS: Lighted. Same Item # was used for the 1980 *Town Church.*

OSRP: $29.00
GBTru: $115.00 ↑5%

Toy Shop

☐ **NAME:** Toy Shop   1986
    ITEM #: 5073-3
    STATUS: Retired 1990

MATERIAL: Ceramic
DESCRIPTION: Front windows display toys. Roof molding brings focus to teddy bear design under pediment. Three story brick.
PARTICULARS: Lighted. Main Street design. Design is based on the Finch Building in Hastings, MN.

OSRP: $36.00
GBTru: $90.00   NC

Apothecary

☐ **NAME:** Apothecary   1986
    ITEM #: 5076-8
    STATUS: Retired 1990

MATERIAL: Ceramic
DESCRIPTION: Two doors flank a central display bow window. Mortar and pestle symbolizes the profession of owner and is on front panel above second floor family windows.
PARTICULARS: Lighted. Main Street design. Based on Hasting, MN's former City Hall. Some sleeves read "Antique Shop." Same Item # was used for the 1981 *Corner Store.*

OSRP: $34.00
GBTru: $100.00 ↑11%

Bakery

☐ **NAME:** Bakery   1986
    ITEM #: 5077-6
    STATUS: Retired 1991

MATERIAL: Ceramic
DESCRIPTION: Corner bakery with two large multi-paned display windows protected by ribbed canopy. Greek key designs around roof edging highlight the bas-relief cupcake topped by a cherry that is centrally placed over entry.
PARTICULARS: Lighted. Main Street design. Designed after Scofield Building in Northfield, MN. Same Item # was used for first Snow Village Bakery–1981 *Bakery.*

OSRP: $35.00
GBTru: $85.00   NC

❐ **NAME:** Diner   1986
ITEM #: 5078-4
STATUS: Retired 1987

MATERIAL: Ceramic
DESCRIPTION: An eating place based on the railroads' famous dining car. Reputation of good, wholesome food. Large windows are a feature. Glass block entry protects diners from weather as customers come in/go out. Diners generally have counter service as well as a dining room.
PARTICULARS: Lighted. Also known as "Mickey's." Designed after Mickey's Diner in St. Paul, MN. Same Item # was used for the 1981 *English Church.*

OSRP: $22.00
GBTru: $650.00 ↑18%

St. Anthony Hotel & Post Office

❐ **NAME:** St. Anthony Hotel & Post Office   1987
ITEM #: 5006-7
STATUS: Retired 1989

MATERIAL: Ceramic–Metal flag
DESCRIPTION: Three story red brick with green trim. Dated 1886, the address of this hotel is "56 Main Street." American flag flies outside the ground floor Post Office.
PARTICULARS: Lighted. Main Street design.

OSRP: $40.00
GBTru: $115.00 ↑5%

Snow Village Factory

❐ **NAME:** Snow Village Factory   1987
ITEM #: 5013-0
STATUS: Retired 1989

MATERIAL: Ceramic
DESCRIPTION: Wood building rises on stone block base with tall smokestack at rear. Factory products were available in small shop at front.
PARTICULARS: Set of 2. Lighted. Smokestack is separate.

OSRP: $45.00
GBTru: $130.00 ↑8%

Cathedral Church

❐ **NAME:** Cathedral Church   1987
ITEM #: 5019-9
STATUS: Retired 1990

MATERIAL: Ceramic
DESCRIPTION: Mosaic "stained glass" decorates the Gothic windows on all sides, as well as the large turret.
PARTICULARS: Lighted.

OSRP: $50.00
GBTru: $105.00 ↑5%

Cumberland House

	NAME:	Cumberland House	1987
	ITEM #:	5024-5	
	STATUS:	Retired 1995	

MATERIAL: Ceramic
DESCRIPTION: Multi-colored curved roof supported by four columns, two chimneys, shuttered windows.
PARTICULARS: Lighted. Same Item # was used for the 1982 *Bank*.

OSRP: $42.00
GBTru: $65.00 ↑44%

Springfield House

	NAME:	Springfield House	1987
	ITEM #:	5027-0	
	STATUS:	Retired 1990	

MATERIAL: Ceramic
DESCRIPTION: Lower level has two multi-paned bay windows, one is bowed. Upper level windows are shuttered. Roof dormers are half-circle sunbursts. Stone chimney completes this clapboard home.
PARTICULARS: Lighted.

OSRP: $40.00
GBTru: $80.00 ↑7%

Lighthouse

	NAME:	Lighthouse	1987
	ITEM #:	5030-0	
	STATUS:	Retired 1988	

MATERIAL: Ceramic
DESCRIPTION: Five story lighthouse beacon rises from sturdy stone slab base and is connected to caretaker's cottage.
PARTICULARS: Lighted.
VARIATIONS: Glazed and Unglazed.

OSRP: $36.00
GBTru: $605.00 ↑2%

Red Barn

	NAME:	Red Barn	1987
	ITEM #:	5081-4	
	STATUS:	Retired 1992	

MATERIAL: Ceramic
DESCRIPTION: Stone base, wooden barn, double cross-buck doors on long side, hayloft doors above main doors. Three ventilator cupolas on roof ridge. Cat sleeps in hayloft.
PARTICULARS: Lighted. Same Item # was used for the 1982 *Gabled House*. Early release to Gift Creations Concepts (GCC).

OSRP: $38.00
GBTru: $85.00 ↑13%

Jefferson School

❑ **NAME:** Jefferson School   1987
     ITEM #: 5082-2
     STATUS: Retired 1991

MATERIAL: Ceramic
DESCRIPTION: Two room schoolhouse with large multi-paned windows with top transoms. Short bell tower incorporated into roof.
PARTICULARS: Lighted. Same Item # was used for the 1982 *Flower Shop*. Early release to Gift Creations Concepts (GCC).

OSRP: $36.00
GBTru: $155.00   ⬆7%

Farm House

❑ **NAME:** Farm House   1987
     ITEM #: 5089-0
     STATUS: Retired 1992

MATERIAL: Ceramic
DESCRIPTION: 2 ¹/₂ story wood frame home with front full-length porch. Roof interest is two low, one high peak with attic window in highest peak.
PARTICULARS: Lighted.

OSRP: $40.00
GBTru: $75.00 ⬆15%

Fire Station No. 2

❑ **NAME:** Fire Station No. 2   1987
     ITEM #: 5091-1
     STATUS: Retired 1989

MATERIAL: Ceramic
DESCRIPTION: Large double doors for station housing two engines, side stair leads to living quarters. Brick building with stone arch design at engine doors and front windows.
PARTICULARS: Lighted. Early release to Gift Creations Concepts (GCC).

OSRP: $40.00
GBTru: $220.00 ⬆19%

Snow Village Resort Lodge

❑ **NAME:** Snow Village Resort Lodge   1987
     ITEM #: 5092-0
     STATUS: Retired 1989

MATERIAL: Ceramic
DESCRIPTION: Bright yellow with green, scalloped roof, covered porch and side entry. Bay windows on front house section. Back section rises to dormered 3 ¹/₂ stories. Ventilator areas directly under roof cap.
PARTICULARS: Lighted.

OSRP: $55.00
GBTru: $145.00   ⬆4%

Village Market

☐	**NAME:**	Village Market	1988
	ITEM #:	5044-0
	STATUS:	Retired 1991

MATERIAL: Ceramic
DESCRIPTION: Silk-screened "glass" windows detail merchandise available, red and white canopy protects shoppers using in/out doors. Sign over second story windows.
PARTICULARS: Lighted. Early release to Gift Creations Concepts (GCC).

OSRP: $39.00
GBTru: $75.00 ↑15%

Kenwood House

☐	**NAME:**	Kenwood House	1988
	ITEM #:	5054-7
	STATUS:	Retired 1990

MATERIAL: Ceramic
DESCRIPTION: Old-fashioned wrap-around veranda with arched openings on three story home. Front facade features scalloped shingles on third story.
PARTICULARS: Lighted. Early release to Gift Creations Concepts (GCC).

OSRP: $50.00
GBTru: $130.00 ↑4%

Maple Ridge Inn

☐	**NAME:**	Maple Ridge Inn	1988
	ITEM #:	5121-7
	STATUS:	Retired 1990

MATERIAL: Ceramic
DESCRIPTION: Replica of Victorian mansion, ornamental roof piece concealed lightning rods.
PARTICULARS: Lighted. Interpretation of an American landmark in Cambridge, NY. 1991 Gift Creations Concepts (GCC) Catalog Exclusive @ $75.00.

OSRP: $55.00
GBTru: $75.00 ↑15%

Village Station And Train

☐	**NAME:**	Village Station And Train	1988
	ITEM #:	5122-5
	STATUS:	Retired 1992

MATERIAL: Ceramic
DESCRIPTION: Station features an outside ticket window, soft drink vending machine, and outside benches, with a three car train.
PARTICULARS: Set of 4. Lighted. Third Original Snow Village train and station design. Train cars do not light.

OSRP: $65.00
GBTru: $115.00 ↑15%

Cobblestone Antique Shop

❒ **NAME:** Cobblestone Antique Shop 1988
ITEM #: 5123-3
STATUS: Retired 1992

MATERIAL: Ceramic
DESCRIPTION: Silk-screened front windows display antiques for sale, bay window fills second story width, building date of 1881 on arched cornice.
PARTICULARS: Lighted.

OSRP: $36.00
GBTru: $70.00 ↑8%

Corner Cafe

❒ **NAME:** Corner Cafe 1988
ITEM #: 5124-1
STATUS: Retired 1991

MATERIAL: Ceramic
DESCRIPTION: "Pie" and "Coffee" silkscreen on windows of corner restaurant with red, white, and blue striped awnings. Building date of 1875 inscribed on turret design.
PARTICULARS: Lighted.

OSRP: $37.00
GBTru: $90.00 NC

Single Car Garage

❒ **NAME:** Single Car Garage 1988
ITEM #: 5125-0
STATUS: Retired 1990

MATERIAL: Ceramic
DESCRIPTION: Double doors open to house car, two outside lights for convenience, designed to look like house, windows have shutters, roof has dormers, roof projects over wood pile.
PARTICULARS: Lighted.

OSRP: $22.00
GBTru: $55.00 ↑10%

Home Sweet Home/House & Windmill

❒ **NAME:** Home Sweet Home/
House & Windmill 1988
ITEM #: 5126-8
STATUS: Retired 1991

MATERIAL: Ceramic–Metal blades of windmill are separate
DESCRIPTION: Based on a landmark historic home, saltbox with asymmetrical arrangement of windows. Doors for root cellar are at front corner, one central brick chimney. Four-bladed windmill.
PARTICULARS: Set of 2. Lighted. Inspired by the East Hampton, NY home of John Howard Payne, composer of "Home Sweet Home".

OSRP: $60.00
GBTru: $120.00 ↑4%

Redeemer Church

☐ **NAME:** Redeemer Church   1988
ITEM #: 5127-6
STATUS: Retired 1992

MATERIAL: Ceramic
DESCRIPTION: Stone corners add strength and support to church and bell tower. Arched windows, heavy wooden double doors.
PARTICULARS: Lighted.

OSRP: $42.00
GBTru: $70.00 ↑17%

Service Station

☐ **NAME:** Service Station   1988
ITEM #: 5128-4
STATUS: Retired 1991

MATERIAL: Ceramic
DESCRIPTION: Two gas pumps, candy machine, restroom, work area and office.
PARTICULARS: Set of 2. Lighted. Also known as "Bill's Service Station." Pumps included. Pumps do not light.

OSRP: $37.50
GBTru: $295.00   NC

Stonehurst House

☐ **NAME:** Stonehurst House   1988
ITEM #: 5140-3
STATUS: Retired 1994

MATERIAL: Ceramic
DESCRIPTION: Red brick punctuated with black and white painted bricks. Half circle sunburst design second story dormers restate the arch shape of first floor windows.
PARTICULARS: Lighted.

OSRP: $37.50
GBTru: $65.00 ↑8%

Palos Verdes

☐ **NAME:** Palos Verdes   1988
ITEM #: 5141-1
STATUS: Retired 1990

MATERIAL: Ceramic–separate potted Sisal miniature tree on porch
DESCRIPTION: Spanish style with green tiled roof, covered entry porch, stucco finish, 2nd floor has shuttered windows. Coming forward from main wing is 2 story round turret and ground floor window alcove.
PARTICULARS: Lighted.

OSRP: $37.50
GBTru: $85.00 ↑6%

Jingle Belle Houseboat

☐ **NAME:** Jingle Belle Houseboat   1989
   ITEM #: 5114-4
   STATUS: Retired 1991

MATERIAL: Ceramic–stamped Metal bell is separate
DESCRIPTION: Floating house sports a Christmas tree on wheelhouse roof and rear deck. Name is stenciled on bow and life preservers.
PARTICULARS: Lighted.

OSRP: $42.00
GBTru: $115.00 ⬆15%

Colonial Church

☐ **NAME:** Colonial Church   1989
   ITEM #: 5119-5
   STATUS: Retired 1992

MATERIAL: Ceramic with Metal cross
DESCRIPTION: Front entry with four floor-to-roof columns supporting roof over porch. Front facade repeats design with four half-columns set into wall. Cross on three tier steeple bell tower.
PARTICULARS: Lighted. Early release to Gift Creations Concepts (GCC).

OSRP: $60.00
GBTru: $80.00 ⬆7%

North Creek Cottage

☐ **NAME:** North Creek Cottage   1989
   ITEM #: 5120-9
   STATUS: Retired 1992

MATERIAL: Ceramic
DESCRIPTION: Cape cod style with colonial columned front porch. Attached garage with deck on top, front dormer, stone chimney.
PARTICULARS: Lighted. Early release to Gift Creations Concepts (GCC).

OSRP: $45.00
GBTru: $70.00 ⬆27%

Paramount Theater

☐ **NAME:** Paramount Theater   1989
   ITEM #: 5142-0
   STATUS: Retired 1993

MATERIAL: Ceramic
DESCRIPTION: Spanish theme Art Deco building, double marques. Ticket booth in center flanked by two double doors. Corner billboards display scenes from movie.
PARTICULARS: Lighted.

OSRP: $42.00
GBTru: $125.00 ⬆47%

☐ **NAME:** Doctor's House   1989
    ITEM #: 5143-8
    STATUS: Retired 1992

MATERIAL: Ceramic
DESCRIPTION: Home and office within house. Rounded turret completes front. Three story home has arched porthole, and bay windows to add to Victorian charm.
PARTICULARS: Lighted.

OSRP: $56.00
GBTru: $100.00 ↑5%

Courthouse

☐ **NAME:** Courthouse   1989
    ITEM #: 5144-6
    STATUS: Retired 1993

MATERIAL: Ceramic
DESCRIPTION: Four corner roof turrets with central clock tower, windows with half-circle sunbursts, decorative molding on second story with two front windows being clear half-circles.
PARTICULARS: Lighted. Design based on Gibson County Courthouse in Princetown, IN.

OSRP: $65.00
GBTru: $150.00 ↑20%

Village Warming House

☐ **NAME:** Village Warming House   1989
    ITEM #: 5145-4
    STATUS: Retired 1992

MATERIAL: Ceramic
DESCRIPTION: Used by skaters to warm up from the chill, small red house has steep front roof. Bench at side for a brief rest.
PARTICULARS: Lighted. Trees detach.

OSRP: $42.00
GBTru: $70.00 ↑17%

J. Young's Granary

☐ **NAME:** J. Young's Granary   1989
    ITEM #: 5149-7
    STATUS: Retired 1992

MATERIAL: Ceramic
DESCRIPTION: Central water wheel for grinding grain, stone silo on one side, and small storage/store on other side.
PARTICULARS: Lighted.

OSRP: $45.00
GBTru: $75.00 ↑15%

The Original Snow Village

Pinewood Log Cabin

☐ **NAME:** Pinewood Log Cabin 1989
ITEM #: 5150-0
STATUS: Retired 1995

MATERIAL: Ceramic
DESCRIPTION: Log construction with two fireplaces for heating/cooking, tree trunk porch pillars, firewood stack, house name on sign above porch, attached tree.
PARTICULARS: Lighted. Early release to Gift Creations Concepts (GCC), Fall 1990.

OSRP: $37.50
GBTru: $60.00 ↑60%

56 Flavors Ice Cream Parlor

☐ **NAME:** 56 Flavors Ice Cream Parlor 1990
ITEM #: 5151-9
STATUS: Retired 1992

MATERIAL: Ceramic
DESCRIPTION: Decorated like a sundae, peppermint pillars flank door, sugar cone roof with a cherry on peak, window boxes hold ice cream cones.
PARTICULARS: Lighted. Early release to Gift Creations Concepts (GCC).

OSRP: $42.00
GBTru: $105.00 ↑31%

Morningside House

☐ **NAME:** Morningside House 1990
ITEM #: 5152-7
STATUS: Retired 1992

MATERIAL: Ceramic with Sisal trees that detach
DESCRIPTION: Pink/coral split level house with one-car garage. Fieldstone chimney, curved front steps, terraced landscaping with movable trees.
PARTICULARS: Lighted. Early release to Showcase Dealers and the National Association Of Limited Edition Dealers (NALED).

OSRP: $45.00
GBTru: $65.00 ↑30%

Mainstreet Hardware Store

☐ **NAME:** Mainstreet Hardware Store 1990
ITEM #: 5153-5
STATUS: Retired 1993

MATERIAL: Ceramic
DESCRIPTION: Three story building with store on ground level. Rental rooms on second and third story with access by outside staircase. Awning covers display window.
PARTICULARS: Lighted. Was originally designed with blue window trim.

OSRP: $42.00
GBTru: $75.00 ↑15%

Village Realty

❏ **NAME:** Village Realty   1990
    ITEM #: 5154-3
    STATUS: Retired 1993

MATERIAL: Ceramic
DESCRIPTION: Two story main building houses real estate office. Front bay display window for available properties. Adjacent building houses small Italian dining place with colorful striped awning.
PARTICULARS: Lighted. "J. Saraceno" over door is a tribute to D56's former National Sales Manager.

OSRP: $42.00
GBTru: $75.00 ⬆7%

Spanish Mission Church

❏ **NAME:** Spanish Mission Church   1990
    ITEM #: 5155-1
    STATUS: Retired 1992

MATERIAL: Ceramic with three Metal crosses for cemetery
DESCRIPTION: Sun-dried clay Spanish-style arcade along one side gives protected access.
PARTICULARS: Lighted. Designed after Enga Memorial Chapel in Minneapolis, MN.

OSRP: $42.00
GBTru: $75.00 ⬆25%

Prairie House

❏ **NAME:** Prairie House   1990
    ITEM #: 5156-0
    STATUS: Retired 1993

MATERIAL: Ceramic
DESCRIPTION: Two story home with upper floor set in and back atop first story. Large chimney rises up through first story. Two large pillars support covered entry.
PARTICULARS: Lighted. American Architecture Series.

OSRP: $42.00
GBTru: $70.00 ⬆17%

Queen Anne Victorian

❏ **NAME:** Queen Anne Victorian   1990
    ITEM #: 5157-8
    STATUS: Current

MATERIAL: Ceramic
DESCRIPTION: Broad steps lead up to pillared porch with unique corner gazebo-style sitting area. Ornate turret on corner of second story decorated with scalloped shingles.
PARTICULARS: Lighted. American Architecture Series.

OSRP: $48.00
GBTru: $50.00   NC

❏ **NAME:** The Christmas Shop 1991
ITEM #: 5097-0
STATUS: Current

MATERIAL: Ceramic
DESCRIPTION: Pediment on brick building advertises the holiday, the French "NOEL." Large teddy bear by front window.
PARTICULARS: Lighted. Early release to Gift Creations Concepts (GCC) and Showcase Dealers.

OSRP: $37.50
GBTru: $37.50 NC

❏ **NAME:** Oak Grove Tudor 1991
ITEM #: 5400-3
STATUS: Retired 1994

MATERIAL: Ceramic
DESCRIPTION: Red brick base with stucco and timbered second story. Fireplace of brick and stone by entry door. Rough stone frames door.
PARTICULARS: Lighted. Early release to Showcase Dealers.

OSRP: $42.00
GBTru: $65.00 ⬆8%

❏ **NAME:** The Honeymooner Motel 1991
ITEM #: 5401-1
STATUS: Retired 1993

MATERIAL: Ceramic
DESCRIPTION: Moon and stars sign above office door is advertisement for motel. White building with blue awnings and doors. Soda and ice machine by office door.
PARTICULARS: Lighted. Early release to Showcase Dealers.

OSRP: $42.00
GBTru: $70.00 NC

❏ **NAME:** Village Greenhouse 1991
ITEM #: 5402-0
STATUS: Retired 1995

MATERIAL: Ceramic with Acrylic panels
DESCRIPTION: Plant growing area has bricked bottom and "glass" roof to allow sunlight in. Attached small store sells accessories. It has brick chimney, shingled roof and covered entry.
PARTICULARS: Lighted.

OSRP: $35.00
GBTru: $75.00 ⬆108%

Southern Colonial

☐ **NAME:** Southern Colonial 1991
  ITEM #: 5403-8
  STATUS: Retired 1994

MATERIAL: Ceramic with Sisal trees that detach
DESCRIPTION: Four columns rise from ground to roof with second story veranda across front. Double chimneys surrounded by a balustrade. Shutters by each window both decorate, and shut out heat of sun. Two urns flank steps of entryway.
PARTICULARS: Lighted. American Architecture Series.

OSRP: $48.00
GBTru: $75.00 ↑15%

Gothic Farmhouse

☐ **NAME:** Gothic Farmhouse 1991
  ITEM #: 5404-6
  STATUS: Current

MATERIAL: Ceramic
DESCRIPTION: Columned front porch and entry. First floor large bay window with second story rising to a gable with carved molding which is repeated on two dormer windows over porch. Clapboard home with roof shingles in diamond pattern.
PARTICULARS: Lighted. American Architecture Series.

OSRP: $48.00
GBTru: $48.00 NC

Finklea's Finery Costume Shop

☐ **NAME:** Finklea's Finery Costume Shop 1991
  ITEM #: 5405-4
  STATUS: Retired 1993

MATERIAL: Ceramic
DESCRIPTION: Pediment over front door repeated in roof design. Red awnings over 1st floor display windows. Dressed stone trims the facade of the three story brick building. Hood projects over third floor windows–an area used by piano teacher. Attached side setback is two stories with decorated rental return door and awning on upper window.
PARTICULARS: Lighted.

OSRP: $45.00
GBTru: $60.00 ↑9%

Jack's Corner Barber Shop

☐ **NAME:** Jack's Corner Barber Shop 1991
  ITEM #: 5406-2
  STATUS: Retired 1994

MATERIAL: Ceramic
DESCRIPTION: Barber Shop also houses M. Schmitt Photography Studio and second floor Tailor Shop. Two story turret separates two identical wings of brick building. Fantail window design repeated on doors and on roof peaks.
PARTICULARS: Lighted. "M. Schmitt Studio" is in honor of Matthew Schmitt, the photographer for D56's *Quarterly*, brochures, etc.

OSRP: $42.00
GBTru: $65.00 ↑18%

Double Bungalow

☐ **NAME:** Double Bungalow   1991
    ITEM #: 5407-0
    STATUS: Retired 1994

MATERIAL: Ceramic
DESCRIPTION: Early two-family home–double entry doors, each side has bow window downstairs, a roof dormer, and own chimney. A brick facade dresses up clapboard house.
PARTICULARS: Lighted.

OSRP: $45.00
GBTru: $65.00 ⬆18%

Grandma's Cottage

☐ **NAME:** Grandma's Cottage   1992
    ITEM #: 5420-8
    STATUS: Current

MATERIAL: Ceramic
DESCRIPTION: Small porch nestled between two identical house sections. Hooded double windows, front side sections with evergreens flanking each area. Chimneys rise off main roof.
PARTICULARS: Lighted. Early release to Gift Creations Concepts (GCC).

OSRP: $42.00
GBTru: $45.00   NC

St. Luke's Church

☐ **NAME:** St. Luke's Church   1992
    ITEM #: 5421-6
    STATUS: Retired 1994

MATERIAL: Ceramic
DESCRIPTION: Brick church features three square based steeples with the central one rising off nave roof. Others are at front corners of church with doors at base and trefoil design on the front/side repeated on main entry doors.
PARTICULARS: Lighted. Early release to Gift Creations Concepts (GCC).

OSRP: $45.00
GBTru: $70.00 ⬆17%

Village Post Office

☐ **NAME:** Village Post Office   1992
    ITEM #: 5422-4
    STATUS: Retired 1995

MATERIAL: Ceramic
DESCRIPTION: Doric columns support porch to double entry doors. Two story brick with two story turret rising above sign. Greek key and incised design separate stories.
PARTICULARS: Lighted. Early release to Showcase Dealers.

OSRP: $35.00
GBTru: $70.00 ⬆87%

Al's TV Shop

☐ **NAME:** Al's TV Shop   1992
    ITEM #: 5423-2
    STATUS: Retired 1995

MATERIAL: Ceramic
DESCRIPTION: TV antenna on roof. Red awnings on upper windows and red canopy over lower display window. Store entry on corner of building.
PARTICULARS: Lighted.

OSRP: $40.00
GBTru: $65.00 ↑62%

Good Shepherd Chapel & Church School

☐ **NAME:** Good Shepherd Chapel & Church School   1992
    ITEM #: 5424-0
    STATUS: Current

MATERIAL: Ceramic
DESCRIPTION: White chapel with red roof rises on stone base. Steeple at front entry. School has double doors with tall windows and small bell tower. Stone chimney on side. Church side door meets school side door.
PARTICULARS: Set of 2. Lighted.

OSRP: $72.00
GBTru: $72.00   NC

Print Shop & Village News

☐ **NAME:** Print Shop & Village News   1992
    ITEM #: 5425-9
    STATUS: Retired 1994

MATERIAL: Ceramic
DESCRIPTION: Stone in front pediment notes 1893 construction. Symmetrical building design emphasized by double chimneys, matching windows and columns. Brick building also houses Muffin Shop.
PARTICULARS: Lighted.

OSRP: $37.50
GBTru: $60.00 ↑9%

Hartford House

☐ **NAME:** Hartford House   1992
    ITEM #: 5426-7
    STATUS: Retired 1995

MATERIAL: Ceramic
DESCRIPTION: Steeply pitched roof with ornate front covered entry pediment design, repeated in steep front gable. Molding surrounds windows, is present on porch columns.
PARTICULARS: Lighted.

OSRP: $55.00
GBTru: $80.00 ↑45%

Village Vet And Pet Shop

☐ **NAME:** Village Vet And Pet Shop   1992
    ITEM #: 5427-5
    STATUS: Retired 1995

MATERIAL: Ceramic
DESCRIPTION: Arched crescents over picture windows that are screened designs depicting dogs, kittens, fish and birds. Ornamental molding outlines roof edge. Dog sits on entry steps to Vet's Office.
PARTICULARS: Lighted.

OSRP: $32.00
GBTru: $65.00 ↑103%

Craftsman Cottage

☐ **NAME:** Craftsman Cottage   1992
    ITEM #: 5437-2
    STATUS: Retired 1995

MATERIAL: Ceramic
DESCRIPTION: Stone based porch extends across front of house ending in stone chimney. Large squared pillars are part of support for second story room above entryway. Small dormer by chimney.
PARTICULARS: Lighted. American Architecture Series.

OSRP: $55.00
GBTru: $75.00 ↑36%

Village Station

☐ **NAME:** Village Station   1992
    ITEM #: 5438-0
    STATUS: Current

MATERIAL: Ceramic
DESCRIPTION: Clock tower rises on one side of two story red brick station. Platform sign behind a stack of luggage announces arrivals and departures. Many-windowed waiting room for travelers extends length of station.
PARTICULARS: Lighted.

OSRP: $65.00
GBTru: $65.00   NC

Airport

☐ **NAME:** Airport   1992
    ITEM #: 5439-9
    STATUS: Current

MATERIAL: Ceramic
DESCRIPTION: Semicircular vaulted roof extends length of plane hangar, with control tower rising off central rear of building. One-engine prop plane sits in hangar entrance. Fuel tank pump at corner, plus thermometer, and crop dusting schedule. Door at opposite front corner for passenger and freight business.
PARTICULARS: Lighted.

OSRP: $60.00
GBTru: $60.00   NC

☐ **NAME:** Nantucket Renovation   1993
ITEM #: 5441-0
STATUS: 1993 Annual

MATERIAL: Ceramic
DESCRIPTION: Matching gabled wing added to original design & greenhouse moved to front of house. Front porch columns now milled. Small evergreens now at front & large tree moved to rear corner, exposing side bay window.
PARTICULARS: Lighted. Available only through retailers who carried Snow Village in 1986, Showcase Dealers & select buying groups. For the original *Nantucket* see 1978, Item #5014-6. Special box & hang tag. Blueprints of renovation included.

OSRP: $55.00
GBTru: $75.00   ↑7%

Mount Olivet Church

☐ **NAME:** Mount Olivet Church   1993
ITEM #: 5442-9
STATUS: Current

MATERIAL: Ceramic
DESCRIPTION: Brick church with large stained glass window above double door entry. Square bell tower with steeple roof.
PARTICULARS: Lighted.

OSRP: $65.00
GBTru: $65.00   NC

Village Public Library

☐ **NAME:** Village Public Library   1993
ITEM #: 5443-7
STATUS: Current

MATERIAL: Ceramic
DESCRIPTION: Brick and stone building with four Greek columns supporting front portico. Entry from side steps to double doors. Brick cupola rises from center of roof.
PARTICULARS: Lighted.

OSRP: $55.00
GBTru: $55.00   NC

Woodbury House

☐ **NAME:** Woodbury House   1993
ITEM #: 5444-5
STATUS: Current

MATERIAL: Ceramic
DESCRIPTION: Turned spindle posts support front porch of clapboard home. Double gable design with lower gable featuring two story bow windows. Brick chimney extends through roof.
PARTICULARS: Lighted.

OSRP: $45.00
GBTru: $45.00   NC

Hunting Lodge

☐ **NAME:** Hunting Lodge   1993
   ITEM #: 5445-3
   STATUS: Current

MATERIAL: Ceramic
DESCRIPTION: Rustic log structure on stone foundation and with stone fireplace. Antlers decorate front gable above porch entry.
PARTICULARS: Lighted.

OSRP: $50.00
GBTru: $50.00   NC

Dairy Barn

☐ **NAME:** Dairy Barn   1993
   ITEM #: 5446-1
   STATUS: Current

MATERIAL: Ceramic
DESCRIPTION: Cow barn with attached silo. Tin mansard roof. Cow weather vane.
PARTICULARS: Lighted.

OSRP: $55.00
GBTru: $55.00   NC

Dinah's Drive-In

☐ **NAME:** Dinah's Drive-In   1993
   ITEM #: 5447-0
   STATUS: Current

MATERIAL: Ceramic
DESCRIPTION: Burger in bun and bubbly soda top circular fast food drive-in.
PARTICULARS: Lighted.

OSRP: $45.00
GBTru: $45.00   NC

Snowy Hills Hospital

☐ **NAME:** Snowy Hills Hospital   1993
   ITEM #: 5448-8
   STATUS: Current

MATERIAL: Ceramic
DESCRIPTION: Brick hospital, steps lead to double main doors with emergency entry drive-up on side.
PARTICULARS: Lighted. Portion of proceeds from sale of piece will be donated to AmFAR through the Gift For Life Foundation.

OSRP: $48.00
GBTru: $48.00   NC

Fisherman's Nook Resort

☐ **NAME:** Fisherman's Nook Resort   1994
ITEM #: 5460-7
STATUS: Current

MATERIAL: Ceramic
DESCRIPTION: Office/store for cabin rental, bait, and gas for boats, plus places for boats to tie up.
PARTICULARS: Lighted.

OSRP: $75.00
GBTru: $75.00   NC

FISHERMAN'S NOOK CABINS

☐ **NAME:** FISHERMAN'S NOOK CABINS   1994
ITEM #: 5461-5
STATUS: Current

MATERIAL: Ceramic
DESCRIPTION: Set of 2 includes *Fisherman's Nook Bass Cabin* and *Fisherman's Nook Trout Cabin*.
PARTICULARS: Set of 2. Lighted. Midyear release.

OSRP: $50.00
GBTru: $50.00   NC

Fisherman's Nook Bass Cabin

Photo—
See Above.

☐ **NAME:** Fisherman's Nook Bass Cabin   1994
ITEM #: 5461-5
STATUS: Current

MATERIAL: Ceramic
DESCRIPTION: Each cabin named for fish–rustic wood cabin with wood pile and fireplace for heat.
PARTICULARS: 1 of a 2 piece set. Sold only as a set. Lighted. Midyear release.

Fisherman's Nook Trout Cabin

Photo—
See Above.

☐ **NAME:** Fisherman's Nook Trout Cabin   1994
ITEM #: 5461-5
STATUS: Current

MATERIAL: Ceramic
DESCRIPTION: Each cabin named for fish–rustic wood cabin with wood pile and fireplace for heat.
PARTICULARS: 1 of a 2 piece set. Sold only as a set. Lighted. Midyear release.

❐ **NAME:** The Original Snow Village Starter Set　1994
　ITEM #: 5462-3
　STATUS: Current

MATERIAL: Ceramic, Sisal trees and Real Plastic Snow
DESCRIPTION: The Original Snow Village Starter Set
includes *Shady Oak Church, Sunday School Serenade*
accessory, three assorted "bottle-brush" sisal trees, and
a bag of Real Plastic Snow.
PARTICULARS: Set of 6. Lighted. Featured at D56 National
Open Houses hosted by participating Gift Creation Concepts
(GCC) retailers the first weekend in November 1994.

OSRP: $49.99
GBTru: $50.00　NC

Wedding Chapel

❐ **NAME:** Wedding Chapel　1994
　ITEM #: 5464-0
　STATUS: Current

MATERIAL: Ceramic
DESCRIPTION: White clapboard church. Brick tower
supports wooden steeple. Bell hangs in tower above door.
Green shutters on arched windows.
PARTICULARS: Lighted.

OSRP: $55.00
GBTru: $55.00　NC

Federal House

❐ **NAME:** Federal House　1994
　ITEM #: 5465-8
　STATUS: Current

MATERIAL: Ceramic
DESCRIPTION: Symmetrical brick structure has white
portico and columns at front door. Dormers and four
chimneys complete the mirrored effect.
PARTICULARS: Lighted. American Architecture Series.

OSRP: $50.00
GBTru: $50.00　NC

Carmel Cottage

❐ **NAME:** Carmel Cottage　1994
　ITEM #: 5466-6
　STATUS: Current

MATERIAL: Ceramic
DESCRIPTION: Stucco walls, steep pitched roof, dormer
on side and chimney at rear. Stone trims door, side passage
and windows.
PARTICULARS: Lighted.

OSRP: $48.00
GBTru: $48.00　NC

Skate & Ski Shop

❒ **NAME:** Skate & Ski Shop   1994
ITEM #: 5467-4
STATUS: Current

MATERIAL: Ceramic
DESCRIPTION: Stone chimney and slate roof on chalet-style shop. Timber trims windows and base.
PARTICULARS: Lighted.

OSRP: $50.00
GBTru: $50.00   NC

Glenhaven House

❒ **NAME:** Glenhaven House   1994
ITEM #: 5468-2
STATUS: Current

MATERIAL: Ceramic
DESCRIPTION: 2 ½ story home with bay windows on first floor. Small porch at entrance. Two trees attached at right front corner.
PARTICULARS: Lighted.

OSRP: $45.00
GBTru: $45.00   NC

Coca-Cola® brand Bottling Plant

❒ **NAME:** Coca-Cola® brand Bottling Plant   1994
ITEM #: 5469-0
STATUS: Current

MATERIAL: Ceramic
DESCRIPTION: Large, red Coca-Cola logo sign set on roof above entry doors. Vending machine sits at back of loading dock, two cases sit at front. Two smoke stacks rise from roof near skylights.
PARTICULARS: Lighted. Prototypes did not have cases of soda on loading dock.

OSRP: $65.00
GBTru: $65.00   NC

Marvel's Beauty Salon

❒ **NAME:** Marvel's Beauty Salon   1994
ITEM #: 5470-4
STATUS: Current

MATERIAL: Ceramic
DESCRIPTION: Brick 1st story houses Beauty Salon. Picture window displays styles. Stucco 2nd story houses Wig Shop.
PARTICULARS: Lighted.

OSRP: $37.50
GBTru: $37.50   NC

The Original Snow Village

Christmas Cove Lighthouse

❏ **NAME:** Christmas Cove Lighthouse 1995
ITEM #: 5483-6
STATUS: Current

MATERIAL: Ceramic
DESCRIPTION: Ship beacon atop white block tower.
Steps lead to brick home of keeper. Attached trees.
PARTICULARS: Lighted. Midyear release. 2-light socket cord.
Lift-off top allows access to bulb in tower.

OSRP: $60.00
GBTru: $60.00 NC

Coca-Cola® brand Corner Drugstore

❏ **NAME:** Coca-Cola® brand Corner Drugstore 1995
ITEM #: 5484-4
STATUS: Current

MATERIAL: Ceramic
DESCRIPTION: Oversize Coke bottle and logo sign is
advertisement for soda shop in drugstore. Stone corner
shop with bow windows and roof cornices.
PARTICULARS: Lighted. Midyear release.

OSRP: $55.00
GBTru: $55.00 NC

Snow Carnival Ice Palace

❏ **NAME:** Snow Carnival Ice Palace 1995
ITEM #: 54850
STATUS: Current

MATERIAL: Ceramic
DESCRIPTION: Turrets trim a fantasy frosty ice palace for
festival King and Queen. Entry welcome gate with snowy
trees leads to the magical creation built of blocks of ice.
PARTICULARS: Set of 2. Lighted.

OSRP: $95.00
GBTru: $95.00

Pisa Pizza

❏ **NAME:** Pisa Pizza 1995
ITEM #: 54851
STATUS: Current

MATERIAL: Ceramic
DESCRIPTION: A replica of the Leaning Tower of Pisa is
central design on restaurant. Flanking doors and window
have striped canopies.
PARTICULARS: Lighted.

OSRP: $35.00
GBTru: $35.00

The Original Snow Village

Peppermint Porch Day Care

❐ **NAME:** Peppermint Porch Day Care 1995
ITEM #: 5485-2
STATUS: Current

MATERIAL: Ceramic
DESCRIPTION: Day care center in white clapboard house. Mint candy theme on pillars and balcony. Boots, teddy bear on porch.
PARTICULARS: Lighted. Midyear release. Prototype had "Peppermint Place" as the name on the building.

OSRP: $45.00
GBTru: $45.00 NC

Village Police Station

❐ **NAME:** Village Police Station 1995
ITEM #: 54853
STATUS: Current

MATERIAL: Ceramic
DESCRIPTION: The 56th Precinct is housed in a 2 story brick building with stone coping capping off roof edge. Arched windows accent double entry design. Awnings on 3 upper windows with Dept. name above. Doughnut shop next door for a quick pick-me-up break.
PARTICULARS: Lighted.

OSRP: $48.00
GBTru: $48.00

Holly Brothers® Garage

❐ **NAME:** Holly Brothers® Garage 1995
ITEM #: 54854
STATUS: Current

MATERIAL: Ceramic
DESCRIPTION: Gas station with two pumps. Coke machine, wall phone, repair stalls, tires, free air, office and rest rooms are housed in a white building. Owners name above gas pumps.
PARTICULARS: Lighted.

OSRP: $48.00
GBTru: $48.00

Ryman Auditorium

❐ **NAME:** Ryman Auditorium 1995
ITEM #: 54855
STATUS: Current

MATERIAL: Ceramic
DESCRIPTION: Nashville's country music auditorium.
PARTICULARS: Lighted.

OSRP: $75.00
GBTru: $75.00

The Original Snow Village

Dutch Colonial

❐ **NAME:** Dutch Colonial   1995
ITEM #: 54856
STATUS: Current

MATERIAL: Ceramic
DESCRIPTION: Second story of colonial home is constructed as part of mansard roof that extends down to first floor level. Shuttered double windows frame front door two steps up from walk. One bedroom accesses an upper balustraded outdoor sitting area.
PARTICULARS: Lighted. American Architecture Series.

OSRP: $45.00
GBTru: $45.00

Beacon Hill Victorian

❐ **NAME:** Beacon Hill Victorian   1995
ITEM #: 54857
STATUS: Current

MATERIAL: Ceramic
DESCRIPTION: Covered porch encloses turret structure that rises up entire height of house and features shuttered windows. Brick home with transverse roof has ornate wood molding trim on gables. Snowy fir trees on front corner.
PARTICULARS: Lighted.

OSRP: $60.00
GBTru: $60.00

Bowling Alley

❐ **NAME:** Bowling Alley   1995
ITEM #: 54858
STATUS: Current

MATERIAL: Ceramic
DESCRIPTION: Bowling pins and ball atop brick building advertise sports activity within. Pins flank Village Lanes sign above archway of double entry doors. Snowy trees next to entrance.
PARTICULARS: Lighted.

OSRP: $42.00
GBTru: $42.00

Starbucks Coffee

❐ **NAME:** Starbucks Coffee   1995
ITEM #: 54859
STATUS: Current

MATERIAL: Ceramic
DESCRIPTION: Corner building features infinite varieties of coffee and treats. Stone structure with starred canopies over upper windows and larger awnings atop windows on street level. Store logo displayed on roof pediment.
PARTICULARS: Lighted.

OSRP: $48.00
GBTru: $48.00

Nick's Tree Farm

❏ **NAME:** Nick's Tree Farm   1996
ITEM #: 54871
STATUS: Current

MATERIAL: Ceramic
DESCRIPTION: Small wood hut provides office and warming area for Nick on a farm where he or you can select a live or cut tree. Nick pulls a cut tree on sled.
PARTICULARS: Set of 10. Lighted. Midyear release.

OSRP: $40.00
GBTru: $40.00

Smokey Mountain Retreat

❏ **NAME:** Smokey Mountain Retreat   1996
ITEM #: 54872
STATUS: Current

MATERIAL: Ceramic
DESCRIPTION: Log structure with two stone fireplaces has exposed log beams, covered entry and porch areas to hold sleds and outdoor gear.
PARTICULARS: Lighted. Midyear release.
With Smoking Chimney.

OSRP: $65.00
GBTru: $65.00

Boulder Springs House

❏ **NAME:** Boulder Springs House   1996
ITEM #: 54873
STATUS: Current

MATERIAL: Ceramic
DESCRIPTION: Clapboard house with 2 ½ stories has covered entry and front porch. Shutters frame front gable windows, attached tree behind side bow window.
PARTICULARS: Lighted. Midyear release.

OSRP: $60.00
GBTru: $60.00

Reindeer Bus Depot

❏ **NAME:** Reindeer Bus Depot   1996
ITEM #: 54874
STATUS: Current

MATERIAL: Ceramic
DESCRIPTION: Depot is two stories with restaurant and waiting room flanking central entry topped by depot name and vertical bus sign.
PARTICULARS: Lighted. Midyear release.

OSRP: $42.00
GBTru: $42.00

Carolers

❑ **NAME:** Carolers   1979
    ITEM #: 5064-1
    STATUS: Retired 1986

MATERIAL: Ceramic
DESCRIPTION: Couple, girl, garlanded lamppost, snowman.
PARTICULARS: Set of 4. First non-lit accessory.

OSRP: $12.00
GBTru: $125.00   NC

Ceramic Car

❑ **NAME:** Ceramic Car   1980
    ITEM #: 5069-0
    STATUS: Retired 1986

MATERIAL: Ceramic
DESCRIPTION: Open roadster holds lap rugs, Christmas tree
and wrapped presents.
PARTICULARS: First vehicle, no other cars were available
until 1985. Did not come in a box.

OSRP: $5.00
GBTru: $55.00 ↑10%

Ceramic Sleigh

❑ **NAME:** Ceramic Sleigh   1981
    ITEM #: 5079-2
    STATUS: Retired 1986

MATERIAL: Ceramic
DESCRIPTION: Patterned after old-fashioned wood sleigh,
holds Christmas tree and wrapped presents.
PARTICULARS: Did not come in a box.

OSRP: $5.00
GBTru: $55.00   NC

Snowman With Broom

❑ **NAME:** Snowman With Broom   1982
    ITEM #: 5018-0
    STATUS: Retired 1990

MATERIAL: Ceramic with Straw broom
DESCRIPTION: Top hat, red nose, snowman holds
straw broom.

OSRP: $3.00
GBTru: $12.00 ↑20%

Monks-A-Caroling

☐ **NAME:** Monks-A-Caroling   1983
ITEM #: 6459-9
STATUS: Retired 1984

MATERIAL: Ceramic
DESCRIPTION: Four friars singing carols.
PARTICULARS: The original Monks, #6460-2, although giftware, was adopted as a Snow Village piece by collectors. It was unglazed, had paper song books and cord sashes. This piece, #6459-9, was retired after just one year due to maker's inability to supply. The Monks have a diffused rosy blush. The Monks were re-introduced in 1984 as Item #5040-7 from another supplier–on this piece the Monks have a distinct pink circle to give cheeks blush.

OSRP: $6.00
GBTru: $65.00 ↓7%

Scottie With Tree

☐ **NAME:** Scottie With Tree   1984
ITEM #: 5038-5
STATUS: Retired 1985

MATERIAL: Ceramic
DESCRIPTION: Black dog waits by snow covered tree with star at top.
VARIATIONS: With and without star at top of tree.

OSRP: $3.00
GBTru: $165.00 ↑10%

Monks-A-Caroling

☐ **NAME:** Monks-A-Caroling   1984
ITEM #: 5040-7
STATUS: Retired 1988

MATERIAL: Ceramic
DESCRIPTION: Four friars singing carols.
PARTICULARS: Replaced 1983 *Monks-A-Caroling*, Item #6459-9.

OSRP: $6.00
GBTru: $38.00 ↓5%

Singing Nuns

☐ **NAME:** Singing Nuns   1985
ITEM #: 5053-9
STATUS: Retired 1987

MATERIAL: Ceramic
DESCRIPTION: Four nuns in habits, sing carols.

OSRP: $6.00
GBTru: $130.00 ↑4%

Original Snow Village Accessories   65

Auto With Tree

<input disabled="" type="checkbox"> **NAME:** Auto With Tree   1985
ITEM #: 5055-5
STATUS: Current

MATERIAL: Ceramic with attached Sisal tree
DESCRIPTION: Red VW Beetle with tree strapped to roof.
PARTICULARS: Did not come in box. First Issue looks as if the tree's weight crushed the car. First Issue is approximately 3 $^3/_8$" long. Second Issue is approximately 3" long.

OSRP: $5.00
GBTru: $6.50 NC

Snow Kids Sled, Skis

<input disabled="" type="checkbox"> **NAME:** Snow Kids Sled, Skis 1985
ITEM #: 5056-3
STATUS: Retired 1987

MATERIAL: Ceramic
DESCRIPTION: Three children on a toboggan and one child on skis.
PARTICULARS: Set of 2. See *Snow Kids*, 1987, Item #5113-6.

OSRP: $11.00
GBTru: $50.00 NC

Family Mom/Kids, Goose/Girl

<input disabled="" type="checkbox"> **NAME:** Family Mom/Kids, Goose/Girl 1985
ITEM #: 5057-1
STATUS: Retired 1988

MATERIAL: Ceramic
DESCRIPTION: Mother holds hands of two children, one girl feeds corn to geese.
PARTICULARS: Set of 2.
VARIATIONS: In size.

OSRP: $11.00
GBTru: $48.00 ⬆7%

Santa/Mailbox

<input disabled="" type="checkbox"> **NAME:** Santa/Mailbox   1985
ITEM #: 5059-8
STATUS: Retired 1988

MATERIAL: Ceramic
DESCRIPTION: Santa with toy bag. Girl mails letter to Santa as dog watches.
PARTICULARS: Set of 2.
VARIATIONS: In size–larger Santa before down-scaled was 3 $^1/_5$", new Santa with trimmer silhouette is 3".

OSRP: $11.00
GBTru: $53.00 ⬆6%

Original Snow Village Accessories

Kids Around The Tree

☐ **NAME:** Kids Around The Tree 1986
ITEM #: 5094-6
STATUS: Retired 1990

MATERIAL: Ceramic
DESCRIPTION: Children join hands to make a ring around the snow covered tree with a gold star.
VARIATIONS: In size. Dramatically scaled down 5 ³/₄" to 4 ¹/₂". Variations affect GREENBOOK Trumarket Price. Larger, pre-1987 pieces–$60.00 (NC), scaled down pieces–$38.00 (↑9%).

OSRP: $15.00
GBTru: See Variations

Girl/Snowman, Boy

☐ **NAME:** Girl/Snowman, Boy 1986
ITEM #: 5095-4
STATUS: Retired 1987

MATERIAL: Ceramic
DESCRIPTION: Girl puts finishing touches on snowman as boy reaches to place decorated hat atop head.
PARTICULARS: Set of 2. See *Snow Kids*, 1987, Item #5113-6.

OSRP: $11.00
GBTru: $62.00 ↓11%

Shopping Girls With Packages

☐ **NAME:** Shopping Girls With Packages 1986
ITEM #: 5096-2
STATUS: Retired 1988

MATERIAL: Ceramic
DESCRIPTION: Girls dressed toasty for shopping– with hats, mittens, coats, boots–stand by some of their wrapped packages.
PARTICULARS: Set of 2.
VARIATIONS: In size–3" vs. 2 ³/₄", pre-1987 pieces are larger.

OSRP: $11.00
GBTru: $48.00 ↑7%

3 Nuns With Songbooks

☐ **NAME:** 3 Nuns With Songbooks 1987
ITEM #: 5102-0
STATUS: Retired 1988

MATERIAL: Ceramic
DESCRIPTION: Three nuns in habits carry songbooks to sing carols.

OSRP: $6.00
GBTru: $128.00 ↑2%

Original Snow Village Accessories

Praying Monks

❑ **NAME:** Praying Monks   1987
ITEM #: 5103-9
STATUS: Retired 1988

MATERIAL: Ceramic
DESCRIPTION: Three monks, standing side-by-side, praying.

OSRP: $6.00
GBTru: $44.00 ⬆10%

Children In Band

❑ **NAME:** Children In Band   1987
ITEM #: 5104-7
STATUS: Retired 1989

MATERIAL: Ceramic
DESCRIPTION: One child conducts three band players:
horn, drum and tuba.

OSRP: $15.00
GBTru: $32.00 ⬆28%

Caroling Family

❑ **NAME:** Caroling Family   1987
ITEM #: 5105-5
STATUS: Retired 1990

MATERIAL: Ceramic
DESCRIPTION: Father holds baby, mother and son,
and girl with pup.
PARTICULARS: Set of 3.

OSRP: $20.00
GBTru: $28.00 ⬇7%

Taxi Cab

❑ **NAME:** Taxi Cab   1987
ITEM #: 5106-3
STATUS: Current

MATERIAL: Ceramic
DESCRIPTION: Yellow Checker cab.
PARTICULARS: Size: 3 $^1/_2$" x 2".

OSRP: $6.00
GBTru: $6.50   NC

Original Snow Village Accessories

Christmas Children

☐ **NAME:** Christmas Children   1987
ITEM #: 5107-1
STATUS: Retired 1990

MATERIAL: Ceramic
DESCRIPTION: Children at outdoor activities: girl and pup on sled pulled by boy, girl holding wreath, girl feeding carrot to bunny.
PARTICULARS: Set of 4.

OSRP: $20.00
GBTru: $35.00 ↑17%

For Sale Sign

☐ **NAME:** For Sale Sign   1987
ITEM #: 5108-0
STATUS: Retired 1989

MATERIAL: Ceramic
DESCRIPTION: Holly trims house For Sale sign.
VARIATIONS: Blank sign for personalization, Item #581-9, Gift Creations Concepts (GCC) 1989 Christmas Catalog Exclusive, free with $100 D56 purchase.

OSRP: $3.50
GBTru: $10.00   NC

Snow Kids

☐ **NAME:** Snow Kids   1987
ITEM #: 5113-6
STATUS: Retired 1990

MATERIAL: Ceramic
DESCRIPTION: Three kids on toboggan, child on skis, boy and girl putting finishing touches on snowman.
PARTICULARS: Set of 4. Set of 4 incorporates 1985, Item #5056-3, and 1986, Item #5095-4, re-scaled to a smaller size.

OSRP: $20.00
GBTru: $50.00 ↑11%

Man On Ladder Hanging Garland

☐ **NAME:** Man On Ladder Hanging Garland   1988
ITEM #: 5116-0
STATUS: Retired 1992

MATERIAL: Man is Ceramic, ladder is Wooden, garland is Fiber
DESCRIPTION: Man carries garland up ladder to decorate eaves of house.

OSRP: $7.50
GBTru: $16.00 ↓11%

Original Snow Village Accessories

Hayride

☐ **NAME:** Hayride   1988
ITEM #: 5117-9
STATUS: Retired 1990

MATERIAL: Ceramic
DESCRIPTION: Farmer guides horse-drawn hay-filled sleigh with children as riders.

OSRP: $30.00
GBTru: $60.00   NC

School Children

☐ **NAME:** School Children   1988
ITEM #: 5118-7
STATUS: Retired 1990

MATERIAL: Ceramic
DESCRIPTION: Three children carrying school books.
PARTICULARS: Set of 3.

OSRP: $15.00
GBTru: $25.00   NC

Apple Girl/Newspaper Boy

☐ **NAME:** Apple Girl/Newspaper Boy   1988
ITEM #: 5129-2
STATUS: Retired 1990

MATERIAL: Ceramic
DESCRIPTION: Girl holds wood tray carrier selling apples for 5¢, newsboy sells the Village News.
PARTICULARS: Set of 2.

OSRP: $11.00
GBTru: $22.00 ↑10%

Woodsman And Boy

☐ **NAME:** Woodsman And Boy   1988
ITEM #: 5130-6
STATUS: Retired 1991

MATERIAL: Ceramic
DESCRIPTION: Man chops and splits logs, and boy prepares to carry supply to fireplace.
PARTICULARS: Set of 2.

OSRP: $13.00
GBTru: $30.00   NC

Doghouse/Cat In Garbage Can

❒ **NAME:** Doghouse/Cat In Garbage Can   1988
ITEM #: 5131-4
STATUS: Retired 1992

MATERIAL: Ceramic
DESCRIPTION: Dog sits outside doghouse decorated with wreath; cat looks at empty boxes and wrappings in garbage can.
PARTICULARS: Set of 2.

OSRP: $15.00
GBTru: $27.00   ⬆8%

Fire Hydrant & Mailbox

❒ **NAME:** Fire Hydrant & Mailbox   1988
ITEM #: 5132-2
STATUS: Current

MATERIAL: Metal
DESCRIPTION: Red fire hydrant and rural curbside mailbox on post.
PARTICULARS: Set of 2. Sizes: 1 $^1/_2$" & 2 $^3/_4$", respectively.

OSRP: $6.00
GBTru: $6.00   NC

Water Tower

❒ **NAME:** Water Tower   1988
ITEM #: 5133-0
STATUS: Retired 1991

MATERIAL: Metal and Ceramic
DESCRIPTION: Metal scaffold base holds red ceramic water container with green top, ladder leads to top.
PARTICULARS: 2 pieces–scaffold base and water container. Special piece, "John Deere Co." Water Tower (1989), Item #2510-4, Original SRP was $24.00 + Shipping. GREENBOOK Trumarket Price is $675.00 (⬆4%).

OSRP: $20.00
GBTru: $70.00   ⬆8%

Nativity

❒ **NAME:** Nativity   1988
ITEM #: 5135-7
STATUS: Current

MATERIAL: Ceramic
DESCRIPTION: Holy Family, lamb, in creche scene.
PARTICULARS: Size: 2 $^1/_4$".

OSRP: $7.50
GBTru: $7.50   NC

Original Snow Village Accessories   71

Woody Station Wagon

☐ **NAME:** Woody Station Wagon   1988
    ITEM #: 5136-5
    STATUS: Retired 1990

MATERIAL: Ceramic
DESCRIPTION: "Wood" paneled sides on station wagon.

OSRP: $6.50
GBTru: $25.00   NC

School Bus, Snow Plow

☐ **NAME:** School Bus, Snow Plow   1988
    ITEM #: 5137-3
    STATUS: Retired 1991

MATERIAL: Ceramic
DESCRIPTION: Yellow school bus and red, sand/gravel truck with snow plow.
PARTICULARS: Set of 2.

OSRP: $16.00
GBTru: $57.00 ↑14%

Tree Lot

☐ **NAME:** Tree Lot   1988
    ITEM #: 5138-1
    STATUS: Current

MATERIAL: Ceramic shack, Wood fence and Sisal trees
DESCRIPTION: Christmas lights on tree lot's fence plus decorated shack and trees for sale.
PARTICULARS: Size: 9 $1/2$" x 5" x 4 $1/2$".

OSRP: $33.50
GBTru: $37.50   NC

Sisal Tree Lot

☐ **NAME:** Sisal Tree Lot   1988
    ITEM #: 8183-3
    STATUS: Retired 1991

MATERIAL: Sisal
DESCRIPTION: A variety of cut trees for sale at a street lot.

OSRP: $45.00
GBTru: $85.00 ↑13%

Village Gazebo

☐ **NAME:** Village Gazebo   1989
    ITEM #: 5146-2
    STATUS: Retired 1995

MATERIAL: Ceramic
DESCRIPTION: Small, open, red roofed garden structure that will protect folks from rain and snow, or be a private place to sit.

OSRP: $27.00
GBTru: $42.00 ↑40%

Choir Kids

☐ **NAME:** Choir Kids   1989
    ITEM #: 5147-0
    STATUS: Retired 1992

MATERIAL: Ceramic
DESCRIPTION: Four kids in white and red robes with green songbooks caroling.

OSRP: $15.00
GBTru: $25.00   NC

Special Delivery

☐ **NAME:** Special Delivery   1989
    ITEM #: 5148-9
    STATUS: Retired 1990

MATERIAL: Ceramic
DESCRIPTION: Mailman and mailbag with his mail truck in USPO colors of red, white and blue with the eagle logo.
PARTICULARS: Set of 2. Discontinued due to licensing problems with the U.S. Postal Service. Replaced with 1990, *Special Delivery*, Item #5197-7.

OSRP: $16.00
GBTru: $40.00 ↓11%

For Sale Sign

☐ **NAME:** For Sale Sign   1989
    ITEM #: 5166-7
    STATUS: Current

MATERIAL: Metal
DESCRIPTION: Enameled metal sign can be "For Sale" or "SOLD." Birds decorate and add color.
PARTICULARS: Size: 3".
VARIATIONS: Item #539-8, **Bachman's Exclusive** Village Gathering 1990 "For Sale" sign. GREENBOOK Trumarket Price is $25.00 (NC).

OSRP: $4.50
GBTru: $4.50   NC

Original Snow Village Accessories

Street Sign

☐ **NAME:** Street Sign   1989
ITEM #: 5167-5
STATUS: Discontinued 1992

MATERIAL: Metal
DESCRIPTION: Green street signs can be personalized to give each village street a unique name.
PARTICULARS: 6 pieces per package. Use street names provided (Lake St., Maple Dr., Park Ave., River Rd., Elm St., Ivy Lane ...) or personalize. Size: 4 ¼" tall.

OSRP: $7.50
GBTru: $12.00 ↑50%

Kids Tree House

☐ **NAME:** Kids Tree House   1989
ITEM #: 5168-3
STATUS: Retired 1991

MATERIAL: Resin
DESCRIPTION: Decorated Club House built on an old dead tree. Steps lead up to hideaway.

OSRP: $25.00
GBTru: $55.00 ↑10%

Bringing Home The Tree

☐ **NAME:** Bringing Home The Tree   1989
ITEM #: 5169-1
STATUS: Retired 1992

MATERIAL: Ceramic with Sisal tree
DESCRIPTION: Man pulls sled holding tree as girl watches to make sure it doesn't fall off.

OSRP: $15.00
GBTru: $27.00   ↑8%

Skate Faster Mom

☐ **NAME:** Skate Faster Mom   1989
ITEM #: 5170-5
STATUS: Retired 1991

MATERIAL: Ceramic
DESCRIPTION: Two children sit in sleigh as skating Mom pushes them across the ice.

OSRP: $13.00
GBTru: $28.00 ↑40%

Crack The Whip

❒ **NAME:** Crack The Whip   1989
ITEM #: 5171-3
STATUS: Current

MATERIAL: Ceramic
DESCRIPTION: Fast moving line of skaters hold tightly to person in front of them. First person does slow patterns but as line snakes out, last people are racing to keep up and they whip out.
PARTICULARS: Set of 3. Sizes: 4 $^1/_4$", 2 $^1/_2$" & 1 $^3/_4$".

OSRP: $25.00
GBTru: $25.00   NC

Through The Woods

❒ **NAME:** Through The Woods   1989
ITEM #: 5172-1
STATUS: Retired 1991

MATERIAL: Ceramic and Sisal
DESCRIPTION: Children bring tree and basket of goodies to Grandma.
PARTICULARS: Set of 2.

OSRP: $18.00
GBTru: $23.00   ↓8%

Statue Of Mark Twain

❒ **NAME:** Statue Of Mark Twain   1989
ITEM #: 5173-0
STATUS: Retired 1991

MATERIAL: Ceramic
DESCRIPTION: Tribute to author who wrote about lives of American folk.

OSRP: $15.00
GBTru: $35.00 ↑17%

Calling All Cars

❒ **NAME:** Calling All Cars   1989
ITEM #: 5174-8
STATUS: Retired 1991

MATERIAL: Ceramic
DESCRIPTION: Police car and patrolman directing traffic.
PARTICULARS: Set of 2.

OSRP: $15.00
GBTru: $35.00   NC

Flag Pole

❒ **NAME:** Flag Pole   1989
ITEM #: 5177-2
STATUS: Current

MATERIAL: Resin base, Metal pole, Cloth flag, Thread rope
DESCRIPTION: Pole with American Flag to display in public.
PARTICULARS: Size: 7" high.

OSRP: $8.50
GBTru: $8.50   NC

Mailbox

❒ **NAME:** Mailbox   1989
ITEM #: 5179-9
STATUS: Retired 1990

MATERIAL: Metal
DESCRIPTION: Freestanding public mailbox in USPO
colors: red, white and blue with logo.
PARTICULARS: Discontinued due to licensing problems
with the U.S. Postal Service. Replaced with
1990 *Mailbox*, Item #5198-5.

OSRP: $3.50
GBTru: $20.00   NC

Village Birds

❒ **NAME:** Village Birds   1989
ITEM #: 5180-2
STATUS: Retired 1994

MATERIAL: Metal
DESCRIPTION: Small red and blue sitting birds.
PARTICULARS: 6 pieces per package.

OSRP: $3.50
GBTru: $5.00 ↑25%

Snow Village Promotional Sign

❒ **NAME:** Snow Village Promotional Sign   1989
ITEM #: 9948-1
STATUS: Discontinued 1990

MATERIAL: Earthenware
DESCRIPTION: Displays Snow Village logo. Brickwork
at base supports sign.
PARTICULARS: Intended to be used by D56 retailers as a
promotional item.

OSRP: Promotional
GBTru: $20.00 ↑33%

Kids Decorating The Village Sign

❑ **NAME:** Kids Decorating The Village Sign   1990
    ITEM #: 5134-9
    STATUS: Retired 1993

MATERIAL: Ceramic
DESCRIPTION: Two children place garland on Snow Village sign.

OSRP: $12.50
GBTru: $22.00 ⬆10%

Down The Chimney He Goes

❑ **NAME:** Down The Chimney He Goes   1990
    ITEM #: 5158-6
    STATUS: Retired 1993

MATERIAL: Ceramic
DESCRIPTION: Santa with bag of toys enters chimney to make delivery on Christmas Eve.

OSRP: $6.50
GBTru: $15.00   ⬆7%

Sno–Jet Snowmobile

❑ **NAME:** Sno–Jet Snowmobile   1990
    ITEM #: 5159-4
    STATUS: Retired 1993

MATERIAL: Ceramic
DESCRIPTION: Snowmobile, red with silver trim, front ski runners and rear caterpillar treads.

OSRP: $15.00
GBTru: $25.00   ⬆4%

Sleighride

❑ **NAME:** Sleighride   1990
    ITEM #: 5160-8
    STATUS: Retired 1992

MATERIAL: Ceramic
DESCRIPTION: Family rides in open, old-fashioned, green sleigh pulled by one horse.

OSRP: $30.00
GBTru: $50.00   ⬇9%

Original Snow Village Accessories

Here We Come A Caroling

☐ **NAME:** Here We Come A Caroling   1990
    ITEM #: 5161-6
    STATUS: Retired 1992

MATERIAL: Ceramic
DESCRIPTION: Children and pet dog sing carols.
PARTICULARS: Set of 3.

OSRP: $18.00
GBTru: $24.00 ↓4%

Home Delivery

☐ **NAME:** Home Delivery   1990
    ITEM #: 5162-4
    STATUS: Retired 1992

MATERIAL: Ceramic
DESCRIPTION: Milkman and milk truck.
PARTICULARS: Set of 2.

OSRP: $16.00
GBTru: $33.00 ↑10%

Fresh Frozen Fish

☐ **NAME:** Fresh Frozen Fish   1990
    ITEM #: 5163-2
    STATUS: Retired 1993

MATERIAL: Ceramic
DESCRIPTION: Ice fisherman, ice house.
PARTICULARS: Set of 2.

OSRP: $20.00
GBTru: $36.00 ↑3%

A Tree For Me

☐ **NAME:** A Tree For Me   1990
    ITEM #: 5164-0
    STATUS: Retired 1995

MATERIAL: Ceramic and Sisal
DESCRIPTION: Snowman with top hat, corn cob pipe, and red muffler carries his own small snow covered tree.
PARTICULARS: 2 pieces per package.

OSRP: $7.50
GBTru: $14.00 ↑75%

A Home For The Holidays

❏ **NAME:** A Home For The Holidays   1990
    ITEM #: 5165-9
    STATUS: Current

MATERIAL: Resin with Metal
DESCRIPTION: Birdhouse with blue bird sitting on roof. Pole decorated with garland and small snow covered evergreen.
PARTICULARS: Size: 4" tall.

OSRP: $6.50
GBTru: $7.00   NC

Special Delivery

❏ **NAME:** Special Delivery   1990
    ITEM #: 5197-7
    STATUS: Retired 1992

MATERIAL: Ceramic
DESCRIPTION: Snow Village postman and truck in red and green Snow Village Mail Service colors.
PARTICULARS: Set of 2. "S.V. Mail" Service replaced discontinued 1985 *Special Delivery*, Item #5148-9.

OSRP: $16.00
GBTru: $36.00   ↑3%

Village Mailbox

❏ **NAME:** Village Mailbox   1990
    ITEM #: 5198-5
    STATUS: Current

MATERIAL: Metal
DESCRIPTION: Snow Village mail receptacle in red and green Snow Village Mail Service colors.
PARTICULARS: "S.V. Mail" Service, replaces discontinued 1985 *Mailbox*, Item #5179-9. Size: 2".

OSRP: $3.50
GBTru: $3.50   NC

Christmas Trash Cans

❏ **NAME:** Christmas Trash Cans   1990
    ITEM #: 5209-4
    STATUS: Current

MATERIAL: Metal, Plastic and Paper
DESCRIPTION: Two galvanized refuse cans filled with holiday wrappings and garbage.
PARTICULARS: Set of 2. Tops come off. Size: 1 ½".

OSRP: $6.50
GBTru: $7.00   NC

Wreaths For Sale

❐ **NAME:** Wreaths For Sale   1991
ITEM #: 5408-9
STATUS: Retired 1994

MATERIAL: Ceramic, Wood and Sisal
DESCRIPTION: Girl holds for sale sign, boy holds up wreaths, child pulls sled. Fence holds wreath.
PARTICULARS: Set of 4.

OSRP: $27.50
GBTru: $40.00 ↓11%

Winter Fountain

❐ **NAME:** Winter Fountain   1991
ITEM #: 5409-7
STATUS: Retired 1993

MATERIAL: Ceramic and Acrylic
DESCRIPTION: Angel holds sea shell with water frozen as it flowed.

OSRP: $25.00
GBTru: $50.00   NC

Cold Weather Sports

❐ **NAME:** Cold Weather Sports   1991
ITEM #: 5410-0
STATUS: Retired 1994

MATERIAL: Ceramic
DESCRIPTION: Three children play ice hockey.
PARTICULARS: Set of 4.

OSRP: $27.50
GBTru: $45.00   NC

Come Join The Parade

❐ **NAME:** Come Join The Parade   1991
ITEM #: 5411-9
STATUS: Retired 1992

MATERIAL: Ceramic
DESCRIPTION: Two children carry parade banner.

OSRP: $12.50
GBTru: $20.00   NC

Village Marching Band

❏ **NAME:** Village Marching Band   1991
ITEM #: 5412-7
STATUS: Retired 1992

MATERIAL: Ceramic
DESCRIPTION: Drum Major, two horn players and two drummers.
PARTICULARS: Set of 3.

OSRP: $30.00
GBTru: $55.00 ↑10%

Christmas Cadillac

❏ **NAME:** Christmas Cadillac   1991
ITEM #: 5413-5
STATUS: Retired 1994

MATERIAL: Ceramic and Sisal
DESCRIPTION: Pink car holds tree and presents.

OSRP: $9.00
GBTru: $15.00 ↑50%

Snowball Fort

❏ **NAME:** Snowball Fort   1991
ITEM #: 5414-3
STATUS: Retired 1993

MATERIAL: Ceramic
DESCRIPTION: One boy behind wall, one hides behind tree, one in open clearing, all with snowballs to throw.
PARTICULARS: Set of 3.

OSRP: $27.50
GBTru: $40.00   NC

Country Harvest

❏ **NAME:** Country Harvest   1991
ITEM #: 5415-1
STATUS: Retired 1993

MATERIAL: Ceramic
DESCRIPTION: Farm folk with market basket and pitchfork. Reminiscent of Grant Wood's *American Gothic* painting.

OSRP: $13.00
GBTru: $18.00 ↓28%

Original Snow Village Accessories

Village Greetings

❐ **NAME:** Village Greetings   1991
ITEM #: 5418-6
STATUS: Retired 1994

MATERIAL: Metal
DESCRIPTION: Holiday banners to hang on side of buildings.
PARTICULARS: Set of 3.

OSRP: $5.00
GBTru: $10.00   NC

Village Used Car Lot

❐ **NAME:** Village Used Car Lot   1992
ITEM #: 5428-3
STATUS: Current

MATERIAL: Ceramic
DESCRIPTION: Small "wooden" office on a stone base with stone chimney. Attached tree. Free standing sign plus office sign advertises used cars and good terms. Three cars in lot.
PARTICULARS: Set of 5. Sizes: 10 $\frac{1}{2}$" x 5 $\frac{1}{2}$" x 6" & 4".

OSRP: $45.00
GBTru: $45.00   NC

Village Phone Booth

❐ **NAME:** Village Phone Booth   1992
ITEM #: 5429-1
STATUS: Current

MATERIAL: Ceramic
DESCRIPTION: Silver and red outdoor phone booth with accordion open/close doors.
PARTICULARS: Size: 4" high.

OSRP: $7.50
GBTru: $7.50   NC

Nanny And The Preschoolers

❐ **NAME:** Nanny And The Preschoolers   1992
ITEM #: 5430-5
STATUS: Retired 1994

MATERIAL: Ceramic
DESCRIPTION: Two girls and boy hold onto Nanny's shopping basket as she pushes carriage with baby.
PARTICULARS: Set of 2.

OSRP: $27.50
GBTru: $38.00 ↑27%

Early Morning Delivery

☐ **NAME:** Early Morning Delivery   1992
ITEM #: 5431-3
STATUS: Retired 1995

MATERIAL: Ceramic
DESCRIPTION: Village kids deliver morning newspaper. One tosses to house, one pushes sled, and Dalmatian holds next paper in mouth.
PARTICULARS: Set of 3.

OSRP: $27.50
GBTru: $34.00 ↑24%

Christmas Puppies

☐ **NAME:** Christmas Puppies   1992
ITEM #: 5432-1
STATUS: Current

MATERIAL: Ceramic
DESCRIPTION: One girl hugs a pup as two kids take box of pups for a ride in red wagon.
PARTICULARS: Set of 2. Sizes: 5 ³/₄" x 3" & 3".

OSRP: $27.50
GBTru: $27.50   NC

Round & Round We Go!

☐ **NAME:** Round & Round We Go!   1992
ITEM #: 5433-0
STATUS: Retired 1995

MATERIAL: Ceramic
DESCRIPTION: Two kids go sledding on round saucer sleds.
PARTICULARS: Set of 2.

OSRP: $18.00
GBTru: $22.00 ↑22%

A Heavy Snowfall

☐ **NAME:** A Heavy Snowfall   1992
ITEM #: 5434-8
STATUS: Current

MATERIAL: Ceramic
DESCRIPTION: Girl stops to look at bird perched on handle of her shovel as boy shovels snow off the walkway.
PARTICULARS: Set of 2. Sizes: 3" x 2 ¹/₄" & 3".

OSRP: $16.00
GBTru: $16.00   NC

Original Snow Village Accessories   83

We're Going To A Christmas Pageant

☐ **NAME:** We're Going To A Christmas Pageant 1992
ITEM #: 5435-6
STATUS: Retired 1994

MATERIAL: Ceramic
DESCRIPTION: Children wear costumes of Santa, a decorated tree and a golden star.

OSRP: $15.00
GBTru: $20.00 ↑11%

Winter Playground

☐ **NAME:** Winter Playground 1992
ITEM #: 5436-4
STATUS: Retired 1995

MATERIAL: Ceramic
DESCRIPTION: Two swings and a playground slide. Two trees and two birds complete piece.

OSRP: $20.00
GBTru: $35.00 ↑75%

Spirit Of Snow Village Airplane

☐ **NAME:** Spirit Of Snow Village Airplane 1992
ITEM #: 5440-2
STATUS: Current

MATERIAL: Ceramic and Metal
DESCRIPTION: Red prop biplane. Metal strap spring on three-tree base allows positioning.
PARTICULARS: Size: 7" x 6 $\frac{1}{2}$" x 5 $\frac{1}{4}$".

OSRP: $32.50
GBTru: $32.50 NC

Safety Patrol

☐ **NAME:** Safety Patrol 1993
ITEM #: 5449-6
STATUS: Current

MATERIAL: Ceramic
DESCRIPTION: Older children are safety guards at street crossing for two younger children.
PARTICULARS: Set of 4. Sizes: 3 $\frac{1}{4}$", 2 $\frac{1}{4}$", 2 $\frac{1}{2}$" & 2".

OSRP: $27.50
GBTru: $27.50 NC

Christmas At The Farm

❐ **NAME:** Christmas At The Farm   1993
   ITEM #: 5450-0
   STATUS: Current

MATERIAL: Ceramic
DESCRIPTION: Calf and lamb greet girl carrying a pail of feed.
PARTICULARS: Set of 2. Sizes: 2 $^3/_4$" x 2 $^3/_4$" & 2 $^3/_4$" x 2 $^1/_4$".

OSRP: $16.00
GBTru: $16.00   NC

Check It Out Bookmobile

❐ **NAME:** Check It Out Bookmobile   1993
   ITEM #: 5451-8
   STATUS: Retired 1995

MATERIAL: Ceramic
DESCRIPTION: Bookmobile van carries stories to children in villages and farms. Boys and girls select books to borrow.
PARTICULARS: Set of 3.

OSRP: $25.00
GBTru: $28.00   ⬆12%

Tour The Village

❐ **NAME:** Tour The Village   1993
   ITEM #: 5452-6
   STATUS: Current

MATERIAL: Ceramic
DESCRIPTION: Tourist information booth with clerk to assist visitors new to the village.
PARTICULARS: "Bayport" is misspelled. Has *q* instead of *p*. Size: 5 $^1/_4$".

OSRP: $12.50
GBTru: $12.50   NC

Pint-Size Pony Rides

❐ **NAME:** Pint-Size Pony Rides   1993
   ITEM #: 5453-4
   STATUS: Current

MATERIAL: Ceramic
DESCRIPTION: One child waits to buy a pony ride as another rides and one offers carrot to pony. Stable building and bench.
PARTICULARS: Set of 3. Sizes: 5 $^3/_4$" x 4 $^3/_4$" x 4 $^1/_2$", 3 $^1/_2$" & 2".

OSRP: $37.50
GBTru: $37.50   NC

Original Snow Village Accessories

Pick-up And Delivery

❑ **NAME:** Pick-up And Delivery   1993
ITEM #: 5454-2
STATUS: Current

MATERIAL: Ceramic
DESCRIPTION: Pick-up truck carries Christmas trees.
PARTICULARS: Size: 4 $\frac{1}{2}$" x 1 $\frac{3}{4}$" x 1 $\frac{3}{4}$".

OSRP: $10.00
GBTru: $10.00   NC

A Herd Of Holiday Heifers

❑ **NAME:** A Herd Of Holiday Heifers   1993
ITEM #: 5455-0
STATUS: Current

MATERIAL: Ceramic
DESCRIPTION: Three Holstein cows.
PARTICULARS: Set of 3. Sizes: 4 $\frac{1}{4}$" x 2", 4 $\frac{1}{4}$" x 2 $\frac{1}{4}$",
& 3" x 2".

OSRP: $18.00
GBTru: $18.00   NC

Classic Cars

❑ **NAME:** Classic Cars   1993
ITEM #: 5457-7
STATUS: Current

MATERIAL: Ceramic
DESCRIPTION: Station wagon with roof rack. Two tone
green sedan with tail fins. Sedan with spare tire mounted
outside trunk.
PARTICULARS: Set of 3.

OSRP: $22.50
GBTru: $22.50   NC

Spirit Of Snow Village Airplane

❑ **NAME:** Spirit Of Snow Village Airplane   1993
ITEM #: 5458-5
STATUS: Current

MATERIAL: Ceramic
DESCRIPTION: Propeller double strut winged planes.
PARTICULARS: 2 Assorted–blue or yellow.
Size: 4 $\frac{1}{2}$" x 5 $\frac{1}{2}$" x 2 $\frac{3}{4}$".

OSRP: $12.50
GBTru: $12.50   NC

Village News Delivery

☐ **NAME:** Village News Delivery 1993
ITEM #: 5459-3
STATUS: Current

MATERIAL: Ceramic
DESCRIPTION: Driver carries newspaper from van to stores and home delivery children carriers.
PARTICULARS: Set of 2. Sizes: 5" x 2" x 2 $\frac{1}{4}$" & 3".

OSRP: $15.00
GBTru: $15.00 NC

Caroling At The Farm

☐ **NAME:** Caroling At The Farm 1994
ITEM #: 5463-1
STATUS: Current

MATERIAL: Ceramic
DESCRIPTION: Farmer drives tractor/pulls carolers on hay covered wagon. One child pulls another onto wagon.
PARTICULARS: Midyear release. First ceramic accessory to be a midyear release. Size: 8 $\frac{1}{4}$" x 3" x 4".

OSRP: $35.00
GBTru: $35.00 NC

Stuck In The Snow

☐ **NAME:** Stuck In The Snow 1994
ITEM #: 5471-2
STATUS: Current

MATERIAL: Ceramic
DESCRIPTION: Dad pushes car, mom watches and son holds shovel and sand.
PARTICULARS: Set of 3. Sizes: 7" x 2 $\frac{1}{2}$", 3" & 2 $\frac{1}{2}$".

OSRP: $30.00
GBTru: $30.00 NC

Pets On Parade

☐ **NAME:** Pets On Parade 1994
ITEM #: 5472-0
STATUS: Current

MATERIAL: Ceramic
DESCRIPTION: Two children walk dogs on cold wintry day.
PARTICULARS: Set of 2. Sizes: 3 $\frac{1}{4}$" x 2 $\frac{1}{2}$" & 2 $\frac{1}{2}$" x 2 $\frac{3}{4}$".

OSRP: $16.50
GBTru: $16.50 NC

Original Snow Village Accessories

Feeding The Birds

❒ **NAME:** Feeding The Birds   1994
    ITEM #: 5473-9
    STATUS: Current

MATERIAL: Ceramic
DESCRIPTION: Woman and children are feeding birds as other birds sit on frozen birdbath.
PARTICULARS: Set of 3. Sizes: 3 $^1/_4$", 2" & 2 $^1/_4$".

OSRP: $25.00
GBTru: $25.00   NC

Mush!

❒ **NAME:** Mush!   1994
    ITEM #: 5474-7
    STATUS: Current

MATERIAL: Ceramic
DESCRIPTION: Small child sits on sled that is harnessed to a St. Bernard. Older child shouts to them from behind mailbox.
PARTICULARS: Set of 2. Sizes: 4" x 2" & 2 $^1/_4$".

OSRP: $20.00
GBTru: $20.00   NC

Skaters & Skiers

❒ **NAME:** Skaters & Skiers   1994
    ITEM #: 5475-5
    STATUS: Current

MATERIAL: Ceramic
DESCRIPTION: One child laces up her skates while another is happy to be able to stand. As one skier looks on, another goes BOOM!
PARTICULARS: Set of 3. Sizes: 4" x 2 $^1/_2$", 3" x 2 $^3/_4$" & 3 $^1/_2$" x 2".

OSRP: $27.50
GBTru: $27.50   NC

Going To The Chapel

❒ **NAME:** Going To The Chapel   1994
    ITEM #: 5476-3
    STATUS: Current

MATERIAL: Ceramic
DESCRIPTION: Family walks to the chapel with gifts and wreath as clergyman waits to greet them.
PARTICULARS: Set of 2. Size: Both are 3 $^1/_4$".

OSRP: $20.00
GBTru: $20.00   NC

Santa Comes To Town, 1995

❏ **NAME:** Santa Comes To Town, 1995   1994
ITEM #: 5477-1
STATUS: 1995 Annual

MATERIAL: Ceramic
DESCRIPTION: Children circle Santa as he hands out presents. He is holding a sack of toys and a book dated "1995."
PARTICULARS: 1st in a Series of Dated Annual Santa pieces.

OSRP: $30.00
GBTru: $34.00 ↑13%

Marshmallow Roast

❏ **NAME:** Marshmallow Roast   1994
ITEM #: 5478-0
STATUS: Current

MATERIAL: Ceramic
DESCRIPTION: Children take skating rest and roast marshmallows over log fire.
PARTICULARS: Set of 3. Lighted. Battery operated or can be used with Adapter, Item #5225-6. Fire glows.
Sizes: 3", 4" x 2" & 2".

OSRP: $32.50
GBTru: $32.50   NC

Coca-Cola® brand Delivery Truck

❏ **NAME:** Coca-Cola® brand Delivery Truck   1994
ITEM #: 5479-8
STATUS: Current

MATERIAL: Ceramic
DESCRIPTION: A large wreath encircles "Coca-Cola" on the back of red & white delivery truck.
PARTICULARS: Size: 5 ¼" x 2 ¾".

OSRP: $15.00
GBTru: $15.00   NC

Coca-Cola® brand Delivery Men

❏ **NAME:** Coca-Cola® brand Delivery Men   1994
ITEM #: 5480-1
STATUS: Current

MATERIAL: Ceramic
DESCRIPTION: One man carries crates to truck as another stops to taste a Coke.
PARTICULARS: Set of 2. Size: Both are 3 ½".

OSRP: $25.00
GBTru: $25.00   NC

Coca-Cola® brand Billboard

❏ **NAME:** Coca-Cola® brand Billboard   1994
ITEM #: 5481-0
STATUS: Current

MATERIAL: Ceramic
DESCRIPTION: Three lights shine on billboard featuring Santa enjoying a Coke. Trees grow in the shade of the sign.
PARTICULARS: Size: 7 ¼" x 3 ¾".

OSRP: $18.00
GBTru: $18.00   NC

A Visit With Santa

❏ **NAME:** A Visit With Santa   1995
ITEM #: 7544
STATUS: 1995 Annual

MATERIAL: Ceramic
DESCRIPTION: Mother and children meet Santa on the street. Mother has shopping bag. Gifts stacked on snow.
PARTICULARS: Store logo on shopping bag. Retailers chose colors for gift packages. Stores and individual Item Numbers as follows:

OSRP: $25.00
GBTru: See Particulars

Store	Item #	GBTru $
Bachman's	#754-4	$60.00
Fortunoff	#767-6	60.00
Pine Cone Christmas Shop	#773-0	60.00
Stat's	#765-0	60.00
The Lemon Tree	#768-4	60.00
The Limited Edition	#764-1	70.00
William Glen	#766-8	65.00
Young's Ltd.	#769-2	60.00

Frosty Playtime

❏ **NAME:** Frosty Playtime   1995
ITEM #: 54860
STATUS: Current

MATERIAL: Ceramic
DESCRIPTION: Child rides on bouncing deer as another holds a hula hoop. Boys make snow and ice houses.
PARTICULARS: Set of 3. Sizes: 3", 2" & 2 ½".

OSRP: $30.00
GBTru: $30.00

❐ **NAME:** Poinsettias For Sale   1995
  ITEM #: 54861
  STATUS: Current

MATERIAL: Ceramic
DESCRIPTION: Vendor offers choice of plants to shoppers.
PARTICULARS: Set of 3. Sizes: 3", 2 ³/₄" & 2 ¹/₂".

OSRP: $30.00
GBTru: $30.00

❐ **NAME:** Santa Comes To Town, 1996   1995
  ITEM #: 54862
  STATUS: Current

MATERIAL: Ceramic
DESCRIPTION: Santa pulls sleigh loaded with gifts as children catch a ride.
PARTICULARS: 2nd in a Series of Dated Annual Santa pieces. Size: 7 ¹/₄" x 3 ³/₄".

OSRP: $32.50
GBTru: $32.50

❐ **NAME:** Chopping Firewood   1995
  ITEM #: 54863
  STATUS: Current

MATERIAL: Ceramic with Wood
DESCRIPTION: Father chops wood as son stacks into ventilated cords.
PARTICULARS: Set of 2. Sizes: 3" & 2 ¹/₂".

OSRP: $16.50
GBTru: $16.50

Firewood Delivery Truck

❐ **NAME:** Firewood Delivery Truck   1995
  ITEM #: 54864
  STATUS: Current

MATERIAL: Ceramic with Wood
DESCRIPTION: Holiday Farms loaded with firewood held in place by slatted wood panels.
PARTICULARS: Size: 5 ¹/₂" x 2 ¹/₂".

OSRP: $15.00
GBTru: $15.00

Original Snow Village Accessories   91

Service With A Smile

❐ **NAME:** Service With A Smile   1995
ITEM #: 54865
STATUS: Current

MATERIAL: Ceramic
DESCRIPTION: One attendant at car service station cleans windshield as other holds new tire.
PARTICULARS: Set of 2.

OSRP: $25.00
GBTru: $25.00

Pizza Delivery

❐ **NAME:** Pizza Delivery   1995
ITEM #: 54866
STATUS: Current

MATERIAL: Ceramic
DESCRIPTION: Pisa Pizza green VW bug auto used for home delivery of fresh pizzas. Delivery person carries stacked boxed pies plus additional take-out.
PARTICULARS: Set of 2. Sizes: 4" & 3 $^1/_4$".

OSRP: $20.00
GBTru: $20.00

Grand Old Opry Carolers

❐ **NAME:** Grand Old Opry Carolers   1995
ITEM #: 54867
STATUS: Current

MATERIAL: Ceramic
DESCRIPTION: Singer and musicians present carols country-style.
PARTICULARS: Size: 3 $^1/_4$".

OSRP: $25.00
GBTru: $25.00

Snow Carnival Ice Sculptures

❐ **NAME:** Snow Carnival Ice Sculptures   1995
ITEM #: 54868
STATUS: Current

MATERIAL: Ceramic
DESCRIPTION: Mother and child get set to photograph ice angel as artist puts final touches on penguins and snowflakes.
PARTICULARS: Set of 2. Sizes: 3 $^1/_4$" & 2 $^1/_2$".

OSRP: $27.50
GBTru: $27.50

Snow Carnival King & Queen

❒ **NAME:** Snow Carnival King & Queen   1995
    ITEM #: 54869
    STATUS: Current

MATERIAL: Ceramic
DESCRIPTION: Ice carnival King and Queen arrive in sled-dog drawn sleigh.
PARTICULARS: Size: 9" x 4".

OSRP: $35.00
GBTru: $35.00

Starbucks Coffee Cart

❒ **NAME:** Starbucks Coffee Cart   1995
    ITEM #: 54870
    STATUS: Current

MATERIAL: Ceramic
DESCRIPTION: Woman stops to purchase hot coffee from vendor with mobile cart.
PARTICULARS: Set of 2. Sizes: 5" & 3 $^1/_4$".

OSRP: $27.50
GBTru: $27.50

Just Married

❒ **NAME:** Just Married   1995
    ITEM #: 54879
    STATUS: Current

MATERIAL: Ceramic
DESCRIPTION: Groom carries bride. Car is decorated in congratulatory balloons, tin cans and banner.
PARTICULARS: Set of 2. Sizes: 3 $^1/_4$" & 5" x 2 $^1/_2$".

OSRP: $25.00
GBTru: $25.00

Notes: _____

_____

_____

_____

_____

_____

Original Snow Village Accessories   93

*Photo
Not Available
At Press Time*

	NAME:	Here Comes Santa	1996
	ITEM #:	Various	
	STATUS:	1996 Annual	

MATERIAL: Ceramic
DESCRIPTION: Santa has red banner with message "Joy To The World." Three children follow Santa and one carries a gift wrapped present.
PARTICULARS: The following stores will have this piece, personalized for their store:

Store	Item #
Bachman's	#07744
Bronner's Wonderland	#07745
Broughton Christmas Shoppe	#07748
Calabash Nautical Gifts	#07753
Carson Pirie Scott	#07763
Dickens' Gift Shoppe	#07750
European Imports	#07762
Fibber Magee's	#07747
Fortunoff	#07741
Gustaf's	#07759
Ingle's Nook	#07754
North Pole City	#07742
Pine Cone Christmas Shop	#07740
Royal Dutch Collectibles	#07760
Russ Country Gardens	#07756
St. Nick's	#07757
Seventh Avenue	#07758
Stat's	#07749
The Cabbage Rose	#07752
The Calico Butterfly	#07751
The Christmas Loft	#07755
The Limited Edition	#07746
William Glen	#07743
Young's Ltd.	#07761

OSRP: $25.00
GBTru: $25.00

A Ride On The Reindeer Lines

	NAME:	A Ride On The Reindeer Lines	1996
	ITEM #:	54875	
	STATUS:	Current	

MATERIAL: Ceramic
DESCRIPTION: Family ready to depart for the holidays. Child and Bus Driver. Reindeer Line Bus with racing deer on front and sides is complete with large chrome bumper, wipers, and windows all around.
PARTICULARS: Set of 3. Midyear release.

OSRP: $35.00
GBTru: $35.00

❏ **NAME:** THE ORIGINAL SHOPS OF
DICKENS' VILLAGE 1984
ITEM #: 6515-3
STATUS: Retired 1988

See below.

MATERIAL: Porcelain
DESCRIPTION: Set of 7 includes *Crowntree Inn, Candle Shop, Green Grocer, Golden Swan Baker, Bean And Son Smithy Shop, Abel Beesley Butcher, Jones & Co. Brush & Basket Shop.*
PARTICULARS: Set of 7. Lighted.

OSRP: $175.00
GBTru: $1325.00 ↑2%

Crowntree Inn

❏ **NAME:** Crowntree Inn 1984
ITEM #: 6515-3
STATUS: Retired 1988

MATERIAL: Porcelain
DESCRIPTION: Large multi-paned windows run length of front of Inn with entry door decorated by wreath, second story stone, attic dormer.
PARTICULARS: 1 of the 7 piece set–THE ORIGINAL SHOPS OF DICKENS' VILLAGE. Lighted.

OSRP: $25.00
GBTru: $305.00 ↑2%

Candle Shop

❏ **NAME:** Candle Shop 1984
ITEM #: 6515-3
STATUS: Retired 1988

MATERIAL: Porcelain
DESCRIPTION: Timber framed windows, plaster on stone small house/store. Attic rental rooms, light over front entry.
PARTICULARS: 1 of the 7 piece set–THE ORIGINAL SHOPS OF DICKENS' VILLAGE. Lighted.
VARIATIONS: Variations in **roof color**–first release was gray, followed by blue.

OSRP: $25.00
GBTru: $195.00 ↑3%

Green Grocer

❏ **NAME:** Green Grocer 1984
ITEM #: 6515-3
STATUS: Retired 1988

MATERIAL: Porcelain
DESCRIPTION: Thatched roof over timber two story grocery/provisions store. Bay window for display. Attached storage room on side of store.
PARTICULARS: 1 of the 7 piece set–THE ORIGINAL SHOPS OF DICKENS' VILLAGE. Lighted.

OSRP: $25.00
GBTru: $185.00 NC

Golden Swan Baker

☐ **NAME:** Golden Swan Baker 1984
ITEM #: 6515-3
STATUS: Retired 1988

MATERIAL: Porcelain
DESCRIPTION: Painted sign with gold swan hangs above large bay window for display. Timbered building, brick chimney, light above entry door.
PARTICULARS: 1 of the 7 piece set–THE ORIGINAL SHOPS OF DICKENS' VILLAGE. Lighted.

OSRP: $25.00
GBTru: $180.00 NC

Bean And Son Smithy Shop

☐ **NAME:** Bean And Son Smithy Shop 1984
ITEM #: 6515-3
STATUS: Retired 1988

MATERIAL: Porcelain
DESCRIPTION: Double wood door, stone first story, second story set on stone with overhang. Steep curved roof with brick chimney.
PARTICULARS: 1 of the 7 piece set–THE ORIGINAL SHOPS OF DICKENS' VILLAGE. Lighted.

OSRP: $25.00
GBTru: $190.00 ↓3%

Abel Beesley Butcher

☐ **NAME:** Abel Beesley Butcher 1984
ITEM #: 6515-3
STATUS: Retired 1988

MATERIAL: Porcelain
DESCRIPTION: Timbered bottom half, second story plaster over stone, two chimneys.
PARTICULARS: 1 of the 7 piece set–THE ORIGINAL SHOPS OF DICKENS' VILLAGE. Lighted.

OSRP: $25.00
GBTru: $130.00 ↑4%

Jones & Co. Brush & Basket Shop

☐ **NAME:** Jones & Co. Brush & Basket Shop 1984
ITEM #: 6515-3
STATUS: Retired 1988

MATERIAL: Porcelain
DESCRIPTION: Cellar shop is a cobbler with small sign by his door to advertise, rest of building is for basketry, mats, and brush. Narrow staircase leads to entry.
PARTICULARS: 1 of the 7 piece set–THE ORIGINAL SHOPS OF DICKENS' VILLAGE. Lighted.

OSRP: $25.00
GBTru: $290.00 ↓3%

Dickens' Village

☐ **NAME:** Dickens' Village Church   1985
   ITEM #: 6516-1
   STATUS: Retired 1989

MATERIAL: Porcelain
DESCRIPTION: Stone entry at base of turret. Exposed stone nave base; timber/plaster upper walls; irregular shingled roof. Entry and nave windows are pointed arch shape.
PARTICULARS: Lighted.
VARIATIONS: There are five variations of the *Village Church:*

OSRP: $35.00
GBTru: See Variations

1) **Winter White:** Off white to cream walls, brown roof matches brown cornerstones–$385.00 (↑3%).

2) **Yellow or Cream:** Cream walls with light yellow coloring in mortar between stones, butterscotch roof–$275.00 (↑22%).

3) **Green:** Very light green tone on walls, butterscotch roof–$325.00 (↓1%).

4) **Tan:** Tan walls, butterscotch roof–$175.00 (↓8%).

5) **"Dark" or Butterscotch:** Walls are same color or nearly the same as roof–$150.00 (↓3%). (Only sleeve to read "Village Church." All others read "Shops Of Dickens' Village.")

☐ **NAME:** DICKENS' COTTAGES   1985
   ITEM #: 6518-8
   STATUS: Retired 1988

See below.

MATERIAL: Porcelain
DESCRIPTION: Set of 3 includes *Thatched Cottage, Stone Cottage, Tudor Cottage.*
PARTICULARS: Set of 3. Lighted. Early release to Gift Creations Concepts (GCC).

OSRP: $75.00
GBTru: $915.00 ↓4%

☐ **NAME:** Thatched Cottage   1985
   ITEM #: 6518-8
   STATUS: Retired 1988

MATERIAL: Porcelain
DESCRIPTION: Double chimneys rise from thatched roof, second story plastered/timbered home with second story extending out on sides.
PARTICULARS: 1 of the 3 piece set–DICKENS' COTTAGES. Lighted. Early release to Gift Creations Concepts (GCC).

OSRP: $25.00
GBTru: $185.00 ↓7%

Stone Cottage

☐ **NAME:** Stone Cottage   1985
ITEM #: 6518-8
STATUS: Retired 1988

MATERIAL: Porcelain
DESCRIPTION: Variegated fieldstone walls and rough-hewn shingle roof. Each house wing has own chimney.
PARTICULARS: 1 of the 3 piece set–DICKENS' COTTAGES. Lighted. Early release to Gift Creations Concepts (GCC).
VARIATIONS: Variations in **color**: "Early Tan" and "Pea Green."

OSRP: $25.00
GBTru: $400.00   NC

Tudor Cottage

☐ **NAME:** Tudor Cottage   1985
ITEM #: 6518-8
STATUS: Retired 1988

MATERIAL: Porcelain
DESCRIPTION: Stone foundation with timbered/plastered walls forming a small house. Two chimneys for heating/cooking.
PARTICULARS: 1 of the 3 piece set–DICKENS' COTTAGES. Lighted. Early release to Gift Creations Concepts (GCC).

OSRP: $25.00
GBTru: $375.00   ↓6%

Dickens' Village Mill

☐ **NAME:** Dickens' Village Mill   1985
ITEM #: 6519-6
STATUS: Limited Edition of 2,500

MATERIAL: Porcelain
DESCRIPTION: Rough-hewn stone makes up 3-section mill with large wooden mill wheel. Two sets double doors–one large set to allow carriage to be brought directly into building, smaller doors open into silo area. Pronounced roof ridges on two sections.
PARTICULARS: Lighted. Early release to Gift Creations Concepts (GCC). Some sleeves read "Dickens' Village Cottage."

OSRP: $35.00
GBTru: $4850.00   ↓3%

CHRISTMAS CAROL COTTAGES

☐ **NAME:** CHRISTMAS CAROL COTTAGES   1986
ITEM #: 6500-5
STATUS: Retired 1995

MATERIAL: Porcelain
DESCRIPTION: Set of 3 includes *Fezziwig's Warehouse, Scrooge & Marley Counting House, The Cottage Of Bob Cratchit & Tiny Tim.*
PARTICULARS: Set of 3. Lighted.

See next page.

OSRP: $75.00
GBTru: $115.00 ↑28%

☐ **NAME:** Fezziwig's Warehouse 1986
ITEM #: 6500-5
STATUS: Retired 1995

MATERIAL: Porcelain
DESCRIPTION: Square brick two-story building has two chimneys. Second story front is plaster over brick. Entire front is windowed.
PARTICULARS: 1 of the 3 piece set–CHRISTMAS CAROL COTTAGES. Lighted.
VARIATIONS: Early pieces have panes cut out of front door.

OSRP: $25.00
GBTru: $40.00 ⬆33%

Scrooge & Marley Counting House

☐ **NAME:** Scrooge & Marley Counting House 1986
ITEM #: 6500-5
STATUS: Retired 1995

MATERIAL: Porcelain
DESCRIPTION: Simple rectangular shape. Bottom brick, second story plastered with shuttered windows. Bay window major decorative design.
PARTICULARS: 1 of the 3 piece set–CHRISTMAS CAROL COTTAGES. Lighted.

OSRP: $25.00
GBTru: $40.00 ⬆33%

The Cottage of Bob Cratchit & Tiny Tim

☐ **NAME:** The Cottage of Bob Cratchit & Tiny Tim 1986
ITEM #: 6500-5
STATUS: Retired 1995

MATERIAL: Porcelain
DESCRIPTION: Small four-room house, main room has fireplace for heat/cooking. Half of house rises two stories to provide sleeping area. Neatly thatched roof.
PARTICULARS: 1 of the 3 piece set–CHRISTMAS CAROL COTTAGES. Lighted.

OSRP: $25.00
GBTru: $50.00 ⬆67%

Norman Church

☐ **NAME:** Norman Church 1986
ITEM #: 6502-1
STATUS: Limited Edition of 3,500

MATERIAL: Porcelain
DESCRIPTION: Solid four-sided tower used as both watch and bell tower. Doors and windows reflect the Romanesque rounded arches.
PARTICULARS: Lighted. Early release to Gift Creations Concepts (GCC).
VARIATIONS: Variations: light to dark gray in **color**.

OSRP: $40.00
GBTru: $3250.00 ⬆8%

Dickens' Village

NAME: DICKENS' LANE SHOPS   1986
ITEM #: 6507-2
STATUS: Retired 1989

MATERIAL: Porcelain
DESCRIPTION: Set of 3 includes *Thomas Kersey Coffee House, Cottage Toy Shop, Tuttle's Pub.*
PARTICULARS: Set of 3. Lighted.

See below.

OSRP:	$80.00
GBTru:	$615.00 ↑3%

Thomas Kersey Coffee House

NAME: Thomas Kersey Coffee House   1986
ITEM #: 6507-2
STATUS: Retired 1989

MATERIAL: Porcelain
DESCRIPTION: Unique roof set upon simple rectangular building rises up to central chimney with four flue pipes. Brick, plaster, and timber with tile or slate roof. Large multi-paned windows predominate front walls.
PARTICULARS: 1 of the 3 piece set–DICKENS' LANE SHOPS. Lighted.

OSRP:	$27.00
GBTru:	$170.00 ↑3%

Cottage Toy Shop

NAME: Cottage Toy Shop   1986
ITEM #: 6507-2
STATUS: Retired 1989

MATERIAL: Porcelain
DESCRIPTION: Small thatched roof cottage. Shop has large bay windows for light and display. Outside side stair/entry for family to living quarters.
PARTICULARS: 1 of the 3 piece set–DICKENS' LANE SHOPS. Lighted.

OSRP:	$27.00
GBTru:	$235.00 ↑4%

Tuttle's Pub

NAME: Tuttle's Pub   1986
ITEM #: 6507-2
STATUS: Retired 1989

MATERIAL: Porcelain
DESCRIPTION: Building rises three stories, ground level has pub for refreshments plus stable area for horse and carriages, second and third story jut out in step fashion. Travelers could rent rooms.
PARTICULARS: 1 of the 3 piece set–DICKENS' LANE SHOPS. Lighted.

OSRP:	$27.00
GBTru:	$225.00 NC

❒ **NAME:** Blythe Pond Mill House   1986
     ITEM #: 6508-0
     STATUS: Retired 1990

MATERIAL: Porcelain
DESCRIPTION: Three story timber house, fieldstone wing holds water wheel gears. Grinding stones rest next to house.
PARTICULARS: Lighted.
VARIATIONS: Name **"By The Pond"** error on bottom–$135.00 (NC). (Variation is more common than the correct piece and therefore is less expensive.)

OSRP: $37.00
GBTru: $280.00 ↓11%

❒ **NAME:** Chadbury Station And Train   1986
     ITEM #: 6528-5
     STATUS: Retired 1989

MATERIAL: Porcelain
DESCRIPTION: Three-car train (engine, coal/wood, and passenger car). Station built of rough stone base and fieldstone. Columns support overhang to keep passengers dry. Indoor room warmed by fireplace. Wooden benches provide waiting area.
PARTICULARS: Set of 4. Lighted.
VARIATIONS: In **size**.

OSRP: $65.00
GBTru: $385.00 ↑3%

❒ **NAME:** BARLEY BREE   1987
     ITEM #: 5900-5
     STATUS: Retired 1989

MATERIAL: Porcelain
DESCRIPTION: Set of 2 includes *Farmhouse* and *Barn*.
PARTICULARS: Set of 2. Lighted.

See below.

OSRP: $60.00
GBTru: $375.00   ↓5%

❒ **NAME:** Farmhouse   1987
     ITEM #: 5900-5
     STATUS: Retired 1989

MATERIAL: Porcelain
DESCRIPTION: Thatched roof on small farmhouse with centralized chimney. Half-story tucked into steeply pitched roof.
PARTICULARS: 1 of the 2 piece set–BARLEY BREE. Lighted. Secondary Market sales data for 2 piece set only.

OSRP: $30.00
GBTru: See Particulars

Dickens' Village

Barn

☐ **NAME:** Barn   1987
    ITEM #: 5900-5
    STATUS: Retired 1989

MATERIAL: Porcelain
DESCRIPTION: Stone foundation, thatched roof, for livestock.
PARTICULARS: 1 of the 2 piece set–BARLEY BREE. Lighted.
Secondary Market sales data for 2 piece set only.

OSRP: $30.00
GBTru: See Particulars

The Old Curiosity Shop

☐ **NAME:** The Old Curiosity Shop   1987
    ITEM #: 5905-6
    STATUS: Current

MATERIAL: Porcelain
DESCRIPTION: Antiques corner shop is adjacent to rare
bookstore. Curiosity shop has large display window and
two chimneys. Book shop is taller and narrower. Wood ribs
support upper story window and roof dormer.
PARTICULARS: Lighted. Designed after the Old Curiosity Shop
on Portsmouth Street in London.

OSRP: $32.00
GBTru: $42.00   NC

Kenilworth Castle

☐ **NAME:** Kenilworth Castle   1987
    ITEM #: 5916-1
    STATUS: Retired 1988

MATERIAL: Porcelain
DESCRIPTION: Stronghold for Kings and Lords, began
as a fortress and converted to Medieval Palace. Stone, thick-
walled, compact. Battlements surround all turrets.
PARTICULARS: Lighted. Inspired by the remains of
Kenilworth Castle, Warwickshire, England.
VARIATIONS: Slight **size** changes over two years.

OSRP: $70.00
GBTru: $695.00   ↑3%

Brick Abbey

☐ **NAME:** Brick Abbey   1987
    ITEM #: 6549-8
    STATUS: Retired 1989

MATERIAL: Porcelain
DESCRIPTION: Two spires flank front doors, rose window
above entry oak doors. Example of a stage of Gothic
architecture.
PARTICULARS: Lighted.

OSRP: $33.00
GBTru: $375.00   ↓5%

𝔇𝔦𝔠𝔨𝔢𝔫𝔰' 𝔙𝔦𝔩𝔩𝔞𝔤𝔢

❒ **NAME:** Chesterton Manor House   1987
ITEM #: 6568-4
STATUS: Limited Edition of 7,500

MATERIAL: Porcelain
DESCRIPTION: Known as a Great House, countryside home of many acres. Stone facade, slate roof, plaster and half-timber, open pediment above wood entry door with double-gable roof design.
PARTICULARS: Lighted. Early release to Gift Creations Concepts (GCC).
VARIATIONS: In **color**.

OSRP: $45.00
GBTru: $1665.00   ⬆1%

❒ **NAME:** Counting House &
           Silas Thimbleton Barrister   1988
ITEM #: 5902-1
STATUS: Retired 1990

MATERIAL: Porcelain
DESCRIPTION: Square, 3-story, 3-chimnied, offices. Equal angle gables create 4-section roof. Attached plaster/timbered 3-story building is smaller and narrower.
PARTICULARS: Lighted.

OSRP: $32.00
GBTru: $90.00   ⬆6%

❒ **NAME:** C. Fletcher Public House   1988
ITEM #: 5904-8
STATUS: Limited Edition of 12,500*

MATERIAL: Porcelain
DESCRIPTION: Pub windows wrap around corner. Wood ribs support wider/longer 2nd story. Sweet Shop tucks in next to pub, is plaster/timber design.
PARTICULARS: Lighted. *Plus Proof Editions. Market Price for Proofs is not established. Early release to Gift Creations Concepts (GCC).

OSRP: $35.00
GBTru: $545.00   ⬇5%

See next page.

❒ **NAME:** COBBLESTONE SHOPS   1988
ITEM #: 5924-2
STATUS: Retired 1990

MATERIAL: Porcelain
DESCRIPTION: Set of 3 includes *The Wool Shop, Booter And Cobbler, T. Wells Fruit & Spice Shop.*
PARTICULARS: Set of 3. Lighted.

OSRP: $95.00
GBTru: $380.00   ⬆4%

The Wool Shop

❏ **NAME:** The Wool Shop   1988
ITEM #: 5924-2
STATUS: Retired 1990

MATERIAL: Porcelain
DESCRIPTION: Low turret rounds out one front corner of shop. Wood framing of three front windows and lattice design. Light by front door.
PARTICULARS: 1 of the 3 piece set–COBBLESTONE SHOPS. Lighted.

OSRP: $32.00
GBTru: $175.00 ↓3%

Booter And Cobbler

❏ **NAME:** Booter And Cobbler   1988
ITEM #: 5924-2
STATUS: Retired 1990

MATERIAL: Porcelain
DESCRIPTION: Shoes made and repaired in this stone building with entry via Tannery where leather is cured and dyed. Outdoor light by main display window, wood hatch on roof opening.
PARTICULARS: 1 of the 3 piece set–COBBLESTONE SHOPS. Lighted. Some box sleeves picture *T. Wells Fruit & Spice Shop.*

OSRP: $32.00
GBTru: $125.00 ↑9%

T. Wells Fruit & Spice Shop

❏ **NAME:** T. Wells Fruit & Spice Shop   1988
ITEM #: 5924-2
STATUS: Retired 1990

MATERIAL: Porcelain
DESCRIPTION: White washed brick and timbered building. Front window has stone ledge. Outdoor covered produce bin for food.
PARTICULARS: 1 of the 3 piece set–COBBLESTONE SHOPS. Lighted. Some box sleeves picture *Booter And Cobbler.*

OSRP: $32.00
GBTru: $100.00 ↑5%

NICHOLAS NICKLEBY

❏ **NAME:** NICHOLAS NICKLEBY   1988
ITEM #: 5925-0
STATUS: Retired 1991

MATERIAL: Porcelain
DESCRIPTION: Set of 2 includes *Nicholas Nickleby Cottage, Wackford Squeers Boarding School.*
PARTICULARS: Set of 2. Lighted.
VARIATIONS: *Set with Nic"k"olas Error–$200.00 (↑8%).

See next page.

OSRP: $72.00
GBTru: $160.00* ↑3%

Nicholas Nickleby Cottage

❑ **NAME:** Nicholas Nickleby Cottage 1988
ITEM #: 5925-0
STATUS: Retired 1991

MATERIAL: Porcelain
DESCRIPTION: Brick, stone and slate-roofed home. Three chimneys, curved timbers decorate second story. Bay window on front room. Two roof dormers.
PARTICULARS: 1 of the 2 piece set–NICHOLAS NICKLEBY. Lighted.
VARIATIONS: Spelling error–Nic"k"olas–$120.00 (↑20%).

OSRP: $36.00
GBTru: $85.00 ↑6%

Wackford Squeers Boarding School

❑ **NAME:** Wackford Squeers Boarding School 1988
ITEM #: 5925-0
STATUS: Retired 1991

MATERIAL: Porcelain
DESCRIPTION: Three chimneys on steeply pitched roof ridge w/many gables. Student rooms above downstairs classrooms. Shuttered attic windows.
PARTICULARS: 1 of the 2 piece set–NICHOLAS NICKLEBY. Lighted.

OSRP: $36.00
GBTru: $85.00 NC

MERCHANT SHOPS

❑ **NAME:** MERCHANT SHOPS 1988
ITEM #: 5926-9
STATUS: Retired 1993

MATERIAL: Porcelain
DESCRIPTION: Set of 5 includes *Poulterer, Geo. Weeton Watchmaker, The Mermaid Fish Shoppe, White Horse Bakery, Walpole Tailors.*
PARTICULARS: Set of 5. Lighted.

See below.

OSRP: $150.00
GBTru: $245.00 ↓4%

Poulterer

❑ **NAME:** Poulterer 1988
ITEM #: 5926-9
STATUS: Retired 1993

MATERIAL: Porcelain
DESCRIPTION: Three-story stone block and timber, fresh geese hang outside front door.
PARTICULARS: 1 of the 5 piece set–MERCHANT SHOPS. Lighted.

OSRP: $32.50
GBTru: $55.00 NC

Dickens' Village

Geo. Weeton Watchmaker

❒ **NAME:** Geo. Weeton Watchmaker   1988
ITEM #: 5926-9
STATUS: Retired 1993

MATERIAL: Porcelain
DESCRIPTION: All brick, rounded bay window, slate roof, fan light window in oak front door.
PARTICULARS: 1 of the 5 piece set–MERCHANT SHOPS. Lighted.

OSRP: $32.50
GBTru: $55.00   NC

The Mermaid Fish Shoppe

❒ **NAME:** The Mermaid Fish Shoppe   1988
ITEM #: 5926-9
STATUS: Retired 1993

MATERIAL: Porcelain
DESCRIPTION: Roadside fish bins, bay windows, angled doors and walls, wooden trap door in roof.
PARTICULARS: 1 of the 5 piece set–MERCHANT SHOPS. Lighted.

OSRP: $32.50
GBTru: $70.00   ↑8%

White Horse Bakery

❒ **NAME:** White Horse Bakery   1988
ITEM #: 5926-9
STATUS: Retired 1993

MATERIAL: Porcelain
DESCRIPTION: Two large windows to display baked goods, roof is hipped and gabled with scalloped shingles.
PARTICULARS: 1 of the 5 piece set–MERCHANT SHOPS. Lighted.

OSRP: $32.50
GBTru: $55.00   NC

Walpole Tailors

❒ **NAME:** Walpole Tailors   1988
ITEM #: 5926-9
STATUS: Retired 1993

MATERIAL: Porcelain
DESCRIPTION: Stone and brick covered by stucco. Large first floor windows have wood panels under sills. Second floor has bow window.
PARTICULARS: 1 of the 5 piece set–MERCHANT SHOPS. Lighted.

OSRP: $32.50
GBTru: $55.00   NC

Dickens' Village

Ivy Glen Church

❐ **NAME:** Ivy Glen Church   1988
    ITEM #: 5927-7
    STATUS: Retired 1991

MATERIAL: Porcelain
DESCRIPTION: Square-toothed parapet tops stone turret by front entry of a thatched roof church. Curved timber design above door is repeated on bell chamber of turret. Arched windows. This church has a chimney.
PARTICULARS: Lighted.

OSRP: $35.00
GBTru: $80.00   ↓6%

DAVID COPPERFIELD

See below.

❐ **NAME:** DAVID COPPERFIELD   1989
    ITEM #: 5550-6
    STATUS: Retired 1992

MATERIAL: Porcelain
DESCRIPTION: Set of 3 includes *Mr. Wickfield Solicitor, Betsy Trotwood's Cottage, Peggotty's Seaside Cottage.*
PARTICULARS: Set of 3. Lighted. Early release to Showcase Dealers, 1990.
VARIATIONS: *Set with "Original Tan" Peggotty's– $230.00 (↑2%).

OSRP: $125.00
GBTru: $165.00*   ↓6%

Mr. Wickfield Solicitor

❐ **NAME:** Mr. Wickfield Solicitor   1989
    ITEM #: 5550-6
    STATUS: Retired 1992

MATERIAL: Porcelain
DESCRIPTION: Well-to-do legal practice and home. Second story has two balcony areas defined by low balustrades. 3 small dormers. Side door for family entry.
PARTICULARS: 1 of the 3 piece set–DAVID COPPERFIELD. Lighted. Early release to Showcase Dealers, 1990.

OSRP: $42.50
GBTru: $95.00   NC

Betsy Trotwood's Cottage

❐ **NAME:** Betsy Trotwood's Cottage   1989
    ITEM #: 5550-6
    STATUS: Retired 1992

MATERIAL: Porcelain
DESCRIPTION: Country home–brick, timbered, whitewash. Two chimneys. Known for variations of wall angles. Roof ridge has unique dogtooth design.
PARTICULARS: 1 of the 3 piece set–DAVID COPPERFIELD. Lighted. Early release to Showcase Dealers, 1990.

OSRP: $42.50
GBTru: $60.00   ↓8%

Peggotty's Seaside Cottage

🗌 **NAME:** Peggotty's Seaside Cottage   1989
ITEM #: 5550-6
STATUS: Retired 1992

MATERIAL: Porcelain
DESCRIPTION: Up-side-down boat into a house, iron funnel as chimney, captain's bridge, crows nest, barrels, boxes, ropes, and boots near entry.
PARTICULARS: 1 of the 3 piece set–DAVID COPPERFIELD. Lighted. Early release to Showcase Dealers, 1990.
VARIATIONS: In **color**–*"Original Tan"–$125.00 (↓17%).

OSRP: $42.50
GBTru: $55.00* ↓8%

Victoria Station

🗌 **NAME:** Victoria Station   1989
ITEM #: 5574-3
STATUS: Current

MATERIAL: Porcelain
DESCRIPTION: Brownstone with granite pillars and facings–central section with domed red tile roof, two side wings, covered front drive-through, gold clock above entry.
PARTICULARS: Lighted. Early release to Showcase Dealers and National Association Of Limited Edition Dealers (NALED), 1990. Designed after Victoria Station in London.

OSRP: $100.00
GBTru: $112.00   NC

Knottinghill Church

🗌 **NAME:** Knottinghill Church   1989
ITEM #: 5582-4
STATUS: Retired 1995

MATERIAL: Porcelain
DESCRIPTION: Beige/honey stone with gray slate roof, arched windows. Turret bell chamber rises where church wings intersect.
PARTICULARS: Lighted.

OSRP: $50.00
GBTru: $65.00 ↑18%

Cobles Police Station

🗌 **NAME:** Cobles Police Station   1989
ITEM #: 5583-2
STATUS: Retired 1991

MATERIAL: Porcelain
DESCRIPTION: Two-story brick, stone outlines front entry and upper windows. Two watch turrets on 2nd story corners.
PARTICULARS: Lighted.

OSRP: $37.50
GBTru: $145.00 ↑16%

☐ **NAME:** Theatre Royal 1989
ITEM #: 5584-0
STATUS: Retired 1992

MATERIAL: Porcelain
DESCRIPTION: Double set of doors fill theatre frontage. Garlands and gold bells add festive touch. Second floor rounded arch windows are separated by pilasters.
PARTICULARS: Lighted. Inspired by the Theatre Royal in Rochester, England where Charles Dickens saw his first Shakespearean play.

OSRP: $45.00
GBTru: $85.00 ↑6%

Ruth Marion Scotch Woolens

☐ **NAME:** Ruth Marion Scotch Woolens 1989
ITEM #: 5585-9
STATUS: Limited Edition of 17,500*

MATERIAL: Porcelain
DESCRIPTION: Herringbone brick design between timbers decorates front of 1 1/2-story shops and home. Small flower shop tucked onto one side. Bay windows repeat diamond and hexagon panes.
PARTICULARS: Lighted. *Plus Proof Editions. Market Price for Proofs is generally 10 to 20% less. Early release to Gift Creations Concepts (GCC). Named for the wife of D56 artist, Neilan Lund.

OSRP: $65.00
GBTru: $390.00 ↑1%

Green Gate Cottage

☐ **NAME:** Green Gate Cottage 1989
ITEM #: 5586-7
STATUS: Limited Edition of 22,500*

MATERIAL: Porcelain
DESCRIPTION: Three-story home. Repeated vault design on chimney, dormers, and third story windows. Balcony above door. Fenced courtyard and two doors give impression of two homes. Small part has steep roof, crooked chimney, and ornamental molding.
PARTICULARS: Lighted. *Plus Proof Editions. Market Price for Proofs is generally 10 to 20% less.

OSRP: $65.00
GBTru: $270.00 ↓2%

Q&A
Ask The Historian

Q. *Is Department 56 sold in other countries?*

A. Yes. Canada is the largest importer of Department 56 products. Other countries include England, Australia, and Japan. At this time, Department 56 is looking for a "partner" in Europe so it can increase its exports to that area of the world.

☐ **NAME:** The Flat Of Ebenezer Scrooge   1989
ITEM #: 5587-5
STATUS: Current

MATERIAL: Porcelain
DESCRIPTION: Four stories, broken balustrades and shutters, front door padlocked and chained, ghostly face on door knocker.
PARTICULARS: Lighted. Early release to National Association Of Limited Edition Dealers (NALED), 1989. Addition to "Christmas Carol" grouping.
VARIATIONS: There are four variations of *The Flat Of Ebenezer Scrooge:*
1) Made in Taiwan. Yellow panes in windows, far left shutter on 4th floor is slightly open allowing light to shine through–$95.00 (↓5%).
2) Made in Taiwan. No panes in windows–$65.00 (↑8%).
3) Made in Philippines. Yellow panes in windows, far left shutter on 4th floor is sealed–SRP @ $37.50.
4) Made in China. Yellow panes in windows–SRP @ $37.50.

OSRP: $37.50
GBTru: See Variations

☐ **NAME:** Bishops Oast House   1990
ITEM #: 5567-0
STATUS: Retired 1992

MATERIAL: Porcelain
DESCRIPTION: Large attached barn, round cobblestone oasts contain a kiln for drying malt or hops to produce ale. Exterior finished as a rough-cast surface over brick.
PARTICULARS: Lighted.

OSRP: $45.00
GBTru: $80.00 ↑7%

☐ **NAME:** KING'S ROAD   1990
ITEM #: 5568-9
STATUS: Current

MATERIAL: Porcelain
DESCRIPTION: Set of 2 includes *Tutbury Printer,* #55690 and *C.H. Watt Physician,* #55691.
PARTICULARS: Set of 2. Lighted. Each piece of set now assigned individual Item Number.

See next page.

OSRP: $72.00
GBTru: $80.00 ↑11%

Tutbury Printer

❏ **NAME:** Tutbury Printer 1990
ITEM #: 55690
STATUS: Current

MATERIAL: Porcelain
DESCRIPTION: Timbered/plaster design with decorative molding between first and second story. Ground floor bay window with smaller bays on second floor. Steeply pitched roof with a dormer.
PARTICULARS: 1 of the 2 piece set–KING'S ROAD. Lighted. Each piece of set now assigned individual Item Number.

OSRP: $36.00
GBTru: $40.00 NC

C. H. Watt Physician

❏ **NAME:** C.H. Watt Physician 1990
ITEM #: 55691
STATUS: Current

MATERIAL: Porcelain
DESCRIPTION: Doctor's office on ground floor, outside staircase leads to family residence, bricks used above most windows as decorative arch, exposed stone edges on four corners of house walls.
PARTICULARS: 1 of the 2 piece set–KING'S ROAD. Lighted. Each piece of set now assigned individual Item Number.

OSRP: $36.00
GBTru: $40.00 NC

Fagin's Hide-A-Way

❏ **NAME:** Fagin's Hide-A-Way 1991
ITEM #: 5552-2
STATUS: Retired 1995

MATERIAL: Porcelain
DESCRIPTION: Two attached buildings in disrepair. Broken shutters, cracks in wall. Barrel warehouse with step roof, gate across doors.
PARTICULARS: Lighted.

OSRP: $68.00
GBTru: $80.00 ↑11%

OLIVER TWIST

See next page.

❏ **NAME:** OLIVER TWIST 1991
ITEM #: 5553-0
STATUS: Retired 1993

MATERIAL: Porcelain
DESCRIPTION: Set of 2 includes *Brownlow House* and *Maylie Cottage.*
PARTICULARS: Set of 2. Lighted.

OSRP: $75.00
GBTru: $135.00 ↑4%

Brownlow House

❒ **NAME:** Brownlow House 1991
ITEM #: 5553-0
STATUS: Retired 1993

MATERIAL: Porcelain
DESCRIPTION: Two-story stone house with two brick chimneys and three front gables. Double doors.
PARTICULARS: 1 of the 2 piece set–OLIVER TWIST. Lighted.

OSRP:	$37.50	
GBTru:	$75.00	↑7%

Maylie Cottage

❒ **NAME:** Maylie Cottage 1991
ITEM #: 5553-0
STATUS: Retired 1993

MATERIAL: Porcelain
DESCRIPTION: Pronounced roof ridge. Curved cone roof shape repeated on dormers and front door. One chimney rises up front facade, second chimney on side of house.
PARTICULARS: 1 of the 2 piece set–OLIVER TWIST. Lighted.

OSRP:	$37.50	
GBTru:	$65.00	NC

Ashbury Inn

❒ **NAME:** Ashbury Inn 1991
ITEM #: 5555-7
STATUS: Retired 1995

MATERIAL: Porcelain
DESCRIPTION: Tudor timbered Inn for coach travelers. Food, lodging, and drink. Double chimneys, two roof dormers, and double peaks over multi-paned windows by entry.
PARTICULARS: Lighted.

OSRP:	$55.00	
GBTru:	$70.00	↑17%

Nephew Fred's Flat

❒ **NAME:** Nephew Fred's Flat 1991
ITEM #: 5557-3
STATUS: Retired 1994

MATERIAL: Porcelain
DESCRIPTION: Four-story home with three-story turret-like bow windows. Planters flank front door. Overhang window above side door with crow stepped coping in gable rising to two chimneys. Ivy grows up corner area–garlands, wreath, and Christmas greetings decorate facade.
PARTICULARS: Lighted. Addition to "Christmas Carol" grouping.
VARIATIONS: Taiwan piece is darker in color and approximately ¼" shorter than pieces from China.

OSRP:	$35.00	
GBTru:	$65.00	NC

Dickens' Village

❏ **NAME:** Old Michaelchurch   1992
    ITEM #: 5562-0
    STATUS: Current

MATERIAL: Porcelain
DESCRIPTION: Stone base with lath and plaster filling space between timbered upper portion. Tower rises up front facade with heavy solid look, a simple four-sided structure. Double wood doors at rear of church.
PARTICULARS: Lighted. Early release to Showcase Dealers and Gift Creations Concepts (GCC).

OSRP: $42.00
GBTru: $48.00   NC

Crown & Cricket Inn

❏ **NAME:** Crown & Cricket Inn   1992
    ITEM #: 5750-9
    STATUS: 1992 Annual

MATERIAL: Porcelain
DESCRIPTION: Three-story brick and stone with pillars flanking covered formal entry. Curved canopy roof on Golden Lion Arms Pub. Wrought iron balustrade outlines triple window on second floor. Dressed stone edges walls. Mansard roof with decorative trim and molding.
PARTICULARS: Lighted. Special collector box and hang tag. 1st Edition in the Charles Dickens' Signature Series.
VARIATIONS: In **color** from light to dark trim.

OSRP: $100.00
GBTru: $145.00 ↓17%

Hembleton Pewterer

❏ **NAME:** Hembleton Pewterer   1992
    ITEM #: 5800-9
    STATUS: Retired 1995

MATERIAL: Porcelain
DESCRIPTION: Timber framed with plaster in Elizabethan style. Bay windows create two story front facade. Chimney Sweep shop with steep pitched roof hugs one side of the pewterer.
PARTICULARS: Lighted.
VARIATIONS: Early issue has two small additions on right side, latter issue has one larger addition.

OSRP: $72.00
GBTru: $75.00 ↑4%

King's Road Post Office

❏ **NAME:** King's Road Post Office   1992
    ITEM #: 5801-7
    STATUS: Current

MATERIAL: Porcelain
DESCRIPTION: Simple four-sided stone three-story building with semi circular turret-like two story rise out of window area. Entrance door surmounted by pediment just below post office sign. Triple-flue chimney rises off back of building.
PARTICULARS: Lighted.

OSRP: $45.00
GBTru: $45.00   NC

Dickens' Village

The Pied Bull Inn

	NAME:	The Pied Bull Inn	1993
	ITEM #:	5751-7	
	STATUS:	1993 Annual	

MATERIAL: Porcelain
DESCRIPTION: Elizabethan style with wood and plaster upper stores canter levered out from stone and brick lower levels. Front entry at side of Inn allows public rooms to be of good size to service guests and local folk.
PARTICULARS: Lighted. Special collector box and hang tag. 2nd Edition in the Charles Dickens' Signature Series.

OSRP: $100.00
GBTru: $150.00 ↑3%

PUMP LANE SHOPPES

See below.

	NAME:	PUMP LANE SHOPPES	1993
	ITEM #:	5808-4	
	STATUS:	Current	

MATERIAL: Porcelain
DESCRIPTION: Set of 3 includes *Bumpstead Nye Cloaks & Canes, #58085; Lomas Ltd. Molasses, #58086* and *W.M. Wheat Cakes & Puddings, #58087.*
PARTICULARS: Set of 3. Lighted. Each piece now assigned individual Item Number.

OSRP: $112.00
GBTru: $112.00 NC

Bumpstead Nye Cloaks & Canes

	NAME:	Bumpstead Nye Cloaks & Canes	1993
	ITEM #:	58085	
	STATUS:	Current	

MATERIAL: Porcelain
DESCRIPTION: Tall narrow shop with timbered 2nd story. Front gable has design etched into trim. Shop was noted for cloaks and capes as well as canes and walking sticks.
PARTICULARS: 1 of the 3 piece set–PUMP LANE SHOPPES. Lighted. Each piece now assigned individual Item Number.

OSRP: $37.50
GBTru: $37.50 NC

Lomas Ltd. Molasses

	NAME:	Lomas Ltd. Molasses	1993
	ITEM #:	58086	
	STATUS:	Current	

MATERIAL: Porcelain
DESCRIPTION: Steps lead up to store above stone lower level where molasses and treacles are refined and stored. Double chimneys rise above thatched roof.
PARTICULARS: 1 of the 3 piece set–PUMP LANE SHOPPES. Lighted. Each piece now assigned individual Item Number.

OSRP: $37.50
GBTru: $37.50 NC

W.M. Wheat Cakes & Puddings

r **NAME:** W.M. Wheat Cakes & Puddings 1993
ITEM #: 58087
STATUS: Current

MATERIAL: Porcelain
DESCRIPTION: Baking-chimney rises from center of main shop roof. Second story rooms are dormered with additional chimney at rear. Wreath hangs above curved front door and arched design is repeated above front windows.
PARTICULARS: 1 of the 3 piece set–PUMP LANE SHOPPES. Lighted. Each piece now assigned individual Item Number.

OSRP: $37.50
GBTru: $37.50 NC

Boarding & Lodging School (#18)

r **NAME:** Boarding & Lodging School (#18) 1993
ITEM #: 5809-2
STATUS: 1993 Annual

MATERIAL: Porcelain
DESCRIPTION: Scrooge's early school, the red brick building is a solid & elegant design w/symmetry of gables, coping, matching chimneys & rooftop balustrade cupola.
PARTICULARS: Lighted. Bottom Stamp of the Charles Dickens' Heritage Foundation commemorates 150th Anniversary of *A Christmas Carol*. Address is #18. Special box & hang tag. Available since 1994 as Item #5810-6, w/o commemorative stamp, & address is #43. Early release to Showcase Dealers & select buying groups. An Edition in the C. Dickens' Signature Collection.

OSRP: $48.00
GBTru: $160.00 ↓20%

Kingsford's Brew House

r **NAME:** Kingsford's Brew House 1993
ITEM #: 5811-4
STATUS: Current

MATERIAL: Porcelain
DESCRIPTION: Stone 3-story building with slate roof. Grain was processed into ale by fermentation. Chimneys rise from both sides from ovens & vats where the beverages were brewed. Banner of Tankard hangs outside.
PARTICULARS: Lighted.

OSRP: $45.00
GBTru: $45.00 NC

Great Denton Mill

r **NAME:** Great Denton Mill 1993
ITEM #: 5812-2
STATUS: Current

MATERIAL: Porcelain
DESCRIPTION: Both grinding of grain for baking and animal feed as well as preparation of wool combed into yarn took place at Mill. Narrow 3-story wood structure with water wheel for power to turn wheels.
PARTICULARS: Lighted.

OSRP: $50.00
GBTru: $50.00 NC

Dedlock Arms

r **NAME:** Dedlock Arms   1994
ITEM #: 5752-5
STATUS: 1994 Annual

MATERIAL: Porcelain
DESCRIPTION: Stone wall courtyard has metal gate and 2 lanterns. 3-story Inn is brightly lit with Inn sign above front window.
PARTICULARS: Lighted. Special collector box and hang tag. 3rd Edition in the Charles Dickens' Signature Series.

OSRP: $100.00
GBTru: $135.00 ↓10%

Boarding & Lodging School (#43)

r **NAME:** Boarding & Lodging School (#43)   1994
ITEM #: 5810-6
STATUS: Current

MATERIAL: Porcelain
DESCRIPTION: Scrooge's early school, the red brick building is a solid and elegant design with symmetry of gables, coping, matching chimneys and rooftop balustrade cupola.
PARTICULARS: Lighted. Features #43 as address. See 1993, #5809-2 for Commemorative version.

OSRP: $48.00
GBTru: $48.00   NC

Whittlesbourne Church

r **NAME:** Whittlesbourne Church   1994
ITEM #: 5821-1
STATUS: Current

MATERIAL: Porcelain
DESCRIPTION: Stone church with a single fortress-like tower rising off front right side. A masonry brace built against left side supports massive stone wall and provides a walkway.
PARTICULARS: Lighted. Midyear release.

OSRP: $85.00
GBTru: $85.00   NC

Giggelswick Mutton & Ham

r **NAME:** Giggelswick Mutton & Ham   1994
ITEM #: 5822-0
STATUS: Current

MATERIAL: Porcelain
DESCRIPTION: Butcher shop concentrates on meats from sheep and pigs. Smokehouse on side cures meat and adds special flavoring. Shop has corner wraparound windows.
PARTICULARS: Lighted. Midyear release. Named after a town in North Yorkshire, England.

OSRP: $48.00
GBTru: $48.00   NC

Dickens' Village

☐ **NAME:** Hather Harness   1994
     ITEM #: 5823-8
     STATUS: Current

MATERIAL: Porcelain
DESCRIPTION: Stone, brick and stucco 3-story shop and family home. Double doors allow entry of horses. Oxen, carriages and wagons to be fixed.
PARTICULARS: Lighted.
VARIATIONS: Color variations in main part of shop/home.

OSRP: $48.00
GBTru: $48.00   NC

See below.

☐ **NAME:** PORTOBELLO ROAD
            THATCHED COTTAGES   1994
     ITEM #: 5824-6
     STATUS: Current

MATERIAL: Porcelain
DESCRIPTION: Set of 3 includes *Mr. & Mrs. Pickle,* #58247, *Cobb Cottage,* #58248 and *Browning Cottage,* #58249.
PARTICULARS: Set of 3. Lighted. Each piece now assigned individual Item Number.

OSRP: $120.00
GBTru: $120.00   NC

☐ **NAME:** Mr. & Mrs. Pickle   1994
     ITEM #: 58247
     STATUS: Current

MATERIAL: Porcelain
DESCRIPTION: Timbered stucco home with attached Antique Store. Home sign highlights a pickle.
PARTICULARS: 1 of the 3 piece set–PORTOBELLO ROAD THATCHED COTTAGES. Lighted. Each piece now assigned individual Item Number.

OSRP: $40.00
GBTru: $40.00   NC

☐ **NAME:** Cobb Cottage   1994
     ITEM #: 58248
     STATUS: Current

MATERIAL: Porcelain
DESCRIPTION: Thatched roof being completed on a stucco, timber and brick home. Unique L-shape with ornate roof ridges.
PARTICULARS: 1 of the 3 piece set–PORTOBELLO ROAD THATCHED COTTAGES. Lighted. Each piece now assigned individual Item Number. First Heritage Village house without snow on the roof.

OSRP: $40.00
GBTru: $40.00   NC

Browning Cottage

☐ **NAME:** Browning Cottage   1994
ITEM #: 58249
STATUS: Current

MATERIAL: Porcelain
DESCRIPTION: 2-story brick, timber and stucco home. Original thatch roof replaced by slate to denote increase in family's wealth. Dutch door entry.
PARTICULARS: 1 of the 3 piece set–PORTOBELLO ROAD THATCHED COTTAGES. Lighted. Each piece now assigned individual Item Number.

OSRP: $40.00
GBTru: $40.00   NC

Sir John Falstaff Inn

☐ **NAME:** Sir John Falstaff Inn   1995
ITEM #: 5753-3
STATUS: 1995 Annual

MATERIAL: Porcelain
DESCRIPTION: 3-story Inn of stucco, timber and brick with slate roof. 2-story bay windows frame front entry.
PARTICULARS: Lighted. Special collector box and hang tag. 4th Edition in the Charles Dickens' Signature Series.

OSRP: $100.00
GBTru: $130.00 ↑30%

Dickens' Village Start A Tradition Set

☐ **NAME:** Dickens' Village Start A Tradition Set   1995
ITEM #: 5832-7
STATUS: Current

MATERIAL: Porcelain
DESCRIPTION:
Faversham Lamps & Oil–2-story shop/home with stone trim on arched door/windows. Crowsteppped roof edges.
Morston Steak And Kidney Pie–Meat pies prepared in small 1 ½-story shop/home. Large paned window by entry.
Set also includes:
   Town Square Carolers accessory,
   5 assorted sisal trees,
   Cobblestone Road and
   Bag of Real Plastic Snow.
PARTICULARS: Set of 13. Lighted. Starter Set is midyear release featured at D56 National Homes For The Holidays Open House Event–Oct/Nov 1995. Special packaging for promotion. Set also available during Event week of November 7-11, 1996.

OSRP: $85.00
GBTru: $85.00   NC

☐ **NAME:** J.D. Nichols Toy Shop   1995
ITEM #: 58328
STATUS: Current

MATERIAL: Porcelain
DESCRIPTION: Brightly lit front window, topped by ledge carrying store name, and trimmed with 3 potted trees highlights toy shop. Tall front gables feature timber design. Brick chimneys rise from steeply pitched roof.
PARTICULARS: Lighted.

OSRP: $48.00
GBTru: $48.00

☐ **NAME:** Dursley Manor   1995
ITEM #: 58329
STATUS: Current

MATERIAL: Porcelain
DESCRIPTION: Two plaques above entry state building name and year cornerstone placed. Brick with stone trim at windows, carriage portico, roof edging and the 3 chimneys.
PARTICULARS: Lighted.

OSRP: $50.00
GBTru: $50.00

☐ **NAME:** Blenham Street Bank   1995
ITEM #: 58330
STATUS: Current

MATERIAL: Porcelain
DESCRIPTION: Many windows bring light and openness to squared building design. Strength and fortress-like solidarity promoted by use of stone, columns, and arches above windows. Double entry doors topped by fanlight window arch.
PARTICULARS: Lighted.

OSRP: $60.00
GBTru: $60.00

☐ **NAME:** WRENBURY SHOPS   1995
ITEM #: 58331
STATUS: Current

MATERIAL: Porcelain
DESCRIPTION: Set of 3 includes *Wrenbury Baker*, #58332, *The Chop Shop*, #58333 and *T. Puddlewick Spectacle Shop*, #58334.
PARTICULARS: Set of 3. Lighted. Each piece now assigned individual Item Number.

See next page.

OSRP: $100.00
GBTru: $100.00

Wrenbury Baker

NAME: Wrenbury Baker   1995
ITEM #: 58332
STATUS: Current

MATERIAL: Porcelain
DESCRIPTION: Cottage shop houses baker. 1 $\frac{1}{2}$-story with roof line coming down to first floor. Single chimney rises through hand hewn roof. Sign outside by entry.
PARTICULARS: 1 of the 3 piece set–WRENBURY SHOPS. Lighted. Each piece now assigned individual Item Number.

OSRP: $35.00
GBTru: $35.00

The Chop Shop

NAME: The Chop Shop   1995
ITEM #: 58333
STATUS: Current

MATERIAL: Porcelain
DESCRIPTION: Large chimney with 4 flue pots rises through rough shingle roof. Sign outside entry advertises wares. Stucco facade.
PARTICULARS: 1 of the 3 piece set–WRENBURY SHOPS. Lighted. Each piece now assigned individual Item Number.

OSRP: $35.00
GBTru: $35.00

T. Puddlewick Spectacle Shop

NAME: T. Puddlewick Spectacle Shop   1995
ITEM #: 58334
STATUS: Current

MATERIAL: Porcelain
DESCRIPTION: Ornate timber tudor style shop selling glasses, lorgnettes, looking glasses, monocles, and spyglasses. Sign outside advertises product.
PARTICULARS: 1 of the 3 piece set–WRENBURY SHOPS. Lighted. Each piece now assigned individual Item Number.

OSRP: $35.00
GBTru: $35.00

The Maltings

NAME: The Maltings   1995
ITEM #: 5833-5
STATUS: Current

MATERIAL: Porcelain
DESCRIPTION: Home, shop and bridge in one construct of stone, stucco and wood. Large doors allow carts to enter.
PARTICULARS: Lighted. Midyear release.

OSRP: $50.00
GBTru: $50.00   NC

❒ **NAME:** Dudden Cross Church   1995
     ITEM #: 5834-3
     STATUS: Current

MATERIAL: Porcelain
DESCRIPTION: Brick church with stone coping. Bell tower rises on one side through roof. Stone archway to courtyard on other side near entry door.
PARTICULARS: Lighted. Midyear release.

OSRP: $45.00
GBTru: $45.00   NC

❒ **NAME:** The Grapes Inn   1996
     ITEM #: 57534
     STATUS: 1996 Annual

MATERIAL: Porcelain
DESCRIPTION: Inn on the waterfront supplies food, drink and lodging for weary travelers. Rowboats are tied up to rear unloading dock. Two staircases outside lead to inn or to pub and dining areas.
PARTICULARS: Lighted. 5th Edition in Charles Dickens' Signature Series.

OSRP: $120.00
GBTru: $120.00

❒ **NAME:** Ramsford Palace   1996
     ITEM #: 58336
     STATUS: Limited Edition of 27,500

MATERIAL: Porcelain
DESCRIPTION: Set of 17 includes: *Ramsford Palace*–Equally proportioned, to symbolize the stability of the royal family in residence. Heraldry symbol above two storied pillars. Main roof topped by dome. Accessories: *Palace Guards, Set/2, Palace Gate, Palace Fountain, Wall Hedge, Set/8, Corner Wall Topiaries, Set/4.*
PARTICULARS: Set of 17. Lighted. Midyear release. Canada will now begin to receive limited edition pieces. Distributor is Millard Lister–approximately 100 pieces allocated.

OSRP: $175.00
GBTru: $175.00

❒ **NAME:** Butter Tub Farmhouse   1996
     ITEM #: 58337
     STATUS: Current

MATERIAL: Porcelain
DESCRIPTION: Three steeply pitched red roof heights set off tall narrow chimneys. Door and windows have wood frames. High gables match roof heights on front facade.
PARTICULARS: Lighted. Midyear release.

OSRP: $40.00
GBTru: $40.00

☐ **NAME:** Butter Tub Barn   1996
ITEM #: 58338
STATUS: Current

MATERIAL: Porcelain
DESCRIPTION: Two separate barn areas share one steep roof. Wagons can enter through double wood doors or into central loading area.
PARTICULARS: Lighted. Midyear release.

OSRP: $48.00
GBTru: $48.00

The Christmas Carol Cottage (Revisited)

☐ **NAME:** The Christmas Carol Cottage
(Revisited)   1996
ITEM #: 58339
STATUS: Current

MATERIAL: Porcelain and Metal
DESCRIPTION: New version of home of Bob and Mary Cratchit. 1 ¹/₂-story, roof comes down to first floor. Dormers on upper loft sleeping area show as rounded sections in roof. Log pile against larger chimney holds smoking element.
PARTICULARS: Lighted. Midyear release. A built-in **Magic Smoking Element** powered by a separate transformer heats a supplied non-toxic liquid causing it to smoke.

OSRP: $60.00
GBTru: $60.00

Q&Ask The Historian

Q. Buildings used to retire and nearly double in price right away. Then they would increase every year. This doesn't seem to be the rule anymore.

A. You're right. Values increased by approximately 100% almost immediately, then decreased slightly a few months later before beginning their ascent. Typically, this is no longer the case. Collectors have learned to purchase the pieces they like, if not before they retire, then on retirement day. The full-page ad that Department 56 runs in the *USA Today* newspaper each retirement day is largely responsible for this. Collectors are immediately aware of what retires and can act accordingly.

The reason that newly retired pieces still increase is because some collectors still don't have the opportunity to purchase them before they retire, or more likely, decide they want them after they have retired. Also, there are new collectors everyday. They, too, may want to purchase pieces that have recently retired.

❏ **NAME:** NEW ENGLAND VILLAGE 1986
ITEM #: 6530-7
STATUS: Retired 1989

MATERIAL: Porcelain
DESCRIPTION: Set of 7 includes *Apothecary Shop, General Store, Nathaniel Bingham Fabrics, Livery Stable & Boot Shop, Steeple Church, Brick Town Hall* and *Red Schoolhouse.*
PARTICULARS: Set of 7. Lighted.

See below.

OSRP: $170.00
GBTru: $1225.00 ↓2%

APOTHECARY SHOP

❏ **NAME:** Apothecary Shop 1986
ITEM #: 6530-7
STATUS: Retired 1989

MATERIAL: Porcelain
DESCRIPTION: Variegated fieldstone with white wood bay window. Gable and lean-to are blue clapboard.
PARTICULARS: 1 of the 7 piece set–NEW ENGLAND VILLAGE. Lighted.

OSRP: $25.00
GBTru: $100.00 NC

GENERAL STORE

❏ **NAME:** General Store 1986
ITEM #: 6530-7
STATUS: Retired 1989

MATERIAL: Porcelain
DESCRIPTION: Round columns support full length covered porch. Two small dormers on roof with central chimney.
PARTICULARS: 1 of the 7 piece set–NEW ENGLAND VILLAGE. Lighted.

OSRP: $25.00
GBTru: $325.00 ↓7%

NATHANIEL BINGHAM FABRICS

❏ **NAME:** Nathaniel Bingham Fabrics 1986
ITEM #: 6530-7
STATUS: Retired 1989

MATERIAL: Porcelain
DESCRIPTION: Clapboard saltbox design fabric store and Post Office. Each shop has own chimney. Living quarters above larger fabric store.
PARTICULARS: 1 of the 7 piece set–NEW ENGLAND VILLAGE. Lighted.

OSRP: $25.00
GBTru: $160.00 ↑7%

LIVERY STABLE & BOOT SHOP

❏ **NAME:** Livery Stable & Boot Shop   1986
ITEM #: 6530-7
STATUS: Retired 1989

MATERIAL: Porcelain
DESCRIPTION: Two-story painted clapboard house with wood planked wing contains tannery and livery stable. Stable has stone chimney, double doors.
PARTICULARS: 1 of the 7 piece set–NEW ENGLAND VILLAGE. Lighted.

OSRP: $25.00
GBTru: $150.00 ⬆3%

STEEPLE CHURCH

❏ **NAME:** Steeple Church   1986
ITEM #: 6530-7
STATUS: Retired 1989

MATERIAL: Porcelain
DESCRIPTION: White clapboard church w/2-tier steeple. Windows have molding above and below. Simple design.
PARTICULARS: 1 of the 7 piece set–NEW ENGLAND VILLAGE. Lighted. Reissued in 1989 as #6539-0.
VARIATIONS: Variations affect GBTru Prices: 1) #6530-7, tree attached with porcelain slip –$185 (⬆6%). 2) #6530-7, tree attached with glue–$95 (⬇5%). 3) Reissue of church as #6539-0, tree attached with glue–$90 (⬆ 6%).

OSRP: $25.00
GBTru: See Variations

BRICK TOWN HALL

❏ **NAME:** Brick Town Hall   1986
ITEM #: 6530-7
STATUS: Retired 1989

MATERIAL: Porcelain
DESCRIPTION: Mansard roof over 2-story Town Hall. Cupola is centered on roof ridge between two brick chimneys. Windows trimmed with ornamental molding.
PARTICULARS: 1 of the 7 piece set–NEW ENGLAND VILLAGE. Lighted.

OSRP: $25.00
GBTru: $220.00 ⬆5%

RED SCHOOLHOUSE

❏ **NAME:** Red Schoolhouse   1986
ITEM #: 6530-7
STATUS: Retired 1989

MATERIAL: Porcelain
DESCRIPTION: Red wood school with stone chimney and open belfry. Hand powered water pump by front door.
PARTICULARS: 1 of the 7 piece set–NEW ENGLAND VILLAGE. Lighted.

OSRP: $25.00
GBTru: $255.00 ⬇2%

JACOB ADAMS FARMHOUSE AND BARN

☐ **NAME:** Jacob Adams Farmhouse And Barn 1986
ITEM #: 6538-2
STATUS: Retired 1989

MATERIAL: Porcelain
DESCRIPTION: Red multi-level wood barn atop a stone foundation. Stone silo attached. Home features front porch, small front bay window, butter churn by door, simple design.
PARTICULARS: Set of 5–2 buildings, 3 animals. Lighted.

OSRP: $65.00
GBTru: $525.00 ↓9%

CRAGGY COVE LIGHTHOUSE

☐ **NAME:** Craggy Cove Lighthouse 1987
ITEM #: 5930-7
STATUS: Retired 1994

MATERIAL: Porcelain
DESCRIPTION: Keeper lives in small white clapboard home attached to lighthouse. Front porch of home features holiday decorated columns. Stone house foundation, whitewashed brick light tower.
PARTICULARS: Lighted.
VARIATIONS: Early issue has **drain hole** directly below light tower, later issue does not.

OSRP: $35.00
GBTru: $60.00 NC

WESTON TRAIN STATION

☐ **NAME:** Weston Train Station 1987
ITEM #: 5931-5
STATUS: Retired 1989

MATERIAL: Porcelain
DESCRIPTION: Luggage ramps lead to platform, where you purchase tickets and wait inside or on benches outside. Wheeled luggage cart stands on side of building. White with blue trim and red roof.
PARTICULARS: Lighted.

OSRP: $42.00
GBTru: $260.00 ↓5%

SMYTHE WOOLEN MILL

☐ **NAME:** Smythe Woolen Mill 1987
ITEM #: 6543-9
STATUS: Limited Edition of 7,500

MATERIAL: Porcelain
DESCRIPTION: Fabric woven for manufacturing into clothing, yard goods. Hydro-powered by water wheel. Stone base with wood upper stories. Bales of wool stacked outside office door. Lower windows each with shutter.
PARTICULARS: Lighted.

OSRP: $42.00
GBTru: $1050.00 ↓9%

NEW ENGLAND VILLAGE

TIMBER KNOLL LOG CABIN

❐ **NAME:** Timber Knoll Log Cabin   1987
ITEM #: 6544-7
STATUS: Retired 1990

MATERIAL: Porcelain
DESCRIPTION: Two stone chimneys and fireplace provide heat and cooking facilities for rustic log cabin, wood shakes comprise roof. One wing rises two stories.
PARTICULARS: Lighted.

OSRP: $28.00
GBTru: $165.00   NC

OLD NORTH CHURCH

❐ **NAME:** Old North Church   1988
ITEM #: 5932-3
STATUS: Current

MATERIAL: Porcelain
DESCRIPTION: Red brick church. First and second floor windows feature sunburst and/or spoke tops. Steeple rises from main entry. Belfry has tiered design.
PARTICULARS: Lighted. Based on Historic Landmark.

OSRP: $40.00
GBTru: $45.00   NC

CHERRY LANE SHOPS

See below.

❐ **NAME:** CHERRY LANE SHOPS   1988
ITEM #: 5939-0
STATUS: Retired 1990

MATERIAL: Porcelain
DESCRIPTION: Set of 3 includes *Ben's Barbershop, Otis Hayes Butcher Shop* and *Anne Shaw Toys.*
PARTICULARS: Set of 3. Lighted.

OSRP: $80.00
GBTru: $330.00   ⬆2%

BEN'S BARBERSHOP

❐ **NAME:** Ben's Barbershop   1988
ITEM #: 5939-0
STATUS: Retired 1990

MATERIAL: Porcelain
DESCRIPTION: A barber pole hangs from front house corner next to a bench for customers. Water tower on roof supplies the shop's needs. Upstairs office used by a lawyer.
PARTICULARS: 1 of the 3 piece set–CHERRY LANE SHOPS. Lighted.

OSRP: $27.00
GBTru: $110.00 ⬆16%

NEW ENGLAND VILLAGE

❐ **NAME:** Otis Hayes Butcher Shop   1988
    ITEM #: 5939-0
    STATUS: Retired 1990

MATERIAL: Porcelain
DESCRIPTION: Dutch-door entry, stone side walls, brick front. Small size and thick walls plus river/lake ice helped keep meat fresh.
PARTICULARS: 1 of the 3 piece set–CHERRY LANE SHOPS. Lighted.

OSRP: $27.00
GBTru: $80.00 ⬆7%

❐ **NAME:** Anne Shaw Toys   1988
    ITEM #: 5939-0
    STATUS: Retired 1990

MATERIAL: Porcelain
DESCRIPTION: Large front windows with window boxes allow a look at toys for sale. Molding beneath floor edge and squared shape give roof a turret look/feel.
PARTICULARS: 1 of the 3 piece set–CHERRY LANE SHOPS. Lighted.

OSRP: $27.00
GBTru: $155.00 ⬇3%

❐ **NAME:** Ada's Bed And Boarding House   1988
    ITEM #: 5940-4
    STATUS: Retired 1991

MATERIAL: Porcelain
DESCRIPTION: Large family home becomes a bed & breakfast for travelers. Double chimneys. Central cupola & wrap-around porch.
PARTICULARS: Lighted.
VARIATIONS: Color & **mold** variations affect GBTru Price: **1st Issue:** Lemon yellow, rear steps part of building's mold, alternating yellow panes on 2nd story windows–$310 (⬇5%). **2nd Issue:** Paler yellow, same mold–$165 (⬆10%). **3rd Issue:** Pale yellow, rear steps added on, 2nd story windows w/yellow panes only on top half– $125 (NC).

OSRP: $36.00
GBTru: See Variations

❐ **NAME:** Berkshire House   1989
    ITEM #: 5942-0
    STATUS: Retired 1991

MATERIAL: Porcelain
DESCRIPTION: Blue Dutch colonial inn, two front entries, half porch, five dormered windows on front, second story mansard roof.
PARTICULARS: Lighted.
VARIATIONS: Variations in **color** affect TRUMARKET Price: "Original Blue"– $160.00 (⬆7%), "Teal"–$110.00 (⬆10%). "Forest Green" price is Not Established.

OSRP: $40.00
GBTru: See Variations

NEW ENGLAND VILLAGE

JANNES MULLET AMISH FARM HOUSE

❐ **NAME:** Jannes Mullet Amish Farm House   1989
    ITEM #: 5943-9
    STATUS: Retired 1992

MATERIAL: Porcelain
DESCRIPTION: White frame house, fenced yard on side, two chimneys, gutter and leader to barrel to collect rain water.
PARTICULARS: Lighted.

OSRP: $32.00
GBTru: $110.00   NC

JANNES MULLET AMISH BARN

❐ **NAME:** Jannes Mullet Amish Barn   1989
    ITEM #: 5944-7
    STATUS: Retired 1992

MATERIAL: Porcelain
DESCRIPTION: Wood and fieldstone with attached sheds and silo, Amish family black buggy stands at barn entrance.
PARTICULARS: Lighted.

OSRP: $48.00
GBTru: $90.00   NC

STEEPLE CHURCH

❐ **NAME:** Steeple Church   1989
    ITEM #: 6539-0
    STATUS: Retired 1990

MATERIAL: Porcelain
DESCRIPTION: White clapboard church with steeple. Windows have molding above and below. Simple design.
PARTICULARS: Lighted. Re-issue. See 1986 *Steeple Church*, #6530-7.

OSRP: $30.00
GBTru: $90.00   NC

SHINGLE CREEK HOUSE

❐ **NAME:** Shingle Creek House   1990
    ITEM #: 5946-3
    STATUS: Retired 1994

MATERIAL: Porcelain
DESCRIPTION: Saltbox design with chimney rising from mid-roof. Windows have shutters and molding on top and base. Attached shed on one side, with storm cellar doors and fenced side entrance.
PARTICULARS: Lighted. Early release to Showcase Dealers and the National Association Of Limited Edition Dealers (NALED).

OSRP: $37.50
GBTru: $55.00   ↑22%

CAPTAIN'S COTTAGE

☐ **NAME:** Captain's Cottage   1990
   ITEM #: 5947-1
   STATUS: Current

MATERIAL: Porcelain
DESCRIPTION: 2 ½-story has balcony full length of 2nd story. Enclosed staircase on house side to second floor. A connected double dormer is centered on front roof between two ridge chimneys.
PARTICULARS: Lighted.

OSRP: $40.00
GBTru: $44.00   NC

SLEEPY HOLLOW

See below.

☐ **NAME:** SLEEPY HOLLOW   1990
   ITEM #: 5954-4
   STATUS: Retired 1993

MATERIAL: Porcelain
DESCRIPTION: Set of 3 includes *Sleepy Hollow School, Van Tassel Manor,* and *Ichabod Crane's Cottage.*
PARTICULARS: Set of 3. Lighted.

OSRP: $96.00
GBTru: $175.00   ⬆3%

SLEEPY HOLLOW SCHOOL

☐ **NAME:** Sleepy Hollow School   1990
   ITEM #: 5954-4
   STATUS: Retired 1993

MATERIAL: Porcelain
DESCRIPTION: Framed stone chimney warms log cabin school. Brick and wood belfry houses bell. Wood pile and bench with bucket near front door.
PARTICULARS: 1 of the 3 piece set–SLEEPY HOLLOW. Lighted.

OSRP: $32.00
GBTru: $90.00 ⬆13%

VAN TASSEL MANOR

☐ **NAME:** Van Tassel Manor   1990
   ITEM #: 5954-4
   STATUS: Retired 1993

MATERIAL: Porcelain
DESCRIPTION: Yellow house with mansard roof with two front dormers. Wood corner posts support porch. Stone lean-to one side. Double chimneys rise off roof ridge. Four ears of corn decorate front entry.
PARTICULARS: 1 of the 3 piece set–SLEEPY HOLLOW. Lighted.

OSRP: $32.00
GBTru: $60.00   NC

ICHABOD CRANE'S COTTAGE

☐ **NAME:** Ichabod Crane's Cottage   1990
ITEM #: 5954-4
STATUS: Retired 1993

MATERIAL: Porcelain
DESCRIPTION: Stone first story topped by wood second story. Rough shingled roof with dip in the middle between two brick chimneys.
PARTICULARS: 1 of the 3 piece set–SLEEPY HOLLOW. Lighted.

OSRP: $32.00
GBTru: $55.00   NC

SLEEPY HOLLOW CHURCH

☐ **NAME:** Sleepy Hollow Church   1990
ITEM #: 5955-2
STATUS: Retired 1993

MATERIAL: Porcelain
DESCRIPTION: Wood church with steeple rising off front. Arched windows with prominent sills. Front steps lead to double doors with ornate hinges and molding.
PARTICULARS: Lighted.

OSRP: $36.00
GBTru: $60.00   NC

McGREBE-CUTTERS & SLEIGHS

☐ **NAME:** McGrebe-Cutters & Sleighs   1991
ITEM #: 5640-5
STATUS: Retired 1995

MATERIAL: Porcelain
DESCRIPTION: Builders of carriages, sleighs, and sleds to move people and goods in snowy New England. Stone and wood building. Large doors in front and side to allow movement of vehicles. Stone half has short tower atop roof. Large loft doors above entry.
PARTICULARS: Lighted.

OSRP: $45.00
GBTru: $65.00 ↑35%

BLUEBIRD SEED AND BULB

☐ **NAME:** Bluebird Seed And Bulb   1992
ITEM #: 5642-1
STATUS: Current

MATERIAL: Porcelain
DESCRIPTION: Covered storage area near entry door has open storage bins. Small shuttered arched window adjacent to door. Outside stairs lead to other storage areas. Two stories with stone block lower level and fieldstone chimney.
PARTICULARS: Lighted.

OSRP: $48.00
GBTru: $48.00   NC

YANKEE JUD BELL CASTING

❏ **NAME:** Yankee Jud Bell Casting   1992
     ITEM #: 5643-0
     STATUS: Retired 1995

MATERIAL: Porcelain
DESCRIPTION: Red brick foundry with steeply pitched gable roof. Projecting side doors on second and third story for lifting heavy, large castings. Tall circular brick chimney rises off rear of foundry.
PARTICULARS: Lighted.

OSRP: $44.00
GBTru: $60.00 ↑36%

STONEY BROOK TOWN HALL

❏ **NAME:** Stoney Brook Town Hall   1992
     ITEM #: 5644-8
     STATUS: Retired 1995

MATERIAL: Porcelain
DESCRIPTION: Rectangular brick building serves as meeting hall for town governance. Side entry with a latch gate, cellar windows with shutters, roof dormers and two chimneys, and many windows on long sides of building complete structure.
PARTICULARS: Lighted.

OSRP: $42.00
GBTru: $60.00 ↑43%

BLUE STAR ICE CO.

❏ **NAME:** Blue Star Ice Co.   1993
     ITEM #: 5647-2
     STATUS: Current

MATERIAL: Porcelain
DESCRIPTION: Stone 1st story with insulated wood upper storage level. Wooden chute enabled ice block to be pulled up where sawdust or salt hay insulated each block.
PARTICULARS: Lighted.

OSRP: $45.00
GBTru: $48.00   NC

A. BIELER FARM

See next page.

❏ **NAME:** A. BIELER FARM   1993
     ITEM #: 5648-0
     STATUS: Current

MATERIAL: Porcelain
DESCRIPTION: Set of 2 includes *Pennsylvania Dutch Farmhouse,* #56481 and *Pennsylvania Dutch Barn,* #56482.
PARTICULARS: Set of 2. Lighted. Each piece now assigned individual Item Number.

OSRP: $92.00
GBTru: $95.00   NC

PENNSYLVANIA DUTCH FARMHOUSE

☐ **NAME:** Pennsylvania Dutch Farmhouse   1993
ITEM #: 56481
STATUS: Current

MATERIAL: Porcelain
DESCRIPTION: Two-story clapboard home. Many windowed to let in light, colorful trim on all windows, roof and wall moldings.
PARTICULARS: 1 of the 2 piece set–A. BIELER FARM. Lighted. Each piece now assigned individual Item Number.

OSRP: $42.00
GBTru: $43.50   NC

PENNSYLVANIA DUTCH BARN

☐ **NAME:** Pennsylvania Dutch Barn   1993
ITEM #: 56482
STATUS: Current

MATERIAL: Porcelain
DESCRIPTION: Red barn with green mansard roof. Two stone silos on one corner. Double door entry reached by stone supported ramp. Hex signs hung on barn outer walls.
PARTICULARS: 1 of the 2 piece set–A. BIELER FARM. Lighted. Each piece now assigned individual Item Number.

OSRP: $50.00
GBTru: $51.50   NC

ARLINGTON FALLS CHURCH

☐ **NAME:** Arlington Falls Church   1994
ITEM #: 5651-0
STATUS: Current

MATERIAL: Porcelain
DESCRIPTION: Wood church with steeple rising in tiers above from entry. Pillars at front doors are wrapped in garlands. Double tier of windows on side of church to let in daylight. Simple structure with a country look.
PARTICULARS: Lighted. Midyear release.

OSRP: $40.00
GBTru: $42.00   NC

CAPE KEAG FISH CANNERY

☐ **NAME:** Cape Keag Fish Cannery   1994
ITEM #: 5652-9
STATUS: Current

MATERIAL: Porcelain
DESCRIPTION: Lobster pots, buoys are stacked on wharf along building front. Brick tower rising on side of factory cannery puts focus on fishing and canning industry.
PARTICULARS: Lighted.

OSRP: $48.00
GBTru: $48.00   NC

PIGEONHEAD LIGHTHOUSE

❐ **NAME:** Pigeonhead Lighthouse   1994
ITEM #: 5653-7
STATUS: Current

MATERIAL: Porcelain
DESCRIPTION: Light shines from porthole windows.
Tower connects to keeper's home. Steps lead down from
rocks to water.
PARTICULARS: Lighted.

OSRP: $50.00
GBTru: $50.00   NC

BREWSTER BAY COTTAGES

See below.

❐ **NAME:** BREWSTER BAY COTTAGES   1995
ITEM #: 5657-0
STATUS: Current

MATERIAL: Porcelain
DESCRIPTION: Set of 2 includes *Jeremiah Brewster House*,
#56568 and *Thomas T. Julian House*, #56569.
PARTICULARS: Set of 2. Lighted. Midyear release.
Each piece now assigned individual Item Number.

OSRP: $90.00
GBTru: $90.00   NC

JEREMIAH BREWSTER HOUSE

❐ **NAME:** Jeremiah Brewster House   1995
ITEM #: 56568
STATUS: Current

MATERIAL: Porcelain
DESCRIPTION: Shed roof side addition attached to main
square 2-story house. Shuttered windows, widow's walk
on roof.
PARTICULARS: 1 of the 2 piece set–BREWSTER BAY
COTTAGES. Lighted. Midyear release. Each piece now
assigned individual Item Number.

OSRP: $45.00
GBTru: $45.00   NC

THOMAS T. JULIAN HOUSE

❐ **NAME:** Thomas T. Julian House   1995
ITEM #: 56569
STATUS: Current

MATERIAL: Porcelain
DESCRIPTION: Central chimney rises where 4-gabled
roof meets. Two-story bay windowed turret next to covered
porch entry.
PARTICULARS: 1 of the 2 piece set–BREWSTER BAY
COTTAGES. Lighted. Midyear release. Each piece now
assigned individual Item Number.

OSRP: $45.00
GBTru: $45.00   NC

CHOWDER HOUSE

❐ **NAME:** Chowder House   1995
ITEM #: 56571
STATUS: Current

MATERIAL: Porcelain
DESCRIPTION: Small cozy eating establishment sits on fieldstone base. Small boats can tie up to one side while another entry serves walk-ins. Blue clapboard with a mansard roof.
PARTICULARS: Lighted.

OSRP: $40.00
GBTru: $40.00

WOODBRIDGE POST OFFICE

❐ **NAME:** Woodbridge Post Office   1995
ITEM #: 56572
STATUS: Current

MATERIAL: Porcelain
DESCRIPTION: Two-story brick post office serves village for mail, stamps, parcels and postal cards. Windows flank double entry doors.
PARTICULARS: Lighted.

OSRP: $40.00
GBTru: $40.00

PIERCE BOAT WORKS

❐ **NAME:** Pierce Boat Works   1995
ITEM #: 56573
STATUS: Current

MATERIAL: Porcelain
DESCRIPTION: Boats for lobstermen and fishermen are built at the boat works. Wooden building with double doors allow boats to be pulled or rolled down ramp. Rowboat held on winch and pulley rig on side of building.
PARTICULARS: Lighted.

OSRP: $55.00
GBTru: $55.00

APPLE VALLEY SCHOOL

❐ **NAME:** Apple Valley School   1996
ITEM #: 56172
STATUS: Current

MATERIAL: Porcelain
DESCRIPTION: Small squared brick and stone village school. Tall central chimney connects to stove to keep schoolrooms heated. Bell tower in front gable.
PARTICULARS: Lighted. Midyear release.

OSRP: $35.00
GBTru: $35.00

ALPINE VILLAGE

☐ **NAME:** ALPINE VILLAGE   1986
   ITEM #: 6540-4
   STATUS: Current

See below.

MATERIAL: Porcelain
DESCRIPTION: Set of 5 includes *Bessor Bierkeller,* #65405, *Gasthof Eisl,* #65406, *Apotheke,* #65407, *E. Staubr Backer,* #65408, *Milch-Käse,* #65409.
PARTICULARS: Set of 5. Lighted. Early release to National Association Of Limited Edition Dealers (NALED), 1987. Each piece now assigned individual Item Number.

OSRP: $150.00
GBTru: $195.00   NC

BESSOR BIERKELLER

☐ **NAME:** Bessor Bierkeller (Beer Cellar)   1986
   ITEM #: 65405
   STATUS: Current

MATERIAL: Porcelain
DESCRIPTION: Window boxes on second story hung with colorful banners. Third story rustic timbered enclosed balcony has garland decoration.
PARTICULARS: 1 of the 5 piece set–ALPINE VILLAGE. Lighted. Early release to National Association Of Limited Edition Dealers (NALED), 1987. Each piece now assigned individual Item Number.

OSRP: $25.00
GBTru: $39.00   NC

GASTHOF EISL

☐ **NAME:** Gasthof Eisl (Guest House)   1986
   ITEM #: 65406
   STATUS: Current

MATERIAL: Porcelain
DESCRIPTION: Rustic inn, fieldstone first floor with two stories of stucco topped by orange/red roof. A third story balcony is decorated with greenery and banners. Window boxes also decorate other rooms.
PARTICULARS: 1 of the 5 piece set–ALPINE VILLAGE. Lighted. Early release to National Association Of Limited Edition Dealers (NALED), 1987. Each piece now assigned individual Item Number.

OSRP: $25.00
GBTru: $39.00   NC

APOTHEKE

☐ **NAME:** Apotheke (Apothecary)   1986
   ITEM #: 65407
   STATUS: Current

MATERIAL: Porcelain
DESCRIPTION: Cream walls topped by blue roof. Banners flying from attic window. Prescriptions and drugstore supplies available from store on ground floor. Building shares with tobacconist.
PARTICULARS: 1 of the 5 piece set–ALPINE VILLAGE. Lighted. Early release to National Association Of Limited Edition Dealers (NALED), 1987. Each piece now assigned individual Item Number.

OSRP: $25.00
GBTru: $39.00   NC

E. STAUBR BACKER

❏ **NAME:** E. Staubr Backer (Bakery)   1986
    ITEM #: 65408
    STATUS: Current

MATERIAL: Porcelain
DESCRIPTION: Three-story building with bakery on ground level. Third story has some timbering design and an oriel window. Tiled roof and two chimneys.
PARTICULARS: 1 of the 5 piece set–ALPINE VILLAGE. Lighted. Only building in which bulb is inserted in the side. Early release to National Association Of Limited Edition Dealers (NALED), 1987. Each piece now assigned individual Item Number.

OSRP: $25.00
GBTru: $39.00   NC

MILCH-KASE

❏ **NAME:** Milch-Käse (Milk & Cheese Shop)   1986
    ITEM #: 65409
    STATUS: Current

MATERIAL: Porcelain
DESCRIPTION: Milk cans by door denotes shop that sells milk and cheese. Rough slate roof tops blue walls and wood planking exterior. Double wood doors allow wagons to bring supplies in/out.
PARTICULARS: 1 of the 5 piece set–ALPINE VILLAGE. Lighted. Early release to National Association Of Limited Edition Dealers (NALED), 1987. Each piece now assigned individual Item Number.

OSRP: $25.00
GBTru: $39.00   NC

JOSEF ENGEL FARMHOUSE

❏ **NAME:** Josef Engel Farmhouse   1987
    ITEM #: 5952-8
    STATUS: Retired 1989

MATERIAL: Porcelain
DESCRIPTION: House and barn are connected. Stucco over stone. Barn has hay loft above animal and equipment area. Shutters swing overhead. Home has balcony above front entry with herringbone planking. Red roof, capped chimneys.
PARTICULARS: Lighted.

OSRP: $33.00
GBTru: $925.00   ↓5%

ALPINE CHURCH

❏ **NAME:** Alpine Church   1987
    ITEM #: 6541-2
    STATUS: Retired 1991

MATERIAL: Porcelain
DESCRIPTION: Onion dome tops steeple which also features a clock on all sides of the tower.
PARTICULARS: Lighted.
VARIATIONS: Variations in **color** affect TRUMARKET Price: "White Trim"– $350.00 (↑19%), "Dark Trim"–$155.00 (↓6%).

OSRP: $32.00
GBTru: See Variations

GRIST MILL

◻ **NAME:** Grist Mill   1988
     ITEM #: 5953-6
     STATUS: Current

MATERIAL: Porcelain
DESCRIPTION: Irregular shingle roofing tops the mill that grinds corn and wheat into meal and flour.
PARTICULARS: Lighted.

OSRP: $42.00
GBTru: $45.00   NC

BAHNHOF

◻ **NAME:** Bahnhof (Train Station)   1990
     ITEM #: 5615-4
     STATUS: Retired 1993

MATERIAL: Porcelain
DESCRIPTION: Stucco upper wall atop tiled lower wall. Ticket window in base of tower rises through roof and repeats tile design.
PARTICULARS: Lighted.
VARIATIONS: Gold trim can be bright or dull in color intensity.

OSRP: $42.00
GBTru: $70.00   NC

ST. NIKOLAUS KIRCHE

◻ **NAME:** St. Nikolaus Kirche   1991
     ITEM #: 5617-0
     STATUS: Current

MATERIAL: Porcelain
DESCRIPTION: Bell tower rises above front entry, topped by onion dome. Set-in rounded arched windows accent nave sides. Pebble-dash finish on surface walls. The home of the Christmas hymn "Silent Night, Holy Night."
PARTICULARS: Lighted. Designed after Church Of St. Nikola in Oberndorf, Austria.

OSRP: $37.50
GBTru: $37.50   NC

ALPINE SHOPS

See next page.

◻ **NAME:** ALPINE SHOPS   1992
     ITEM #: 5618-9
     STATUS: Current

MATERIAL: Porcelain
DESCRIPTION: Set of 2 includes *Metterniche Wurst,* #56190 and *Kukuck Uhren,* #56191.
PARTICULARS: Set of 2. Lighted. Each piece now assigned individual Item Number.

OSRP: $75.00
GBTru: $75.00   NC

ALPINE VILLAGE

METTERNICHE WURST

❒ **NAME:** Metterniche Wurst (Sausage Shop) 1992
ITEM #: 56190
STATUS: Current

MATERIAL: Porcelain
DESCRIPTION: Stucco over stone and brick with steeply
pitched roof coming down to first floor on sides. Front
facade framed by ornamental curved coping.
PARTICULARS: 1 of the 2 piece set–ALPINE SHOPS. Lighted.
Each piece now assigned individual Item Number.

OSRP: $37.50
GBTru: $37.50 NC

KUKUCK UHREN

❒ **NAME:** Kukuck Uhren (Clock Shop) 1992
ITEM #: 56191
STATUS: Current

MATERIAL: Porcelain
DESCRIPTION: Franc Schiller displays his trademark clock
on shop sign above recessed entry door. Small shop has
wood timbers that outline the stone, brick and stucco exterior.
PARTICULARS: 1 of the 2 piece set–ALPINE SHOPS. Lighted.
Each piece now assigned individual Item Number.

OSRP: $37.50
GBTru: $37.50 NC

SPORT LADEN

❒ **NAME:** Sport Laden 1993
ITEM #: 5612-0
STATUS: Current

MATERIAL: Porcelain
DESCRIPTION: Shop for skiing and winter sports equipment.
Small shop tucked away on one side. Roof-overhangs
protect facade and chimneys are capped to keep out snow,
ice and rain.
PARTICULARS: Lighted.

OSRP: $50.00
GBTru: $50.00 NC

BAKERY & CHOCOLATE SHOP

❒ **NAME:** Bakery & Chocolate Shop
(Konditorei Schokolade) 1994
ITEM #: 5614-6
STATUS: Current

MATERIAL: Porcelain
DESCRIPTION: Garland and banners hang down from
the second story balcony. The extended eaves protect the
building from heavy snows.
PARTICULARS: Lighted.

OSRP: $37.50
GBTru: $37.50 NC

ALPINE VILLAGE

❐ **NAME:** Kamm Haus   1995
ITEM #: 56171
STATUS: Current

MATERIAL: Porcelain
DESCRIPTION: House on the crest is the translation of this Alpine building's name. Long stairs lead up to the main balcony and front door of the skiers inn. Roof-overhangs offer protection from icing. Large fireplace at rear of roof has a cap to keep snow from falling in.
PARTICULARS: Lighted.

OSRP: $42.00
GBTru: $42.00

OTHER GUIDES FROM GREENBOOK:

GREENBOOK Guide to
>> The Enesco PRECIOUS MOMENTS Collection

GREENBOOK Guide to
>> Hallmark KEEPSAKE Ornaments

GREENBOOK Guide to
>> Hallmark MERRY MINIATURES

GREENBOOK Guide to
>> DEPARTMENT 56 Snowbabies

GREENBOOK Guide to
>> the WALT DISNEY Classics Collection

GREENBOOK Guide to
>> Enesco's CHERISHED TEDDIES

Coming in early 1997:

GREENBOOK Guide to
>> SWAROVSKI

GREENBOOK Guide to
>> BOYD'S BEARS

ALPINE VILLAGE

SUTTON PLACE BROWNSTONES

☐ **NAME:** Sutton Place Brownstones   1987
   ITEM #: 5961-7
   STATUS: Retired 1989

MATERIAL: Porcelain
DESCRIPTION: Three multi-storied homes, attached via shared common walls. Three shops occupy semi-below ground level space. Attic dormer windows have iron grillwork.
PARTICULARS: Lighted.

OSRP: $80.00
GBTru: $845.00 ↑2%

THE CATHEDRAL

☐ **NAME:** The Cathedral   1987
   ITEM #: 5962-5
   STATUS: Retired 1990

MATERIAL: Porcelain
DESCRIPTION: Twin spires, early Gothic design and decorated windows set this Cathedral apart. Stone church incorporates a fortress-like solidness.
PARTICULARS: Lighted.
VARIATIONS: Two versions: 1) Smaller, darker, snow on sides of steps. 2) Larger, lighter, no snow on steps.

OSRP: $60.00
GBTru: $340.00 ↑1%

PALACE THEATRE

☐ **NAME:** Palace Theatre   1987
   ITEM #: 5963-3
   STATUS: Retired 1989

MATERIAL: Porcelain
DESCRIPTION: Mask of Comedy & Tragedy are bas-reliefs on brick building featuring Christmas Show of Nutcracker. Stage entrance on side of building.
PARTICULARS: Lighted.
VARIATIONS: In **size**, paint **trim** and **snow**.

OSRP: $45.00
GBTru: $890.00 ↓4%

CHRISTMAS IN THE CITY

See next page.

☐ **NAME:** CHRISTMAS IN THE CITY   1987
   ITEM #: 6512-9
   STATUS: Retired 1990

MATERIAL: Porcelain
DESCRIPTION: Set of 3 includes *Toy Shop And Pet Store, Bakery* and *Tower Restaurant.*
PARTICULARS: Set of 3. Lighted.
VARIATIONS: All three buildings vary from dark to light in **color**.

OSRP: $112.00
GBTru: $565.00 ↑19%

CHRISTMAS IN THE CITY

TOY SHOP AND PET STORE

❏ **NAME:** Toy Shop And Pet Store   1987
ITEM #: 6512-9
STATUS: Retired 1990

MATERIAL: Porcelain
DESCRIPTION: Side-by-side Pet Store and Toy Shop. Tucked in at side is Tailor Shop. Ground floor has extra high ceiling with half-circle windows.
PARTICULARS: 1 of the 3 piece set–CHRISTMAS IN THE CITY. Lighted.

OSRP: $37.50
GBTru: $235.00 ⬆7%

BAKERY

❏ **NAME:** Bakery   1987
ITEM #: 6512-9
STATUS: Retired 1990

MATERIAL: Porcelain
DESCRIPTION: Four-story building with Bakery on first two levels. Iron grill work for safety and decor on smaller windows. Two different height chimneys.
PARTICULARS: 1 of the 3 piece set–CHRISTMAS IN THE CITY. Lighted.

OSRP: $37.50
GBTru: $100.00 ⬆5%

TOWER RESTAURANT

❏ **NAME:** Tower Restaurant   1987
ITEM #: 6512-9
STATUS: Retired 1990

MATERIAL: Porcelain
DESCRIPTION: Multi-sided tower structure is integral part of residential building. Double door entry to restaurant/cafe. Iron grillwork on upper tower windows.
PARTICULARS: 1 of the 3 piece set–CHRISTMAS IN THE CITY. Lighted.

OSRP: $37.50
GBTru: $235.00 ⬆18%

CHOCOLATE SHOPPE

❏ **NAME:** Chocolate Shoppe   1988
ITEM #: 5968-4
STATUS: Retired 1991

MATERIAL: Porcelain
DESCRIPTION: Paneled roof between first and second story extends to shop signs. Building over Chocolate Shoppe rises three stories plus attic. Above Brown Brothers Bookstore is one short story plus attic. Stone facade has heart panels at base while bookstore has sign and canopy over window.
PARTICULARS: Lighted.
VARIATIONS: Vary from dark to light in **color**.

OSRP: $40.00
GBTru: $135.00 ⬆35%

CHRISTMAS IN THE CITY

CITY HALL

☐ **NAME:** City Hall   1988
ITEM #: 5969-2
STATUS: Retired 1991

MATERIAL: Porcelain
DESCRIPTION: Imposing fortress with four towers at corners plus repeat design on clock tower. Broad steps plus large columns establish entry doors. Stone arches accent first floor windows plus tower window. Planters with evergreens on either side of steps.
PARTICULARS: Lighted.
VARIATIONS: Smaller in **size** "Proof" version (none of the boxes had sleeves)–$195.00 (↑5%).

OSRP: $65.00
GBTru: $160.00   ↑3%

HANK'S MARKET

☐ **NAME:** Hank's Market   1988
ITEM #: 5970-6
STATUS: Retired 1992

MATERIAL: Porcelain
DESCRIPTION: Grocery store as corner shop with boxes/barrels of produce on display. Rolled awnings over sign. Brick building with painted brick on upper sections of second story. Two upper windows are multi-paned with half-circle sunburst, other window has awning. Two chimneys on steeply pitched roof.
PARTICULARS: Lighted. aka "Corner Grocery".

OSRP: $40.00
GBTru: $85.00   ↑6%

VARIETY STORE

☐ **NAME:** Variety Store   1988
ITEM #: 5972-2
STATUS: Retired 1990

MATERIAL: Porcelain
DESCRIPTION: Corner store in two-story brick building. Garland decorated awnings extend out to shelter display windows and shoppers. Separate door for upper story. Second floor corner window projects out, as rounded tower and support column underneath becomes part of entry. Next door shop is barbershop with striped pole outside. Small eyeglass shop completes trio.
PARTICULARS: Lighted. Same mold as the Bachman's Hometown Series, *Drugstore* #672-6.

OSRP: $45.00
GBTru: $165.00 ↑10%

RITZ HOTEL

☐ **NAME:** Ritz Hotel   1989
ITEM #: 5973-0
STATUS: Retired 1994

MATERIAL: Porcelain
DESCRIPTION: Red doors complete columned entryway, red window canopy over each second story French window. Stone, block, and brick building. Cupola on attic window. Slate roof.
PARTICULARS: Lighted.

OSRP: $55.00
GBTru: $75.00 ↑15%

CHRISTMAS IN THE CITY

DOROTHY'S DRESS SHOP

❐ **NAME:** Dorothy's Dress Shop   1989
    ITEM #: 5974-9
    STATUS: Limited Edition of 12,500

MATERIAL: Porcelain
DESCRIPTION: Bright green door and awning, bay windows on first and second floor, mansard roof.
PARTICULARS: Lighted.

OSRP: $70.00
GBTru: $375.00 ↑7%

5607 PARK AVENUE TOWNHOUSE

❐ **NAME:** 5607 Park Avenue Townhouse   1989
    ITEM #: 5977-3
    STATUS: Retired 1992

MATERIAL: Porcelain
DESCRIPTION: Four stories with ground floor card and gift shop, curved·corner turret, blue canopy over double French door entry.
PARTICULARS: Lighted.
VARIATIONS: Earlier pieces had gilded trim at top of building, later production had dull gold colored paint.

OSRP: $48.00
GBTru: $80.00 NC

5609 PARK AVENUE TOWNHOUSE

❐ **NAME:** 5609 Park Avenue Townhouse   1989
    ITEM #: 5978-1
    STATUS: Retired 1992

MATERIAL: Porcelain
DESCRIPTION: Four stories with ground floor art gallery, double wood doors lead to apartments, blue canopy over entry.
PARTICULARS: Lighted.
VARIATIONS: Earlier pieces had gilded trim at top of building, later production has dull gold colored paint.

OSRP: $48.00
GBTru: $80.00 NC

RED BRICK FIRE STATION

❐ **NAME:** Red Brick Fire Station   1990
    ITEM #: 5536-0
    STATUS: Retired 1995

MATERIAL: Porcelain
DESCRIPTION: Brick Station House for Hook & Ladder Company. Large wood doors lead to equipment with separate door for upper level. Stone block detailing on turret and above upper floor windows. Formal pediment at front gate.
PARTICULARS: Lighted.

OSRP: $55.00
GBTru: $75.00 ↑36%

WONG'S IN CHINATOWN

❑ **NAME:** Wong's In Chinatown   1990
ITEM #: 5537-9
STATUS: Retired 1994

MATERIAL: Porcelain
DESCRIPTION: Chinese restaurant and a laundry in brick building. Canopy over entry and at roof feature pagoda shape. Fire escape for second and third story tenants. Chinese characters highlight signs and entry.
PARTICULARS: Lighted.
VARIATIONS: In **color**: 1st issue–Top window is red. 2nd issue–Top window is gold.

OSRP: $55.00
GBTru: $70.00   NC

HOLLYDALE'S DEPARTMENT STORE

❑ **NAME:** Hollydale's Department Store   1991
ITEM #: 5534-4
STATUS: Current

MATERIAL: Porcelain
DESCRIPTION: Corner curved front with awnings on windows, domed cupola, skylights on roof, and carved balustrade design on second story windows highlight store.
PARTICULARS: Lighted.
VARIATIONS: Holly on **canopies**–3 main entrance only vs. both main entrance and 2nd floor canopies.

OSRP: $75.00
GBTru: $85.00   NC

"LITTLE ITALY" RISTORANTE

❑ **NAME:** "Little Italy" Ristorante   1991
ITEM #: 5538-7
STATUS: Retired 1995

MATERIAL: Porcelain
DESCRIPTION: Three-story tall, narrow, stucco finish upper level above brick street level entry. Outdoor cafe serving pizza is on side.
PARTICULARS: Lighted.

OSRP: $50.00
GBTru: $75.00 ↑44%

ALL SAINTS CORNER CHURCH

❑ **NAME:** All Saints Corner Church   1991
ITEM #: 5542-5
STATUS: Current

MATERIAL: Porcelain
DESCRIPTION: Gothic style. Carved support frame arched windows, tall steeple with corners capped by small steeple design. Large windows exhibit tracery pattern.
PARTICULARS: Lighted.

OSRP: $96.00
GBTru: $110.00   NC

CHRISTMAS IN THE CITY

ARTS ACADEMY

☐ **NAME:** Arts Academy   1991
   ITEM #: 5543-3
   STATUS: Retired 1993

MATERIAL: Porcelain
DESCRIPTION: Two-story brick building has classrooms and practice halls. Curved canopy over entrance repeats design of arched triple window, skylight & small tower window.
PARTICULARS: Lighted.

OSRP: $45.00
GBTru: $75.00   NC

THE DOCTOR'S OFFICE

☐ **NAME:** The Doctor's Office   1991
   ITEM #: 5544-1
   STATUS: Retired 1994

MATERIAL: Porcelain
DESCRIPTION: Four-story brick building for Doctor, Dentist, and office space. Bow window is first level Doctor. Dentist windows have broad awning.
PARTICULARS: Lighted.

OSRP: $60.00
GBTru: $75.00   NC

CATHEDRAL CHURCH OF ST. MARK

☐ **NAME:** Cathedral Church Of St. Mark   1991
   ITEM #: 5549-2
   STATUS: Limited Edition of 3,024*

MATERIAL: Porcelain
DESCRIPTION: Front has look of fortification with two towers rising next to entry. Moldings are richly carved above double doors. Stone and brick with accented stone work framing walls and towers. Triple windows on each upper tower side.
PARTICULARS: Lighted. Early release to Gift Creations Concepts (GCC), Fall 1992. *Announced Edition of 17,500– closed at 3,024 pieces due to production problems.

OSRP: $120.00
GBTru: $1860.00 ↓19%

UPTOWN SHOPPES

See next page.

☐ **NAME:** UPTOWN SHOPPES   1992
   ITEM #: 5531-0
   STATUS: Current

MATERIAL: Porcelain
DESCRIPTION: Set of 3 includes *Haberdashery*, #55311, *Music Emporium*, #55312, and *City Clockworks*, #55313.
PARTICULARS: Set of 3. Lighted. Each piece now assigned individual Item Number.

OSRP: $150.00
GBTru: $150.00   NC

CHRISTMAS IN THE CITY

HABERDASHERY

☐ **NAME:** Haberdashery   1992
ITEM #: 55311
STATUS: Current

MATERIAL: Porcelain
DESCRIPTION: Squared corner of three-story building is men's clothier entry. First story front window topped by canopy and store sign. Second floor triple windows topped by ornamental molding and side windows have triangular canopies. Brick, stone, and roughcast pepple-dash facade.
PARTICULARS: 1 of the 3 piece set–UPTOWN SHOPPES. Lighted. Each piece now assigned individual Item Number.

OSRP: $40.00
GBTru: $40.00   NC

MUSIC EMPORIUM

☐ **NAME:** Music Emporium   1992
ITEM #: 55312
STATUS: Current

MATERIAL: Porcelain
DESCRIPTION: Brick store decorates side wall with a musical score. Store name is superimposed and trimmed for holidays. Other signs advertise violins, flutes, and horns. Tallest of the three shops, building has 3 floors and attic dormer. Street level window tall and narrow topped by sign.
PARTICULARS: 1 of the 3 piece set–UPTOWN SHOPPES. Lighted. Each piece now assigned individual Item Number.

OSRP: $54.00
GBTru: $54.00   NC

CITY CLOCKWORKS

☐ **NAME:** City Clockworks   1992
ITEM #: 55313
STATUS: Current

MATERIAL: Porcelain
DESCRIPTION: Triangular shaped building. Front angle blunted by semi-circular windows above entry to shop. Large clock hangs at right angles to store between sign and windows. Second clock next to entrance.
PARTICULARS: 1 of the 3 piece set–UPTOWN SHOPPES. Lighted. Each piece now assigned individual Item Number.

OSRP: $56.00
GBTru: $56.00   NC

WEST VILLAGE SHOPS

See next page.

☐ **NAME:** WEST VILLAGE SHOPS   1993
ITEM #: 5880-7
STATUS: Current

MATERIAL: Porcelain
DESCRIPTION: Set of 2 includes *Potter's Tea Seller,* #58808 and *Spring St. Coffee House,* #58809.
PARTICULARS: Set of 2. Lighted. Each piece now assigned individual Item Number.

OSRP: $90.00
GBTru: $90.00   NC

POTTER'S TEA SELLER

❐ **NAME:** Potter's Tea Seller   1993
ITEM #: 58808
STATUS: Current

MATERIAL: Porcelain
DESCRIPTION: Stone 3-story shop serves tea by the cup or pot. Stone arches decorate windows. Green awning covers upper window above entry. Sign hangs in front of door to alert shoppers.
PARTICULARS: 1 of the 2 piece set–WEST VILLAGE SHOPS. Lighted. Each piece now assigned individual Item Number.

OSRP: $45.00
GBTru: $45.00   NC

SPRING ST. COFFEE HOUSE

❐ **NAME:** Spring St. Coffee House   1993
ITEM #: 58809
STATUS: Current

MATERIAL: Porcelain
DESCRIPTION: Four-story narrow building. Steps lead to entry door covered by small pillared portico. Buy beans ground to order & blended for taste, or have a cup at the shop. Lower level is brick, upper stories are stucco.
PARTICULARS: 1 of the 2 piece set–WEST VILLAGE SHOPS. Lighted. Each piece now assigned individual Item Number.

OSRP: $45.00
GBTru: $45.00   NC

BROKERAGE HOUSE

❐ **NAME:** Brokerage House   1994
ITEM #: 5881-5
STATUS: Current

MATERIAL: Porcelain
DESCRIPTION: Stone building gives impression of invincibility. Four pillars support large entry pediment which has name of Exchange carved into stone. Feeling of wealth is reinforced by gold embellishments.
PARTICULARS: Lighted. "18" is symbolic of initial D56 stock offering at $18.00.

OSRP: $48.00
GBTru: $48.00   NC

FIRST METROPOLITAN BANK

❐ **NAME:** First Metropolitan Bank   1994
ITEM #: 5882-3
STATUS: Current

MATERIAL: Porcelain
DESCRIPTION: Domed, 3-story building presents solid edifice. Four columns reach to third story and create covered entry and area for name inscription. Bank has gilt trim on dome, windows and door.
PARTICULARS: Lighted.

OSRP: $60.00
GBTru: $60.00   NC

CHRISTMAS IN THE CITY

HERITAGE MUSEUM OF ART

❐ **NAME:** Heritage Museum Of Art   1994
ITEM #: 5883-1
STATUS: Current

MATERIAL: Porcelain
DESCRIPTION: A stately, symmetrical structure with large windows. Names of famous artists are displayed around the top of the building and Thomas Nast's rendition of Santa Claus is on display above the entrance.
PARTICULARS: Lighted.

OSRP: $96.00
GBTru: $96.00   NC

IVY TERRACE APARTMENTS

❐ **NAME:** Ivy Terrace Apartments   1995
ITEM #: 5887-4
STATUS: Current

MATERIAL: Porcelain
DESCRIPTION: Three-story brick building with two canopy covered entries. Third floor apartment has terrace with wrought iron enclosure.
PARTICULARS: Lighted. Midyear release.

OSRP: $60.00
GBTru: $60.00   NC

HOLY NAME CHURCH

❐ **NAME:** Holy Name Church   1995
ITEM #: 58875
STATUS: Current

MATERIAL: Porcelain
DESCRIPTION: Brick church with entry and steeple with ornate pediment and molding topped by golden dome and cross. Stained glass fills rose window and lancet windows. Niche for statuary in steeple. Ribbed roof with carved design in ridge edging.
PARTICULARS: Lighted. Design adaptation–Cathedral of the Immaculate Conception, Kansas City, MO.

OSRP: $96.00
GBTru: $96.00

BRIGHTON SCHOOL

❐ **NAME:** Brighton School   1995
ITEM #: 58876
STATUS: Current

MATERIAL: Porcelain
DESCRIPTION: Brick school with small flag flying atop clock tower. Stone foundation with steps that lead to front doors. School name above doors. Banner over windows tells children date of winter recess.
PARTICULARS: Lighted.

OSRP: $52.00
GBTru: $52.00

CHRISTMAS IN THE CITY

☐ **NAME:** BROWNSTONES ON THE SQUARE 1995
ITEM #: 58877
STATUS: Current

See below.

MATERIAL: Porcelain
DESCRIPTION: Set of 2 includes *Beekman House,* #58878 and *Pickford Place,* #58879.
PARTICULARS: Set of 2. Lighted. Each piece now assigned individual Item Number.

OSRP: $90.00
GBTru: $90.00

☐ **NAME:** Beekman House 1995
ITEM #: 58878
STATUS: Current

MATERIAL: Porcelain
DESCRIPTION: Four-story walk-up with entry canopy, decorated with script 'B'. Building name above paned first level window with lamp close by. Second story arched window has wrought iron ornamentation, while other front windows are canopied. Date appears on ornate roof molding.
PARTICULARS: 1 of the 2 piece set—BROWNSTONES ON THE SQUARE. Lighted. Each piece now assigned individual Item Number.

OSRP: $45.00
GBTru: $45.00

☐ **NAME:** Pickford Place 1995
ITEM #: 58879
STATUS: Current

MATERIAL: Porcelain
DESCRIPTION: Four-story walk-up with entry canopy, decorated with script 'P'. Building name above paned first level window with lamp close by. Second story arched window has potted plant while other front windows have wrought iron ornamentation. Date appears on ornate roof molding.
PARTICULARS: 1 of the 2 piece set—BROWNSTONES ON THE SQUARE. Lighted. Each piece now assigned individual Item Number.

OSRP: $45.00
GBTru: $45.00

☐ **NAME:** Washington Street Post Office 1996
ITEM #: 58880
STATUS: Current

MATERIAL: Porcelain
DESCRIPTION: Three-story brick with roof and edges of building finished in dressed stone. This office can receive and send letters, packages and airmail as well as sell stamps.
PARTICULARS: Lighted. Midyear release.

OSRP: $52.00
GBTru: $52.00

❑ **NAME:** Little Town Of Bethlehem   1987
ITEM #: 5975-7
STATUS: Current

See below.

MATERIAL: Porcelain
DESCRIPTION: Replica of Holy Family Manger Scene with Three Wise Men and Shepherd. Stone and sun-dried brick homes and shelters add Mid-East simplicity. Animals attentive to Holy Family.
PARTICULARS: Set of 12. Lighted.
VARIATIONS: With and without **snow** on manger.

OSRP: $150.00
GBTru: $150.00   NC

 **Q&Ask The Historian**

Q.   Do you think that the newer pieces will ever be as valuable on the secondary market as the older ones?

A.   That depends on what you mean by "as valuable." If you mean both pieces selling for the same amount at the same time, it's not probable. It does happen, however. Take Santa's Workshop, for example. Its value has passed those of many older pieces. This is because it was sold for a relatively short time and is highly sought after—it is considered to be the cornerstone of the North Pole series.

Will a newly retired piece have the same value in five years as a piece that retired five years ago is worth now? It is very possible. It's true that D56 is manufacturing more pieces now than they did five years ago, but there are more collectors buying them. Five years from now, there will be even more collectors. Some of them will want a piece that retired this year.

Santa's Workshop

❏ **NAME:** Santa's Workshop 1990
ITEM #: 5600-6
STATUS: Retired 1993

MATERIAL: Porcelain
DESCRIPTION: Multi-chimnied, many gabled home and workshop. Stone foundation with stucco and timber upper stories. Balconies extend off windows and hold garlands. Mailbox by front door.
PARTICULARS: Lighted.

OSRP: $72.00
GBTru: $485.00 ↑29%

North Pole

See below.

❏ **NAME:** NORTH POLE 1990
ITEM #: 5601-4
STATUS: Current

MATERIAL: Porcelain
DESCRIPTION: Set of 2 includes *Reindeer Barn,* #56015 and *Elf Bunkhouse,* #56016.
PARTICULARS: Set of 2. Lighted. Each piece now assigned individual Item Number.

OSRP: $70.00
GBTru: $80.00 NC

Reindeer Barn

❏ **NAME:** Reindeer Barn 1990
ITEM #: 56015
STATUS: Current

MATERIAL: Porcelain
DESCRIPTION: Stone and stucco has stalls for all reindeer. Steeply pitched roof has cupola on ridge and step design on front of dormers. Roof vents and Dutch stall doors provide ventilation.
PARTICULARS: 1 of the 2 piece set–NORTH POLE. Lighted.

OSRP: $35.00 Each piece now assigned individual Item Number.
GBTru: $40.00 NC **VARIATIONS:** Common variation: a name duplicated, another omitted on reindeer stalls.

Elf Bunkhouse

❏ **NAME:** Elf Bunkhouse 1990
ITEM #: 56016
STATUS: Current

MATERIAL: Porcelain
DESCRIPTION: Home for Santa's helpers, 3 stories with steeply pitched roof and protected chimney. Made of wood, stone, and stucco featuring bay windows, dormers, and a balcony.
PARTICULARS: 1 of the 2 piece set–NORTH POLE. Lighted. Each piece now assigned individual Item Number.

OSRP: $35.00
GBTru: $40.00 NC

NeeNee's Dolls And Toys

☐ **NAME:** NeeNee's Dolls And Toys   1991
ITEM #: 5620-0
STATUS: Retired 1995

MATERIAL: Porcelain
DESCRIPTION: Rough finish stucco and stone house. Steeply pitched rear roof, red shuttered lattice-paned front second story windows, monogram within wreaths.
PARTICULARS: Lighted. Early release to Showcase Dealers and Gift Creations Concepts (GCC).

OSRP: $36.00
GBTru: $55.00 ↑47%

North Pole Shops

See below.

☐ **NAME:** NORTH POLE SHOPS   1991
ITEM #: 5621-9
STATUS: Retired 1995

MATERIAL: Porcelain
DESCRIPTION: Set of 2 includes *Orly's Bell & Harness Supply* and *Rimpy's Bakery*.
PARTICULARS: Set of 2. Lighted.

OSRP: $75.00
GBTru: $105.00 ↑40%

Orly's Bell & Harness Supply

☐ **NAME:** Orly's Bell & Harness Supply   1991
ITEM #: 5621-9
STATUS: Retired 1995

MATERIAL: Porcelain
DESCRIPTION: Stone steps lead to bell shop doorway with brick work design to frame it. Sleigh strap with bells above sign. Harness area has large wood doors that open to allow horse drawn carriage or wagon to enter. Window with balcony above, on 2nd story.
PARTICULARS: 1 of the 2 piece set–NORTH POLE SHOPS. Lighted.

OSRP: $37.50
GBTru: $55.00 ↑47%

Rimpy's Bakery

☐ **NAME:** Rimpy's Bakery   1991
ITEM #: 5621-9
STATUS: Retired 1995

MATERIAL: Porcelain
DESCRIPTION: Three storied, half wood timbered narrow building. Hipped-roof with gable on facade. Large eight paned front window with wood crib in front and on side.
PARTICULARS: 1 of the 2 piece set–NORTH POLE SHOPS. Lighted.

OSRP: $37.50
GBTru: $55.00 ↑47%

❏ **NAME:** Tassy's Mittens & Hassel's Woolies 1991
ITEM #: 5622-7
STATUS: Retired 1995

MATERIAL: Porcelain
DESCRIPTION: Two shops in connected buildings. Hassel's has corner turret window and oriel turret upper window. Tassy's has angled front window at ground and three arched windows on overhanging second story. Gable has carved bough and berry design–roof angles steeply pitched.
PARTICULARS: Lighted.

OSRP: $50.00
GBTru: $75.00 ↑50%

Post Office

❏ **NAME:** Post Office 1992
ITEM #: 5623-5
STATUS: Current

MATERIAL: Porcelain
DESCRIPTION: Basis for building is turret with what appears to be a half-house on one side of main tower. Second floor features multi-paned windows, small curved turret between second and third floor could hold staircase and take up little wall space. Third floor has low balcony outside windows.
PARTICULARS: Lighted. Early release to Showcase Dealers.

OSRP: $45.00
GBTru: $50.00 NC

Obbie's Books & Letrinka's Candy

❏ **NAME:** Obbie's Books & Letrinka's Candy 1992
ITEM #: 5624-3
STATUS: Current

MATERIAL: Porcelain
DESCRIPTION: The tall narrow books and toys shop contrast sharply with the shorter, wider, candy shop. Both shops have steep pitched roofs. A bay window on Obbie's side wall plus a number of dormer windows reinforce the angular look of the shop. Onion dome shaped chimney and cupola on roof ridge are unique to Letrinka's which also has a vertical timbered ground level design. Both shops have lettered wreaths by front entries.
PARTICULARS: Lighted.

OSRP: $70.00
GBTru: $70.00 NC

Elfie's Sleds & Skates

❏ **NAME:** Elfie's Sleds & Skates 1992
ITEM #: 5625-1
STATUS: Current

MATERIAL: Porcelain
DESCRIPTION: Distinctive roof design with chimneys that are only visible outside from the second story. Roof hood projects out from walls to protect windows on house sides as well as sweeping down to help form large front window. Wreath with letter "E" in addition to shop signs.
PARTICULARS: Lighted.

OSRP: $48.00
GBTru: $48.00 NC

North Pole Chapel

NAME: North Pole Chapel   1993
ITEM #: 5626-0
STATUS: Current

MATERIAL: Porcelain
DESCRIPTION: Spire, containing brass bell rises at rear of Chapel. Fieldstone topped by timbered upper story. Double door front entry flanked by evergreens. Side chimney rises through roof with flue pipe capped by onion cap. Large wreath circled clock above entry.
PARTICULARS: Lighted. Early release to Showcase Dealers and select buying groups.

OSRP: $45.00
GBTru: $45.00   NC

North Pole Express Depot

❐ **NAME:** North Pole Express Depot   1993
ITEM #: 5627-8
STATUS: Current

MATERIAL: Porcelain
DESCRIPTION: Receiving area for people and deliveries in and out of North Pole, not going by Santa's sled. Roof line at lowest point is pagoda-like with an A-frame gable transversing a ridge. Stone chimney rises at rear of roof. Separate doors for passengers and freight.
PARTICULARS: Lighted.

OSRP: $48.00
GBTru: $48.00   NC

Santa's Woodworks

❐ **NAME:** Santa's Woodworks   1993
ITEM #: 5628-6
STATUS: Current

MATERIAL: Porcelain
DESCRIPTION: Lower level contains heavy equipment for sawing, debarking and trimming wood. Main level reached by wood stairs at side of open porch. Structure is a log house.
PARTICULARS: Lighted.

OSRP: $42.00
GBTru: $45.00   NC

Santa's Lookout Tower

❐ **NAME:** Santa's Lookout Tower   1993
ITEM #: 5629-4
STATUS: Current

MATERIAL: Porcelain
DESCRIPTION: Pennants fly above door and top of tower, which rises above trees to give Santa a clear picture of flight conditions. Balcony around highest story lets Santa check wind velocity.
PARTICULARS: Lighted.

OSRP: $45.00
GBTru: $48.00   NC

❒ **NAME:** Elfin Snow Cone Works 1994
ITEM #: 5633-2
STATUS: Current

MATERIAL: Porcelain
DESCRIPTION: Snow cones on shutters and sign of steep roofed shop. Roof molding trim resembles icing. Oriel window extends from 3rd floor to rooftop.
PARTICULARS: Lighted.

OSRP: $40.00
GBTru: $40.00 NC

Beard Barber Shop

❒ **NAME:** Beard Barber Shop 1994
ITEM #: 5634-0
STATUS: Current

MATERIAL: Porcelain
DESCRIPTION: Small shop with 3 tall front windows allowing light to enter. Barber pole at entry and banner of shears establish function of shop.
PARTICULARS: Lighted.

OSRP: $27.50
GBTru: $27.50 NC

North Pole Dolls & Santa's Bear Works

❒ **NAME:** North Pole Dolls & Santa's
Bear Works 1994
ITEM #: 5635-9
STATUS: Current

MATERIAL: Porcelain
DESCRIPTION: Set of 3 consists of *North Pole Dolls, Santa's Bear Works* and *Entrance.* Two 3-story mirror image buildings with 2-story center connecting entrance way. Shops have signs by doors. A *NP* pennant flies from the cupola in the center.
PARTICULARS: Set of 3. Entrance is non-lit.

OSRP: $96.00
GBTru: $96.00 NC

Tin Soldier Shop

❒ **NAME:** Tin Soldier Shop 1995
ITEM #: 5638-3
STATUS: Current

MATERIAL: Porcelain
DESCRIPTION: Tall, narrow shop with garland draped balcony. Toy soldiers decorate base of 2-story turret at side of entry.
PARTICULARS: Lighted. Midyear release.

OSRP: $42.00
GBTru: $42.00 NC

Elfin Forge & Assembly Shop

☐ **NAME:** Elfin Forge & Assembly Shop   1995
ITEM #: 56384
STATUS: Current

MATERIAL: Porcelain
DESCRIPTION: North Pole folks make all the necessary iron works at the forge. Steps lead up to entry that connects two building wings. The forge furnaces are housed in the 3-story building with the tall furnace pipes. Design and assembly takes place in attached turret, with finished product exiting through large double doors.
PARTICULARS: Lighted.

OSRP: $65.00
GBTru: $65.00

Weather & Time Observatory

☐ **NAME:** Weather & Time Observatory   1995
ITEM #: 56385
STATUS: Current

MATERIAL: Porcelain
DESCRIPTION: Santa has to know all time zones and prevailing climate to plan his big sleigh trip, as well as conditions for visiting folk, elves and animals. Telescope located in rooftop observatory, clocks are set for all time zones. Satellite dish brings in news on weather. Fortress-like turret for astronomy and smaller attached areas for offices.
PARTICULARS: Lighted.

OSRP: $50.00
GBTru: $50.00

Santa's Rooming House

☐ **NAME:** Santa's Rooming House   1995
ITEM #: 56386
STATUS: Current

MATERIAL: Porcelain
DESCRIPTION: Visitors to the North Pole stay at this red clapboard inn. Stairs lead up to entry door for bedrooms. Lower level houses kitchen, dining and sitting rooms, as well as the cloak room.
PARTICULARS: Lighted.

OSRP: $50.00
GBTru: $50.00

Elves' Trade School

☐ **NAME:** Elves' Trade School   1995
ITEM #: 56387
STATUS: Current

MATERIAL: Porcelain
DESCRIPTION: All Toy Workshop, Forge & Assembly, Astronomy and Charting skills are taught at the school for elves. Stone pillars form part of sturdy base to support wood structure. Hammer holds school sign above red door.
PARTICULARS: Lighted.

OSRP: $50.00
GBTru: $50.00

North Pole

Popcorn & Cranberry House

❑ **NAME:** Popcorn & Cranberry House   1996
    ITEM #: 56388
    STATUS: Current

MATERIAL: Porcelain
DESCRIPTION: Tall chimney separates front part of house from rear work area. Elves work on the berries and corn preparing them for stringing into garlands and creation of holiday trim. Berries trim front sign accented by red roof, door and windows.
PARTICULARS: Lighted. Midyear release.

OSRP: $45.00
GBTru: $45.00

Santa's Bell Repair

❑ **NAME:** Santa's Bell Repair   1996
    ITEM #: 56389
    STATUS: Current

MATERIAL: Porcelain
DESCRIPTION: Bells that no longer ring, chime or jingle are sent to the repair shop to be fixed and shined. Brass bells over entry, tall fieldstone chimney, and combination bell tower/dormer set this design apart.
PARTICULARS: Lighted. Midyear release.

OSRP: $45.00
GBTru: $45.00

North Pole Start A Tradition Set

❑ **NAME:** North Pole Start A Tradition Set   1996
    ITEM #: 56390
    STATUS: Current

MATERIAL: Porcelain
DESCRIPTION: Set of 12 includes: CANDY CANE LANE, Set of 2–*Candy Cane & Peppermint Shop* and *Gift Wrap & Ribbons*.
Accessories: Set /2–*Candy Cane Elves*,
6 Trees and a Bag of Snow.
PARTICULARS: Set of 12. Lighted.
Starter Set is midyear release featured at D56 National Homes For The Holidays Open House Event, November 7-11, 1996.
Special packaging for promotion.
Starter Set will be priced at $65.00 only during Event and then will be listed at SRP of $85.00.
The 1996 Retirement Announcement has been scheduled to be announced on 11/8/96 as part of the Event.

OSRP: $85.00
GBTru: $85.00

Mickey's Christmas Carol

❐ **NAME:** Mickey's Christmas Carol   1994
   ITEM #: 5350-3
   STATUS: Retired May 1996

MATERIAL: Porcelain
DESCRIPTION: Replica of the building in Fantasyland at Disney World in Orlando, Florida. Gold trim and blue roof along with multiple turrets and gables make this a very distinctive building.
PARTICULARS: Set of 2. Lighted.
VARIATIONS: Disney Theme Park Release is Item #742-0 and has "Holiday Collection" Bottom Stamp on larger piece.

OSRP: $144.00
GBTru: $144.00   NC

OLDE WORLD ANTIQUES SHOPS

See below.

❐ **NAME:** OLDE WORLD ANTIQUES SHOPS 1994
   ITEM #: 5351-1
   STATUS: Retired May 1996

MATERIAL: Porcelain
DESCRIPTION: Set of 2 includes *Olde World Antiques I* and *Olde World Antiques II*.
PARTICULARS: Set of 2. Lighted.
VARIATIONS: Disney Theme Park Release is Item #743-9 and has "Holiday Collection" Bottom Stamp.

OSRP: $90.00
GBTru: $90.00   NC

Olde World Antiques I

❐ **NAME:** Olde World Antiques I   1994
   ITEM #: 5351-1
   STATUS: Retired May 1996

MATERIAL: Porcelain
DESCRIPTION: Similar building can be seen in Disney World's Liberty Square. Long staircase in front leads to second floor.
PARTICULARS: 1 of the 2 piece set—OLDE WORLD ANTIQUES SHOPS. Lighted.
VARIATIONS: Disney Theme Park Release is Item #743-9 and has "Holiday Collection" Bottom Stamp.

OSRP: $45.00
GBTru: $45.00   NC

Olde World Antiques II

❐ **NAME:** Olde World Antiques II   1994
   ITEM #: 5351-1
   STATUS: Retired May 1996

MATERIAL: Porcelain
DESCRIPTION: Replica of the building in Liberty Square in Orlando's Disney World. Windows vary from arched to rectangular.
PARTICULARS: 1 of the 2 piece set—OLDE WORLD ANTIQUES SHOPS. Lighted.
VARIATIONS: Disney Theme Park Release is Item #743-9 and has "Holiday Collection" Bottom Stamp.

OSRP: $45.00
GBTru: $45.00   NC

Disney Parks Village

Disneyland Fire Department #105

❏ **NAME:** Disneyland Fire Department #105   1994
ITEM #: 5352-0
STATUS: Retired May 1996

MATERIAL: Porcelain
DESCRIPTION: Inspired by the fire station on Main Street in Disneyland. Brick station's large front doors allow fire equipment in and out.
PARTICULARS: Lighted.
VARIATIONS: Disney Theme Park Release is Item #744-7 and has "Holiday Collection" Bottom Stamp.

OSRP: $45.00
GBTru: $45.00   NC

Silversmith

❏ **NAME:** Silversmith   1995
ITEM #: 53521
STATUS: Retired May 1996

MATERIAL: Porcelain
DESCRIPTION: Five-sided building of fieldstone. Many windows on all sides. Dormers in each roof section. Hanging sign above double entry doors. Potted trees flank door.
PARTICULARS: Lighted. Item #7448 was an exclusive for Disney Theme Parks.

OSRP: $50.00
GBTru: $50.00

Tinker Bell's Treasures

❏ **NAME:** Tinker Bell's Treasures   1995
ITEM #: 53522
STATUS: Retired May 1996

MATERIAL: Porcelain
DESCRIPTION: Timbered and stucco building with twin chimneys. Porcelain trees in raised stone garden beds flank front and sides. Roof line slopes down to trees to frame front entry.
PARTICULARS: Lighted. Item #7449 was an exclusive for Disney Theme Parks.

OSRP: $60.00
GBTru: $60.00

Q. *Who is the artist that designs the Department 56 buildings and accessories?*

A. For the most part, the buildings and accessories are designed with a team concept. A number of designers and artists may work on a given piece as it advances through the production stages. There is one village artist, however, whom Department 56 has featured at events–Neilan Lund. Mr. Lund is responsible for designs of Dickens' Village, New England Village, Alpine Village and the North Pole.

Disney Parks Village

☐ **NAME:** Carolers 1984
ITEM #: 6526-9
STATUS: Retired 1990

MATERIAL: Porcelain
DESCRIPTION: Group of village people sing or listen to carols.
PARTICULARS: Set of 3. Dickens' Village accessory.
VARIATIONS: There are three versions (sculpting/painting) of this set. 1st Issue "White Post"–Viola is very light with dark brown trim, very little detail in figures, made in Taiwan–$120.00* (NC). 2nd Issue–Black post, viola is one color, slightly more detail in figures, made in Taiwan. 3rd Issue– Black post, viola has darker trim, largest of 3 sets, made in Philippines.

OSRP: $10.00
GBTru: $40.00* ↑5%

Village Train

☐ **NAME:** Village Train 1985
ITEM #: 6527-7
STATUS: Retired 1986

MATERIAL: Porcelain
DESCRIPTION: Three car porcelain train.
PARTICULARS: Set of 3. Dickens' Village accessory.
aka "Brighton Village Train".

OSRP: $12.00
GBTru: $395.00 ↓17%

Christmas Carol Figures

☐ **NAME:** Christmas Carol Figures 1986
ITEM #: 6501-3
STATUS: Retired 1990

MATERIAL: Porcelain
DESCRIPTION: Ebenezer Scrooge, Bob Cratchit carrying Tiny Tim, boy with poulterer/goose.
PARTICULARS: Set of 3. Dickens' Village accessory.

OSRP: $12.50
GBTru: $85.00 ↑6%

Lighted Tree W/Children And Ladder

☐ **NAME:** Lighted Tree W/Children And Ladder 1986
ITEM #: 6510-2
STATUS: Retired 1989

MATERIAL: Porcelain
DESCRIPTION: Children climb ladder to decorate tree.
PARTICULARS: Set of 3. Lighted. Christmas In The City accessory. Original sleeve reads, "Christmas In The City".

OSRP: $35.00
GBTru: $320.00 ↓9%

He

	NAME:	Sleighride	1986
	ITEM #:	6511-0	
	STATUS:	Retired 1990	

MATERIAL: Porcelain
DESCRIPTION: Couple enjoys ride in old fashioned sleigh drawn by two horses.
PARTICULARS: Dickens' and New England Village accessory.
VARIATIONS: There are 2 versions of the Sleighride: 1st Issue–Original sleeve reads, "Dickens Sleighride"– man has a narrow white scarf with red polka dots. 2nd Issue–Man's scarf and lapels are white with red polka dots. Gray horse is more spotted.

OSRP: $19.50
GBTru: $50.00   NC

Covered Wooden Bridge

	NAME:	Covered Wooden Bridge	1986
	ITEM #:	6531-5	
	STATUS:	Retired 1990	

MATERIAL: Porcelain
DESCRIPTION: Simple wooden bridge with shingle roof, protects travelers from weather while crossing river.
PARTICULARS: New England Village accessory.
VARIATIONS: In **color** from light to dark.

OSRP: $10.00
GBTru: $38.00   ↑9%

New England Winter Set

	NAME:	New England Winter Set	1986
	ITEM #:	6532-3	
	STATUS:	Retired 1990	

MATERIAL: Porcelain
DESCRIPTION: Stone well, man pushes sleigh as woman rides, snow covered trees, man pulls cut tree.
PARTICULARS: Set of 5.

OSRP: $18.00
GBTru: $47.00   ↑4%

Porcelain Trees

	NAME:	Porcelain Trees	1986
	ITEM #:	6537-4	
	STATUS:	Retired 1992	

MATERIAL: Porcelain
DESCRIPTION: Two different size snow covered evergreens.
PARTICULARS: Set of 2.

OSRP: $14.00
GBTru: $35.00   NC

NAME: Alpine Villagers   1986
ITEM #: 6542-0
STATUS: Retired 1992

MATERIAL: Porcelain
DESCRIPTION: Seated man, walking woman carrying book, dog pulling wagon with milk cans.
PARTICULARS: Set of 3.
VARIATIONS: Later years of production thinned size of figurines.

OSRP: $13.00
GBTru: $38.00   ↑9%

Farm People & Animals

NAME: Farm People & Animals   1987
ITEM #: 5901-3
STATUS: Retired 1989

MATERIAL: Porcelain
DESCRIPTION: Man hauling logs. Woman and girl feeding geese. Goat pulls wagon and deer eat winter hay.
PARTICULARS: Set of 5. Dickens' Village accessory.

OSRP: $24.00
GBTru: $94.00   ↑4%

Blacksmith

NAME: Blacksmith   1987
ITEM #: 5934-0
STATUS: Retired 1990

MATERIAL: Porcelain
DESCRIPTION: One man tends fire while smithy shoes horse. Boy holds pail of nails.
PARTICULARS: Set of 3. Dickens' Village accessory.

OSRP: $20.00
GBTru: $75.00   ↑7%

Silo & Hay Shed

NAME: Silo & Hay Shed   1987
ITEM #: 5950-1
STATUS: Retired 1989

MATERIAL: Porcelain
DESCRIPTION: Stone and stucco grain storage silo and elevated wood hay building.
PARTICULARS: Set of 2. Dickens' Village accessory.
VARIATIONS: Color: 1st Issue–The roof of silo has stripes of rust, gold and brown, 2nd Issue–Silo roof is almost solid brown.

OSRP: $18.00
GBTru: $160.00   NC

Ox Sled

☐ **NAME:** Ox Sled 1987
ITEM #: 5951-0
STATUS: Retired 1989

MATERIAL: Porcelain
DESCRIPTION: Oxen team pulls heavy wood wagon on sled runners. Driver plus a small boy holding Christmas tree.
PARTICULARS: Dickens' Village accessory.
VARIATIONS: Variations in **color** affect TRUMARKET Price: Tan pants and Green seat cushion–$250.00 (NC), Blue pants and Black seat cushion–$140.00 (↓3%).

OSRP: $20.00
GBTru: See Variations

Christmas In The City Sign

☐ **NAME:** Christmas In The City Sign 1987
ITEM #: 5960-9
STATUS: Retired 1993

MATERIAL: Porcelain

OSRP: $6.00
GBTru: $15.00 NC

Automobiles

☐ **NAME:** Automobiles 1987
ITEM #: 5964-1
STATUS: Current

MATERIAL: Porcelain
DESCRIPTION: City delivery truck, checkered taxi, and roadster.
PARTICULARS: Set of 3. Christmas In The City accessory. Size: 3".

OSRP: $15.00
GBTru: $22.00 NC

City People

☐ **NAME:** City People 1987
ITEM #: 5965-0
STATUS: Retired 1990

MATERIAL: Porcelain
DESCRIPTION: Police officer, man walking dog*, pretzel man with pushcart, mother and daughter with shopping bag, and woman collecting for the needy.
PARTICULARS: Set of 5. Christmas In The City accessory. (*missing from photo)

OSRP: $27.50
GBTru: $55.00 ↑10%

Heritage Village Accessories

Shopkeepers

❒ **NAME:** Shopkeepers   1987
ITEM #: 5966-8
STATUS: Retired 1988

MATERIAL: Porcelain
DESCRIPTION: Vendors of fruits, vegetables, breads, cakes.
PARTICULARS: Set of 4. Dickens' Village accessory.
Shopkeepers and *City Workers* are the only figures to have
"snow" sprinkled on them.

OSRP: $15.00
GBTru: $38.00   NC

City Workers

❒ **NAME:** City Workers   1987
ITEM #: 5967-6
STATUS: Retired 1988

MATERIAL: Porcelain
DESCRIPTION: Police constable, nurse, driver, tradesman
with packages.
PARTICULARS: Set of 4. Dickens' Village accessory.
Shopkeepers and *City Workers* are the only figures to have
"snow" sprinkled on them. Some boxes read "City People".

OSRP: $15.00
GBTru: $35.00 ↓12%

Village Express Train–Black

❒ **NAME:** Village Express Train–Black   1987
ITEM #: 5997-8
STATUS: Retired 1988

Photo Not Available.

DESCRIPTION: Black locomotive pulls a coal car, two
passenger cars and a caboose.
PARTICULARS: Set of 22. Manufactured by Tyco.

OSRP: $90.00
GBTru: $265.00 ↓12%

Skating Pond

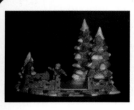

❒ **NAME:** Skating Pond   1987
ITEM #: 6545-5
STATUS: Retired 1990

MATERIAL: Porcelain
DESCRIPTION: Low stone wall circles pond. One child
watches other child skating. Two snow covered trees.
PARTICULARS: Dickens', New England & Christmas In
The City accessory.
VARIATIONS: 1st Issue–Made in Taiwan, ice is generally very
light blue streaks, 2nd Issue–Made in Philippines, blue covers
most of ice surface.

OSRP: $24.00
GBTru: $75.00   NC

Stone Bridge

☐ **NAME:** Stone Bridge 1987
ITEM #: 6546-3
STATUS: Retired 1990

MATERIAL: Porcelain
DESCRIPTION: Variegated fieldstone arches over river.
Corner post has lamp.
VARIATIONS: In **color** from light to dark.

OSRP: $12.00
GBTru: $80.00 NC

Village Well & Holy Cross

☐ **NAME:** Village Well & Holy Cross 1987
ITEM #: 6547-1
STATUS: Retired 1989

MATERIAL: Porcelain
DESCRIPTION: Old fashioned hand pump for water, housed
in small gazebo. Cross upon pedestal on stone step base.
PARTICULARS: Set of 2. Dickens' Village accessory.
VARIATIONS: 1st Issue–Water is blue, birds are dark;
2nd Issue–Water has no color, birds are light.

OSRP: $13.00
GBTru: $165.00 ↑3%

Dickens' Village Sign

☐ **NAME:** Dickens' Village Sign 1987
ITEM #: 6569-2
STATUS: Retired 1993

MATERIAL: Porcelain

OSRP: $6.00
GBTru: $18.00 ↓10%

New England Village Sign

☐ **NAME:** New England Village Sign 1987
ITEM #: 6570-6
STATUS: Retired 1993

MATERIAL: Porcelain

OSRP: $6.00
GBTru: $16.00 ↑7%

Heritage Village Accessories

Alpine Village Sign

❐ **NAME:** Alpine Village Sign   1987
     ITEM #: 6571-4
     STATUS: Retired 1993

MATERIAL: Porcelain

OSRP: $6.00
GBTru: $17.00 ↓15%

Maple Sugaring Shed

❐ **NAME:** Maple Sugaring Shed   1987
     ITEM #: 6589-7
     STATUS: Retired 1989

MATERIAL: Porcelain
DESCRIPTION: Two tapped trees, sled with bucket of syrup, and open walled shed with cooking vat.
PARTICULARS: Set of 3. New England Village accessory.

OSRP: $19.00
GBTru: $215.00 ↓12%

Dover Coach

❐ **NAME:** Dover Coach   1987
     ITEM #: 6590-0
     STATUS: Retired 1990

MATERIAL: Porcelain
DESCRIPTION: Passenger coach with horse, driver, & coachman.
PARTICULARS: Dickens' Village accessory.
VARIATIONS: Variations affect GBTru Prices. There are 3 versions: 1st Issue–Made in Taiwan, coachman has no mustache, wheels are crude–$98.00 (↓11%). 2nd Issue–Made in Taiwan, coachman has mustache, wheels are rounder, two long recesses on underside of base–$60.00 (↓8%). 3rd issue–Made in Sri Lanka, coachman has mustache, wheels are round– $64.00 (↓15%).

OSRP: $18.00
GBTru: See Variations

Childe Pond And Skaters

❐ **NAME:** Childe Pond And Skaters   1988
     ITEM #: 5903-0
     STATUS: Retired 1991

MATERIAL: Porcelain
DESCRIPTION: Brick warming-house, shutters latch against wind, wooden benches for skaters, birdhouse above door.
PARTICULARS: Set of 4. Dickens' Village accessory.
VARIATIONS: **Color** of warming hut varies.

OSRP: $30.00
GBTru: $80.00   NC

Fezziwig And Friends

❒ **NAME:** Fezziwig And Friends   1988
ITEM #: 5928-5
STATUS: Retired 1990

MATERIAL: Porcelain
DESCRIPTION: Husband and wife bringing food to elderly neighbors.
PARTICULARS: Set of 3. Dickens' Village accessory. Addition to "Christmas Carol" grouping.

OSRP: $12.50
GBTru: $52.00   ↑4%

Nicholas Nickleby Characters

❒ **NAME:** Nicholas Nickleby Characters   1988
ITEM #: 5929-3
STATUS: Retired 1991

MATERIAL: Porcelain
DESCRIPTION: Nicholas and sister Kate, Wackford Squeers with schoolbook, three children playing, and four-wheeled wagon.
PARTICULARS: Set of 4. Dickens' Village accessory. Misspelled as Nicholas Nick"el"by on sleeve.

OSRP: $20.00
GBTru: $32.00   ↓11%

Snow Children

❒ **NAME:** Snow Children   1988
ITEM #: 5938-2
STATUS: Retired 1994

MATERIAL: Porcelain
DESCRIPTION: Girl finishes snowman while dog watches. Two boys push off on sled, another belly flops on his sled.
PARTICULARS: Set of 3.

OSRP: $15.00
GBTru: $28.00   ↑27%

Village Harvest People

❒ **NAME:** Village Harvest People   1988
ITEM #: 5941-2
STATUS: Retired 1991

MATERIAL: Porcelain
DESCRIPTION: Woman with butter churn, man loads pumpkins on cart, corn shocks, and pumpkins.
PARTICULARS: Set of 4. New England Village accessory. Sleeve reads "Harvest Time".

OSRP: $27.50
GBTru: $45.00   NC

Heritage Village Accessories

City Newsstand

❐ **NAME:** City Newsstand   1988
ITEM #: 5971-4
STATUS: Retired 1991

MATERIAL: Porcelain
DESCRIPTION: News vendor, magazine and newspaper wooden stand, woman reading paper, newsboy showing headlines.
PARTICULARS: Set of 4. Christmas In The City accessory.

OSRP: $25.00
GBTru: $52.00 ⬆8%

Village Express Train

❐ **NAME:** Village Express Train   1988
ITEM #: 5980-3
STATUS: Current

DESCRIPTION: Red, black and silver locomotive pulls the cars around the track.
PARTICULARS: Set of 22. Manufactured by Bachmann Trains.

OSRP: $95.00
GBTru: $100.00   NC

Village Train Trestle

❐ **NAME:** Village Train Trestle   1988
ITEM #: 5981-1
STATUS: Retired 1990

MATERIAL: Porcelain
DESCRIPTION: Double arch trestle spans river. Single track on stone train overpass.
PARTICULARS: Sleeve reads "Stone Train Trestle".

OSRP: $17.00
GBTru: $70.00 ⬆17%

One Horse Open Sleigh

❐ **NAME:** One Horse Open Sleigh   1988
ITEM #: 5982-0
STATUS: Retired 1993

MATERIAL: Porcelain
DESCRIPTION: Couple out for a ride in sleigh with canopy. Lap robes protect against cold.

OSRP: $20.00
GBTru: $38.00 ⬆9%

City Bus & Milk Truck

❒ **NAME:** City Bus & Milk Truck   1988
ITEM #: 5983-8
STATUS: Retired 1991

MATERIAL: Porcelain
DESCRIPTION: Open back milk truck carries large
milk cans. Old fashioned city bus.
PARTICULARS: Set of 2. Christmas In The City accessory.
Box reads "Transport".

OSRP: $15.00
GBTru: $32.00   NC

Salvation Army Band

❒ **NAME:** Salvation Army Band   1988
ITEM #: 5985-4
STATUS: Retired 1991

MATERIAL: Porcelain
DESCRIPTION: Five uniformed musicians and conductor
represent charitable organization.
PARTICULARS: Set of 6. Christmas In The City accessory.

OSRP: $24.00
GBTru: $75.00   ↑15%

Woodcutter And Son

❒ **NAME:** Woodcutter And Son   1988
ITEM #: 5986-2
STATUS: Retired 1990

MATERIAL: Porcelain
DESCRIPTION: Father splits logs as son carries firewood.
PARTICULARS: Set of 2. New England Village accessory.

OSRP: $10.00
GBTru: $42.00   ↑5%

Red Covered Bridge

❒ **NAME:** Red Covered Bridge   1988
ITEM #: 5987-0
STATUS: Retired 1994

MATERIAL: Porcelain
DESCRIPTION: Wooden bridge spans Maple Creek,
supported by stone bases.
PARTICULARS: New England Village accessory.

OSRP: $15.00
GBTru: $24.00   ↑9%

Heritage Village Accessories

Town Square Gazebo

❐ **NAME:** Town Square Gazebo   1989
ITEM #: 5513-1
STATUS: Current

MATERIAL: Resin
DESCRIPTION: Eight posts support the roof that rises to a spire. Stone work on floor follows the shape of the roof.

OSRP: $19.00
GBTru: $19.00   NC

Boulevard

❐ **NAME:** Boulevard   1989
ITEM #: 5516-6
STATUS: Retired 1992

DESCRIPTION: Forms a tree-lined sidewalk. Trees provide shade at benches.
PARTICULARS: Set of 14. Christmas In The City accessory. 4 sidewalk pieces, 4 removable 5" trees, 2 benches, 4 hitching posts.

OSRP: $25.00
GBTru: $50.00   NC

Mailbox & Fire Hydrant

❐ **NAME:** Mailbox & Fire Hydrant   1989
ITEM #: 5517-4
STATUS: Retired 1990

MATERIAL: Metal
DESCRIPTION: Red, white and blue mail box features "U.S. Mail" sign and eagle logo.
PARTICULARS: Christmas In The City accessory. US Post Office colors of Red, White & Blue. Replaced in 1990 by #5214-0, a green and red HV mail box.

OSRP: $6.00
GBTru: $22.00 ↑10%

David Copperfield Characters

❐ **NAME:** David Copperfield Characters   1989
ITEM #: 5551-4
STATUS: Retired 1992

MATERIAL: Porcelain
DESCRIPTION: David Copperfield, Agnes, Mr. Wickfield, Peggotty with young David and Emily, Betsy Trotwood with Mr. Dick.
PARTICULARS: Set of 5. Dickens' Village accessory.

OSRP: $32.50
GBTru: $44.00 ↓8%

Village Sign With Snowman

❏ **NAME:** Village Sign With Snowman   1989
ITEM #: 5572-7
STATUS: Retired 1994

MATERIAL: Porcelain
DESCRIPTION: Snowman with top hat and scarf next to brick pillars and Heritage Village Sign.
PARTICULARS: Size: 3".

OSRP: $10.00
GBTru: $20.00 ↑67%

Lamplighter With Lamp

❏ **NAME:** Lamplighter With Lamp   1989
ITEM #: 5577-8
STATUS: Current

MATERIAL: Porcelain
DESCRIPTION: Man carries lit torch to light street lamps at dusk. Old fashioned lamp post, small tree by post.
PARTICULARS: Set of 2. Dickens' Village accessory. Size: 3 ¹/₂".

OSRP: $9.00
GBTru: $10.00   NC

Royal Coach

❏ **NAME:** Royal Coach   1989
ITEM #: 5578-6
STATUS: Retired 1992

MATERIAL: Porcelain and Metal
DESCRIPTION: Gold filigree decorates red coach with Royal Coat Of Arms on door. Wheel base and undercarriage are cast metal, four gray horses have red and gold harnesses.
PARTICULARS: Dickens' Village accessory. Early release to National Association Of Limited Edition Dealers (NALED).

OSRP: $55.00
GBTru: $75.00   NC

Constables

❏ **NAME:** Constables   1989
ITEM #: 5579-4
STATUS: Retired 1991

MATERIAL: Porcelain
DESCRIPTION: One holds club, one with seated dog, one tips hat and stands by lamppost.
PARTICULARS: Set of 3. Dickens' Village accessory.

OSRP: $17.50
GBTru: $62.00 ↑3%

Heritage Village Accessories   171

Violet Vendor/Carolers/Chestnut Vendor

❑ **NAME:** Violet Vendor/Carolers/
Chestnut Vendor   1989
ITEM #: 5580-8
STATUS: Retired 1992

MATERIAL: Porcelain
DESCRIPTION: Elderly woman sells violet bunches from basket, man sells fresh roasted nuts, and two women singing carols.
PARTICULARS: Set of 3. Dickens' Village accessory.

OSRP: $23.00
GBTru: $40.00   NC

King's Road Cab

❑ **NAME:** King's Road Cab   1989
ITEM #: 5581-6
STATUS: Current

MATERIAL: Porcelain
DESCRIPTION: Two-wheeled horse drawn carriage. Driver sits high and behind cab. Passengers protected from weather.
PARTICULARS: Dickens' Village accessory. Size: 7 $\frac{1}{4}$".

OSRP: $30.00
GBTru: $30.00   NC

Christmas Morning Figures

❑ **NAME:** Christmas Morning Figures   1989
ITEM #: 5588-3
STATUS: Current

MATERIAL: Porcelain
DESCRIPTION: Scrooge transformed–smiling, small boy by fence and lamppost–waving, couple carrying presents.
PARTICULARS: Set of 3. Dickens' Village accessory. Early release to National Association Of Limited Edition Dealers (NALED). Addition to "Christmas Carol" grouping.
Size: 2" high.

OSRP: $18.00
GBTru: $18.00   NC

Christmas Spirits Figures

❑ **NAME:** Christmas Spirits Figures   1989
ITEM #: 5589-1
STATUS: Current

MATERIAL: Porcelain
DESCRIPTION: Scrooge with Ghost Of...1) Christmas Past, 2) Christmas Present, and 3) Future...&...Marley.
PARTICULARS: Set of 4. Dickens' Village accessory. Addition to "Christmas Carol" grouping. Size: 2" high.

OSRP: $27.50
GBTru: $27.50   NC

	NAME:	Farm Animals	1989
	ITEM #:	5945-5	
	STATUS:	Retired 1991	

MATERIAL: Porcelain
DESCRIPTION: Chickens, geese, sheep, ewe and lamb.
PARTICULARS: Set of 4. New England Village accessory.

OSRP: $15.00
GBTru: $40.00   NC

Organ Grinder

	NAME:	Organ Grinder	1989
	ITEM #:	5957-9	
	STATUS:	Retired 1991	

MATERIAL: Porcelain
DESCRIPTION: Man turns handle to produce music for little monkey to dance. Woman and girl watch monkey.
PARTICULARS: Set of 3. Christmas In The City accessory.

OSRP: $21.00
GBTru: $36.00   ↑3%

Popcorn Vendor

	NAME:	Popcorn Vendor	1989
	ITEM #:	5958-7	
	STATUS:	Retired 1992	

MATERIAL: Porcelain
DESCRIPTION: Truck with red and white striped top. Vendor fills red and white bag. Little girl has a full popcorn bag.
PARTICULARS: Set of 3. Christmas In The City accessory.

OSRP: $22.00
GBTru: $32.00   ↓20%

River Street Ice House Cart

	NAME:	River Street Ice House Cart	1989
	ITEM #:	5959-5	
	STATUS:	Retired 1991	

MATERIAL: Porcelain
DESCRIPTION: Horse pulls a blue and gray ice wagon for ice man.
PARTICULARS: Christmas In The City accessory.

OSRP: $20.00
GBTru: $50.00   NC

☐ **NAME:**	Central Park Carriage	1989
ITEM #:	5979-0	
STATUS:	Current	

MATERIAL: Porcelain
DESCRIPTION: Gray horse pulls red and black carriage. Driver has mother and child as passengers.
PARTICULARS: Christmas In The City accessory. Size: 7 $^1/_4$".

OSRP: $30.00
GBTru: $30.00 NC

HV Promotional Sign

☐ **NAME:**	HV Promotional Sign	1989
ITEM #:	9953-8	
STATUS:	Retired 1990	

MATERIAL: Earthenware
DESCRIPTION: Vertical sign with arched top and brick base. Gold lettering on white facade.
VARIATION: Green lettering on green facade.

OSRP: $5.00
GBTru: $25.00 ↑25%

Mailbox & Fire Hydrant

☐ **NAME:**	Mailbox & Fire Hydrant	1990
ITEM #:	5214-0	
STATUS:	Current	

MATERIAL: Metal
DESCRIPTION: Red & green mail box & red fire hydrant.
PARTICULARS: Set of 2. Christmas In The City accessory. Green & Red HV Mail Box. Replaced #5517-4.

OSRP: $5.00
GBTru: $5.00 NC

Busy Sidewalks

☐ **NAME:**	Busy Sidewalks	1990
ITEM #:	5535-2	
STATUS:	Retired 1992	

MATERIAL: Porcelain
DESCRIPTION: Delivery boy, doorman, two elderly ladies, mother with toddler and baby in carriage.
PARTICULARS: Set of 4. Christmas In The City accessory.

OSRP: $28.00
GBTru: $45.00 NC

Heritage Village Accessories

'Tis The Season

❒ **NAME:** 'Tis The Season   1990
     ITEM #: 5539-5
     STATUS: Retired 1994

MATERIAL: Porcelain
DESCRIPTION: Santa with bell and iron kettle for Season donations. Little girl gives to the needy.
PARTICULARS: Christmas In The City accessory.

OSRP: $12.50
GBTru: $20.00   NC

Rest Ye Merry Gentleman

❒ **NAME:** Rest Ye Merry Gentleman   1990
     ITEM #: 5540-9
     STATUS: Current

MATERIAL: Porcelain and Metal
DESCRIPTION: Man sits on bench reading newspaper with purchases all around him.
PARTICULARS: Christmas In The City accessory. Size: 1 ³/₄".

OSRP: $12.50
GBTru: $12.95   ↑4%

Town Crier & Chimney Sweep

❒ **NAME:** Town Crier & Chimney Sweep   1990
     ITEM #: 5569-7
     STATUS: Current

MATERIAL: Porcelain
DESCRIPTION: Crier rings bell and reads out announcements. A Sweep in top hat and tails carries chimney brush.
PARTICULARS: Set of 2. Dickens' Village accessory. Sizes: 2 ¹/₂" & 2 ¹/₂".

OSRP: $15.00
GBTru: $16.00   NC

Carolers On The Doorstep

❒ **NAME:** Carolers On The Doorstep   1990
     ITEM #: 5570-0
     STATUS: Retired 1993

MATERIAL: Porcelain
DESCRIPTION: Four children sing carols to elderly man and woman, boys carry lanterns, girls have song books.
PARTICULARS: Set of 4. Dickens' Village accessory.

OSRP: $25.00
GBTru: $40.00   NC

Heritage Village Accessories

Holiday Travelers

☐ **NAME:** Holiday Travelers   1990
ITEM #: 5571-9
STATUS: Current

MATERIAL: Porcelain
DESCRIPTION: Train conductor, baggage handler, and man and woman passengers.
PARTICULARS: Set of 3. Dickens' Village accessory. Sizes: 2 ¹/₂", 2 ¹/₂", & 2 ¹/₂".

OSRP: $22.50
GBTru: $25.00   NC

The Flying Scot Train

☐ **NAME:** The Flying Scot Train   1990
ITEM #: 5573-5
STATUS: Current

MATERIAL: Porcelain
DESCRIPTION: Engine and wood supply car and two passenger cars with luggage carriers atop cars.
PARTICULARS: Set of 4. Dickens' Village accessory. Size: 14".

OSRP: $48.00
GBTru: $50.00   NC

Victoria Station Train Platform

☐ **NAME:** Victoria Station Train Platform   1990
ITEM #: 5575-1
STATUS: Current

MATERIAL: Porcelain and Metal
DESCRIPTION: Six-sided ticket booth with windows all around, long metal roof to protect passengers.
PARTICULARS: Dickens' Village accessory.
Size: 6 ¹/₂" x 3 ³/₄".

OSRP: $20.00
GBTru: $22.00   NC

Trimming The North Pole

☐ **NAME:** Trimming The North Pole   1990
ITEM #: 5608-1
STATUS: Retired 1993

MATERIAL: Porcelain
DESCRIPTION: One elf holds another to hang greenery on North Pole sign while blue bird watches.
PARTICULARS: North Pole accessory.

OSRP: $10.00
GBTru: $25.00 ↑14%

Santa & Mrs. Claus

❒ **NAME:** Santa & Mrs. Claus   1990
ITEM #: 5609-0
STATUS: Current

MATERIAL: Porcelain
DESCRIPTION: Mrs. Claus and elf wave good-bye to Santa as he does a final check of delivery book before leaving North Pole.
PARTICULARS: Set of 2. North Pole accessory. Size: 2 1/4".
VARIATIONS: Variation exists in title on book: "Good Boys" instead of "Good Kids."

OSRP: $15.00
GBTru: $15.00   NC

Santa's Little Helpers

❒ **NAME:** Santa's Little Helpers   1990
ITEM #: 5610-3
STATUS: Retired 1993

MATERIAL: Porcelain
DESCRIPTION: Elf stands on presents to hang wreath. Two elves move toy sack. One elf brings two reindeer to sleigh.
PARTICULARS: Set of 3. North Pole accessory.

OSRP: $28.00
GBTru: $52.00   ⬆8%

Sleigh & Eight Tiny Reindeer

❒ **NAME:** Sleigh & Eight Tiny Reindeer   1990
ITEM #: 5611-1
STATUS: Current

MATERIAL: Porcelain
DESCRIPTION: Toys fill sleigh harnessed to Santa's eight reindeer.
PARTICULARS: Set of 5. North Pole accessory. Size: 13 1/2".

OSRP: $40.00
GBTru: $42.00   NC

The Toy Peddler

❒ **NAME:** The Toy Peddler   1990
ITEM #: 5616-2
STATUS: Current

MATERIAL: Porcelain
DESCRIPTION: Toy peddler carries tray with toys. Mother and son look at toy horse. Little girl holds top.
PARTICULARS: Set of 3. Alpine Village accessory. Sizes: 2 1/2", 2 1/2" & 2 1/4".

OSRP: $22.00
GBTru: $22.00   NC

Heritage Village Accessories   177

Amish Family

☐ **NAME:** Amish Family   1990
    ITEM #: 5948-0
    STATUS: Retired 1992

MATERIAL: Porcelain
DESCRIPTION: Mother carries apples in apron, father stacks boxes, children sort apples.
PARTICULARS: Set of 3. New England accessory. Early release to Showcase Dealers and the National Association Of Limited Edition Dealers (NALED).
VARIATION: Amish man with **mustache**–$55.00* (↑10%).

OSRP: $20.00
GBTru: $35.00*   NC

Amish Buggy

☐ **NAME:** Amish Buggy   1990
    ITEM #: 5949-8
    STATUS: Retired 1992

MATERIAL: Porcelain
DESCRIPTION: Amish man feeds brown horse harnessed to family carriage, curtained for privacy.
PARTICULARS: New England Village accessory.

OSRP: $22.00
GBTru: $50.00   NC

Sleepy Hollow Characters

☐ **NAME:** Sleepy Hollow Characters   1990
    ITEM #: 5956-0
    STATUS: Retired 1992

MATERIAL: Porcelain
DESCRIPTION: Man carving pumpkin. Squire and Mrs. VanTassel, Ichabod Crane with children.
PARTICULARS: Set of 3. New England Village accessory.

OSRP: $27.50
GBTru: $42.00   ↓7%

Skating Party

☐ **NAME:** Skating Party   1991
    ITEM #: 5523-9
    STATUS: Current

MATERIAL: Porcelain
DESCRIPTION: Skating couple, boy, and girl.
PARTICULARS: Set of 3. New England Village accessory. Size: 2 ¼".

OSRP: $27.50
GBTru: $27.50   NC

All Around The Town

☐ **NAME:** All Around The Town   1991
    ITEM #: 5545-0
    STATUS: Retired 1993

MATERIAL: Porcelain
DESCRIPTION: Man with "sandwich boards" as a walking ad for "White Christmas." Man with packages stops to get a shoeshine from young boy.
PARTICULARS: Set of 2. Christmas In The City accessory.

OSRP: $18.00
GBTru: $28.00   ↓7%

The Fire Brigade

☐ **NAME:** The Fire Brigade   1991
    ITEM #: 5546-8
    STATUS: Retired 1995

MATERIAL: Porcelain
DESCRIPTION: Two firemen carry ladder and ax. Fireman with pail takes moment to pet mascot Dalmatian.
PARTICULARS: Set of 2. Christmas In The City accessory.

OSRP: $20.00
GBTru: $24.00   ↑20%

"City Fire Dept." Fire Truck

☐ **NAME:** "City Fire Dept." Fire Truck   1991
    ITEM #: 5547-6
    STATUS: Retired 1995

MATERIAL: Porcelain
DESCRIPTION: Ladder attached to side, hose and nozzle assembly on top and rear of red fire truck.
PARTICULARS: Christmas In The City accessory.

OSRP: $18.00
GBTru: $22.00   ↑22%

Caroling Thru The City

☐ **NAME:** Caroling Thru The City   1991
    ITEM #: 5548-4
    STATUS: Current

MATERIAL: Porcelain
DESCRIPTION: Singing man pulls sled with two boys, two women with young girl, man (alone), all with song books.
PARTICULARS: Set of 3. Christmas In The City accessory.
Size: 2 ¼".

OSRP: $27.50
GBTru: $27.50   NC

Heritage Village Accessories

Oliver Twist Characters

❐ **NAME:** Oliver Twist Characters   1991
ITEM #: 5554-9
STATUS: Retired 1993

MATERIAL: Porcelain
DESCRIPTION: Mr. Brownlow in long coat, stovepipe hat, walks with cane. Oliver in rags next to food cart, as another boy reaches to steal food, third boy holds sack.
PARTICULARS: Set of 3. Dickens' Village accessory.

OSRP: $35.00
GBTru: $45.00   NC

Bringing Home The Yule Log

❐ **NAME:** Bringing Home The Yule Log   1991
ITEM #: 5558-1
STATUS: Current

MATERIAL: Porcelain
DESCRIPTION: Two boys pull on ropes to haul log. One girl holds lantern to light way and another walks alongside.
PARTICULARS: Set of 3. Dickens' Village accessory.
Size: 2" high.

OSRP: $27.50
GBTru: $28.00   NC

Poultry Market

❐ **NAME:** Poultry Market   1991
ITEM #: 5559-0
STATUS: Retired 1995

MATERIAL: Porcelain
DESCRIPTION: Aproned poulterer holds game bird. Covered stand with display of turkeys and geese. Woman holds purchase as child watches.
PARTICULARS: Set of 3. Dickens' Village accessory.
VARIATION: Original "proof" version with patches on drape.

OSRP: $30.00
GBTru: $37.00 ⬆16%

Come Into The Inn

❐ **NAME:** Come Into The Inn   1991
ITEM #: 5560-3
STATUS: Retired 1994

MATERIAL: Porcelain
DESCRIPTION: Innkeeper's wife pauses to read note as she sweeps snow from entry. Young boy with lantern lights way for coach driver. Gentleman stands by luggage.
PARTICULARS: Set of 3. Dickens' Village accessory.

OSRP: $22.00
GBTru: $27.00 ⬆4%

☐ **NAME:**	Holiday Coach	1991
ITEM #:	5561-1
STATUS:	Current

MATERIAL: Porcelain
DESCRIPTION: Four horses pull coach full of travelers who ride inside and on topside seats. Coachman blows horn on arrival as driver guides horses.
PARTICULARS: Dickens' Village accessory.
Size: 11" x 3" x 4 ¾".
VARIATION: Gold chains vs. silver chains.

OSRP: $68.00
GBTru: $70.00   NC

Toymaker Elves

☐ **NAME:**	Toymaker Elves	1991
ITEM #:	5602-2
STATUS:	Retired 1995

MATERIAL: Porcelain
DESCRIPTION: Two elves carry trunk of toys. One elf balances stack of toys. One elf has apron filled with toys.
PARTICULARS: Set of 3. North Pole accessory.

OSRP: $27.50
GBTru: $42.00 ↑53%

Baker Elves

☐ **NAME:**	Baker Elves	1991
ITEM #:	5603-0
STATUS:	Retired 1995

MATERIAL: Porcelain
DESCRIPTION: One elf holds piece of belled harness from sleigh. One elf holds tray of baked goods. One elf takes a cookie from Sweets Cart.
PARTICULARS: Set of 3. North Pole accessory.

OSRP: $27.50
GBTru: $43.00 ↑56%

Market Day

☐ **NAME:**	Market Day	1991
ITEM #:	5641-3
STATUS:	Retired 1993

MATERIAL: Porcelain
DESCRIPTION: Mother carries baby and basket while daughter holds bread basket. Aproned merchant tips hat as he pushes sledge with bagged food. Man and boy rest on goat-pulled cart while standing boy holds bag.
PARTICULARS: Set of 3. New England Village accessory.

OSRP: $35.00
GBTru: $45.00   NC

NAME: Gate House   1992
ITEM #: 5530-1
STATUS: Available at 1992 Village Gatherings and select Showcase Dealer Open Houses.

MATERIAL: Porcelain
DESCRIPTION: Originated as tower fortified entrance of a castle's outside wall. Brick base with arched entry allowed passage of carriages/wagons and foot soldiers. Windows narrow and shuttered to protect against weather and attack.
VARIATIONS: In **color** of stone brick between shades of gray or blue.

OSRP: $22.50
GBTru: $60.00 ↑9%

Don't Drop The Presents!

NAME: Don't Drop The Presents!   1992
ITEM #: 5532-8
STATUS: Retired 1995

MATERIAL: Porcelain
DESCRIPTION: Mother cautions father to take care as dog jumps up to sniff presents in father's arms. Daughter peeks out from mother's skirt as full shopping bag rests on snow. Son slips and tumbles in snow.
PARTICULARS: Set of 2. Christmas In The City accessory.

OSRP: $25.00
GBTru: $36.00 ↑44%

Welcome Home

NAME: Welcome Home   1992
ITEM #: 5533-6
STATUS: Retired 1995

MATERIAL: Porcelain
DESCRIPTION: Boy reaches to hug Grandmother visiting for holiday as girl and Grandfather reach out to hug each other. Family pet joins the greeting.
PARTICULARS: Set of 3. Christmas In The City accessory.

OSRP: $27.50
GBTru: $34.00 ↑24%

Notes: _____
_____
_____
_____
_____
_____

☐ **NAME:** Churchyard Fence & Gate   1992
ITEM #: 5563-8
STATUS: Discontinued in 1992

MATERIAL: Porcelain
DESCRIPTION: Wrought iron rails atop stone base, acted as barrier to protect church land and graveyard.
PARTICULARS: Set of 3. Early release to Gift Creations Concepts (GCC).
VARIATIONS: Two different sets of Churchyard Gate & Fences introduced in 1992:

OSRP: $15.00
GBTru: $45.00 ↑13%

Version #1–"Churchyard Fence & Gate" (1992 - 1992), Set/3, Item #5563-8 was a midyear introduction and a GCC Exclusive. It included one gate, one wall, and one corner. This version was pictured in the *Quarterly* in gray, but was shipped in brown.

Version #2–"Churchyard Gate & Fence" (1992 - Current), Set/3, is Item #5806-8. It includes one gate and two corners. There are also "Churchyard Fence Extensions" (1992 - Current), Set/4, Item #5807-6, which are 4 straight wall pieces.

Letters For Santa

☐ **NAME:** Letters For Santa   1992
ITEM #: 5604-9
STATUS: Retired 1994

MATERIAL: Porcelain
DESCRIPTION: One elf carries bundles of letters, as another elf tries to lift sack of letters. Two additional elves arrive with reindeer cart filled with mail bags of letters for Santa.
PARTICULARS: Set of 3. North Pole accessory.

OSRP: $30.00
GBTru: $50.00   NC

Testing The Toys

☐ **NAME:** Testing The Toys   1992
ITEM #: 5605-7
STATUS: Current

MATERIAL: Porcelain
DESCRIPTION: One elf rides downhill on a sled as two others try out a toboggan.
PARTICULARS: Set of 2. North Pole accessory.
Sizes: 1 ¹/₂" & 2".

OSRP: $16.50
GBTru: $16.50   NC

NAME: Buying Baker's Bread   1992
ITEM #: 5619-7
STATUS: Retired 1995

MATERIAL: Porcelain
DESCRIPTION: Man and woman lift basket together to carry loaves, she also carries basket on arm. Man carries basket tray of bread while rest of loaves are carried in his basket backpack.
PARTICULARS: Set of 2. Alpine Village accessory.

OSRP: $20.00
GBTru: $32.00 ↑60%

Harvest Seed Cart

NAME: Harvest Seed Cart   1992
ITEM #: 5645-6
STATUS: Retired 1995

MATERIAL: Porcelain
DESCRIPTION: Boy lifts sack of corn to place on barrow. Man lifts barrow filled with corn sacks as one chicken pecks at sack and one chicken walks next to him. Girl holds white rooster and has basket resting on ground by her feet.
PARTICULARS: Set of 3. Dickens' and New England Village accessory.

OSRP: $27.50
GBTru: $42.00 ↑52%

Town Tinker

NAME: Town Tinker   1992
ITEM #: 5646-4
STATUS: Retired 1995

MATERIAL: Porcelain
DESCRIPTION: Traveling peddler with covered cart he moves manually. He sold pots, pans, trinkets, and all manner of odds and ends. He made repairs as well, going from house to house, village to village.
PARTICULARS: Set of 2. Dickens' Village and New England Village accessory.

OSRP: $24.00
GBTru: $25.00 ↑4%

The Old Puppeteer

NAME: The Old Puppeteer   1992
ITEM #: 5802-5
STATUS: Retired 1995

MATERIAL: Porcelain
DESCRIPTION: Children watch puppet show. Stage on wheels with man moving the stringed marionettes to tell stories to audiences of all ages.
PARTICULARS: Set of 3. Dickens' Village accessory.

OSRP: $32.00
GBTru: $36.00 ↑13%

☐ **NAME:** The Bird Seller   1992
ITEM #: 5803-3
STATUS: Retired 1995

MATERIAL: Porcelain
DESCRIPTION: Woman holds up two bird cages. Delighted child and mother with woman who has made a purchase.
PARTICULARS: Set of 3. Dickens' Village accessory.

OSRP: $25.00
GBTru: $28.00 ↑12%

Village Street Peddlers

☐ **NAME:** Village Street Peddlers   1992
ITEM #: 5804-1
STATUS: Retired 1994

MATERIAL: Porcelain
DESCRIPTION: One man carries pole of fresh dressed rabbits. Second peddler wears wooden tray of spices to be sold in small pinches and ounces.
PARTICULARS: Set of 2. Dickens' Village accessory.

OSRP: $16.00
GBTru: $25.00 ↑14%

English Post Box

☐ **NAME:** English Post Box   1992
ITEM #: 5805-0
STATUS: Current

MATERIAL: Metal
DESCRIPTION: Red, six-sided, English-style post box.
PARTICULARS: Dickens' Village accessory. Size: 2 1/4".

OSRP: $4.50
GBTru: $4.50   NC

Churchyard Gate And Fence

☐ **NAME:** Churchyard Gate And Fence   1992
ITEM #: 5806-8
STATUS: Current

MATERIAL: Porcelain
DESCRIPTION: Wrought iron rails atop stone base, acted as barrier to protect church land and graveyard.
PARTICULARS: Set of 3. See 1992 *Churchyard Fence Gate*, Item #5563-8. Sizes: 3 3/4" x 2 1/4", 4 1/4" & 3".

OSRP: $15.00
GBTru: $15.00   NC

	NAME:	Churchyard Fence Extensions	1992
	ITEM #:	5807-6	
	STATUS:	Current	

MATERIAL: Porcelain
DESCRIPTION: Stone base with wrought iron posts and connectors to extend fence around church and graveyard.
PARTICULARS: Set of 4. Size: 4".

OSRP: $16.00
GBTru: $16.00 NC

Lionhead Bridge

	NAME:	Lionhead Bridge	1992
	ITEM #:	5864-5	
	STATUS:	Current	

MATERIAL: Porcelain
DESCRIPTION: Massive bridge with two stone lions, each with one raised paw resting on a sphere.
PARTICULARS: Dickens' Village accessory. Size: 7" x 3 ³/₄" x 2 ³/₄".

OSRP: $22.00
GBTru: $22.00 NC

Village Express Van

	NAME:	Village Express Van	1992
	ITEM #:	5865-3	
	STATUS:	Current	

MATERIAL: Porcelain
DESCRIPTION: Green delivery van advertises On Time Service. Rack on van roof holds wrapped packages.
PARTICULARS: Christmas In The City accessory. Color is green. License plate is abbreviated address of D56 headquarters: 6436 City West Parkway. Size: 4 ¹/₂" x 3".

OSRP: $25.00
GBTru: $25.00 NC

Village Express Van

	NAME:	Village Express Van	1992
	ITEM #:	9951-1	
	STATUS:	Promotional	

MATERIAL: Porcelain
DESCRIPTION: Advertises On Time Service. Rack on van roof holds wrapped packages.
PARTICULARS: Christmas In The City accessory. Special black van. Size is 4 ¹/₂"x 3". Bachman's Gathering & given to Sales Representatives as a gift at National Sales Conference, 12/92.

OSRP: $25.00
GBTru: $185.00 ↑48%

Playing In The Snow

☐ **NAME:** Playing In The Snow   1993
    ITEM #: 5556-5
    STATUS: Current

MATERIAL: Porcelain
DESCRIPTION: Children build and dress a snowman.
PARTICULARS: Set of 3. Christmas In The City accessory.
Sizes: 2 ¹/₄", 2 ¹/₄" & 2".

OSRP: $25.00
GBTru: $25.00   NC

Street Musicians

☐ **NAME:** Street Musicians   1993
    ITEM #: 5564-6
    STATUS: Current

MATERIAL: Porcelain
DESCRIPTION: Girl gives coin to the street musicians.
PARTICULARS: Set of 3. Christmas In The City accessory.
Sizes: 2 ¹/₂" & 1 ¹/₂".

OSRP: $25.00
GBTru: $25.00   NC

Town Tree

☐ **NAME:** Town Tree   1993
    ITEM #: 5565-4
    STATUS: Current

MATERIAL: Porcelain
DESCRIPTION: Decorated town tree and stone sections
to encircle tree.
PARTICULARS: Set of 5. Lighted. Christmas In The City
accessory. Sizes: 11 ³/₄" & 4 ¹/₂".

OSRP: $45.00
GBTru: $45.00   NC

Town Tree Trimmers

☐ **NAME:** Town Tree Trimmers   1993
    ITEM #: 5566-2
    STATUS: Current

MATERIAL: Porcelain
DESCRIPTION: Ladder and three helpers to decorate
town tree.
PARTICULARS: Set of 4. Christmas In The City accessory.
Sizes: 8 ¹/₂", 2 ³/₄" & 2".

OSRP: $32.50
GBTru: $32.50   NC

Heritage Village Accessories

Climb Every Mountain

❐ **NAME:** Climb Every Mountain   1993
    ITEM #: 5613-8
    STATUS: Current

MATERIAL: Porcelain
DESCRIPTION: Three climbers and companion St. Bernard dog roped together for safety.
PARTICULARS: Set of 4. Alpine Village accessory.
Sizes: 1 1/2", 2", 2 1/4" & 3".

OSRP: $27.50
GBTru: $27.50   NC

Woodsmen Elves

❐ **NAME:** Woodsmen Elves   1993
    ITEM #: 5630-8
    STATUS: Retired 1995

MATERIAL: Porcelain
DESCRIPTION: Elves cut tree and wood to warm North Pole buildings.
PARTICULARS: Set of 3. North Pole Village accessory.

OSRP: $30.00
GBTru: $47.00 ↑57%

Sing A Song For Santa

❐ **NAME:** Sing A Song For Santa   1993
    ITEM #: 5631-6
    STATUS: Current

MATERIAL: Porcelain
DESCRIPTION: Caroling North Pole elves.
PARTICULARS: Set of 3. North Pole Village accessory.
Sizes: 2", 2" & 1 1/2".

OSRP: $28.00
GBTru: $28.00   NC

North Pole Gate

❐ **NAME:** North Pole Gate   1993
    ITEM #: 5632-4
    STATUS: Current

MATERIAL: Porcelain
DESCRIPTION: Entry gate to North Pole Village.
PARTICULARS: North Pole Village accessory.
Size: 6" x 5 1/2" x 6".

OSRP: $32.50
GBTru: $32.50   NC

Heritage Village Accessories

NAME: Knife Grinder   1993
ITEM #: 5649-9
STATUS: Current

MATERIAL: Porcelain
DESCRIPTION: Man with pedal-powered grinding wheel keeps sharp edges on knives and tools.
PARTICULARS: Set of 2. New England Village accessory. Sizes: 3" x 2 1/4" & 2 1/2".

OSRP: $22.50
GBTru: $22.50   NC

Blue Star Ice Harvesters

NAME: Blue Star Ice Harvesters   1993
ITEM #: 5650-2
STATUS: Current

MATERIAL: Porcelain
DESCRIPTION: Men cut up pond, lake, and river ice to stack in icehouse for food storage and cooling.
PARTICULARS: Set of 2. New England Village accessory. Sizes: 2 1/2" & 2 3/4".

OSRP: $27.50
GBTru: $27.50   NC

Chelsea Market Fruit Monger & Cart

NAME: Chelsea Market Fruit Monger & Cart   1993
ITEM #: 5813-0
STATUS: Current

MATERIAL: Porcelain
DESCRIPTION: Pushcart vendor of fresh fruit and vegetables.
PARTICULARS: Set of 2. Dickens' Village accessory. Sizes: 2 1/2" & 4".

OSRP: $25.00
GBTru: $25.00   NC

Chelsea Market Fish Monger & Cart

NAME: Chelsea Market Fish Monger & Cart   1993
ITEM #: 5814-9
STATUS: Current

MATERIAL: Porcelain
DESCRIPTION: Pushcart vendor of fresh fish.
PARTICULARS: Set of 2. Dickens' Village accessory. Sizes: 2 1/2" & 3 1/2".

OSRP: $25.00
GBTru: $25.00   NC

❐ **NAME:** Chelsea Market Flower Monger & Cart   1993
  ITEM #: 5815-7
  STATUS: Current

MATERIAL: Porcelain
DESCRIPTION: Pushcart vendor of fresh cut flowers and nosegays.
PARTICULARS: Set of 2. Dickens' Village accessory. Size: 2 ¹/₂" & 3 ¹/₂".

OSRP: $27.50
GBTru: $27.50   NC

Chelsea Lane Shoppers

❐ **NAME:** Chelsea Lane Shoppers   1993
  ITEM #: 5816-5
  STATUS: Current

MATERIAL: Porcelain
DESCRIPTION: Woman and girl, each with flowers. Couple walking with package and basket. Gentleman with walking stick.
PARTICULARS: Set of 4. Dickens' Village accessory. Sizes: 2 ¹/₄", 2 ¹/₄", 2 ¹/₂" & 2 ³/₄".

OSRP: $30.00
GBTru: $30.00   NC

Vision Of A Christmas Past

❐ **NAME:** Vision Of A Christmas Past   1993
  ITEM #: 5817-3
  STATUS: Current

MATERIAL: Porcelain
DESCRIPTION: Innkeeper with coach dogs, traveling merchant, 2 young travelers.
PARTICULARS: Set of 3. Dickens' Village accessory. Sizes: 2 ¹/₂", 2 ¹/₂" & 2".

OSRP: $27.50
GBTru: $27.50   NC

C. Bradford, Wheelwright & Son

❐ **NAME:** C. Bradford, Wheelwright & Son   1993
  ITEM #: 5818-1
  STATUS: Current

MATERIAL: Porcelain
DESCRIPTION: Father and son wagon wheel makers and repairers.
PARTICULARS: Set of 2. Dickens' Village accessory. Sizes: 2" & 2 ¹/₂".

OSRP: $24.00
GBTru: $24.00   NC

NAME: Bringing Fleeces To The Mill   1993
ITEM #: 5819-0
STATUS: Current

MATERIAL: Porcelain
DESCRIPTION: Shepherd takes wagon load of fleeces to market. Child stands with sheep.
PARTICULARS: Set of 2. Dickens' Village accessory. Sizes: 1 3/4" & 5".

OSRP: $35.00
GBTru: $35.00   NC

Dashing Through The Snow

NAME: Dashing Through The Snow   1993
ITEM #: 5820-3
STATUS: Current

MATERIAL: Porcelain
DESCRIPTION: Horse drawn sleigh takes couple for ride across snowy roads.
PARTICULARS: Dickens' Village accessory. Size: 8 1/4".

OSRP: $32.50
GBTru: $32.50   NC

Christmas At The Park

NAME: Christmas At The Park   1993
ITEM #: 5866-1
STATUS: Current

MATERIAL: Porcelain
DESCRIPTION: Seated father, mother and child. Seated boy and girl with dog.
PARTICULARS: Set of 3. Christmas In The City accessory. Sizes: 2 1/4", 2 1/4" & 1 3/4".

OSRP: $27.50
GBTru: $27.50   NC

Village Express Van - Gold

NAME: Village Express Van - Gold   1993
ITEM #: 9977-5
STATUS: Promotional

MATERIAL: Porcelain
DESCRIPTION: Rack on van holds wrapped packages.
PARTICULARS: Gold "Road Show" Edition. Packed in gold box. Presented to potential investors before initial public offering.

OSRP: $25.00
GBTru: $945.00   ↓21%

❏ **NAME:** Village Express Van For Gatherings   1994
   ITEM #: See Particulars
   STATUS: Promotional

MATERIAL: Porcelain
DESCRIPTION: Black van for store delivery service. Right side is D56 logo and left side features specific D56 dealer name logo.
PARTICULARS:
1994:
14 Vans were produced–13 for dealer D56 sponsored Village Gatherings where Van was sold. Suggested Retail Price was $25.00. The Lemon Tree received the other Van to be sold to Members of the store's Collector's Club:

OSRP: See Particulars
GBTru: See Particulars

STORE	ITEM #	GBTru
Bachman's	#729-3	$75.00
Bronner's Christmas Wonderland	#737-4	$60.00
European Imports	#739-0	$60.00
Fortunoff	#735-8	$125.00
Lemon Tree	#721-8	$50.00
Lock, Stock & Barrel	#731-5	$125.00
North Pole City	#736-6	$60.00
Robert's Christmas Wonderland	#734-0	$60.00
Stats	#741-2	$60.00
The Christmas Dove	#730-7	$60.00
The Incredible Christmas Place	#732-3	$80.00
The Limited Edition	#733-1	$100.00
The Windsor Shoppe	#740-4	$60.00
William Glen	#738-2	$60.00

1995:
1) Van, #7560, was produced for St. Nick's, Littleton, CO. This Van does not say D56 on passenger door. Both doors read "1995." GBTru: $70.00.
2) Van, #7522, was produced for the NALED affiliated Parkwest Catalog Group to Commemorate their 10th Anniversary. The group has 350 dealers. The panel of the Van featured the symbol of a running deer, "Parkwest, 10th Anniversary" was printed below. GBTru: $200.00.
3) Van, #21637, was produced for Canadian dealers, and distributed by Millard Lister Sales Ltd. The 10 Canadian Provinces were listed on the Van top rail. One side panel says "On-Time Delivery Since 1976: The Village Express." Other panel has Red Maple Leaf, Canadian Event 1995. Doors have "1995." SRP was $40.00, GBTru: $55.00.

Mickey & Minnie

❏ **NAME:** Mickey & Minnie   1994
   ITEM #: 5353-8
   STATUS: Retired May 1996

MATERIAL: Porcelain
DESCRIPTION: Mickey and Minnie characters welcome guests to the Disney Theme Parks.
PARTICULARS: Set of 2. Disney Parks Village accessory. Size: 2 ½".

OSRP: $22.50
GBTru: $22.50   NC

Disney Parks Family

❐ **NAME:** Disney Parks Family   1994
ITEM #: 5354-6
STATUS: Retired May 1996

MATERIAL: Porcelain
DESCRIPTION: Family of 7, enjoys a day at a Disney Park.
Mom photographs kids in Mouse ears, as 2 others eat ice
cream cones, and one tot is seated on Dad's shoulders for
best view.
PARTICULARS: Set of 3. Sizes: 3", 2 ¹/₂" & 2 ¹/₄".

OSRP: $32.50
GBTru: $32.50   NC

Olde World Antiques Gate

❐ **NAME:** Olde World Antiques Gate   1994
ITEM #: 5355-4
STATUS: Retired May 1996

MATERIAL: Porcelain
DESCRIPTION: Entry gate with wooden door. Brick
frames door and is base for wrought iron fencing.
PARTICULARS: Disney Parks Village accessory.
Size: 5 ³/₄" x 3 ¹/₄".

OSRP: $15.00
GBTru: $15.00   NC

Polka Fest

❐ **NAME:** Polka Fest   1994
ITEM #: 5607-3
STATUS: Current

MATERIAL: Porcelain
DESCRIPTION: Musicians play polka as a couple dances.
Boy sings and yodels to the music.
PARTICULARS: Set of 3. Alpine Village accessory. Size: 2 ¹/₂".

OSRP: $30.00
GBTru: $30.00   NC

Last Minute Delivery

❐ **NAME:** Last Minute Delivery   1994
ITEM #: 5636-7
STATUS: Current

MATERIAL: Porcelain
DESCRIPTION: Elves hand-power a rail car pulling doll car
and teddy car as another elf hangs onto rear bumper.
PARTICULARS: Set of 3. North Pole Village accessory.
Shipping delayed until 1996 due to production problems.
Size: 6" x 2 ¹/₂".

OSRP: $35.00
GBTru: $35.00   NC

Heritage Village Accessories

Snow Cone Elves

❒ **NAME:** Snow Cone Elves   1994
ITEM #: 5637-5
STATUS: Current

MATERIAL: Porcelain
DESCRIPTION: Elves taste test new batch of snow cones. Cart holds more flavors. Icicles form on snow cone sign.
PARTICULARS: Set of 4. North Pole Village accessory. Sizes: 2 $^1/_4$", 2", 2 $^1/_2$" & 1 $^1/_2$".

OSRP: $30.00
GBTru: $30.00   NC

Over The River And Through The Woods

❒ **NAME:** Over The River And Through The Woods   1994
ITEM #: 5654-5
STATUS: Current

MATERIAL: Porcelain
DESCRIPTION: After cutting tree for home, father and kids use horse-drawn sleigh to bring it in. Their dog runs along side.
PARTICULARS: New England Village accessory. Size: 8" x 3 $^1/_2$".

OSRP: $35.00
GBTru: $35.00   NC

The Old Man And The Sea

❒ **NAME:** The Old Man And The Sea   1994
ITEM #: 5655-3
STATUS: Current

MATERIAL: Porcelain
DESCRIPTION: Two children listen closely as the man tells stories of the sea. Boy holds telescope.
PARTICULARS: Set of 3. New England Village accessory. Sizes: 2 $^1/_4$", 2 $^1/_4$" & 2".

OSRP: $25.00
GBTru: $25.00   NC

Two Rivers Bridge

❒ **NAME:** Two Rivers Bridge   1994
ITEM #: 5656-1
STATUS: Current

MATERIAL: Porcelain and Resin
DESCRIPTION: Wooden bridge on 3 sets of pilings spans 2 rivers. Horses, carriages and carts use center. Walkers use side passages.
PARTICULARS: New England Village accessory. Size: 8 $^1/_2$" x 4 $^1/_2$" x 4".

OSRP: $35.00
GBTru: $35.00   NC

NAME: Winter Sleighride   1994
ITEM #: 5825-4
STATUS: Current

MATERIAL: Porcelain
DESCRIPTION: Ice-skating boys give a sleigh ride to a friend.
PARTICULARS: Dickens' Village accessory. Size: 7 1/4" long.

OSRP: $18.00
GBTru: $18.00   NC

Chelsea Market Mistletoe Monger & Cart

NAME: Chelsea Market Mistletoe Monger & Cart   1994
ITEM #: 5826-2
STATUS: Current

MATERIAL: Porcelain
DESCRIPTION: Vendor sells greens from basket as wife sells from cart.
PARTICULARS: Set of 2. Dickens' Village accessory. Size: 3".

OSRP: $25.00
GBTru: $25.00   NC

Chelsea Market Curiosities Monger & Cart

NAME: Chelsea Market Curiosities Monger & Cart   1994
ITEM #: 5827-0
STATUS: Current

MATERIAL: Porcelain
DESCRIPTION: Vendor stands next to cart playing concertina. He sells everything from toys to clocks to quilts.
PARTICULARS: Set of 2. Dickens' Village accessory. Sizes: 2 1/2" & 4".

OSRP: $27.50
GBTru: $27.50   NC

Portabello Road Peddlers

NAME: Portobello Road Peddlers   1994
ITEM #: 5828-9
STATUS: Current

MATERIAL: Porcelain
DESCRIPTION: Peddlers sell toys and carol song sheets to passing villagers.
PARTICULARS: Set of 3. Dickens' Village accessory. Size: 3".

OSRP: $27.50
GBTru: $27.50   NC

Heritage Village Accessories

☐ **NAME:** Thatchers   1994
    ITEM #: 5829-7
    STATUS: Current

MATERIAL: Porcelain
DESCRIPTION: Workers gather up and place thatch bundles on cart.
PARTICULARS: Set of 3. Dickens' Village accessory.
Sizes: 5" x 3", 3", 4".

OSRP: $35.00
GBTru: $35.00   NC

A Peaceful Glow On Christmas Eve

☐ **NAME:** A Peaceful Glow On Christmas Eve   1994
    ITEM #: 5830-0
    STATUS: Current

MATERIAL: Porcelain
DESCRIPTION: Clergyman watches children sell candles for church service.
PARTICULARS: Set of 3. Dickens' Village accessory.
Size: 5" x 2 ³/₄".

OSRP: $30.00
GBTru: $30.00   NC

Christmas Carol Holiday Trimming Set

☐ **NAME:** Christmas Carol Holiday
                 Trimming Set   1994
    ITEM #: 5831-9
    STATUS: Current

MATERIAL: Porcelain
DESCRIPTION: 21 piece holiday trimming set with gate, fence, lamppost, trees, garlands, wreaths, and 3 figurine groupings.
PARTICULARS: Set of 21. Dickens' Village accessory.

OSRP: $65.00
GBTru: $65.00   NC

Chamber Orchestra

☐ **NAME:** Chamber Orchestra   1994
    ITEM #: 5884-0
    STATUS: Current

MATERIAL: Porcelain
DESCRIPTION: Conductor and four musicians play holiday music outdoors.
PARTICULARS: Set of 4. Christmas In The City accessory.
Size: 3".

OSRP: $37.50
GBTru: $37.50   NC

Holiday Field Trip

❐ **NAME:** Holiday Field Trip   1994
   ITEM #: 5885-8
   STATUS: Current

MATERIAL: Porcelain
DESCRIPTION: Five students walk with their teacher as they visit the City sights.
PARTICULARS: Set of 3. Christmas In The City accessory. Sizes: 2 ¼", 1 ½" & 1 ½".

OSRP: $27.50
GBTru: $27.50   NC

Hot Dog Vendor

❐ **NAME:** Hot Dog Vendor   1994
   ITEM #: 5886-6
   STATUS: Current

MATERIAL: Porcelain
DESCRIPTION: Mother buys hot dog for son from a street vendor.
PARTICULARS: Set of 3. Christmas In The City accessory. Size: 3".

OSRP: $27.50
GBTru: $27.50   NC

Postern

❐ **NAME:** Postern   1994
   ITEM #: 9871-0
   STATUS: 1994 Annual

MATERIAL: Porcelain
DESCRIPTION: Arched, timbered entryway connected to gatehouse. Flag flies from atop the arch; village sign hangs below it. Posterns were entrances to important places or village gathering areas.
PARTICULARS: Dickens' Village Ten Year Anniversary Piece. Cornerstone with dates. Special commemorative imprint on bottom.

OSRP: $17.50
GBTru: $25.00   NC

Dedlock Arms Ornament

❐ **NAME:** Dedlock Arms Ornament   1994
   ITEM #: 9872-8
   STATUS: 1994 Annual

MATERIAL: Porcelain
DESCRIPTION: Miniature version of 1994 Signature Collection lit piece. Special Keepsake box.

OSRP: $12.50
GBTru: $18.00 ⬆13%

Heritage Village Accessories

Squash Cart

❑ **NAME:** Squash Cart   1995
ITEM #: 0753-6
STATUS: Bachman's Village Gathering
Event Piece, 1995

Photo Not Available.

MATERIAL: Porcelain
DESCRIPTION: Green squash collected by Bachman's workers are taken to market in horse drawn burgundy wagon.
PARTICULARS: New England Village accessory. Commemorates 110th Anniversary of Bachman's–Special Bottom Stamp. Heritage Dealers piece is the Harvest Pumpkin Wagon, #56591, $45.00, released in 1995.

OSRP: $50.00
GBTru: $95.00 ↑90%

Balloon Seller

❑ **NAME:** Balloon Seller   1995
ITEM #: 53539
STATUS: Retired May, 1996

DESCRIPTION: Girl buys her brother a helium balloon from park vendor.
PARTICULARS: Set of 2. Disney Parks Village accessory. Sizes: 3 $1/2$" & 2 $1/4$".

OSRP: $25.00
GBTru: $25.00

"Silent Night" Music Box

❑ **NAME:** "Silent Night" Music Box   1995
ITEM #: 56180
STATUS: Current

MATERIAL: Porcelain
DESCRIPTION: Styled like the Alpine Church with onion dome, commemorates Christmas song "Silent Night." Compliments St. Nickolaus Kirche in architecture and color.
PARTICULARS: Music Box debuted at Bronner's Christmas Wonderland, Frankenmuth, MI, a Gold Key Dealer. Accessory is based on Silent Night Memorial Chapel in Oberndorf, Austria and Silent Night Memorial Chapel at Bronner's. Accessory available to all Heritage Village Dealers as of 6/1/96. Size: 5" x 7 $1/4$".

OSRP: $32.50
GBTru: $32.50

"Alpen Horn Player" Alpine Village Sign

❑ **NAME:** "Alpen Horn Player"
Alpine Village Sign   1995
ITEM #: 56182
STATUS: Current

MATERIAL: Porcelain
DESCRIPTION: Alpen horn player in tyrolean outfit plays long mountain horn.
PARTICULARS: Size: 4" x 3 $1/4$" x 4 $3/4$".

OSRP: $20.00
GBTru: $20.00

Charting Santa's Course

❐ **NAME:** Charting Santa's Course 1995
ITEM #: 56364
STATUS: Current

MATERIAL: Porcelain
DESCRIPTION: Elves plan Santa's sleighride. One checks skies with telescope as other checks constellation maps with globe of earth.
PARTICULARS: Set of 2. North Pole Village accessory. Sizes: 2" & 2".

OSRP: $25.00
GBTru: $25.00

I'll Need More Toys

❐ **NAME:** I'll Need More Toys 1995
ITEM #: 56365
STATUS: Current

MATERIAL: Porcelain and Acrylic
DESCRIPTION: Santa tells elf that more toys are needed from the workshop.
PARTICULARS: Set of 2. North Pole Village accessory. Sizes: 3 ³/₄" & 1 ³/₄".

OSRP: $25.00
GBTru: $25.00

"A Busy Elf" North Pole Sign

❐ **NAME:** "A Busy Elf" North Pole Sign 1995
ITEM #: 56366
STATUS: Current

MATERIAL: Porcelain and Acrylic
DESCRIPTION: Red bird watches Carver elf create village sign.
PARTICULARS: Size: 5".

OSRP: $20.00
GBTru: $20.00

Farm Animals

❐ **NAME:** Farm Animals 1995
ITEM #: 56588
STATUS: Current

MATERIAL: Porcelain
DESCRIPTION: Cows, horses, sheep, pig, goat, hen, rooster and hay bales.
PARTICULARS: Set of 8 with 8 hay bales. New England Village accessory. Sizes: 2", 1 ¹/₂" & 1".

OSRP: $32.50
GBTru: $32.50

Heritage Village Accessories

Lobster Trappers

❐ **NAME:** Lobster Trappers   1995
    ITEM #: 56589
    STATUS: Current

MATERIAL: Porcelain
DESCRIPTION: Boat at dock with traps filled with lobsters. Boy checks traps and lobsterman holds up three pounder.
PARTICULARS: Set of 4. New England Village accessory. Sizes: 5 $\frac{1}{4}$", 3 $\frac{1}{2}$", 2 $\frac{1}{2}$" & 1 $\frac{1}{2}$".

OSRP: $35.00
GBTru: $35.00

Lumberjacks

❐ **NAME:** Lumberjacks   1995
    ITEM #: 56590
    STATUS: Current

MATERIAL: Porcelain and Wood
DESCRIPTION: One man chops tree with ax as second worker saws trunk into logs.
PARTICULARS: Set of 2. New England Village accessory. Sizes: 5 $\frac{3}{4}$" & 2 $\frac{1}{2}$".

OSRP: $30.00
GBTru: $30.00

Harvest Pumpkin Wagon

❐ **NAME:** Harvest Pumpkin Wagon   1995
    ITEM #: 56591
    STATUS: Current

MATERIAL: Porcelain
DESCRIPTION: Driver and helper with horse drawn wagon– loaded with pumpkins gathered by farm workers.
PARTICULARS: New England Village accessory. Size: 6" x 3 $\frac{1}{4}$" x 4 $\frac{1}{2}$".
VARIATIONS: 1995 Squash Cart commemorates 110th Anniversary of Bachman's, Exclusive for their Village Gathering– Item # 0753-6, $50.00. The Bachman piece has a special Bottom Stamp. Squash are green, otherwise the pieces look the same.

OSRP: $45.00
GBTru: $45.00

"Fresh Paint" New England Village Sign

❐ **NAME:** "Fresh Paint" New England Village Sign   1995
    ITEM #: 56592
    STATUS: Current

MATERIAL: Porcelain
DESCRIPTION: Sign maker completes lettering of village sign.
PARTICULARS: New England Village accessory. Size: 4 $\frac{1}{4}$" x 2 $\frac{3}{4}$" x 4".

OSRP: $20.00
GBTru: $20.00

❒ **NAME:** The 12 Days Of Dickens' Village,
A Partridge In A Pear Tree–#I   1995
ITEM #: 5835-1
STATUS: Current

MATERIAL: Porcelain
DESCRIPTION: Three children dance around tree
as a partridge sits on top.
PARTICULARS: Dickens' Village accessory. Size: 4 ¼".

OSRP: $35.00
GBTru: $35.00   NC

The 12 Days Of Dickens' Village, Two Turtle Doves

❒ **NAME:** The 12 Days Of Dickens' Village,
Two Turtle Doves–#II   1995
ITEM #: 5836-0
STATUS: Current

MATERIAL: Porcelain
DESCRIPTION: Woman carries two turtle doves and
boy carries cage. Another woman and daughter watch.
PARTICULARS: Set of 4. Dickens' Village accessory.
Sizes: 2 ½", 2 ¼" & 2".

OSRP: $32.50
GBTru: $32.50   NC

The 12 Days Of Dickens' Village, Three French Hens–#III

❒ **NAME:** The 12 Days Of Dickens' Village,
Three French Hens –#III   1995
ITEM #: 58378
STATUS: Current

MATERIAL: Porcelain
DESCRIPTION: Farmyard with water pump, farm worker
collecting eggs, farm worker scattering grain feed for hen
and rooster.
PARTICULARS: Set of 3. Dickens' Village accessory.
Sizes: 2", 2 ½" & 3".

OSRP: $32.50
GBTru: $32.50

The 12 Days Of Dickens' Village, Four Calling Birds–#IV

❒ **NAME:** The 12 Days Of Dickens' Village,
Four Calling Birds–#IV   1995
ITEM #: 58379
STATUS: Current

MATERIAL: Porcelain
DESCRIPTION: Street musicians play violin and bass
as birds atop clock respond with song.
PARTICULARS: Set of 2. Dickens' Village accessory.

OSRP: $32.50
GBTru: $32.50

Heritage Village Accessories

The 12 Days Of Dickens' Village, Five Golden Rings–#V

❒ **NAME:** The 12 Days Of Dickens' Village,
Five Golden Rings–#V   1995
ITEM #: 58381
STATUS: Current

MATERIAL: Porcelain
DESCRIPTION: Townsfolk watch as juggler balances
five rings.
PARTICULARS: Set of 2. Dickens' Village accessory.
Sizes: 3 1/4" & 2".

OSRP: $27.50
GBTru: $27.50

The 12 Days Of Dickens' Village, Six Geese A-Laying–#VI

❒ **NAME:** The 12 Days Of Dickens' Village,
Six Geese A-Laying–#VI   1995
ITEM #: 58382
STATUS: Current

MATERIAL: Porcelain
DESCRIPTION: Six geese follow boy and girl.
PARTICULARS: Set of 2. Dickens' Village accessory.
Sizes: 2 1/2" & 1 1/4".

OSRP: $30.00
GBTru: $30.00

Brixton Road Watchman

❒ **NAME:** Brixton Road Watchman   1995
ITEM #: 58390
STATUS: Current

MATERIAL: Porcelain
DESCRIPTION: Early method for protection and enforcement
of village rules and regulation. Watchman provides warning,
gives assistance and monitors activities. Small guard house
used for rest and foul weather.
PARTICULARS: Set of 2. Dickens' Village accessory.
Sizes: 4 1/2" & 2 1/2".

OSRP: $25.00
GBTru: $25.00

"Tally Ho!"

❒ **NAME:** "Tally Ho!"   1995
ITEM #: 58391
STATUS: Current

MATERIAL: Porcelain
DESCRIPTION: Country aristocracy riding to the hounds to
hunt fox for the sport. Riders on hunters leap fences and
hedges as they follow scent hounds. Whipper-in sounds
tally-ho.
PARTICULARS: Set of 5. Dickens' Village accessory.

OSRP: $50.00
GBTru: $50.00

Chelsea Market Hat Monger & Cart

❐ **NAME:** Chelsea Market Hat Monger & Cart   1995
       ITEM #: 58392
       STATUS: Current

MATERIAL: Porcelain
DESCRIPTION: Hat maker seated on trunk holds up hats for sale for every occasion. Apprentice sits on hand cart with cat on lap.
PARTICULARS: Set of 2. Dickens' Village accessory.

OSRP: $27.50
GBTru: $27.50

"Ye Olde Lamplighter"

❐ **NAME:** "Ye Olde Lamplighter"
                Dickens' Village Sign   1995
       ITEM #: 58393
       STATUS: Current

MATERIAL: Porcelain
DESCRIPTION: Lamplighter reaches up to light lamp wick in lantern on village sign.
PARTICULARS: Size: 4 $^{1}/_{4}$".

OSRP: $20.00
GBTru: $20.00

Cobbler & Clock Peddler

❐ **NAME:** Cobbler & Clock Peddler   1995
       ITEM #: 58394
       STATUS: Current

MATERIAL: Porcelain
DESCRIPTION: Clock peddler sells and repairs clocks and timepieces while cobbler makes and repairs shoes.
PARTICULARS: Set of 2. Dickens' Village accessory. Size: 2 $^{1}/_{2}$".

OSRP: $25.00
GBTru: $25.00

"Yes, Virginia..."

❐ **NAME:** "Yes, Virginia..."   1995
       ITEM #: 58890
       STATUS: Current

MATERIAL: Porcelain
DESCRIPTION: Young girl speaks to gentleman with close resemblance to Santa Claus. Famous letter to the editor once written by Virginia is remembered every holiday.
PARTICULARS: Set of 2. Christmas In The City accessory. Sizes: 2 $^{1}/_{2}$" & 1 $^{3}/_{4}$".

OSRP: $12.50
GBTru: $12.50

Heritage Village Accessories

One-Man Band And The Dancing Dog

☐ **NAME:** One-Man Band And
The Dancing Dog   1995
ITEM #: 58891
STATUS: Current

MATERIAL: Porcelain and Metal
DESCRIPTION: Man wears contraption to allow playing of 5 instruments as costumed dog dances to the music.
PARTICULARS: Set of 2. Christmas In The City accessory. Sizes: 3" & 1 ¹/₂".

OSRP: $17.50
GBTru: $17.50

Choir Boys All-In-A-Row

☐ **NAME:** Choir Boys All-In-A-Row   1995
ITEM #: 58892
STATUS: Current

MATERIAL: Porcelain
DESCRIPTION: Choir boys in red, white and gold robes sing Christmas service.
PARTICULARS: Christmas In The City accessory.
Size: 2 ¹/₂".

OSRP: $20.00
GBTru: $20.00

"A Key To The City"

☐ **NAME:** "A Key To The City"
Christmas In The City Sign   1995
ITEM #: 58893
STATUS: Current

MATERIAL: Porcelain and Metal
DESCRIPTION: Mayor stands at city gate to welcome dignitary and give the key to the city.

OSRP: $20.00
GBTru: $20.00

Sir John Falstaff Inn Ornament

☐ **NAME:** Sir John Falstaff Inn Ornament   1995
ITEM #: 9870-1
STATUS: 1995 Annual

MATERIAL: Porcelain
DESCRIPTION: Miniature version of 1995 Signature Collection lit piece. Special Keepsake box.

OSRP: $15.00
GBTru: $18.00 ↑20%

Elves On Ice

☐ **NAME:** Elves On Ice   1996
    ITEM #: 52298
    STATUS: Current

MATERIAL: Resin
DESCRIPTION: Four skating elves can be used on Village Animated Skating Pond. One elf skates as he rings bells. One elf pushes another on skates. One elf speeds on ice with stocking hat blown by wind. One hatless elf glides along ice.
PARTICULARS: Set of 4. North Pole Village accessory. Midyear release.

OSRP: $7.50
GBTru: $7.50

Tending The New Calves

☐ **NAME:** Tending The New Calves   1996
    ITEM #: 58395
    STATUS: Current

DESCRIPTION: Boy leads calf. Girl churns butter from fresh milk. Small building to house young calves.
PARTICULARS: Set of 3. Dickens' Village accessory. Midyear release.

OSRP: $30.00
GBTru: $30.00

Caroling With The Cratchit Family (Revisited)

☐ **NAME:** Caroling With The Cratchit Family
                    (Revisited)   1996
    ITEM #: 58396
    STATUS: Current

PARTICULARS: Set of 3. Dickens' Village accessory. Midyear release.

OSRP: 37.50
GBTru: 37.50

Yeomen Of The Guard

☐ **NAME:** Yeomen Of The Guard   1996
    ITEM #: 58397
    STATUS: Current

DESCRIPTION: Head Warder and Guards that protect royal buildings and residences.
PARTICULARS: Set of 5. Dickens' Village accessory. Midyear release.

OSRP: $30.00
GBTru: $30.00

Heritage Village Accessories

Christmas Bells

❐ **NAME:** Christmas Bells   1996
    ITEM #: 98711
    STATUS: Current

Photo Not Available.

DESCRIPTION: Gazebo with boy ringing town bell as one child holds ears and another watches.
PARTICULARS: Start A Tradition, November 1996 Event piece.

OSRP: $35.00
GBTru: $35.00

The Grapes Inn Ornament

❐ **NAME:** The Grapes Inn Ornament   1996
    ITEM #: 98729
    STATUS: 1996 Annual

DESCRIPTION: Miniature version of Signature Collection lit piece.
PARTICULARS: Midyear release.

OSRP: $15.00
GBTru: $15.00

Crown & Cricket Inn Ornament

❐ **NAME:** Crown & Cricket Inn Ornament   1996
    ITEM #: 98730
    STATUS: 1996 Annual

DESCRIPTION: Miniature version of Signature Collection lit piece.
PARTICULARS: Midyear release.

OSRP: $15.00
GBTru: $15.00

The Pied Bull Inn Ornament

❐ **NAME:** The Pied Bull Inn Ornament   1996
    ITEM #: 98731
    STATUS: 1996 Annual

DESCRIPTION: Miniature version of Signature Collection lit piece.
PARTICULARS: Midyear release.

OSRP: $15.00
GBTru: $15.00

5175-6
Frosted Norway Pines
Set of 3.
Sizes: 7", 9" & 11".

$12.95/set

5203-5
Village Frosted Topiary Trees, Small
Set of 8.
Sizes: 4 @ 2" round,
4 @ 3" high.

$7.50/set

5200-0
Village Frosted Topiary Cone Trees, Large
2 pieces per package.
Size: 11 $\frac{1}{2}$".

$12.50/pkg

5205-1
Village Evergreen Trees
Set of 3.
Sizes: 3 $\frac{1}{4}$", 4 $\frac{1}{4}$" &
6 $\frac{1}{2}$".
Cold-Cast Porcelain

$12.95/set

5201-9
Village Frosted Topiary Cone Trees, Medium
Set of 4.
Sizes: 2 @ 7 $\frac{1}{2}$" &
2 @ 6".

$10.00/set

5216-7
Village Winter Birch Tree
Size: 11 $\frac{1}{2}$".

$12.50/ea

5202-7
Village Frosted Topiary Trees, Large
Set of 8. Sizes: 4 cones
& 4 oblong, 4" each.

$12.50/set

5218-3
Village Porcelain Pine, Large
Size: 8 $\frac{1}{2}$".
Porcelain

$12.50/ea

Add'l Village Accessories–Trees

5219-1
Village Porcelain Pine Tree, Small
Size: 7".
Porcelain

$10.00/ea

5242-6
Village Frosted Bare Branch Tree, Large
Size: 13".

$12.50/ea

5231-0
Village Frosted Spruce Tree
Size: 15".

$12.50/ea

5243-4
Village Bare Branch Tree, with 25 Lights
This item is Battery Operated or can be used with Adapter, Item #5225-6.
Size: 9".

$17.50/ea

5232-9
Village Frosted Spruce Tree
Size: 22".

$27.50/ea

5246-9
Village Pencil Pines
Set of 3. Sizes: 12", 8" & 5".
Resin

$15.00/set

5241-8
Village Frosted Bare Branch Tree, Small
Size: 9 1/2".

$6.50/ea

5248-5
Spruce Tree Forest
Set of 4. Size: 16" x 14".

$25.00/set

5249-3
Village Frosted Zig-Zag Tree, White
Set of 3.
Sizes: 9", 7" & 4 1/2".

$15.00/set

5255-8
Snowy White Pine Tree, Small
Size: 18".

$15.00/ea

5250-7
Village Frosted Zig-Zag Tree, Green
Set of 3.
Sizes: 9", 7" & 4 1/2".

$15.00/set

5256-6
Snowy White Pine Tree, Large
Size: 24".

$20.00/ea

5251-5
Porcelain Pine Tree
Set of 2.
Sizes: 4 3/4" & 3 3/4".
Porcelain

$15.00/set

5419-4
Sisal Wreaths
6 pieces per package.
Size: 1" diameter.

$4.00/pkg

5254-0
Village Autumn Maple Tree
Size: 11".

$15.00/ea

5527-1
Village Pole Pine Forest
Set of 5.
Size: 4 trees in a snow base, 10" x 5" x 12".

$48.00/set

Add'l Village Accessories–Trees

209

5528-0
Pole Pine Tree, Small
Size: 8".

$10.00/ea

5529-8
Pole Pine Tree, Large
Size: 10 $\frac{1}{2}$".

$12.50/ea

6582-0
Frosted Evergreen Trees
Set of 3.
Sizes: 8 $\frac{1}{2}$", 6 $\frac{1}{2}$" &
4 $\frac{1}{2}$".
Papier-Mache

$16.00/set

52590
Village Landscape
Set of 14.

$16.50/set

52596
Village Flexible Sisal Hedge
3 pieces per package.
Size: Each piece is
12" long.
Sisal

$7.50/pkg

52600
Village Hybrid Landscape
Set of 22.

$35.00/set

52603
Lighted Snowcapped Revolving Tree
Lighted. Battery
Operated or can be
used with Adapter,
Item #5225-6.
Size: 8".
Resin

$35.00/ea

52604
Lighted Snowcapped Trees
Set of 2. Lighted.
Sizes: 10" & 8".
Resin

$45.00/set

52605
Village Frosted Fir Trees
Set of 4.
Sizes: 15", 12", 9" &
6 $^1/_4$".
Sisal with Wood trunks

$15.00/set

52610
Village FALLen Leaves
Size: 3-oz. bag.
Fabric

$5.00/bag

52606
Village Cedar Pine Forest
Set of 3.
Sizes: 12", 10" & 8".
Sisal

$15.00/set

52612
Village Snowy Evergreen Trees, Small
Set of 6.
Sizes: 3 $^1/_2$", 3", 2 $^1/_4$"
& 2".
Resin

$8.50/set

52607
Village Ponderosa Pines
Set of 3.
Sizes: 12", 10" & 9".
Sisal

$13.00/set

52613
Village Snowy Evergreen Trees, Medium
Set of 6.
Sizes: 7 $^1/_4$", 5 $^1/_2$", 5 $^1/_4$",
5" & 4 $^1/_4$".
Resin

$25.00/set

52608
Village Arctic Pines
Set of 3.
Sizes: 10", 8" & 6".
Sisal

$12.00/set

52614
Village Snowy Evergreen Trees, Large
Set of 5.
Sizes: 9 $^1/_4$", 9", 7 $^1/_4$"
& 7".
Resin

$32.50/set

52615
Village Snowy Scotch Pines
Set of 3.
Sizes: 7", 5 $^1/_4$" & 5".
Resin

$15.00/set

52619
Village Double Pine Trees
Size: 5 $^1/_4$" x 5 $^1/_2$" x 6".
Resin

$13.50

52616
Village Autumn Trees
Set of 3.
Sizes: 7 $^3/_4$", 6" & 4 $^3/_4$".
Resin

$13.50/set

5229-9
Village Animated Skating Pond
Set of 15.
UL Approved.
Size: 17 $^1/_2$" x 14".

$60.00/set

52617
Village Wagon Wheel Pine Grove
Size:
6 $^3/_4$" x 6 $^1/_4$" x 6 $^1/_2$".
Resin

$22.50

5240-0
Village Streetcar
Set of 10.
Midyear release.

$65.00/set

52618
Village Pine Point Pond
Size: 9 $^1/_4$" x 8" x 5 $^3/_4$".
Resin

$37.50

5247-7
Village Animated All Around The Park
Set of 18.
UL Approved.
Size: 19" x 15" x 16".

$95.00/set

Add'l Village Accessories–Trees/Electrical

5502-6
AC/DC Adapter, For Battery Operated Accessories
Not for use with Brites Lites.

$14.00

9933-3
Village Multi-Outlet Plug Strip, 6 Outlets
UL Approved.
Size: 12" x 2" x 1 ½".

$10.00/ea

9902-8
Single Cord Set, With Switched Cord And Bulb

$3.50/set

52593
Village Up, Up & Away, Animated Sleigh
UL Approved.
Size: 17" tall.

$40.00

9924-4
Village Replacement Light Bulbs
3 pieces per package.
6 Watt, 12 Volt.

$2.00/pkg

59803
"Village Express" HO Scale Train Set
Set of 22 With Transformer.

$100.00

9927-9
Village 6 Socket Lite Set With Bulbs, White Switched Cord
Size: 12'.

$12.50/set

3636-6
Street Lamps
6 pieces per package.
Battery Operated
(2 "AA" Batteries) or can be used with Adapter, Item #5502-6.
Size: Cord 60" long, lamps 2 ¼" tall.

$10.00/pkg

Add'l Village Accessories–Electrical

5215-9
Village Mini Lights
14 bulbs. Battery Operated or can be used with Adapter, Item #5502-6.
Size: 27" long cord.

$12.50

5996-0
Double Street Lamps
4 pieces per package. Battery Operated (2 "C" Batteries) or can be used with Adapter, Item #5502-6.
Size: 3 ½".

$13.00/pkg

5500-0
Traffic Light
2 lights per package. Battery Operated (2 "C" Batteries) or can be used with Adapter, Item #5502-6.
Size: 4 ¼".

$11.00/pkg

52611
Village Spotlight
Battery Operated or can be used with Adapter, Item #5225-6.
Size: 1 ¾".

$7.00

5501-8
Railroad Crossing Sign
2 signs per package. Battery Operated or can be used with Adapter, Item # 5502-6.
Size: 4 ¼".

$12.50/pkg

52621
Candy Cane Lampposts
Set of 4.

$13.00

Photograph Not Available

5504-2
Turn Of The Century Lamppost
4 pieces per package. Battery Operated (2 "C" Batteries) or can be used with Adapter, Item #5502-6.
Size: 4".

$16.00/pkg

Notes:

4995-6
Village "Blanket Of New Fallen Snow"
Size: 2' x 5' x 1".

$7.50

49980
Fresh Fallen Snow
Size: 2-lb. box.

$12.00/box

4998-1
Real Plastic Snow
Size: 7-oz. bag.

$3.00/bag

52592
Village Let It Snow Machine, With 1-lb. Bag Village Fresh Fallen Snow
Size: 38 $\frac{1}{2}$" x 9" x 5 $\frac{1}{2}$".

$85.00

Photograph
Not Available

4999-9
Real Plastic Snow
Size: 2-lb. box.

$10.00/box

5100-4
White Picket Fence
One of the first metal accessories (other was *Park Bench*). Also available in a Set of 4, Item #5101-2, @$12.00.
Size: 6" x 1 $\frac{3}{4}$".
Cast Iron

$3.00/ea

49979
Village Fresh Fallen Snow
Size: 7-oz. bag.

$4.00/bag

5101-2
White Picket Fence
Set of 4.
Size: Each piece is 6" x 1 $\frac{3}{4}$".
Cast Iron

$12.00/set

5204-3
Village Snow Fence,
Flexible Wood & Wire
Size: 2" high x 36" long.

$7.00/ea

5234-5
Chain Link Fence
with Gate
Set of 3.
Sizes: 2" & 4 $^1/_2$".
Metal

$12.00/set

5207-8
Frosty Tree-Lined
Picket Fence
Size: 5 $^3/_4$" x 2 $^1/_2$",
3 posts & 3 attached
trees.
Metal with Resin

$6.50/ea

5235-3
Chain Link Fence
Extensions
Set of 4.
Size: 4 $^1/_2$".

$15.00/set

5212-4
Tree-Lined Courtyard
Fence
Size: 1 $^1/_2$" high x 4" long.
Metal with Resin

$4.00/ea

5252-3
Victorian Wrought Iron
Fence and Gate
Set of 5.
Size: 5 $^1/_2$" x 3".
Metal

$15.00/set

5220-5
Courtyard Fence
with Steps
Size:
1 $^1/_4$" high x 4 $^1/_4$" long.
Metal with Resin

$4.00/ea

5253-1
Victorian Wrought Iron
Fence Extension
Size: 3".
Metal

$2.50/ea

Add'l Village Accessories–Fences

5514-0
Village Wrought Iron Gate and Fence
Set of 9. Gate & 4 fence pieces with 4 posts.
Size: 9 1/4" x 3".
Metal

$15.00/set

5999-4
Wrought Iron Fence
4 pieces per package.
White & Black.
Size: 4" long.
Metal

$10.00/pkg

5515-8
Village Wrought Iron Fence Extensions
Set of 9. 4 fence pieces & 5 posts.
Size: 9 1/4" x 3".
Metal

$12.50/set

52597
Village Split Rail Fence, With Mailbox
Set of 4.
Size: 10 1/4" x 2 1/2".
Hand-Hewn Wood

$12.50/set

5541-7
City Subway Entrance
Size:
4 1/2" x 2 3/4" x 4 1/2".
Metal

$15.00/ea

52598
Village Twig Snow Fence, Wood
Size: 4' x 2 3/4".
Wood

$6.00

5998-6
Wrought Iron Fence
White & Black or White & Green.
Size: 4" long.

$2.50/ea

5226-4
Village Mountain with Frosted Sisal Trees, Small
Set of 5. With 4 trees.
Size: 12" x 10 1/2" x 8".
Foam and Sisal

$32.50/set

5227-2
Village Mountain with Frosted Sisal Trees, Medium
Set of 8. With 7 trees and 1 niche to display Village piece.
Size: 22" x 12" x 10 ¹/₂".
Foam and Sisal

$65.00/set

5110-1
Town Clock
2 Assorted–Green or Black.
Size: 3 ¹/₂".

$3.00/ea

5228-0
Village Mountains with Frosted Sisal Trees, Large
Set of 14. With 13 trees. Can accommodate 3 lighted pieces.
Size: 35" x 13" x 15 ¹/₂".
Foam and Sisal

$150.00/set

5139-0
"Up On A Roof Top"
2 pieces–Santa hitches onto sleigh.
Size: 4".
Pewter

$6.50

5257-4
Village Mountain Backdrop
Set of 2. Without trees.
Sizes: 27" x 11" & 22" x 9 ¹/₂".
Foam

$65.00

5176-4
Stop Sign
2 pieces per package.
Size: 3" tall.
Metal

$5.00/pkg

52582
Village Mountain Tunnel
Size:
19 ¹/₂" x 9 ¹/₂" x 5 ¹/₂".
Foam

$37.50

5178-0
Parking Meter
4 pieces per package.
Size: 2" tall.
Metal

$6.00/pkg

5208-6
Village Mylar Skating Pond
2 sheets per package.
Size: Each sheet is
25 ¼" x 18".

$6.00/pkg

5230-2
Wrought Iron Park Bench
Size: 2 ¼".
Metal

$5.00/ea

5210-8
Village Brick Road
2 strips per package.
Size: Each strip is
4 ¾" x 36".
Vinyl

$10.00/pkg

5233-7
Village Sled & Skis
Set of 2.
Sizes: 2 & 2 ¼".
Metal

$6.00/set

5211-6
Village Acrylic Icicles
4 pieces per package.
Size: Each piece is
18" long.

$4.50/pkg

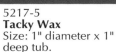

5417-8
"It's A Grand Old Flag"
Pair.
Size: 2 ¼".
Metal

$4.00/pkg

5217-5
Tacky Wax
Size: 1" diameter x 1"
deep tub.

$2.00/tub

5456-9
Windmill
Size: 11 ½" high.
Metal with Earthen base

$20.00

Add'l Village Accessories–Trims

5511-5
'Christmas Eave' Trim
Non-electric bulb
garland.
Size: 24" long.

$3.50/ea

52595
Village Pink Flamingos
4 pieces per package.
Size: 1 3/4".
Resin

$7.50/pkg

5512-3
**Heritage Village Utility
Accessories**
Set of 8. 2 stop signs,
4 parking meters,
2 traffic lights.
Sizes: 1 3/4", 2" & 3".
Metal

$12.50/set

52599
**Village Election Yard
Signs**
Set of 6, Assorted.
Size: 2 1/4".
Metal

$10.00/set

5984-6
**Village Cobblestone
Road**
2 strips per package.
Size: Each strip is
4 3/4" x 36".
Vinyl

$10.00/pkg

52601
**Village Brick Town
Square**
Size: 23 1/2" square.
Vinyl

$15.00

52594
**Village Let It Snow
Snowman Sign**
Size: 6".
Resin

$12.50

52602
**Village Cobblestone
Town Square**
Size: 23 1/2" square.
Vinyl

$15.00

Add'l Village Accessories–Trims

52620
Village Magic Smoke
6-oz. bottle

$2.50

5224-8
**Village Brite Lites
Reindeer, Animated**
Battery Operated or can
be used with Adapter,
Item #5225-6.
Size: 3 $1/4$".

$13.50/ea

98841
**"The Building Of A
Village Tradition"
Video, With Instruction
Booklet**
35 Minutes.

$19.95

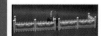

5225-6
**Village Brite Lites
Adapter**
For use with 2
"Brites Lites" only.

$10.00/ea

5222-1
**Village Brite Lites
'I Love My Village',
Animated**
Battery Operated or can
be used with Adapter,
Item #5225-6.
Size: 6 $1/2$".

$15.00/ea

5236-1
**Village Brite Lites Fence,
Animated**
Set of 4. Battery Oper-
ated or can be
used with Adapter,
Item #5225-6.
Size: 11".

$25.00/set

5223-0
**Village Brite Lites
'Merry Christmas',
Animated**
Battery Operated or can
be used with Adapter,
Item #5225-6.
Size: 7 $1/2$".

$15.00/ea

5237-0
**Village Brite Lites
Snowman, Animated**
Battery Operated or can
be used with Adapter,
Item #5225-6.
Size: 3 $3/4$".

$20.00/ea

5238-8
Village Brite Lites Tree, Animated
Battery Operated or can be used with Adapter, Item #5225-6.
Size: 3 1/2".

$13.50/ea

5482-8
Coca-Cola® brand Neon Sign
Battery Operated or can be used with Adapter, Item #5225-6.
Size: 4 1/2" x 2".

$22.50/ea

5239-6
Village Brite Lites Santa, Animated
Battery Operated or can be used with Adapter, Item #5225-6.
Size: 3 1/2".

$20.00/ea

9846-9
Village Brite Lites 'Department 56', Animated
Battery Operated or can be used with Adapter, Item #5225-6.
Size: 5".

$10.00/ea

5244-2
Village Brite Lites Waving Flag, Animated
Battery Operated or can be used with Adapter, Item #5225-6.
Size: 5".

$12.50/ea

Notes:

5245-0
Village Brite Lites Set of 20 Red Lights, Flashing
Battery Operated or can be used with Adapter, Item #5225-6.

$9.00/ea

Notes:

Add'l Village Accessories–Brite Lites

Discontinued Village Accessories

	Item #	Name	Type
	5111-0	**Christmas Wreaths** Set of 8. Sizes: 1" & 3/4".	trees
	5112-8	**SV Garland Trim** 3 pieces per package. Size: Each piece is 24" long.	trees
	5115-2	**Frosted Topiary Village Garden** Set of 8. 4 cones, 4 ovals.	trees
	5181-0	**Bare Branch Winter Oak, Small** Size: 4 1/4".	trees
	5182-9	**Bare Branch Winter Oak, Large** Size: 7 3/4".	trees
	5183-7	**Sisal Tree Set** Set of 7. 4 cones & 3 ovals.	trees
	5184-5	**Winter Oak Tree with 2 Red Birds**	trees
	5185-3	**Topiary Garden Sisal** 36 pieces assorted. Sizes: 2 1/2", 4", 6", 8" & 12".	trees
	5192-6	**Village Potted Topiary Pair** 2 pieces per package. Size: 4 3/4".	trees
	5221-3	**Pine Cone Trees** Set of 2. Sizes: 8 3/4" & 7 1/4".	trees
	6595-1	**Spruce Tree with Wooden Base, Small** Size: 6".	trees

	Item #	Name	Type
	6597-8	**Spruce Tree with Wooden Base, Medium** Size: 9".	trees
	6598-6	**Spruce Tree with Wooden Base, Large** Size: 12".	trees
	5213-2	**"Lights Out" Remote Control** Turns lights on/off in up to 60 houses at once. Size: 4" x 2 $3/4$".	electrical
	9926-0	**Battery Operated Light** 6 watts, 12 volts.	electrical
	5206-0	**Candles by the Doorstep** 4 pieces per package. 2 "AA" Batteries. Size: 2 $1/4$".	lights
	5416-0	**Yard Lights (2 Santas, 2 Snowmen)** Set of 4. Size: 1 $3/4$".	lights
	5503-4	**Old World Streetlamp** 4 pieces per package. 2 "C" Batteries. Size: 4".	lights
	5505-0	**Turn of the Century Lamppost** 6 pieces per package. 2 "C" Batteries. Size: 4".	lights
	5993-5	**Streetlamp Wrapped in Garland** 2 pieces per package. Size: 4".	lights
	4996-4	**"Let It Snow" Crystals, Plastic Snow** Size: 8 oz. box.	snow
	5506-9	**Lamp Post Fence** Set of 10. 2 lamps, 4 posts, 4 fence pieces.	fence
	5508-5	**Lamp Post Fence Extension** Set of 12. 6 posts & 6 fence pieces.	fence

Discontinued Village Accessories

	Item #	Name	Type
	5109-8	**Village Park Bench** Size: 2 ¹/₂".	trims
	5524-7	**"Village Sounds" Tape** **with Speakers** 23 minute tape. Size: 12' cord.	trims
	5525-5	**"Village Sounds" Tape** 23 minutes, continuous play.	trims
	5526-3	**Heritage Banners** Set of 4, 2 each of 2. Size: 1 ¹/₄".	trims
	948-2	**Heritage Village Collection** **Promotional Logo Banner** Giveaway at 1992 events.	trims

Discontinued Village Accessories

❏ **NAME:** **Gingerbread House** 1983
ITEM#: 5025-3
STATUS: Retired 1984

MATERIAL: Ceramic
DESCRIPTION: Designed like a Christmas edible treat. Cookies trim sides while candy canes and sugar heart decorate roof.
PARTICULARS: In 1983, Department 56 issued the *Gingerbread House* with all intentions of it being a lit house. After realizing it did not fit well with the other Snow Village houses, D56 decided to close the light hole in the back, put a slot for coins and create a bank.
Some of the original lit pieces made their way to consumers through the Bachman's stores, leading to much of the confusion. Adding to the confusion, is the fact that the *Gingerbread House* is listed as a Snow Village piece on the Snow Village History List. (Note it does not appear on the 1994 Snow Village poster).

OSRP: $24.00
GBTru: $280.00 ↑4%

□ **NAME:**   **Thatched Cottage**   1979
      ITEM #:   5050-0
      STATUS: Retired 1980

MATERIAL: Ceramic
DESCRIPTION: Small thatched cottage with attached tree.

OSRP: $30.00   Chimney at rear of stucco and timber trim.
GBTru: $725.00 ↓9% **PARTICULARS:** Lighted.

□ **NAME:**   **Countryside Church**   1979
      ITEM #:   5051-8
      STATUS: Retired 1980

MATERIAL: Ceramic
DESCRIPTION: Countryside Church in a springtime setting.
Large green tree against a simple white wood church with
steeple rising from entry to nave.

OSRP: $25.00   **PARTICULARS:** Lighted.
GBTru: $685.00 ↓14% **VARIATION:** For snow version see OSV, 1979, #5058-3.

□ **NAME:**   **Aspen Trees** (Accessory)   1979
      ITEM #:   5052-6
      STATUS: Retired 1980

MATERIAL: Ceramic
OSRP: $16.00   **DESCRIPTION:** The trees that shiver and tremble in the wind.
GBTru: NE   Small leaves on a hardwood tree.

□ **NAME:**   **Sheep** (Accessory)   1979
      ITEM #:   5053-4
      STATUS: Retired 1980

MATERIAL: Ceramic
OSRP: $12.00   **DESCRIPTION:** Grazing white and black sheep.
GBTru: NE   **PARTICULARS:** Set of 12. 9 white, 3 black.

OSRP: $34.00
GBTru: $300.00 ↓8%

❒ **NAME:**   **Hometown Boarding House**   1987
    ITEM #:   670-0
    STATUS: Retired 1988

MATERIAL: Porcelain
DESCRIPTION: Three-story brick building with rented rooms above main floor parlor and dining room. Ground floor has front bay window adjacent to covered entry porch, which extends around side to windowed area. Second story features arched windows. Brick turret-like structures appear attached to rectangular design. Taller turret has windows on all four sides of roof with attic used for rental or storage.
PARTICULARS: Lighted. Inspired by Sprague House in Red Wing, Mn.

OSRP: $40.00
GBTru: $305.00 ↓6%

❒ **NAME:**   **Hometown Church**   1987
    ITEM #:   671-8
    STATUS: Retired 1988

MATERIAL: Porcelain
DESCRIPTION: Cross-shaped floor plan with spire rising from one side of transept. Simple entry door at base of spire in contrast to large arched windows that fill end walls.
PARTICULARS: Lighted. Designed after a St. Paul, MN Church.

OSRP: $40.00
GBTru: $565.00 ↓10%

❒ **NAME:**   **Hometown Drugstore**   1988
    ITEM #:   672-6
    STATUS: Retired 1989

MATERIAL: Porcelain
DESCRIPTION: Drugstore is corner store in a 2-attached buildings structure. Taller 3-story building houses barber shop on main level and eye glass shop above. Entry to drugstore is at corner of shorter building with three support columns providing an open area to entry and for support of upper windowed turret design. Garlands decorate the awnings over display windows
PARTICULARS: Lighted. Same mold as the Christmas In The City *Variety Store*, #5972-2. Inspired by a store in Stillwater, MN.

The Original Snow Village

Retired Buildings

5000-8	1984	Town Hall
5001-3	1979	Mountain Lodge
5001-6	1985	Grocery
5002-1	1979	Gabled Cottage
5002-4	1984	Victorian Cottage
5003-2	1985	Governor's Mansion
5003-9	1979	The Inn
5004-0	1986	Turn Of The Century
5004-7	1979	Country Church
5005-4	1979	Steepled Church
5005-9	1986	Main Street House
5006-2	1979	Small Chalet
5006-7	1989	St. Anthony Hotel & Post Office
5007-0	1979	Victorian House
5007-5	1986	Stratford House
5008-3	1987	Haversham House
5008-8	1979	Mansion
5009-1	1985	Galena House
5009-6	1979	Stone Church
5010-5	1987	River Road House
5011-2	1984	Homestead
5012-0	1980	General Store
5012-1	1986	Delta House
5013-0	1989	Snow Village Factory
5013-8	1980	Cape Cod
5014-6	1986	Nantucket
5015-3	1979	Skating Rink/Duck Pond Set
5015-6	1986	Bayport
5016-1	1989	Small Double Trees
5017-2	1984	Skating Pond
5019-9	1984	Street Car
5019-9	1990	Cathedral Church
5020-2	1984	Centennial House
5021-0	1984	Carriage House
5022-9	1984	Pioneer Church
5023-7	1984	Swiss Chalet
5024-5	1983	Bank
5024-5	1995	Cumberland House
5026-1	1984	Village Church
5027-0	1990	Springfield House
5028-8	1986	Gothic Church
5029-6	1985	Parsonage
5030-0	1988	Lighthouse
5031-8	1985	Wooden Church
5032-6	1984	Fire Station
5033-4	1985	English Tudor
5034-2	1985	Congregational Church
5035-0	1986	Trinity Church
5036-9	1985	Summit House
5037-7	1986	New School House
5039-3	1986	Parish Church
5041-5	1986	Waverly Place
5042-3	1986	Twin Peaks
5043-1	1986	2101 Maple
5044-0	1991	Village Market
5045-8	1986	Stucco Bungalow
5046-6	1988	Williamsburg House
5047-4	1987	Plantation House
5048-2	1988	Church Of The Open Door
5049-0	1987	Spruce Place
5050-4	1987	Duplex
5051-2	1988	Depot And Train With 2 Train Cars
5052-0	1987	Ridgewood
5054-2	1982	Victorian
5054-7	1990	Kenwood House
5055-9	1981	Knob Hill
5056-7	1981	Brownstone
5057-5	1981	Log Cabin
5058-3	1984	Countryside Church
5059-1	1980	Stone Church
5060-1	1988	Lincoln Park Duplex
5060-9	1982	School House
5061-7	1981	Tudor House
5062-5	1980	Mission Church
5062-8	1988	Sonoma House
5063-3	1980	Mobile Home
5063-6	1988	Highland Park House
5065-2	1988	Beacon Hill House
5065-8	1982	Giant Trees
5066-0	1988	Pacific Heights House

...continued

OSV Retired Buildings Continued

5066-6	1980	Adobe House
5067-4	1981	Cathedral Church
5067-9	1989	Ramsey Hill House
5068-2	1982	Stone Mill House
5068-7	1988	Saint James Church
5070-9	1982	Colonial Farm House
5071-7	1982	Town Church
5071-7	1988	Carriage House
5072-5	1984	Wooden Clapboard
5073-3	1982	English Cottage
5073-3	1990	Toy Shop
5074-1	1984	Barn
5076-8	1983	Corner Store
5076-8	1990	Apothecary
5077-6	1983	Bakery
5077-6	1991	Bakery
5078-4	1982	English Church
5078-4	1987	Diner
5080-6	1989	Large Single Tree
5081-4	1983	Gabled House
5081-4	1992	Red Barn
5082-2	1983	Flower Shop
5082-2	1991	Jefferson School
5083-0	1984	New Stone Church
5084-9	1984	Chateau
5085-6	1985	Train Station With 3 Train Cars
5089-0	1992	Farm House
5091-1	1989	Fire Station No. 2
5092-0	1989	Snow Village Resort Lodge
5114-4	1991	Jingle Belle Houseboat
5119-5	1992	Colonial Church
5120-9	1992	North Creek Cottage
5121-7	1990	Maple Ridge Inn
5122-5	1992	Village Station And Train
5123-3	1992	Cobblestone Antique Shop
5124-1	1991	Corner Cafe
5125-0	1990	Single Car Garage
5126-8	1991	Home Sweet Home/ House & Windmill
5127-6	1992	Redeemer Church
5128-4	1991	Service Station
5140-3	1994	Stonehurst House
5141-1	1990	Palos Verdes
5142-0	1993	Paramount Theater
5143-8	1992	Doctor's House
5144-6	1993	Courthouse
5145-4	1992	Village Warming House
5149-7	1992	J. Young's Granary
5150-0	1995	Pinewood Log Cabin
5151-9	1992	56 Flavors Ice Cream Parlor
5152-7	1992	Morningside House
5153-5	1993	Mainstreet Hardware Store
5154-3	1993	Village Realty
5155-1	1992	Spanish Mission Church
5156-0	1993	Prairie House
5400-3	1994	Oak Grove Tudor
5401-1	1993	The Honeymooner Motel
5402-0	1995	Village Greenhouse
5403-8	1994	Southern Colonial
5405-4	1993	Finklea's Finery Costume Shop
5406-2	1994	Jack's Corner Barber Shop
5407-0	1994	Double Bungalow
5421-6	1994	St. Luke's Church
5422-4	1995	Village Post Office
5423-2	1995	Al's TV Shop
5425-9	1994	Print Shop & Village News
5426-7	1995	Hartford House
5427-5	1995	Village Vet And Pet Shop
5437-2	1995	Craftsman Cottage

Quikreference

Original Snow Village

Retired Accessories

5018-0	1990	Snowman With Broom	5158-6	1993	Down The Chimney
5038-5	1985	Scottie With Tree			He Goes
5040-7	1988	Monks–A–Caroling	5159-4	1993	Sno–Jet Snowmobile
5053-9	1987	Singing Nuns	5160-8	1992	Sleighride
5056-3	1987	Snow Kids Sled, Skis	5161-6	1992	Here We Come A
5057-1	1988	Family Mom/Kids,			Caroling
		Goose/Girl	5162-4	1992	Home Delivery
5059-8	1988	Santa/Mailbox	5163-2	1993	Fresh Frozen Fish
5064-1	1986	Carolers	5164-0	1995	A Tree For Me
5069-0	1986	Ceramic Car	5168-3	1991	Kids Tree House
5079-2	1986	Ceramic Sleigh	5169-1	1992	Bringing Home The
5094-6	1990	Kids Around The Tree			Tree
5095-4	1987	Girl/Snowman, Boy	5170-5	1991	Skate Faster Mom
5096-2	1988	Shopping Girls With	5172-1	1991	Through The Woods
		Packages	5173-0	1991	Statue Of Mark Twain
5102-0	1988	3 Nuns With	5174-8	1991	Calling All Cars
		Songbooks	5179-9	1990	Mailbox
5103-9	1988	Praying Monks	5180-2	1994	Village Birds
5104-7	1989	Children In Band	5197-7	1992	Special Delivery
5105-5	1990	Caroling Family	5408-9	1994	Wreaths For Sale
5107-1	1990	Christmas Children	5409-7	1993	Winter Fountain
5108-0	1989	For Sale Sign	5410-0	1994	Cold Weather Sports
5113-6	1990	Snow Kids	5411-9	1992	Come Join The Parade
5116-0	1992	Man On Ladder	5412-7	1992	Village Marching Band
		Hanging Garland	5413-5	1994	Christmas Cadillac
5117-9	1990	Hayride	5414-3	1993	Snowball Fort
5118-7	1990	School Children	5415-1	1993	Country Harvest
5129-2	1990	Apple Girl/Newspaper	5418-6	1994	Village Greetings
		Boy	5430-5	1994	Nanny And The
5130-6	1991	Woodsman And Boy			Preschoolers
5131-4	1992	Doghouse/Cat In	5431-3	1995	Early Morning Delivery
		Garbage Can	5433-0	1995	Round & Round We
5133-0	1991	Water Tower			Go!
5134-9	1993	Kids Decorating The	5435-6	1994	We're Going To A
		Village Sign			Christmas Pageant
5136-5	1990	Woody Station Wagon	5436-4	1995	Winter Playground
5137-3	1991	School Bus, Snow Plow	5451-8	1995	Check It Out Bookmo-
5146-2	1995	Village Gazebo			bile
5147-0	1992	Choir Kids	6459-9	1984	Monks–A–Caroling
5148-9	1990	Special Delivery	8183-3	1991	Sisal Tree Lot

Dickens' Village

Retired Buildings

5550-6	1992	DAVID COPPERFIELD	5926-9	1993	White Horse Bakery
5550-6	1992	Mr. Wickfield Solicitor	5926-9	1993	Walpole Tailors
5550-6	1992	Betsy Trotwood's Cottage	5927-7	1991	Ivy Glen Church
5550-6	1992	Peggotty's Seaside Cottage	6500-5	1995	CHRISTMAS CAROL COTTAGES
5552-2	1995	Fagin's Hide-A-Way	6500-5	1995	Fezziwig's Warehouse
5553-0	1993	OLIVER TWIST	6500-5	1995	Scrooge & Marley Counting House
5553-0	1993	Brownlow House	6500-5	1995	The Cottage of Bob Cratchit & Tiny Tim
5553-0	1993	Maylie Cottage			
5555-7	1995	Ashbury Inn			
5557-3	1994	Nephew Fred's Flat	6507-2	1989	DICKENS' LANE SHOPS
5567-0	1992	Bishops Oast House	6507-2	1989	Thomas Kersey Coffee House
5582-4	1995	Knottinghill Church			
5583-2	1991	Cobles Police Station	6507-2	1989	Cottage Toy Shop
5584-0	1992	Theatre Royal	6507-2	1989	Tuttle's Pub
5800-9	1995	Hembleton Pewterer	6508-0	1990	Blythe Pond Mill House
5900-5	1989	BARLEY BREE			
5900-5	1989	Farmhouse	6515-3	1988	THE ORIGINAL SHOPS OF DICKENS' VILLAGE
5900-5	1989	Barn			
5902-1	1990	Counting House & Silas Thimbleton Barrister			
5916-1	1988	Kenilworth Castle	6515-3	1988	Crowntree Inn
5924-2	1990	COBBLESTONE SHOPS	6515-3	1988	Candle Shop
			6515-3	1988	Green Grocer
5924-2	1990	The Wool Shop	6515-3	1988	Golden Swan Baker
5924-2	1990	Booter And Cobbler	6515-3	1988	Bean And Son Smithy Shop
5924-2	1990	T. Wells Fruit & Spice Shop	6515-3	1988	Abel Beesley Butcher
5925-0	1991	NICHOLAS NICKLEBY	6515-3	1988	Jones & Co. Brush & Basket Shop
5925-0	1991	Nicholas Nickleby Cottage	6516-1	1989	Dickens' Village Church
5925-0	1991	Wackford Squeers Boarding School	6518-8	1988	DICKENS' COTTAGES
5926-9	1993	MERCHANT SHOPS	6518-8	1988	Thatched Cottage
5926-9	1993	Poulterer	6518-8	1988	Stone Cottage
5926-9	1993	Geo. Weeton Watch-maker	6518-8	1988	Tudor Cottage
5926-9	1993	The Mermaid Fish Shoppe	6528-5	1989	Chadbury Station And Train
			6549-8	1989	Brick Abbey

Quikreference

NEW ENGLAND VILLAGE

Retired Buildings

5640-5	1995	McGrebe-Cutters & Sleighs	5954-4	1993	SLEEPY HOLLOW
			5954-4	1993	Sleepy Hollow School
5643-0	1995	Yankee Jud Bell Casting	5954-4	1993	Van Tassel Manor
5644-8	1995	Stoney Brook Town Hall	5954-4	1993	Ichabod Crane's Cottage
5930-7	1994	Craggy Cove Lighthouse	5955-2	1993	Sleepy Hollow Church
			6530-7	1989	NEW ENGLAND VILLAGE
5931-5	1989	Weston Train Station			
5939-0	1990	CHERRY LANE SHOPS	6530-7	1989	Apothecary Shop
5939-0	1990	Ben's Barbershop	6530-7	1989	General Store
5939-0	1990	Otis Hayes Butcher Shop	6530-7	1989	Nathaniel Bingham Fabrics
5939-0	1990	Anne Shaw Toys	6530-7	1989	Livery Stable & Boot Shop
5940-4	1991	Ada's Bed And Boarding House			
			6530-7	1989	Steeple Church
5942-0	1991	Berkshire House	6530-7	1989	Brick Town Hall
5943-9	1992	Jannes Mullet Amish Farm House	6530-7	1989	Red Schoolhouse
			6538-2	1989	Jacob Adams Farmhouse And Barn
5944-7	1992	Jannes Mullet Amish Barn			
			6539-0	1990	Steeple Church
5946-3	1994	Shingle Creek House	6544-7	1990	Timber Knoll Log Cabin

ALPINE VILLAGE

Retired Buildings

5615-4	1993	Bahnhof (Train Station)
5952-8	1989	Josef Engel Farmhouse
6541-2	1991	Alpine Church

Quikreference

CHRISTMAS IN THE CITY
Retired Buildings

5536-0	1995	Red Brick Fire Station	5972-2	1990	Variety Store
5537-9	1994	Wong's In Chinatown	5973-0	1994	Ritz Hotel
5538-7	1995	"Little Italy" Ristorante	5977-3	1992	5607 Park Avenue
5543-3	1993	Arts Academy			Townhouse
5544-1	1994	The Doctor's Office	5978-1	1992	5609 Park Avenue
5961-7	1989	Sutton Place Brown-			Townhouse
		stones	6512-9	1990	CHRISTMAS IN THE
5962-5	1990	The Cathedral			CITY
5963-3	1989	Palace Theatre	6512-9	1990	Toy Shop And Pet Store
5968-4	1991	Chocolate Shoppe	6512-9	1990	Bakery
5969-2	1991	City Hall	6512-9	1990	Tower Restaurant
5970-6	1992	Hank's Market			

NortH PoLe
Retired Buildings

5600-6	1993	Santa's Workshop	5621-9	1995	Orly's Bell & Harness
5620-0	1995	NeeNee's Dolls And			Supply
		Toys	5621-9	1995	Rimpy's Bakery
5621-9	1995	NORTH POLE SHOPS	5622-7	1995	Tassy's Mitten &
					Hassel's Woolies

Disney Parks Village
Retired Buildings

5350-3	1996	Mickey's Christmas	5351-1	1996	Olde World Antiques II
		Carol	5352-0	1996	Disneyland Fire
5351-1	1996	OLDE WORLD			Department #105
		ANTIQUES SHOPS	53521	1996	Silversmith
5351-1	1996	Olde World Antiques I	53522	1996	Tinker Bell's Treasures

Heritage Village

Retired Accessories

5353-8	1996	Mickey & Minnie
5353-9	1996	Balloon Seller
5354-6	1996	Disney Parks Family
5355-4	1996	Olde World Antiques Gate
5516-6	1992	Boulevard
5517-4	1990	Mailbox & Fire Hydrant
5532-8	1995	Don't Drop The Presents!
5533-6	1995	Welcome Home
5535-2	1992	Busy Sidewalks
5539-5	1994	'Tis The Season
5545-0	1993	All Around The Town
5546-8	1995	The Fire Brigade
5547-6	1995	"City Fire Dept." Fire Truck
5551-4	1992	David Copperfield Characters
5554-9	1993	Oliver Twist Characters
5559-0	1995	Poultry Market
5560-3	1994	Come Into The Inn
5570-0	1993	Carolers On The Doorstep
5572-7	1994	Village Sign With Snowman
5578-6	1992	Royal Coach
5579-4	1991	Constables
5580-8	1992	Violet Vendor/Carolers/ Chestnut Vendor
5602-2	1995	Toymaker Elves
5603-0	1995	Baker Elves
5604-9	1994	Letters For Santa
5608-1	1993	Trimming The North Pole
5610-3	1993	Santa's Little Helpers
5619-7	1995	Buying Baker's Bread
5630-8	1995	Woodsmen Elves
5641-3	1993	Market Day
5645-6	1995	Harvest Seed Cart
5646-4	1995	Town Tinker
5802-5	1995	The Old Puppeteer
5803-3	1995	The Bird Seller
5804-1	1994	Village Street Peddlers
5901-3	1989	Farm People & Animals
5903-0	1991	Childe Pond And Skaters
5928-5	1990	Fezziwig And Friends
5929-3	1991	Nicholas Nickleby Characters
5934-0	1990	Blacksmith
5938-2	1994	Snow Children
5941-2	1991	Village Harvest People
5945-5	1991	Farm Animals
5948-0	1992	Amish Family
5949-8	1992	Amish Buggy
5950-1	1989	Silo & Hay Shed
5951-0	1989	Ox Sled
5956-0	1992	Sleepy Hollow Characters
5957-9	1991	Organ Grinder
5958-7	1992	Popcorn Vendor
5959-5	1991	River Street Ice House Cart
5960-9	1993	Christmas In The City Sign
5965-0	1990	City People
5966-8	1988	Shopkeepers
5967-6	1988	City Workers
5971-4	1991	City Newsstand
5981-1	1990	Village Train Trestle
5982-0	1993	One Horse Open Sleigh
5983-8	1991	City Bus & Milk Truck
5985-4	1991	Salvation Army Band
5986-2	1990	Woodcutter And Son
5987-0	1994	Red Covered Bridge
5997-8	1988	Village Express Train– Black
6501-3	1990	Christmas Carol Figures
6510-2	1989	Lighted Tree W/ Children And Ladder
6511-0	1990	Sleighride
6526-9	1990	Carolers
6527-7	1986	Village Train
6531-5	1990	Covered Wooden Bridge

...continued

HV Retired Accessories Continued

6532-3	1990	New England Winter Set
6537-4	1992	Porcelain Trees
6542-0	1992	Alpine Villagers
6545-5	1990	Skating Pond
6546-3	1990	Stone Bridge
6547-1	1989	Village Well & Holy Cross
6569-2	1993	Dickens' Village Sign
6570-6	1993	New England Village Sign
6571-4	1993	Alpine Village Sign
6589-7	1989	Maple Sugaring Shed
6590-0	1990	Dover Coach
9953-8	1990	HV Promotional Sign

Meadowland

Retired

5050-0	1980	Thatched Cottage
5051-8	1980	Countryside Church
5052-6	1980	Aspen Trees (Accessory)
5053-4	1980	Sheep (Accessory)

Bachman's

Retired

670-0	1988	Hometown Boarding House
671-8	1988	Hometown Church
672-6	1989	Hometown Drugstore

Limited Editions

Dickens' Village

5585-9	Ruth Marion Scotch Woolens	17,500
5586-7	Green Gate Cottage	22,500
58336	Ramsford Palace	27,500
5904-8	C. Fletcher Public House	12,500
6502-1	Norman Church	3,500
6519-6	Dickens' Village Mill	2,500
6568-4	Chesterton Manor House	7,500

New England Village

6543-9	Smythe Woolen Mill	7,500

CHRISTMAS IN THE CITY

5549-2	Cathedral Church Of St. Mark	3,024
5974-9	Dorothy's Dress Shop	12,500

Charles Dickens Signature Series

5750-9	Crown & Cricket Inn	1992
5751-7	The Pied Bull Inn	1993
5752-5	Dedlock Arms	1994
5753-3	Sir John Falstaff Inn	1995
57534	The Grapes Inn	1996
5809-2	Boarding & Lodging (#18)	1993

American Architecture Series

5156-0	Prairie House
5157-8	Queen Anne Victorian
5403-8	Southern Colonial
5404-6	Gothic Farmhouse
5437-2	Craftsman Cottage
5465-8	Federal House
54856	Dutch Colonial

SNOW VILLAGE

SNOW VILLAGE

SNOW VILLAGE

SNOW VILLAGE

Alphabetical by Name–Page Number Index

SNOW VILLAGE

SNOW VILLAGE ACCESSORIES

Alphabetical by Name–Page Number Index

SNOW VILLAGE ACCESSORIES

SNOW VILLAGE ACCESSORIES

Alphabetical by Name–Page Number Index

HERITAGE VILLAGE

HERITAGE VILLAGE

Alphabetical by Name–Page Number Index

HERITAGE VILLAGE

HERITAGE VILLAGE

Alphabetical by Name–Page Number Index

HERITAGE VILLAGE

HERITAGE VILLAGE

HERITAGE VILLAGE ACCESSORIES

HERITAGE VILLAGE ACCESSORIES

Alphabetical by Name–Page Number Index

HERITAGE VILLAGE ACCESSORIES

HERITAGE VILLAGE ACCESSORIES

Alphabetical by Name–Page Number Index

ADDITIONAL VILLAGE ACCESSORIES

ADDITIONAL VILLAGE ACCESSORIES

D56 Item Number–Page Number Index

D56 Item Number–Page Number Index

NOTES